GROUNDWORK FOR COLLEGE READING

THIRD EDITION

GROUNDWORK FOR COLLEGE READING

THIRD EDITION

BILL BRODERICK

CERRITOS COLLEGE

TOWNSEND PRESS

Books in the Townsend Press Reading Series:

Groundwork for College Reading
Ten Steps to Building College Reading Skills
Ten Steps to Improving College Reading Skills
Ten Steps to Advancing College Reading Skills

Books in the Townsend Press Vocabulary Series:

Vocabulary Basics
Groundwork for a Better Vocabulary
Building Vocabulary Skills
Building Vocabulary Skills, Short Version
Improving Vocabulary Skills
Improving Vocabulary Skills, Short Version
Advancing Vocabulary Skills
Advancing Vocabulary Skills, Short Version
Advanced Word Power

Supplements Available for Most Books:

Instructor's Edition
Instructor's Manual, Test Bank and Computer Guide
Set of Computer Disks (MS-DOS, Windows, or Macintosh)

Copyright © 2000 by Townsend Press, Inc.
Printed in the United States of America
9 8 7 6 5 4 3 2

Send book orders and requests for desk copies or supplements to:
Townsend Press
1038 Industrial Drive
West Berlin, New Jersey 08091-9164

For even faster service, call us at our toll-free number:
1-800-772-6410

Or fax your request to:
1-800-225-8894

Or you may send us E-mail at:
townsendcs@aol.com

For more information about Townsend Press, visit our website:
www.townsendpress.com

ISBN 0-944210-48-1

Contents

Preface:
To the Instructor

We all know that many of today's beginning college students do not have the reading skills needed to do effective work in their courses. For any one of a number of reasons, their background in reading is limited. At the same time, their concerns and interests are those of other college students. These students need to develop their reading skills through the use of adult-level materials. A related problem, evident even in class discussions, is that they often lack the skills required to think consistently in a clear and analytic way.

Groundwork for College Reading, Third Edition, is designed to develop effective reading *and* clear thinking. To do so, the book is divided into three parts, each described below.

Part I presents a sequence of word and reading skills that are widely recognized as forming the basis for sound comprehension. The first four chapters focus on word skills:

1 Phonics I: Consonants. The rules governing consonants, including single consonants, consonant blends, digraphs, and silent letter combinations.

2 Phonics II: Vowels. When a vowel is likely to be long or short.

3 Phonics III: Syllables. Principles of breaking words into syllables.

4 Dictionary Use. Guide words and the contents of dictionary entries.

Literal comprehension, the basic level of understanding, is then taught in the remaining six chapters in Part I:

5 Vocabulary in Context. How to determine the meaning of an unfamiliar word.

6 Main Ideas. The steps to finding the topic and the main idea of a paragraph.

7 Supporting Details. The difference between major and minor details; how to outline and prepare maps.

8 Finding Main Ideas. Locations of topic sentences.

9 Relationships I. Relationships of addition and time.

10 Relationships II. Relationships of comparison and contrast, cause and effect, and illustration.

In every chapter in Part I, the key aspects of a skill are explained and illustrated clearly and simply. Each explanation is followed by a series of practices, and four review tests end each chapter. The last review test centers on a reading selection so that students can apply the skill just learned to real-life reading materials, including book excerpts and textbook selections. Each reading is followed by word and comprehension questions that focus on the skill learned in the chapter and, from Chapter 2 on, in prior chapters. Together, the ten chapters provide students with the skills needed for a solid understanding of reading materials.

Following each chapter in Part I are six mastery tests on the skill being learned. The tests progress in difficulty, giving students additional challenging practice. Designed for quick grading, they also require careful thought on the part of the student.

Part II consists of ten additional readings that will help improve both reading and thinking skills. Each reading is followed by a series of *Word Skill Questions* and *Reading Comprehension Questions* that ask students to apply the skills presented in Part I. In addition, an *Outlining* or *Mapping Activity* helps students think carefully about the basic content and organization of the selection. *Discussion Questions* then provide instructors the opportunity to engage students in various reading and thinking skills. The readings in Parts I and II have been chosen not only for the clarity of the writing but also for their compelling content. They thus give your students two key reading experiences: inspiration and simple enjoyment.

Part III begins with a chapter titled "Word Parts" that is formatted much the same as the chapters in Part I. You may want to use this chapter as part of your syllabus.

This chapter is followed by six *Combined Skills Tests* that let students test their knowledge of the word skills and comprehension skills they learned in Part I of the book. Next are six *Advanced Combined Skills Tests* that have no phonics and dictionary questions, and concentrate on comprehension questions.

Finally, there are two *Writing Assignments* for each selection in the text. These questions will help students to focus on the message contained in the selection and to provide personal insights to the selection's content. Just as important, students will begin to understand that reading, writing, and thinking are closely connected skills.

Important Features of the Book

- **Focus on the basics.** The book seeks to explain in a clear, step-by-step way the essential elements of each skill. Many examples are provided to ensure that students understand each point. In general, the focus is on *teaching* the skills, not just on explaining them and not just on testing them.

- **Frequent practice and feedback.** In the belief that progress is made largely through abundant practice and careful feedback, this book includes numerous activities. Students can get immediate feedback on the practice exercises in Part I by turning to the Limited Answer Key in the back of the book. The answers to the review and mastery tests in Part I, the questions for the reading selections in parts II and III, and the review and mastery tests in Part III are in the *Instructor's Manual,* as well as the *Instructor's Edition.*

  The Limited Answer Key increases the active role that students take in their own learning. And they are likely to use the answer key in an honest and positive way if they know that they may be tested on the many activities and selections for which answers are not provided. (Answers not in the book can be easily copied from the *Instructor's Manual* and handed out at the your discretion.)

- **High interest level.** Dull readings and exercises work against learning. The reading selections in this book have been chosen not only for the appropriateness of their reading level but also for their compelling content. This should facilitate the learning process. The selections are meant to appeal to a wide range of students—developmental students, students for whom English is a second language, and Adult Basic Education students. They also take into account the diverse backgrounds of such students.

- **Ease of use.** The logical sequence in each chapter—from explanation to example to practice to review tests to mastery tests—helps make the skills easy to teach. The organization of the book into distinct parts also makes for ease of use. Within a single class, for instance, instructors can work on a particular skill in Part I, review another skill with a mastery test, and provide variety by assigning one of the selections in Part II. The Limited Answer Key at the back of the book also makes for versatility: It means that you can assign parts of each chapter for self-teaching. Finally, the review tests, mastery tests, and combined-skills tests—each on its own tear-out page—make it simple for you to test and evaluate student progress.

- **Integration of skills.** Students do more than learn the skills individually in Part I. They also learn to apply the skills together through the reading selections in Parts I, II, and III and through the combined-skills tests in Part III. In other words, students become effective readers and thinkers through a great deal of practice in applying a combination of skills.

- **Thinking activities.** There are many kinds of thinking activities in *Groundwork for College Reading*, Third Edition. First are the three discussion questions that end each reading selection. They are designed to encourage diverse points of view regarding the selection. Next is the mapping or outlining activity at the end of each reading selection in Part II. These will help students see and understand the organizational pattern of each selection. And third are the two writing activities in Part III for each reading, which allow students to further express their opinions on some aspect of the selection.

  The book is designed, then, to create activities that truly involve students in the processes of reading and thinking while enabling you to provide feedback easily. This practice and feedback on interesting, challenging material will help your students to become effective readers and thinkers.

- **Supplementary materials.** The three helpful supplements listed below are available at no charge to instructors using the text. Any or all can be obtained quickly by contacting Townsend Press in any of the ways indicated on the copyright page.

  1 The *Instructor's Edition*—chances are that you are holding it in your hand—is identical to the student book except that it also provides hints for teachers (see the front of the book), answers to all the practices and tests, and comments on selected items.

  2 A combined *Instructor's Manual and Test Bank* includes suggestions for teaching the course, a model syllabus, readability levels, and answers to the review and mastery tests in Parts I and III and to the questions on the reading selections in Parts II and III. The test bank contains four additional mastery tests for each of the ten skills—all on letter-sized sheets so they can be copied easily for use with students.

  3 *Computer software* (in IBM-DOS, Windows, or Macintosh format) provides two additional mastery tests for each of the ten chapters in Part I of the book. The disks contain a number of user-and instructor-friendly features: brief explanations of answers, a sound option, frequent mention of the user's first name, a running score, and a record-keeping score file.

- **One of a sequence of books.** *Groundwork for College Reading* is the basic text in a series that includes these other books:

     Ten Steps to Building College Reading Skills is suited for an early college reading course. This book provides one word skill (dictionary use) and nine comprehension chapters.

     Ten Steps to Improving College Reading Skills is an intermediate text. It is appropriate for the core developmental reading course offered at most colleges.

     Ten Steps to Advancing College Reading Skills is a higher level developmental text than the *Improving* book. It can be used as the core book for a more advanced class, as a sequel to the intermediate book, or as a second-semester alternative to it.

     A companion set of vocabulary books, listed on page iv, has been designed to go with each book listed above. Recommended to accompany this book is *Groundwork for a Better Vocabulary.*

     Together, the books and their full range of supplements form a sequence that should be ideal for any college reading program.

To summarize, *Groundwork for College Reading*, Third Edition, provides ten word and reading skills to help developmental college students, English as a second language students, and Adult Basic Education students to become independent readers and thinkers. Through an appealing collection of readings and a carefully designed series of activities and tests, students receive considerable guided practice in the skills. The result is an integrated approach to learning that will bring about better readers and stronger thinkers.

Changes in the Third Edition

- **Fresh materials.** About half of the practice materials in the book are new, along with eleven new and highly inspirational readings. The questions used in choosing these selections included these: "Are students going to be moved by this?" "Will students learn from this?" and "Does this selection clearly teach the skill in question?"

- **Major chapter revisions.** Several chapters, most notably "Supporting Details," have been expanded. Two chapters on relationships will make it clearer for students to see the connection between ideas in sentences and within paragraphs. And each chapter in Part I ends with a concise summary, to give students an overview of the chapter and a chance to review the key ideas in it.

- **Integration of transitions with patterns of organization.** The previous edition of the book presented transitions and patterns of organizations in separate chapters. The book now emphasizes the connection between relationships on the sentence level and on the paragraph level. Students will see that transitions signal relationships between two ideas and that certain patterns organize relationships among ideas in paragraphs and longer selections. Specifically, "Relationships I" shows relationships that involve addition and time; "Relationships II" looks at relationships of comparison and contrast, cause and effect, and illustration.

- **Addition of outlining and mapping explanations.** The relationship between main ideas and supporting details is further solidified in "Supporting Details" by explanations of outlining and mapping.

- **Relocation of mastery tests.** For greater ease of use, the six mastery tests for each skill now immediately follow the chapter on that skill.

- **New design elements.** To increase readability, a slightly larger typeface than the one in the previous edition has been used for this text, and a two-column format is now used for the reading selections.

Acknowledgments

Thanks to the exceptional design skills of Janet M. Goldstein, the book enjoys a remarkably clear and "user-friendly" format. I owe appreciation to Janet and to Susan Gamer and Eliza Comodromos for editing and proofreading help. I also appreciate the editorial role played by Carole Mohr, who has worked closely with me on every page of the book. Finally, I am grateful to my wife, Tari, for her inspiration, her confidence in me, and her patience.

Bill Broderick

How to Become a Better Reader and Thinker

The chances are that you are not as good a reader as you should be to do well in college. If so, it's not surprising. You live in a culture where people watch an average of *over seven hours of television every day!* All that passive viewing does not allow much time for reading. Reading is a skill that must be actively practiced. The simple fact is that people who do not read very often are not likely to be strong readers.

- How much television do you watch on an average day? _____ hours

Here are two points to consider about reading. First, a skilled reader is an active reader, one who understands that there must be interaction between the reader and the writer. You can't stare at the words on a page and hope that meaning will come to you. You must work to find the meaning that is intended. This means thinking about what the words and phrases mean and about the message the author is sending you.

Second, you must understand that reading is a key to a successful life. Regular reading improves vocabulary, spelling, reading speed, and comprehension. It develops the command of language so necessary to succeed in today's job world. In short, reading is crucial for people who want to make something of themselves. People who are achievers *make* time to read, even though their responsibilities, including job and family, are often very challenging ones.

Answer these questions about your reading habits. Be honest in your responses.

- Do you read on a regular basis (including newspapers, weekly magazines, and novels)? _____

- What are you most likely to read? _____

- Do you enjoy reading? _____

- Do you feel you have problems with reading? _____

- When are you most likely to do your reading? _____

If you feel you need to improve your reading, *Groundwork for College Reading*, Third Edition, should help you a lot. The book will help you build a solid foundation in the most important skills you need to become a better reader. In addition, this book will help you to strengthen your ability to think clearly and logically. Reading and thinking are closely related skills, and both are vital for your success in college. And writing activities will help you to see the important connection between two vital skills—reading and writing.

To find out just how this book will help you learn these essential skills, read the next several pages and do the brief activities as well. The activities are easily completed and will give you a good sense of how the book is arranged, what it will do for you, and what is expected of you as you interact with the book.

HOW THE BOOK IS ORGANIZED

There are three parts to the book. Each part is described below.

Part I: Ten Steps to College Reading (pages 7–374)

To help you become a more effective reader and thinker, this book first presents a series of ten key word and reading skills. They are listed in the table of contents starting on page v. Turn to that page to fill in the skills missing below:

   1 Phonics I: Consonants

   2 _____

   3 Phonics III: Syllables

   4 _____

   5 Vocabulary in Context

   6 Main Ideas

   7 _____

   8 Finding Main Ideas

   9 Relationships I

  10 _____

Each chapter is developed in the same way. First of all, clear explanations and examples help you *understand* each skill. Next, numerous practices give you the "hands-on" experience needed to *review* the skill.

- How many practices are there in the third chapter, "Phonics III: Syllables" (pages 83–112)? _____

At the end of each chapter are four review tests. The first one reviews the information presented in the chapter.

- On which page is Review Test 1 for "Phonics III: Syllables"? _____

The second and third review tests consist of activities that help you practice the skill presented in the chapter.

- On which pages are Review Tests 2 and 3 for "Phonics III: Syllables"?

  _____

The fourth review test centers on a reading selection that gives you the chance both to practice the skill you learned in the chapter and to perfect skills you learned in previous chapters.

- What is the title of the reading selection in "Phonics III: Syllables"?

  _____

The reading selection is followed by a series of questions that focus on the skill taught in the chapter and on skills you have already learned. These questions are followed by three discussion questions that your instructor may use to strengthen understanding of the selection and to give you a chance to voice your opinion about some aspect of the selection.

Also note that there is a "Check Your Performance" box at the end of each chapter so you can track your progress on the four review tests. Your scores can also be entered on the "Reading Performance Chart" on the inside back cover of the book.

Following each chapter are six mastery tests that gradually increase in difficulty.

- On what pages are the mastery tests for "Phonics III: Syllables"?

  _____

The mastery tests are on tear-out pages that can be easily removed and handed in to your instructor. So that you can track your progress, there is a score box at the top of the first page of each test. As with the review tests, your scores for the mastery tests can also be entered into the "Reading Performance Chart" on the inside back cover of the book.

Part II: Ten Reading Selections (pages 375–476)

Part II is made up of ten reading selections followed by questions that will help you to sharpen all of the skills you learned in Part I.

Each reading selection is organized in the same way. Look, for example, at "Rosa: A Success Story," which starts on page 429. What are the headings of the two sections that come before the reading itself?

- _____

- _____

Note that the vocabulary words in "Words to Watch" are followed by the numbers of the paragraphs where the words appear. Now look again at "Rosa: A Success Story," and explain how each vocabulary word is set off in the reading:

- _____

Activities Following Each Reading Selection

After each selection, there are four kinds of activities that will improve your reading and thinking skills.

1. The first activity is **Word Skills Questions**—questions involving phonics, dictionary use, and vocabulary in context.

   - Look at the word skills questions for "Rosa: A Success Story." Note that the first two questions deal with phonics and the next three focus on dictionary use. How many questions deal with vocabulary in context? _____

2. The second activity is **Reading Comprehension Questions**—questions involving central point, main idea, supporting details, and relationships.

   - Look at the reading comprehension questions for "Rosa: A Success Story." How many questions are there in all? _____

   - How many questions focus on supporting details? _____

3. The third activity involves **outlining or mapping**. Each activity is designed to get you to think logically and clearly about what you have read.

   - How many answers must you fill in for the mapping activity that follows "Rosa: A Success Story?" _____

4. The fourth activity consists of **discussion questions**. These questions provide a chance for you to deepen your understanding of each selection.

   - How many discussion questions are there for "Rosa: A Success Story"?

_____

Part III: For Further Study (pages 477–552)

This part of the book contains additional materials that can help improve your reading.

1. The first chapter is titled **"Word Parts"** and may be included by your instructor as part of your semester's work.

   - This chapter also includes, on page 511, a special offer to students who are using *Groundwork for College Reading*. What is this special offer?

     _____

2. The second chapter is titled **"Combined-Skills Tests."** Here you will find short reading selections followed by questions that focus on the skills you learned in Part I of the book.

   - How many combined-skills tests are there? _____

   - How many questions are there for each combined-skills test? _____

3. The final chapter is made up of **Writing Activities** for all the reading selections in the book. Reading and writing are closely connected skills, and writing practice will improve your ability to read carefully and to think more clearly.

   - How many writing activities are there for "Rosa: A Success Story?"

     _____

HELPFUL FEATURES OF THE BOOK

1 The book centers on *what you really need to know* to become a better reader and thinker. It presents ten key word and comprehension skills, and it explains the most important points about each skill.

2 The book gives you *lots of practice.* We seldom learn a skill only by hearing or reading about it; we make it part of us by repeated practice. There are, then, numerous activities in the text. They are not "busy work," but carefully designed materials that should help you truly learn each skill.

   Notice that after you learn each skill in Part I, you move through a series of review tests, you read a selection that focuses on that skill, and you conclude with mastery tests where you must apply the skill. And as you move from one skill to the next, you continue to practice and reinforce the ones already learned.

3 The selections throughout the book are *motivational and appealing.* Dull and unvaried readings work against learning, so subjects have been carefully chosen for their high interest level. Almost all the selections are

excellent examples of how what we read can capture our attention. For example, read the first three paragraphs of "A Lesson in Love" (page 66) and then try to *stop* reading.

HOW TO USE THIS BOOK

1 A good way to proceed is to read and reread the explanations and examples in a given chapter in Part I until you feel you understand the ideas presented. Then carefully work through the practices. As you finish each one, check your answers with the "Limited Answer Key" that starts on page 553.

   For your own sake, don't just copy in the answers without trying to do the practices! The only way to learn a skill is to practice it first and *then* check the answer key to give yourself feedback. Also, take whatever time is needed to figure out just why you got some answers wrong. By using the answer key to help teach yourself the skills, you will prepare yourself for the review tests at the end of each chapter as well as for the mastery tests and the reading selection questions in the book. Your instructor can supply you with answers to those tests.

   If you have trouble catching on to a particular skill, stick with it. In time, you will learn each of the ten skills.

2 Read the selections with the intent of simply enjoying them. There will be time afterwards for rereading each selection and using it to develop your comprehension skills.

3 Keep track of your progress. Fill in the charts at the end of each chapter in Part I and each reading selection in Parts II and III. And complete the "Reading Performance Chart" on the inside back cover by entering your scores for the review tests and mastery tests in Parts I and III and the reading selections in Parts II and III. These scores can give you a good view of your overall performance as you work through the book.

In summary, *Groundwork for College Reading*, Third Edition, has been designed to interest and benefit you as much as possible. Its format is straight-forward, its explanations are clear, its readings are appealing, and its many practices will help you learn through doing. *It is a book that has been created to reward effort,* and if you provide that effort, you will make yourself a better reader and a stronger thinker. I wish you success.

Bill Broderick

Part I

TEN STEPS TO COLLEGE READING

1

Phonics I: Consonants

What do you do when you are reading and come across a word you can't pronounce? Do you ignore the word, hoping it isn't important? Do you ask someone how the word is pronounced? What you should do is look at the word, break it into syllables, sound out each syllable, and put the word back together again. To put it another way, you should use a very helpful method known as phonics.

Phonics tells you how to break a word into parts called syllables and how to pronounce each syllable. It is true that English letters don't always sound the way you expect them to. But phonics can help you figure out the sounds of most words. And when phonics isn't enough, you can use a dictionary (which is the topic of Chapter 4).

This chapter explains the pronunciation of consonants. Chapter 2 will cover the most important points about vowels. Chapter 3 will show you how to break words into syllables. What you learn in each of these chapters will help you in the ones that follow. In these first three chapters, the keys to improvement are practice and patience. By working carefully on each activity, you will sharpen your ability to pronounce words.

But you'll also need to practice using phonics in everyday reading. You'll find it helpful to read the selections that end each chapter in Part I as well as the selections in Part II of this book. And you should also get into the habit of reading, every day, something that interests you—in magazines, newspapers, and books. Slowly but surely, you will improve your reading.

CONSONANTS

Twenty-one of the twenty-six letters in the English alphabet are **consonants**. (The others are vowels, which will be discussed in Chapter 2.) The consonants are shown on the next page.

Consonants

b	c	d	f	g	h	j
k	l	m	n	p	q	r
s	t	v	w	x	y	z

The sounds of consonants are made when the tongue, lips, or teeth block the air that comes out of your mouth as you speak. In this chapter, you'll learn about the most common sounds of consonants. These three areas will be covered:
- Single Consonants with Just One Sound
- Single Consonants with More Than One Sound
- Three Types of Consonant Combinations

SINGLE CONSONANTS WITH ONLY ONE SOUND

The fifteen consonants listed below generally have only one sound. Each letter is followed by three examples. See if you can add a fourth example of the sound, using the space provided. The first additional example is done for you.

b	bed	able	crab	*best*
f	fan	gift	grief	
h	hog	behave	reheat	
j	jab	jaw	banjo	
k	kiss	bakery	peek	
l	lump	delay	heel	
m	mud	dime	ram	
n	neck	unit	lemon	
p	pat	paper	creep	
r	rub	roar	dear	
t	tub	note	street	
v	vine	river	hive	
w	web	award	sewer	
y	yell	yawn	mayor	
z	zoom	crazy	quiz	

SINGLE CONSONANTS WITH MORE THAN ONE SOUND

The following consonants have more than one sound:

c	g	d	q	s	x

Common sounds for each of these letters are explained below.

1   Sounds of *c*

When **c** is followed by **e, i,** or **y**, it usually has the sound of **s** as in *salt*. This is called the **soft sound** of **c**. Below are five words with the soft sound of **c**. See if you can add a sixth example of the soft sound in the space provided.

cell   circus   city

cereal   bicycle   _____

Whenever **c** is not followed by **e, i,** or **y**, it sounds like **k**. This is known as the **hard sound** of **c**. Below are five words with the hard sound of **c**. See if you can add a sixth example of the hard sound in the space provided.

can   cub   actor

arc   circus   _____

➣ *Practice 1*

Use a check mark to show whether the boldfaced **c** in each word has the soft sound (like the sound of **s** in *cell*) or the hard sound (like the sound of **k** in *can*). The first one is done for you as an example.

	Soft sound of **c** (sounds like **s**)	Hard sound of **c** (sounds like **k**)
1. **c**igarette	✓	
2. **c**are		
3. i**c**e		
4. **c**ustom		
5. pea**c**e		
6. post**c**ard		

	Soft sound of **c** (sounds like **s**)	Hard sound of **c** (sounds like **k**)
7. de**c**ide	_____	_____
8. re**c**ord	_____	_____
9. pani**c**	_____	_____
10. de**c**ent	_____	_____

2   Sounds of *g*

The consonant **g** has two common sounds. These sounds follow the same principle as **c**. When **g** is followed by **e, i** or **y**, it often has the sound of the letter **j**. This is the **soft sound** of **g**. Below are five words with the soft sound of **g**. See if you can add a sixth example of the soft sound in the space provided.

gem	**gin**	**gym**
an**gel**	ma**gic**	_____

(There are some common exceptions to this rule, including such words as *get, girl,* and *gift.*)

When **g** is not followed by **e, i** or **y**, it usually has its **hard sound**, as in *gum* and *leg*. Below are five words with the hard sound of **g**. See if you can add a sixth example of the hard sound in the space provided.

game	**goal**	**guess**
a**go**	pi**g**	_____

➤ *Practice 2*

Use a check mark to show whether the boldfaced **g** in each word has the soft sound (like the **g** in *gem*) or the hard sound (like the **g** in *game*). The first one is done for you as an example.

	Soft sound of **g** (as in *gem*)	Hard sound of **g** (as in *game*)
1. **g**entle	✓	_____
2. **g**uest	_____	_____
3. ra**g**e	_____	_____

	Soft sound of **g** (as in *gem*)	Hard sound of **g** (as in *game*)
4. green	_____	_____
5. pigeon	_____	_____
6. fog	_____	_____
7. frigid	_____	_____
8. gesture	_____	_____
9. legal	_____	_____
10. fragment	_____	_____

3 Sounds of *d*

The consonant **d** usually sounds like the **d** in *dot.* Here are some words with the usual sound of **d**:

    date   si**d**e   blee**d**

At times **d** sounds like **j**. Here are some words in which **d** sounds like **j**:

    e**d**ucate   sche**d**ule   sol**d**ier

There is no sure guideline for knowing when **d** sounds like **j**. But once in a while, you will find that giving a **d** the sound of **j** will be the key to recognizing a word.

4 Sounds of *q (qu)*

The consonant **q** is always followed by **u**. **Qu** is always followed by a vowel and usually sounds like **kw**. Here are some words in which **qu** sounds like **kw**:

    queen   **qu**ilt   re**qu**ire

Sometimes **qu** sounds like **k**. Here are some words in which **qu** sounds like **k**:

    anti**qu**e   pla**qu**e   mos**qu**ito

Qu will usually sound like **k** when a word ends in **que** or in a word that comes to us directly from a foreign language, such as *mosquito* (from Spanish) or *quiche* (from French).

5   Sounds of *s*

The consonant **s** usually sounds like the **s** in *salt.* Here are some other words in which **s** has its usual sound:

soup   unsafe   cost

Sometimes **s** sounds like **z**, as in the word *those.* The **z** sound is common in two situations: 1) when **s** comes between two vowels (as in *rose*), and 2) at the end of a word that shows possession or ownership (such as *his*). Here are some words in which **s** sounds like **z**:

nose   reason   hers

6   Sounds of *x*

The consonant **x** usually sounds like **ks**. Here are some words in which **x** sounds like **ks**:

fox   next   toxic

When the combination **ex** is followed by a vowel, then **x** usually sounds like **gz**. Here are some words in which **x** sounds like **gz**:

exact   exam   exist

Finally, when **x** begins a word (which is rare), it has the sound of **z**, as in the word *Xerox.*

THREE TYPES OF CONSONANT COMBINATIONS

A **consonant combination** is two or more consonants that work together. There are three kinds of consonant combinations:

- **Consonant blends**: Combinations that blend the sounds of single consonants.
  Examples: **sp**it   fe**lt**   **scr**een

- **Consonant digraphs**: Consonant pairs that combine to make a new sound.
  Examples: rou**gh**   wi**sh**   **th**in

- **Silent consonants**: Consonants that are silent in certain combinations.
  Examples: lam**b**   si**ck**   **wr**ong

Each type of consonant combination is explained on the following pages.

Consonant Blends

Consonant blends are two or more neighboring consonants that keep their own sounds but are spoken together. The sounds blend with each other, or run together. For example, the letters **sm** are a consonant blend. To pronounce this blend, just pronounce the **s** and then glide into the sound of the **m**. This is the sound you say at the beginning of the word *smile*.

Below are some words that begin with consonant blends. Read the words to yourself, and notice that you can hear the sound of each of the boldfaced consonants.

bread   **fl**y   **st**eam

Consonant blends also occur in the middle and at the end of words. Read the following words to yourself, and notice that you can hear the sound of each boldfaced consonant.

mo**nst**er   pi**nk**   sou**nd**

Here are four major types of consonant blends:

1 Blends that begin with **s**
2 Blends that end in **l**
3 Blends that end in **r**
4 Other blends in the middle or at the end of a word

Each type of consonant blend is listed and illustrated below and on the following pages. Read the words given as examples, and note the sounds of their consonant blends.

1   Blends that begin with *s*

sc-	scr-	sk-	sl-	sm-
sn-	sp-	spl-	spr-	squ-
st-	str-	sw-		

The consonant blends in the box above are found at the beginning and in the middle of words. In addition, three of them are found at the ends of a word: **-sk**, **-sp**, and **-st**.

Below, two words illustrate each type of blend that begins with **s**. In the space provided, add a third example of each blend.

sc   **sc**ore   **sc**ab   _____

scr   **scr**ap   **scr**eam   _____

sk	**sk**ate	a**sk**	_____
sl	**sl**am	a**sl**eep	_____
sm	**sm**all	**sm**og	_____
sn	**sn**ore	un**sn**ap	_____
sp	**sp**ank	wa**sp**	_____
spl	**spl**ash	**spl**it	_____
spr	**spr**out	re**spr**ay	_____
squ	**squ**eak	**squ**are	_____
st	**st**eel	be**st**	_____
str	**str**eet	in**str**uct	_____
sw	**sw**ear	**sw**eet	_____

➤ _Practice 3_

A. Find the five words below that have a consonant blend beginning with **s**. Remember that this blend may occur anywhere in a word. Write the words in the blank spaces.

asleep	crisp	mask	pints	seat
sew	side	some	squeal	west

_____   _____   _____

_____   _____

B. Find the five words below that have a consonant blend beginning with **s**, and write them in the blank spaces.

   The time it takes to burn a hundred calories varies greatly from activity to activity. Some activities take a long time. For instance, volleyball takes nineteen minutes. Golf takes seventeen. Bowling takes twenty-nine. Other sports take much less time. If you row, you can burn one hundred calories in seven minutes. A strenuous game of racquetball will burn a hundred calories in eight minutes. And downhill skiing will burn a hundred calories in just six minutes.

_____   _____   _____

_____   _____

2 Blends that end in *l*

bl-	cl-	fl-	gl-	pl-

These consonant blends may be at the beginning or in the middle of a word. Examples are *bless* and *apply*.

Below, two words illustrate each type of blend ending in l. In the space provided, add a third example of each blend.

bl	**bl**ess	un**bl**ock	_____
cl	**cl**am	de**cl**ine	_____
fl	**fl**ag	re**fl**ect	_____
gl	**gl**ad	re**gl**ue	_____
pl	**pl**ay	ap**pl**y	_____

➤ *Practice 4*

A. Find the five words below that have a consonant blend ending with l. Remember that this blend may occur at the beginning or in the middle of a word. Write the words in the blank spaces.

ablaze	boil	class	deal	glass
imply	inflame	lame	lick	lug

_____   _____   _____

_____   _____

B. Read the paragraph below, and find the five words that have a consonant blend ending with l. Write them in the blank spaces.

A flag in the half-mast position (halfway down the pole) is a sign of respect for a national leader who has died or for an acclaimed citizen who has been killed in the line of duty. Many first saw this sad sight after President Kennedy was killed. Since that black day, "Old Glory" has been lowered plenty of times. But for those who first witnessed the country's banner at half-mast after John Kennedy's death, the feeling will never be the same as with that first shock.

_____   _____   _____

_____   _____

3   Blends that end in *r*

br-	cr-	dr-	fr-	gr-
pr-	tr-			

These consonant blends may be at the beginning or in the middle of a word. Examples are *brain* and *contract.*

Below, two words illustrate each type of blend ending in **r**. In the space provided, add a third example of each blend.

br	**br**oke	emb**r**ace	_____
cr	**cr**ime	inc**r**ease	_____
dr	**dr**eam	add**r**ess	_____
fr	**fr**ee	af**r**aid	_____
gr	**gr**eed	tele**gr**am	_____
pr	**pr**ay	exp**r**ess	_____
tr	**tr**ain	cont**r**act	_____

➤ *Practice 5*

A. Find the five words below that have a consonant blend ending with **r**. Remember that this blend may occur at the beginning or middle of a word. Write the words in the blank spaces.

across	entrance	frog	jawbreaker	liar
rage	revert	rope	target	trade

_____   _____   _____

_____   _____

B. Read the paragraph below and find the five words that have a consonant blend ending in **r.** Write them in the blank spaces.

If you are looking at a used car, make sure to give it more than a simple visual inspection. Most used cars look good just sitting on a lot or in a driveway. Take the car out on the road. This will help you to see if the important parts of the car are in good shape. For instance, you'll be able to see if the steering system is on-center. You'll be able to tell if the brakes grab or if they are loose. You'll find out how the transmission is acting. And pushing down on the gas pedal will help you see if there are any problems in picking up speed. A road test is a must if you want to make sure you are buying the right used car.

_____   _____   _____

_____   _____

4   Other blends in the middle or at the end of a word

-ft	-ld	-lt	-mp	-nd
-nk	-nt			

These consonant blends may be at the end of a word, as in *lift,* or at the end of a syllable within the word, as in *wanted.*

Below, two words illustrate each type of blend at the end of a syllable or word. In the space provided, add a third example of each blend.

ft	li**ft**	so**ft**ly	_____
ld	chi**ld**	go**ld**en	_____
lt	be**lt**	me**lt**down	_____
mp	la**mp**	du**mp**ster	_____
nd	ha**nd**	wi**nd**shield	_____
nk	i**nk**	ba**nk**book	_____
nt	fro**nt**	pai**nt**ing	_____

➤ *Practice 6*

A. Find the five words below that have a consonant blend at the end of a syllable or at the end of a word. Write the words in the blank spaces.

bumper	glad	handcuff	mild	prod
punt	sank	sweep	very	wire

_____   _____   _____

_____   _____

B. Complete the passage by filling in each blank with the word that contains a consonant blend at the end of a syllable or at the end of the word.

Miguel and Maria were having a *(tough, difficult)* _____ time deciding where to take their family for their vacation. Miguel suggested that they *(stay, camp)* _____ near Las Vegas, where the kids would enjoy the warm weather and he and Maria could enjoy the shows. Maria, however, wanted to go on a *(raft, hike)* _____ in northern California, even though the weather was *(chillier, colder)* _____. But the kids had the final say, and the family ended up going to *(Hawaii, Disneyland)* _____.

Consonant Digraphs

You have just learned that in consonant blends, each consonant is pronounced. In the blend **nt**, for example, two sounds are heard. However, there are some pairs of consonants with only one sound. And that sound is very different from the sound of either of the two letters. A pair of consonants with only one sound is called a **digraph**.

Three types of digraphs are explained below:

1 Digraphs that sound like **f**: **gh** and **ph**
2 Digraphs with new sounds of their own: **sh** and **th**
3 A digraph with three sounds: **ch**

1   Digraphs that sound like *f: gh* and *ph*

The digraphs **gh** and **ph** do not sound like either of the letters they contain. Instead, they each have the sound of a single consonant: **f**.

Following are examples of words in which **gh** sounds like **f**. Note that this digraph appears at the end of a syllable or word.

lau**gh**ing   enou**gh**   tou**gh**

Following are examples of words in which **ph** sounds like **f**. Note that this digraph may appear at the beginning, in the middle, and at the end of words.

phone   dol**ph**in   gra**ph**

2   Digraphs with new sounds of their own: *sh* and *th*

The digraphs **sh** and **th** do not sound like any single letter. Instead, they have sounds of their own.

Below are some words that include the digraph **sh**. Pronounce the words to yourself, and note that **sh** is not a blended sound of **s** plus the sound of **h**. It is a completely different sound.

show　　　　　　　**washer**　　　　　　　**fish**

The digraph **th** has two sounds of its own that are similar to each other. Say the following two groups of words out loud (not in a whisper), and you will hear the slight difference in the two **th** sounds. If you pronounce these words correctly, you will feel a slight vibration of your tongue as you say the words with the "voiced **th** sound." There is no vibration when you say the words with an "unvoiced **th** sound." Instead, you should feel a rush of air between your teeth when you complete the unvoiced **th**.

*Voiced **th** sound*	*Unvoiced **th** sound*
their	**th**ird
they	**th**in
there	**th**ank
ba**th**e	ba**th**

3   A digraph with three sounds: *ch*

The digraph **ch** has three different sounds. The most common is the sound that you hear in the word *achieve*. Here are some other words in which **ch** has that sound. As you pronounce each word, note that the sound of **ch** is hard and short.

chip　　　　　　　**ch**ief　　　　　　　ran**ch**

Ch can also sound like another digraph: **sh**. Here are some words in which **ch** sounds like **sh**:

chef　　　　　　　**ch**ute　　　　　　　Mi**ch**elle

These two sounds, **ch** and **sh**, are very different from each other. If you have trouble hearing the difference between them, think of the **ch** as being a short, forceful sound, such as the one you might make if you are sneezing: "Ah-**ch**oo!" The **sh** is a much more gentle sound, like the sound you would make if you were trying to quiet a young child: "**Sh**hhh."

Finally, **ch** can also have the same sound as a single consonant: **k**. Here are some words in which **ch** sounds like **k**:

chorus	**ch**emist	**ch**aracter
Christian	**ch**rome	**ch**ronic

Notice that all the words in the second line above begin with **chr**. Whenever **ch** is followed by **r**, **ch** will sound like **k**.

➤ *Practice 7*

Complete each sentence by filling in the blank with the word that has a consonant digraph.

1. Professor Vasquez stopped lecturing when a bug flew into her *(eye, nose, mouth)* _____.

2. The *(Chinese, Swedes, Indians)* _____ once trained lions to help them hunt large animals.

3. If you cut off a piece of a *(starfish, lizard, spider)* _____, the piece will grow into a new animal.

4. Kim's new job didn't leave her much time to *(exercise, shop, travel)* _____.

5. The catchy *(words, phrase, tune)* _____ from the ad he heard on the radio stayed with Domingo all day.

6. Bianca forgot to take the car out of gear, and it kept going until it *(hit, crashed, bumped)* _____ against the garage wall.

7. Scientists have developed dairy products that are low in *(fat, calories, cholesterol)* _____.

8. The excuse that Mike missed his date with Karina because he was studying sounded *(phony, made-up, false)* _____ to her.

9. One of the largest cities in the United States is *(New York, Chicago, San Francisco)* _____.

10. If you have a *(bad, hard, rough)* _____ day at work, it may help to come home and take a hot bath.

Silent Consonants

See if you can pronounce these two common words:

    knee   comb

If you pronounced them correctly, you did not hear all of the consonants. In the first word, the **k** is silent. In the second word, the **b** is silent.

    In certain letter combinations, one consonant is pronounced and one is silent. Below are some common consonant combinations where you will find one letter pronounced and one letter silent. Examples of each combination are also included. Say the words to yourself so you can hear that one letter is silent.

- **mb**   **b** is silent after **m**:

  bo**mb**   li**mb**   cli**mb**

- **ck**   **c** is silent before **k**:

  de**ck**   sti**ck**   pa**ck**er

- **gn**   **g** is silent before **n**:

  gnaw   **gn**at   si**gn**

- **wh**   **h** is often silent after **w** when **wh** begins a word:

  white   **wh**isper   **wh**ip

- **who**   **w** is often silent when a word begins with **who**:

  who   whose   whole

- **kn**   **k** is silent before **n**:

  know   **kn**ife   **kn**ick-**kn**ack

- **wr**   **w** is silent before **r**:

  wreck   **wr**ite   un**wr**ap

- When two of the same consonant are next to each other, one of them is silent:

  be**ll**   a**dd**   na**rr**ow   fu**ss**

➤ *Practice 8*

Complete each sentence by filling in the word that has a silent consonant.

1. To *(know, believe, think)* _____ that something is true, scientists need to see proof.

2. When Dominick woke up, he was so hungry that he ate an entire box of *(granola, cereal, Wheaties)* _____.

3. If you visit a petting zoo, be careful that a baby *(goat, pony, lamb)* _____ does not nibble too hard on your fingers.

4. A key to making good bread is knowing how to *(bake, prepare, knead)* _____ it.

5. When Alexei called to find out where his *(bonus, order, check)* _____ was, he was told, "It's in the mail."

6. Many types of birds enjoy leftover bread *(crumbs, pieces, bits)* _____ that people throw their way.

7. Canada is a beautiful country, but its short summers are *(hot, humid, muggy)* _____ and full of insects.

8. Merchandise that is sold at *(discount, retail, wholesale)* _____ prices often attracts people looking for the best bargain.

9. Andre was glad to get the greeting card until he read its *(contents, poem, message)* _____ : "Roses are red, violets are blue; because of you, I caught the flu."

10. Lewis Carroll, author of *Alice's Adventures in Wonderland*, liked to *(eat, write, sleep)* _____ standing up.

An Important Final Note

You have learned a lot of guidelines in this chapter, and more are coming in the next two chapters. You may wonder if it is possible to remember them all. If so, it may interest you to know that skillful readers don't think about guidelines as they read. In fact, most don't remember what the guidelines are.

This doesn't mean that guidelines are not helpful at first. You will make better progress if you review the principles and words in this chapter and the next two chapters often. Even when your instructor is finished with the first three chapters, review the words in them until these words are easy for you to read. When you can read the words, you will be able to read many others that are like them. And once you know how to pronounce the words with ease, you won't need to think about the guidelines.

If you feel your progress is too slow, get help from your school's learning resource center or a tutor. But if you have done the work in this chapter carefully, you are probably reading better already. Progress happens slowly, and you are usually not aware of it. One way to keep track of your progress is to read a paragraph or two into a tape recorder. Then play the tape back to yourself at the end of this course to see how much you have improved.

Finally, don't forget the one activity that builds good readers best—reading. Read not only school material but as much nonschool material as you can—in newspapers, magazines, and books. Read something every day that especially interests you, even if it's only for a few minutes on the bus, during a coffee break, or before you go to sleep. If you do, you will find before long that you can read faster and understand better what you are reading.

CHAPTER SUMMARY

In this chapter, you learned the following:

- Fifteen consonants have *only one sound* when they stand alone:
  b, f, h, j, k, l, m, n, p, r, t, v, w, y, and **z.**

- Six consonants have *more than one sound:*
  c, g, d, q, s, and **x.**

c	certain, curtain	**q**	queen, antique
g	wage, wags	**s**	soup, nose
d	date, educate	**x**	fox, exact, Xerox

- There are three types of consonant combinations:

  Consonant blends are combinations that blend the sounds of single consonants, as in the following:

  Blends beginning with **s:**
  score, **sc**rap, **sk**ate, **sl**am, **sm**all, **sn**ore, **sp**ank, **spl**ash, **spr**out, **squ**eak, **st**eel, **str**eet, **sw**ear

  Blends ending in **l:**
  bless, **cl**am, **fl**ag, **gl**ad, **pl**ay

  Blends ending in **r:**
  broke, **cr**ime, **dr**eam, **fr**ee, **gr**eed, **pr**ay, **tr**ain

  Blends at the end of a syllable or word:
  li**ft**, chi**ld**, be**lt**, dum**p**ster, win**d**bag, ban**k**book, wan**t**ing

  Consonant digraphs are consonant pairs that combine to make a new sound, such as the following:

  Digraphs that sound like **f:**
  gh: lau**gh**ing   **ph**: **ph**one

  Digraphs with sounds of their own:
  sh: fi**sh**   **th** *(voiced):* **th**eir   **th** *(unvoiced):* **th**ird

  A digraph with three sounds—**ch:**
  chip   **ch**ef   **ch**orus

  Silent consonants are consonants that are silent in certain combinations, including the following:

mb: co**mb**	**gn**: **g**naw	**who**: **w**hose	**wr**: **w**rite
ck: dec**k**	**wh**: **wh**ite	**kn**: **k**now	

  Two consonants together: be**ll**, narro**w**, fu**ss**

➤ Review Test 1

To review what you have learned in this chapter, answer each of the following questions. Fill in the blank, or circle the letter of the correct answer.

1. Two consonants that have more than one sound are
   a. **b** and **f**.
   b. **p** and **r**.
   c. **c** and **g**.

2. The consonant **q** (**qu**) usually sounds like
   a. **k**.
   b. **kw**.
   c. **c**.

3. Which of the following is an example of a consonant blend?
   a. **wh**
   b. **cr**
   c. **qu**

4. A consonant digraph is a consonant combination that
   a. blends together.
   b. makes a new sound.
   c. always sounds the same.

5. _____ TRUE OR FALSE? In the consonant combination **wr**, **w** is silent.

➤ Review Test 2

A. Find the five words that have the *hard* sound of **c** (as in *can*) or of **g** (as in *game*). Write them in the blank spaces.

| cider | come | curse | cut | gun |
| hug | huge | twice | Lucy | page |

1. _____   4. _____

2. _____   5. _____

3. _____

B. Find and write down the five words that contain consonant blends.

| bribe | found | heater | motion | repair |
| smile | stain | unplug | visit | voice |

6. _____   9. _____

7. _____   10. _____

8. _____

C. Complete each sentence by filling in the word that has a consonant digraph.

11. *(Ketchup, milk)* _____ was once sold as a medicine.

12. *(Elephants, Ants)* _____ need only two hours of sleep a day.

13. A *(blinking, flashing)* _____ light makes a good fire alarm for the deaf.

14. An ancient remedy for a bad *(cold, cough)* _____ is to breathe oil of wintergreen.

15. "When in doubt," said Mark Twain, "tell the *(truth, facts)* _____."

D. Find and write down the five words with silent consonants.

alert	bitten	blend	bounce	cheese
reign	slug	truck	whole	wrong

16. _____   19. _____

17. _____   20. _____

18. _____

➤ Review Test 3

A. Find the five words in which **c** has a soft sound (as in *city)* or **g** has a soft sound (as in *gem),* and write them in the blank spaces.

cent	comma	cost	ego	gentle
germ	giant	great	rice	tact

1. _____   4. _____

2. _____   5. _____

3. _____

B. Complete each sentence by filling in the word that has a consonant blend.

6. Do you think it is funny when people *(fall, slip)* _____ on a wet pavement?

7. Surprising as it may seem, some Eskimos use refrigerators to keep food from *(mice, freezing)* _____.

8. Working out can be painful when you have a *(groin, foot)* _____ injury.

9. After much thought, Jian decided to buy the *(oval, round)* _____ purple earrings.

10. Maya was bilingual, fluent in both English and *(Russian, Spanish)* _____.

C. Underline the consonant digraph in each of the following words. Then use each word to complete one of the sentences below. (Use each word only once.)

chimney   laugh   nephews   shout   thumb

11. If someone says, "I love you," it is not polite to _____.

12. When you use a hammer, be careful not to hit your _____.

13. Using a cellular phone can be convenient unless there is a lot of static, and you are forced to _____ into the phone.

14. If your house has a fireplace, remember that the _____ must be cleaned regularly so it does not get clogged with soot.

15. Our family gatherings include all our relatives—sons, daughters, _____, nieces, grandparents, and so on.

D. Complete the passage by filling in each blank with the word that contains at least one silent consonant.

When you go outside, do you (16. *know, detect)* _____ what the exact temperature is? Probably not. When the weather is cold, we often think that it is colder—so much so that at times we can become (17. *numb, unfeeling)* _____. This is because of the wind. The "wind (18. *chill, bite)* _____ index" tells us what the temperature feels like (19. *when, if)* _____ combined with current wind conditions. There is a similar index when the weather is hot. The "heat index" combines temperature with humidity readings. The more humidity there is, the warmer you will (20. *doubtless, certainly)* _____ feel.

➤ *Review Test 4*

Here is a chance to apply your understanding of consonant sounds to a full-length reading. This selection is about the obstacles in one man's life, from childhood to adulthood. Juan Angel decided to get past these obstacles, one by one, so that he could make his life better. What enables Juan to keep facing obstacle after obstacle? Think about this question as you read "The Struggle Continues." Then answer the phonics questions that follow.

Words to Watch

Following are some words in the reading that do not have strong context support. Each word is followed by the number of the paragraph in which it appears and its meaning there. These words are indicated in the reading by a small circle (°).

    intentions (2): plans
    intensely (5): with great strength
    deliberation (7): careful thought
    acute (9): sharp
    GED (11) general equivalency diploma (equal to a high-school diploma)

THE STRUGGLE CONTINUES

Juan Angel

1   My name is Juan Angel. I am thirty years old, and I was born in Mexico.

2   As a child, I was alone for most of the time. My father was an alcoholic, and he abandoned my family and me when I was three years old. My mother had to struggle to survive by working from place to place in Mexico. Her good intentions° to support me economically were not enough because of low salaries, so she eventually ended up working here in the United States.

3   I lived with some of my relatives in a little village in Mexico and worked from dawn to sunset and ate sometimes once a day. I felt totally condemned to die of starvation and hard work. My relatives spent the money that my mother sent me, claiming that I was just a child and didn't need it. As a defenseless child, I was innocent, ignorant, and lacked the courage to stand up against the abuse and the injustice. My grandmother, who lived in another little village, couldn't do anything about the oppression I suffered, and she probably didn't even know what was really happening in my life. My relatives covered everything up, and the complaints I made were ignored while my suffering continued to get worse. After five years of being mistreated, humiliated, and abused by my relatives, I decided to put an end to it, and I went to live with my grandmother.

4   When I moved into my grandmother's house, I started living a new lifestyle. By then, I was eight years old, and I felt proud of myself for the first time because I had made my first big decision in life.

5   My grandmother had some pigs, so I had to feed them. One day I was feeding them close to a water stream when I saw two boys passing by. They carried some books with them. I saw them every day walking down a grassy road while I fed those pigs. My curiosity grew intensely°, and one day I stopped them on their way back home. I asked them what they were doing, and they told me that they were attending school. I wanted to know if they knew how to read, and immediately they started reading and writing to show me. I simply couldn't believe it. When they left, I scratched my head and nodded for a moment, looking toward the sky. I said, "Going to school! That's exactly the next step I have to work on." After I finished feeding those pigs, I went home. While I was walking home, I thought about how I would convince my grandmother to allow me to to go school. I knew it was going to be hard to convince her because there were around twenty boys in the village, and they were not attending school either, except those two whom I admired.

6   When I talked to her about my decision on going to school, she got very upset, and she immediately thought about who would care for her pigs. I calmed her down by telling her that I would continue feeding them. She didn't accept my proposal at first, so I looked for the two boys and talked to them about my interest in going to school. They encouraged me to leave the house and forget about the pigs; they would help me to go. I thought it was not a bad idea, but I opposed it because my grandmother and I were living alone. In addition, the closest school was two miles away from the village. For those reasons I hesitated to make such a decision. I had spent two years raising pigs and hesitated about my next step.

7   Finally, I gave up and left my grandmother alone in the house. My friends helped me find a place to sleep in town where the school was, and they gave me some food every day. They took me to the school, and I explained my situation to the

principal; to my surprise, his name was Juan, also. He told me that my age (ten years old) wouldn't match the rules of the school. "You're too old," he said. He questioned me for about five minutes, and then he told me to come back the next day. He met with all the teachers, and after some deliberation°, they approved my enrollment as a new student. I was excited and happy about my achievement as a ten-year-old boy. On the other hand, I couldn't sleep very well at night because I remembered my grandmother very much. She was desperately looking for me, and she found me after a week. I cried while I explained to her why I had left home. She hugged me very hard, and then she went to talk to the principal about my desire to attend school. I never expected her to talk to the principal, but she did. I have never experienced so much happiness in my life as when I was ten years old.

8   I walked the two miles back and forth to school every day. In addition, I had to feed the pigs early in the morning before I went to school and after I came home from school. I also chopped wood for cooking. I did chores at home as a responsible man in charge of a household. My grandmother and I lived happily for six years while I was in primary school.

9   After I finished my first six years in school, I had to make another tough decision. I had to leave my grandmother completely alone because the secondary school I wished to attend was in another town about three hours away by bus. A few months before I took off, she began to suffer from an acute° pain in her chest. I didn't want to leave her, but I did. I wanted to stay in school as much as I could. I used to visit her every weekend, but sometimes the lack of money made it impossible. When I started my second year in the school, I began to worry about my grandmother's health. Her chest pains were getting worse, and I received a letter in which she said that she missed me very much.

10   A week later a friend of mine was looking for me at the school. He told me that my grandmother was very sick. I immediately went to see her. She was lying down with a blanket on the floor. When she saw me, she hugged me very hard, and then she began to ask how my school was. I could hardly answer her because my tears ran down my cheeks as never before. She asked me not to cry, but I couldn't stop. She told me to continue in school, and I promised her I would. A few minutes later, she died in my arms, and I felt that everything was torn apart inside me. I thought that I could never overcome the painful experience of losing my grandmother forever.

11   My mother, who was here in the United States, got there in time for the funeral. She asked me to go back with her, but I refused her offer. So she returned to the United States, and I stayed in Mexico for another four years of school. She continued asking me to join her. Finally, I gave in and immigrated to the United States in 1988. I immediately attended an English class at night and worked

days. At the end of the year I got here, my English teacher recommended me to a Hispanic program where I could get my GED° diploma. When I enrolled in the program, everything was free, including a room in a dormitory. When I finished the program, I had my GED. I then returned to my mother's house. I was unemployed, and three months later, I started working on an irrigated farm, growing alfalfa. I worked three years, and I quit because I wanted to find a more flexible job which would allow me to go to college.

12   Now I'm working in a feed department on swing shift, and I'm attending college in the morning. This department where I'm working operates just in the wintertime, so I'm on the verge of being laid off. I'm a part-time student at Blue Mountain Community College, and I would like to continue attending college. I will keep trying to find ways to stay in college.

13   I have been confronting many obstacles in my life since my childhood. I have challenged those obstacles, and I know by experience how to overcome them. It has not been easy, but I always believe in success through education. Even though I know the struggle is not over yet, I will keep an optimistic smile toward the future.

On his job at the alfalfa farm, Juan Angel spent part of his time repairing harvest equipment.

Phonics Questions

Use phonics clues you learned from this chapter to answer the following questions. Circle the letter of your choice for each question.

1. Which word from the sentence below has a consonant digraph?
   a. *thirty*
   b. *old*
   c. *Mexico*

   "I am thirty years old, and I was born in Mexico." (Paragraph 1)

2. The word *alcoholic*, used in the sentence below, contains
   a. two soft **c** sounds.
   b. a hard **c** sound and a soft **c** sound.
   c. two hard **c** sounds.

   "My father was an alcoholic, and he abandoned my family and me when I was three years old." (Paragraph 2)

3. The word *good*, used in the sentence below, contains
   a. a soft **g** sound.
   b. a hard **g** sound.

   "Her good intentions to support me economically were not enough because of low salaries." (Paragraph 2)

4. The word *spent,* used in the sentence below, contains
   a. two consonant blends.
   b. two consonant digraphs.
   c. one consonant blend and one consonant digraph.

   "My relatives spent the money that my mother sent me, claiming that I was just a child and didn't need it." (Paragraph 3)

5. Which word from the sentence below has an **s** that sounds like **z**?
   a. *grandmother's*
   b. *started*
   c. *lifestyle*

   "When I moved into my grandmother's house, I started living a new lifestyle." (Paragraph 4)

6. Which word from the sentence below has a consonant blend?
   a. *then*
   b. *eight*
   c. *felt*

   "By then, I was eight years old, and I felt proud of myself for the first time because I had made my first big decision in life." (Paragraph 4)

7. Which word from the sentence below has a silent letter combination?
   a. *they*
   b. *writing*
   c. *show*

   "I wanted to know if they knew how to read, and immediately they started reading and writing to show me." (Paragraph 5)

8. The word *chores*, used in the sentence below, contains a
   a. consonant blend.
   b. consonant digraph.
   c. silent letter combination.

   "I did chores at home as a responsible man in charge of a household." (Paragraph 8)

9. Which word from the sentence below has a soft **c** sound?
   a. *could*
   b. *overcome*
   c. *experience*

   "I thought that I could never overcome the painful experience of losing my grandmother forever." (Paragraph 10)

10. The word *experience*, used in the sentence below, has an **x** that sounds like
    a. **ks**.
    b. **gz**.

    "I have challenged those obstacles, and I know by experience how to overcome them." (Paragraph 13)

With Juan and his wife, Hilda, are their children
(left to right), Vianey, Danny, and Juan, Jr.

Discussion Questions

1. Why do you think Juan's grandmother did not want him to go to school—even after he told her he would continue feeding the pigs? Do you think Juan was right in going to school against her wishes?

2. When Juan's grandmother died, Juan's mother asked him to move to the United States with her, but Juan refused her offer. What reasons might he have had for refusing her? Do you think he was right to refuse her? Explain your answer.

3. Based on the reading, what do you think are Juan's strongest personal characteristics? Tell what parts of the story reveal each characteristic you mention.

Note: Writing assignments for this selection appear on page 539.

Check Your Performance   CONSONANTS

Activity	Number Right	Points	Score
Review Test 1 (5 items)	_____	× 2 =	_____
Review Test 2 (20 items)	_____	× 1.5 =	_____
Review Test 3 (20 items)	_____	× 1.5 =	_____
Review Test 4 (10 items)	_____	× 3 =	_____
		TOTAL SCORE =	_____%

Enter your total score into the **Reading Performance Chart: Review Tests** on the inside back cover.

CONSONANTS: Test 1

A. Use a check mark to show whether the boldfaced letter in each word has the soft sound of **c** or **g** (as in *city* or *gem)* or the hard sound of **c** or **g** (as in *can* or *game).*

	Soft sound	*Hard sound*
1. **c**oat	_____	_____
2. re**c**ent	_____	_____
3. i**g**nite	_____	_____
4. pa**g**e	_____	_____
5. **c**igar	_____	_____

B. Fill in each blank with the word that contains a consonant blend.

Some very (6. *unusual, strange)* _____ messages have been (7. *found, seen)* _____ on gravestones. For example, the gravestone of one (8. *teacher, professor)* _____ reads: "School is out. Teacher has gone home." Written on another (9. *grave, tomb)* _____ is this message: "I told you I was sick!" One that is especially (10. *brief, odd)* _____ is "That is all."

C. Find the five words that contain a consonant digraph, and write them in the blank spaces. (A reminder: a digraph is a pair of consonants with one sound that differs from the sound of either of the letters.)

depart	enough	grain	Joseph	kitten
pamphlet	rose	she	think	toy

11. _____   14. _____

12 _____   15. _____

13. _____

(Continues on next page)

D. Complete each sentence by filling in the word that has at least one silent consonant.

16. (*Knitting, Painting*) _____ can be a relaxing activity.

17. Leaving your homework where the dog can get at it would be a (*stupid, dumb*) _____ mistake.

18. By the time you finish playing a tough set of tennis, you may be soaked with sweat. Even your (*wristband, headband*) _____ may be all wet.

19. Being (*lost, stuck*) _____ in traffic is not an acceptable excuse for missing a final exam.

20. The chief of a Midwestern Native American tribe was buried (*sitting, lying*) _____ on his favorite horse.

CONSONANTS: Test 2

A. Complete each sentence by filling in the word that has the *hard* sound of **c** (as in *can*) or of **g** (as in *game*).

1. Most people should include high fiber in their diet, including *(celery, cabbage)* _____.

2. In one unusual hairstyle, the hair stands up straight and the ends are tinted *(gold, orange)* _____.

3. Many *(castles, palaces)* _____ have secret rooms and passageways.

4. Raleigh is the capital of *(North Carolina, Georgia)* _____.

5. Many *(geniuses, great people)* _____ did poorly in school, including Thomas Edison and Albert Einstein.

B. Find the five words that contain one or more consonant blends, and write them in the blank spaces.

comet	glad	grin	parade	pathway
prank	redwood	silly	skill	slim

6. _____   9. _____

7. _____   10. _____

8. _____

C. Find the five words below that have a consonant digraph (a pair of consonants with one sound that differs from the sound of either of the letters). Write the words in the blank spaces.

Phil had planned for this day for two years. He had worked evenings and summers, saving all he could. Finally, he had enough money to buy a car he had dreamed of. He walked into a local showroom, pointed to a red Corvette, and wrote a check for a down payment.

11. _____   14. _____

12 _____   15. _____

13. _____   *(Continues on next page)*

D. (16–25.) Circle the ten words in the box that contain a silent consonant. The words are either straight across or straight down. Here are the words you are looking for:

comb	duck	knock	knot	numb
sign	tack	wrap	wreck	write

w	r	a	p	x	s	i	g	n
z	f	w	f	l	g	o	f	h
c	h	r	t	a	c	k	p	z
o	u	i	m	s	t	p	q	f
m	c	t	s	w	r	e	c	k
b	n	e	h	o	t	z	o	n
q	u	e	d	u	c	k	o	o
z	m	t	h	e	i	u	m	c
o	b	k	k	n	o	t	t	k

CONSONANTS: Test 3

A. Use a check mark to show whether the boldfaced letter in each word has the soft sound of **c** or **g** (as in *city* or *gem)* or the hard sound of **c** or **g** (as in *can* or *game).*

	Soft sound	*Hard sound*
1. sa**g**a	_____	_____
2. **c**eiling	_____	_____
3. **g**inger	_____	_____
4. lettu**c**e	_____	_____
5. re**c**ord	_____	_____

B. Fill in each blank space with the word that contains a consonant blend.

Have you been to the zoo lately? If your answer is "no," you are in for a (6. *surprise, shock)* _____ on your next visit. Zoos are changing. They were first (7. *created, used)* _____ to show off rare animals, which were housed in (8. *tiny, small)* _____ cages. Now, zoos (9. *raise, breed)* _____ animals that are in danger of disappearing. Also, the animals are now housed in spaces that are larger and more like the (10. *environments, areas)* _____ they are used to in their homelands.

C. Find the five words that have a silent consonant, and write them in the blank spaces.

chewing	expect	knob	limb	manhunt
memory	perform	pudding	sack	wrist

11. _____   14. _____

12 _____   15. _____

13. _____

(Continues on next page)

D. (16–25.) Circle the ten words in the box that contain a consonant digraph (a pair of consonants with one sound that differs from the sound of either of the letters). The words are either straight across or straight down. Here are the words you are looking for:

ashore	bath	death	dish	gopher
photo	show	them	tough	with

a	b	a	t	h	q	u	u	w
w	r	x	h	n	u	s	d	t
i	f	d	e	a	t	h	c	o
t	p	u	m	c	r	o	f	u
h	h	n	f	o	b	w	r	g
g	o	p	h	e	r	z	y	h
l	t	m	g	p	c	w	z	m
g	o	t	a	s	h	o	r	e
d	i	s	h	u	i	n	g	b

CONSONANTS: Test 4

A. Find the five words that contain a *soft* **c** (as in *city)* or a *soft* **g** (as in *gem),* and write them in the blank spaces.

A recent concert held to benefit earthquake victims made many people angry. First, the price of admission was too high. Next, it seemed like ages before each band set up and was ready to perform. Finally, the seats were so far away from the stage that people could barely see the performers.

1. _____   4. _____

2. _____   5. _____

3. _____

B. (6–15.) Circle the ten words in the box that contain a consonant blend. The words are either straight across or straight down. Here are the words you are looking for:

blush	brief	faint	hunt	round
skate	sneeze	special	stamp	trip

h	o	h	z	s	t	a	m	p
u	f	t	x	n	w	h	y	s
n	b	r	i	e	f	n	k	f
t	h	i	s	e	v	n	t	a
i	o	p	b	z	x	s	l	i
s	k	a	t	e	f	r	q	n
k	a	t	r	o	u	n	d	t
b	l	u	s	h	i	h	e	r
r	u	s	p	e	c	i	a	l

(Continues on next page)

C. Find the five words that have a consonant digraph (a pair of consonants with one sound that differs from the sound of either of the letters). Write the five words in the blank spaces.

bullfrog	cartoon	cheap	desk	eagle
flush	phase	rough	thousand	violet

16. _____   19. _____

17 _____   20. _____

18. _____

D. Fill in each blank with the word that contains at least one silent consonant.

Have you ever tried to (21. *compose, write*) _____ an essay, only to stare at a blank sheet of paper because no ideas come to your mind? This happens to everyone, even (22. *well-known, famous*) _____ authors. Some say it is helpful to get away from the project for a while and do something (23. *entirely, wholly*) _____ different. Others say that this approach is (24. *wrong, poor*) _____. They prefer to jot down anything on paper. They feel that (25. *with luck, in time*) _____, jotting down ideas will help them to gather their thoughts and get on with the writing.

CONSONANTS: Test 5

A. Complete each sentence by filling in the word which has the *soft* sound of **c** (as in *city)* or of **g** (as in *gem).*

1. Just when I thought I had finally won a game of Blackjack, my sister tossed out a(n) *(jack, ace)* _____ and yelled, "That makes 21!"

2. It is generally better to be *(courteous, civil)* _____ than hostile to people you dislike.

3. Most schools require teachers to know basic life-saving *(procedures, techniques)* _____, such as CPR and the Heimlich maneuver.

4. Too much rain can make a mess of a yard's *(vegetation, garden)* _____.

5. Martina was proud when she was named the outstanding *(principal, educator)* _____ of her district.

B. Complete each sentence by filling in the word that has a consonant blend.

6. President Teddy Roosevelt once said, "Speak *(softly, now)* _____ and carry a big stick."

7. In ancient Egypt, cats were so *(respected, admired)* _____ that anyone killing a cat could be punished by death.

8. Whenever my father said, "This is going to hurt me more than you," I knew I was about to be *(punished, spanked)* _____.

9. A hurricane can be so *(powerful, strong)* _____ that it can knock over trees as if they were toothpicks.

10. If you *(run, bump)* _____ into another car, it is a good idea to check for damage.

(Continues on next page)

C. Complete each sentence by filling in the word that has a consonant digraph.

11. Some *(fish, birds)* _____ can be frozen alive and then brought back to life by being defrosted.

12. A research paper can look more impressive if you insert a *(diagram, graph)* _____ into the text.

13. If you are not satisfied with your meal at a restaurant, ask your waiter or waitress to send it back to the *(chef, cook)* _____.

14. When she heard her class *(giggle, laugh)* _____, Professor McNee realized that she was lecturing on the wrong subject.

15. I *(thought, believed)* _____ that ice-skating would be easy—until I tried it.

D. Complete each sentence by filling in the word that has at least one silent consonant.

16. Even experienced skaters sometimes *(fall, trip)* _____ unexpectedly.

17. A dog is considered a *(dumb, friendly)* _____ animal because it cannot speak.

18. A loud *(knocking, pounding)* _____ on the door woke me from a sound sleep.

19. Once I catch a cold, I am likely to begin *(coughing, wheezing)* _____.

20. In Africa, there is a large type of antelope called a *(gnu, wildebeest)* _____.

CONSONANTS: Test 6

A. Read the passage below and fill in each blank with the word that has a *hard* **c** or **g** sound.

Various professional sports are competing for the attention of the American (1. *audience, public*) _____. Baseball and football are still the two most popular sports. However, increasing media coverage has opened the door for other sports. For example, basketball has won over (2. *countless, large*) _____ numbers of fans. Hockey, the national sport of (3. *Iceland, Canada*) _____, has (4. *advanced, gained*) _____ in popularity as well. And on the horizon is the world's most popular sport— (5. *auto races, soccer*) _____.

B. Read the passage below and fill in each blank with a word that has a consonant blend.

In 1965, a seventeen-year-old named (6. *Fred, Guido*) _____ DeLuca borrowed $1,000 from a (7. *bank, relative*) _____ and used it to (8. *start, open*) _____ a (9. *sandwich, doughnut*) _____ shop in Bridgeport, Connecticut. Within a year, he had opened two others. By 1973, there were sixteen shops. Five years later, DeLuca had (10. *ninety, one hundred*) _____ shops operating. You probably recognize the name of these shops: Subway.

(Continues on next page)

C. Read the passage below and fill in each blank with the word that has at least one consonant digraph.

It is not uncommon for college students to want to help people become successful. Yet there are differing opinions on the best way to (11. *accomplish, attain*) _____ this end. Some students choose education as their major, believing that this career choice will give them the (12. *chance, opportunity*) _____ to help people to gain (13. *enough, sufficient*) _____ knowledge to reach their own goals. Other students turn to business as the major most suited to helping others. This (14. *view, philosophy*) _____ says that the best way to help people is to first become (15. *prosperous, rich*) _____ and then use part of your fortune to help them start their own businesses. What do you think?

D. Read the passage below and fill in each blank with the word that has a silent consonant.

Parker Ranch is on the island of Hawaii. It is the (16. *biggest, largest*) _____ privately owned cattle ranch in the United States. The ranch was once open space used mostly by Hawaiian (17. *ducks, geese*) _____. It became a ranch over a hundred years ago, (18. *after, when*) _____ the king of Hawaii was given a gift of five cows and a bull. The animals multiplied and the king needed help in (19. *controlling, managing*) _____ them. He asked a friend, Mr. Parker, to oversee the animals. Parker did so, and the king (20. *signed over, granted*) _____ two acres of land to Parker. The ranch continued to grow, and it is now over 330 square miles.

2

Phonics II:
Vowels

The sounds of vowels are made with an open mouth, unblocked by teeth, tongue, or lips. Here are the five **vowels** in the English language:

   a   **e**   **i**   **o**   **u**

In addition, **y** is sometimes a vowel.

In this chapter, you'll learn about the most common sounds of vowels. Following are the areas that will be covered:

- Short Vowel Sounds
- Long Vowel Sounds
- Other Vowel Sounds

SHORT VOWEL SOUNDS

The list below shows how the short vowel sounds are pronounced. Note that a common symbol for the short sound of a vowel is a cup-shaped curve over the vowel. This symbol is used in many dictionaries to show that a vowel has a short sound.

ă	sounds like the **a** in *pat.*
ĕ	sounds like the **e** in *pet.*
ĭ	sounds like the **i** in *pit.*
ŏ	sounds like the **o** in *pot.*
ŭ	sounds like the **u** in *cut.*

Remembering these words will help you keep each short vowel sound in mind.

➤ *Practice 1*

A. Practice with the Short a Sound

Say each word below to yourself. Write an **a** with a cup symbol (**ă**) beside each word that contains a short **a** sound, like the **a** in *pat*. Put an X beside words that do not have the short **a** sound. The first two are done for you as examples.

1. crack	ă		6. tame	_____
2. stay	X		7. jam	_____
3. land	_____		8. Spain	_____
4. tap	_____		9. bank	_____
5. face	_____		10. pane	_____

B. Practice with the Short e Sound

Say each word below to yourself. Write an **e** with a cup symbol (**ĕ**) beside each word that contains a short **e** sound, like the **e** in *pet*. Put an X beside words that do not have the short **e** sound. The first two are done for you as examples.

1. bent	ĕ		6. less	_____
2. feed	X		7. sea	_____
3. cream	_____		8. speed	_____
4. get	_____		9. end	_____
5. here	_____		10. fret	_____

C. Practice with the Short i Sound

Say each word below to yourself. Write an **i** with a cup symbol (**ĭ**) beside each word that contains a short **i** sound, like the **i** in *pit*. Put an X beside words that do not have the short **i** sound. The first two are done for you as examples.

1. wig	ĭ		6. file	_____
2. spike	X		7. lint	_____
3. slim	_____		8. ride	_____
4. lime	_____		9. pin	_____
5. disk	_____		10. mice	_____

D. Practice with the Short o Sound

Say each word below to yourself. Write an **o** with a cup symbol (ŏ) beside each word that contains a short **o** sound, like the **o** in *pot.* Put an X beside words that do not have the short **o** sound. The first two are done for you as examples.

1. coat	_____X_____		6. stock	_____
2. stop	_____ŏ_____		7. load	_____
3. cone	_____		8. rock	_____
4. soak	_____		9. grow	_____
5. fox	_____		10. bond	_____

E. Practice with the Short u Sound

Say each word below to yourself. Write a **u** with a cup symbol (ŭ) beside each word that contains a short **u** sound, like the **u** in *cut.* Put an X beside words that do not have the short **u** sound. The first two are done for you as examples.

1. bulb	_____ŭ_____		6. bump	_____
2. fuse	_____X_____		7. sure	_____
3. rum	_____		8. blue	_____
4. tune	_____		9. uncle	_____
5. hug	_____		10. cute	_____

Rule for Short Vowel Sounds

Compare the sounds of the words in columns 1 and 2 below. Which column lists words with the short sound of the vowels?

	Column 1	*Column 2*
a	hat	hate
e	pet	Pete
i	fill	file
o	rob	robe
u	cut	cute

Column 1 lists words with the short vowel sound. Notice that there is only one vowel in each word in the first column and that each vowel is followed by one or more consonants. That is the pattern of the **rule for short vowel sounds**:

When a word or syllable has only one vowel and that vowel is followed by one or more consonants, the vowel is usually short.

A **syllable** is a word or part of a word having one vowel sound. The word *hatbox,* for instance, has two syllables: hat-box. Each syllable has one vowel, and each vowel is followed by one consonant. This tells you that the vowel in each part of *hatbox* is short. You will learn more about syllables in Chapter 3.

Below are two examples of this rule for each of the vowels, **a**, **e**, **i**, **o**, and **u**. See if you can add a third example in each space provided.

Short-vowel rule with **a**:	ham	back	_____
Short-vowel rule with **e**:	end	let	_____
Short-vowel rule with **i**:	sit	bill	_____
Short-vowel rule with **o**:	hop	lot	_____
Short-vowel rule with **u**:	dull	sunup	_____

➤ *Practice 2*

Complete each sentence below by filling in the word that contains a short vowel sound. The short vowel may be **a**, **e**, **i**, **o**, or **u**.

1. When you're driving, the last thing you want is for the engine to *(die, stop)* _____.

2. The floodwaters came up to the *(back, rear)* _____ of our house.

3. An old saying says, "A crying baby is a *(fine, hungry)* _____ baby."

4. It is not healthy to eat too much *(meat, fat)* _____.

5. The first *(real, rubber)* _____ tires were invented long before automobiles—they were used on bicycles.

6. Gambling is legal in the state of *(Nevada, Maine)* _____.

7. Margarine and *(oil, butter)* _____ contain the same amount of fat.

8. Even a person with a great personality can wake up in a *(bad, mean)* _____ mood.

9. Many bald men *(believe, think)* _____ that a hat makes a good fashion statement.

10. The *(frame, body)* _____ of a blue whale contains so much blubber that the whale can go for months without eating.

LONG VOWEL SOUNDS

The list below shows how the long vowel sounds are pronounced. Read them to yourself, and you'll see that **each vowel sounds like the letter's name**.

Notice that the symbol for the long sound is a straight line over the letter.

ā   sounds like the **a** in *pay.*
ē   sounds like the **e** in *bee.*
ī   sounds like the **i** in *pie.*
ō   sounds like the **o** in *toe.*
ū   sounds like the **u** in *fuse.*

Note: Some dictionaries show the long **u** sound as **yōō** rather than **ū**. But for the activities here, you can simply use **ū**.

➤ Practice 3

A. Practice with the Long a Sound

Say each word below to yourself. Write an **a** with a line on top of it (**ā**) beside each word that contains a long **a** sound, like the **a** in *pay.* Put an X beside words that do not have the long **a** sound. The first two are done for you as examples.

1. rake	ā	6. pain	_____
2. stack	X	7. ram	_____
3. plant	_____	8. span	_____
4. tape	_____	9. seed	_____
5. race	_____	10. stay	_____

B. *Practice with the Long* e *Sound*

Say each word below to yourself. Write an **e** with a line on top of it (**ē**) beside each word that contains a long **e** sound, like the **e** in *bee*. Put an X beside words that do not have the long **e** sound. The first two are done for you as examples.

1. beam	ē		6. meat	_____
2. fed	X		7. spend	_____
3. creed	_____		8. street	_____
4. wet	_____		9. bent	_____
5. her	_____		10. free	_____

C. *Practice with the Long* i *Sound*

Say each word below to yourself. Write an **i** with a line on top of it (**ī**) beside each word that contains a long **i** sound, like the **i** in *pie*. Put an X beside words that do not have the long **i** sound. The first two are done for you as examples.

1. wine	ī		6. fist	_____
2. sip	X		7. lint	_____
3. slime	_____		8. bride	_____
4. list	_____		9. pink	_____
5. die	_____		10. mile	_____

D. *Practice with the Long* o *Sound*

Say each word below to yourself. Write an **o** with a line on top of it (**ō**) beside each word that contains a long **o** sound, like the **o** in *toe*. Put an X beside words that do not have the long **o** sound. The first two are done for you as examples.

1. code	ō		6. flock	_____
2. stoop	X		7. loan	_____
3. bone	_____		8. lock	_____
4. float	_____		9. blow	_____
5. pox	_____		10. strong	_____

E. Practice with the Long u Sound

Say each word below to yourself. Write a **u** with a line on top of it (**ū**) beside each word that contains a long **u** sound, like the **u** in *fuse*. Put an X beside words that do not have the long **u** sound. The first two are done for you as examples.

1.	flub	__X__	6.	thump	_____
2.	use	__ū__	7.	mute	_____
3.	runt	_____	8.	blunt	_____
4.	huge	_____	9.	cube	_____
5.	cure	_____	10.	cut	_____

Rules for Long Vowel Sounds

Rule 1: Silent *e*

Compare the sounds of the words in column 1 and column 2. Which column lists words with a long vowel sound?

	Column 1	Column 2
a	hat	hate
e	pet	Pete
i	fill	file
o	rob	robe
u	cut	cute

The second column lists words with a long vowel sound. The **e** that ends each word makes the first vowel long, and the final **e** itself is not pronounced. That is the pattern of the **silent-*e* rule**:

> **When a word or syllable ends in a vowel-consonant-*e*, the vowel before the consonant is long and the final *e* is silent.**

Below are two examples of this rule for each of the vowels **a, e, i, o,** and **u.** See if you can add a third example in each space provided.

Silent-**e** rule with **a**:	name	flake	_____
Silent-**e** rule with **e**:	scene	mere	_____
Silent-**e** rule with **i**:	ride	mine	_____
Silent-**e** rule with **o**:	hope	nose	_____
Silent-**e** rule with **u**:	cube	refuse	_____

➤ *Practice 4*

Complete each sentence by filling in the word that has at least one syllable which follows the silent-**e** rule.

1. The forest fire burned many *(oak, elm, pine)* _____ and maple trees.

2. When we first meet someone, we decide whether he or she is a person we can *(trust, like, enjoy)* _____.

3. When you go to class, make sure you have your *(notebook, textbook, pen)* _____ with you.

4. It's *(dangerous, risky, unsafe)* _____ to fall asleep on top of an electric blanket.

5. Is climbing a tall mountain a *(brave, fearless, bold)* _____ adventure or a foolish one?

Rule 2: Two Vowels Together

Each word below has two vowels together that produce a long vowel sound. Pronounce each word, and then read the explanation that follows.

seed	plea	play
see	hail	tie
please	road	toe

The words above follow the **rule for two vowels together**:

When two of certain vowels are together, the first vowel is long and the second is silent.

Below are vowel combinations that usually follow this rule. Two examples are provided for each. Add a third example in the space provided.

ai	aid	aim	_____
ay	pay	stay	_____

Note: In the **-ay** combination, **y** is a vowel.
(See page 58.)

ea	eat	cream	_____
ee	knee	feet	_____

ie	lie	tied	_____
oa	oat	toad	_____
oe	hoe	goes	_____

➤ *Practice 5*

Complete each sentence by filling in the word that has one syllable which follows the two-vowels-together rule.

1. You must be patient if you want to *(train, ride, own)* _____ a horse.

2. In 1896, the first modern Olympics were held in *(Italy, Greece, France)* _____.

3. The entire life span of some insects can last all of a *(minute, day, month)* _____.

4. Before taking a shower, make sure you have enough *(time, soap, hot water)* _____.

5. Some people like individual sports such as tennis, while others prefer *(team, group, joint)* _____ sports like softball.

Rule 3: Final Single Vowel

In each example below, a single vowel ends a word or syllable. Pronounce each word, and listen to the sound of each boldfaced vowel.

m**e**	sh**e**	h**i**
n**o**tice	m**u**sic	b**a**sic

The words above follow the **rule for a final single vowel**:

> **A single vowel at the end of a word or syllable (other than silent *e*) usually has a long sound.**

➤ *Practice 6*

In each item, three words are underlined. In the space provided, write the one underlined word that is an example of the final single vowel rule.

1. Gold was one of the first precious <u>metals</u> discovered by <u>humankind</u>. It is <u>also</u> one of the rarest metals. _____

2. Scientists have learned that the web of a <u>spider</u> can be <u>three</u> times stronger than iron of the same <u>thickness</u>. _____

3. On the average, Americans today sleep <u>over</u> an hour <u>less</u> than Americans of fifty <u>years</u> ago. _____

4. A computer <u>crash</u> can <u>erase</u> valuable information, which <u>may</u> then be lost forever. _____

5. In a <u>famous</u> magic trick, the magician <u>escapes</u> from a locked cell by using a key <u>hidden</u> on his body. _____

OTHER VOWEL SOUNDS

The Vowel *y*

When **y** starts a word (as in *yell*), it is considered a consonant. Otherwise, **y** is a vowel and usually has one of the following three vowel sounds:

- In the middle of a word or syllable, **y** usually sounds like short **i**, as in *myth, gym,* and *syllable*.
- At the end of a one-syllable word, **y** sounds like long **i**, as in *my, sty,* and *fry*.
- At the end of a word with more than one syllable, **y** sounds like long **e**, as in *many, baby,* and *city*.

(Remember that **y** is also considered a vowel when it follows the letter **a**. The combination **ay**, as in *play* and *stay*, follows the rule for two vowels together: the **a** is long and the **y** is silent.)

➤ *Practice 7*

In the space provided, show whether the **y** in each word sounds like a consonant (**y**), short **i** (ĭ), long **i** (ī), or long **e** (ē). The first three are done for you.

1. stingy	ē	6. lynch	_____
2. hymn	ĭ	7. yellow	_____
3. yes	y	8. marry	_____
4. sadly	_____	9. youth	_____
5. by	_____	10. cyst	_____

Sounds of Vowels Followed by *r*

When **r** follows a vowel, it changes the sound of the vowel. A vowel that comes just before an **r** is usually neither long nor short, but in between. To see how this works, say the words below to yourself. Notice how the sound of the vowel— and the shape of your mouth—change a bit when the vowel is followed by **r**.

Long vowels	*Short vowels*	*Vowels followed by* **r**
cane	can	car
Steve	set	her
site	sit	sir
code	cod	cord
fuel	fun	fur

➤ *Practice 8*

Identify each boldfaced vowel with one of the following:

- the symbol for a long vowel sound (¯)
- the symbol for a short vowel sound (˘)
- an **r** if the vowel sound is changed by an **r**

The first three have been done for you.

1. g**a**s	ă	6. f**i**rm	_____
2. h**a**rd	r	7. gl**e**e	_____
3. p**a**ge	ā	8. r**u**n	_____
4. s**ai**nt	_____	9. sp**o**rt	_____
5. t**e**rm	_____	10. tr**i**ck	_____

Long and Short *oo*

When two **o**'s appear together, they are pronounced in one of two ways. One pronunciation is called the **long double o sound**, as in *boot*. Here are some other words with the long sound of **oo**:

spo**oo**n   r**oo**m   kangar**oo**

The other pronunciation is called the **short double o sound**, as in *foot*. Here are some other words with the short sound of **oo**:

st**oo**d   g**oo**d   c**oo**k

➤ *Practice 9*

In the space provided, show whether each **oo** vowel sound is long (o͞o) or short (o͝o). The first two are done for you as examples.

1. choose	o͞o		6 foot	_____
2. shook	o͝o		7. wool	_____
3. loose	_____		8. proof	_____
4. brook	_____		9. zoo	_____
5. cartoon	_____		10. crook	_____

CHAPTER SUMMARY

In this chapter you learned the following:

- **Short vowels** are shown in some dictionaries by a cup-shaped symbol over the vowel: **ă, ĕ, ĭ, ŏ, ŭ**.

  Rule for short vowel sounds: When a word or syllable has only one vowel and that vowel is followed by one or more consonants, the vowel is usually short: *pat, pet, pit, pot, cut.*

- **Long vowels** have the sound of their own name and are shown in some dictionaries by a line over the vowel: **ā, ē, ī, ō, ū**.

  Here are the rules for long vowels:

  *The silent-**e** rule:* When a word or syllable ends with vowel-consonant-**e**, the vowel before the consonant is long and the final **e** is silent: *hate, Pete, bite, robe, cute.*

  The two-vowels-together rule: When two of certain vowels are together, the first vowel is long and the second is silent: ***aim, pay, eat, knee, lie, oat, hoe.***

The final single vowel rule: A single vowel at the end of a word or syllable (other than silent **e**) usually has a long sound: *me, hi, notice, music.*

- **Y is a vowel** when it does not begin a word.

  Here are the rules for the sounds of the vowel **y**:

  *Short-***i** *sound:* In the middle of a word or syllable, **y** usually sounds like short **i**: *myth.*

  *Long-***i** *sound:* At the end of a one-syllable word, **y** sounds like long **i**: *my.*

  *Long-***e** *sound:* At the end of a word with more than one syllable, **y** sounds like long **e**: *many.*

- **The sound of a vowel followed by r** is usually neither long nor short, but in between: *car.*

- The **long double o sound** is the vowel sound in *boot.* The **short double o sound** is the vowel sound in *foot.*

➤ Review Test 1

To review what you have learned in this chapter, answer each of the following questions. Fill in the blank, or circle the letter of the correct answer.

1. A word or syllable usually has a short vowel sound when
   a. a consonant is followed by a single vowel.
   b. a single vowel is followed by one or more consonants.
   c. a vowel is followed by a consonant and then the letter e.

2. TRUE OR FALSE? _____ The silent-**e** rule states that when a word or syllable ends in vowel-consonant-**e**, the first vowel is long and the **e** ending the word is silent.

3. The two-vowels-together rule states that when two of certain vowels are together in a word,
   a. the first is long and the second is short.
   b. both vowels are long.
   c. the first is long and the second is silent.

4. When **y** is in the middle of a word,
   a. it is a consonant.
   b. it usually sounds like short **i**.
   c. it usually sounds like short **e**.

5. TRUE OR FALSE? _____ A vowel followed by **r** is usually short.

➤ *Review Test 2*

A. For each item below, write a word with the vowel sound shown. Choose from the words in the box; use each word once.

cram	dress	dust	file	green
home	mix	nod	place	used

1. Short **a** sound: _____

2. Long **a** sound: _____

3. Short **e** sound: _____

4. Long **e** sound: _____

5. Short **i** sound: _____

6. Long **i** sound: _____

7. Short **o** sound: _____

8. Long **o** sound: _____

9. Short **u** sound: _____

10. Long **u** sound: _____

B. Here are the rules for long vowel sounds:

> *Silent* **e:** When a word or syllable ends in a vowel-consonant-e, the vowel before the consonant is long and the final **e** is silent.
>
> *Two vowels together:* When two of certain vowels are together, the first vowel is long and the second is silent.
>
> *Final single vowel:* A single vowel at the end of a word or syllable (other than a silent **e**) usually has a long sound.

Beside each word, write the name of the rule that applies: Silent **e**, Two Vowels Together, or Final Single Vowel. In the second space, write a short explanation of the rule. Note the example.

Example

	toast	*Two Vowels Together*	*The "o" is long, and the "a" is silent.*
11.	face	_____	_____
12.	go	_____	_____
13.	road	_____	_____
14.	steal	_____	_____
15.	plane	_____	_____

C. Here are the rules for **y** as a vowel:

Sounds of y

> ***Short*-i** *sound:* In the middle of a word or syllable, **y** usually sounds like short **i**.
>
> ***Long*-i** *sound:* At the end of a one-syllable word, **y** sounds like long **i**.
>
> ***Long*-e** *sound:* At the end of a word with more than one syllable, **y** sounds like long **e**.

Beside each word, identify the **y** sound by writing in one of the following:

     ĭ (short **i**)   ī (long **i**)   ē (long **e**).

In the second space, write a short explanation of the rule that applies. Note the example.

Example

     ready   __ē__   _____*At end of word with more than one syllable*_____

16. sky   _____   _____

17. party   _____   _____

18. system   _____   _____

19. hurry   _____   _____

20. dry   _____   _____

➤ *Review Test 3*

A. Beside each word, write its vowel sound.

- If the vowel is short, write ă, ĕ, ĭ, ŏ, or ŭ.
- If the vowel is long, write ā, ē, ī, ō, or ū.
- If the vowel is followed by r, write **r**.

1. seen	_____	6. knock	_____
2. click	_____	7. slang	_____
3. felt	_____	8. wave	_____
4. glide	_____	9. stove	_____
5. pump	_____	10. yard	_____

B. Complete each sentence by filling in the word with a **short** vowel. Remember that a vowel followed by an **r** is neither long nor short.

11. Makeup could not hide the mosquito bite on Nina's *(cheek, chin, nose)*

_____.

12. Some people like to start the day with a breakfast that includes *(eggs, oatmeal, sweets)* _____.

13. A good class president should be well-informed, intelligent, and *(fair, sincere, warm)* _____.

14. The FBI can tell the *(model, year, age)* _____ of a car from only a chip of paint left at the scene of an accident.

15. I *(clip, save, keep)* _____ coupons to use at the super-market, but many expire before I use them.

C. Here are the rules for long vowel sounds:

Silent e: When a word or syllable ends with vowel-consonant-e, the vowel before the consonant is long and the final **e** is silent.

Two vowels together: When two of certain vowels are together, the first vowel is long and the second is silent.

Final single vowel: A single vowel at the end of a word or syllable (other than a silent **e**) usually has a long sound.

Use the rules to help you write the words below in the right spaces.

be	close	greed
lake	mean	

	Silent-e rule	Two-vowels-together rule	Final vowel rule
	16. _____	18. _____	20. _____
	17. _____	19. _____	

D. Use a check mark (✓) to indicate whether the **oo** in each word is long or short.

	Long **oo**	Short **oo**
21. book	_____	_____
22. balloon	_____	_____
23. food	_____	_____
24. baboon	_____	_____
25. hook	_____	_____

➤ Review Test 4

Here is a chance to apply your understanding of vowel and consonant sounds to a full-length reading. Can you imagine a more terrifying experience than being on a plane that appears destined to crash? What if you were traveling with your young child and had to prepare him or her for what seemed inevitable? Which emotion would take over—love or terror? This selection is a true story of such an event, one that taught the author how strong the bond can be between a mother and her daughter. After reading the selection, answer the phonics questions that follow.

Words to Watch

Following are some words in the reading that do not have strong context support. Each word is followed by the number of the paragraph in which it appears and its meaning there. These words are indicated in the reading by a small circle (°).

chipper (2): cheerful

trimmings (2): accessories; extras worn

seasoned (2): experienced

stoic (8): seemingly not affected

wailed (10): cried loudly

composure (10): calm manner

babble (10): language not able to be understood

compelled (12): forced

unwavering (17): steady

A LESSON IN LOVE

Casey Hawley

1   I learned a lesson about terror, and about love that is stronger than terror. I learned it on a flight I took six years ago, and only now can I speak of it without tears filling my eyes.

2   When our L1011 left the Orlando airport that Friday, we were a chipper°, high-energy group. The early-morning flight hosted mainly professional people going to Atlanta for a day or two of business. There were lots of designer suits, expensive haircuts, leather briefcases—all the trimmings° of seasoned° business travelers. I settled back, intending to do some light reading on the brief flight.

3   But I put down my magazine as it became apparent this was not going to be a calm flight. The aircraft bumped up and down and from side to side. Many of the experienced travelers, including me, looked around with knowing grins. Our expressions indicated that we had experienced such minor problems before. As experienced travelers, we took such things in stride.

4   Our good-humored tolerance soon vanished, however. The plane began dipping wildly, one wing lunging downward. Passengers, bags, and coffee cups lurched and banged around the little cabin. As the plane continued climbing, the frightening motion continued. Then we heard our pilot over the loudspeaker.

5   "We are having some difficulties," he announced. "At this time, we appear to have no nose-wheel steering. Our indicators show that our hydraulic system has failed. We will be returning to the Orlando airport at this time. Because of the lack of hydraulics, we are not sure our landing gear will lock, so the flight attendants will prepare you for a bumpy landing. Also, if you look out the windows, you will see that we are dumping fuel from our fuel tanks. We want to have as little on board as possible in the event of a rough touchdown."

6   In other words, we were about to crash.

7   Nothing had ever seemed so grim to me as the sight of that fuel, hundreds of gallons of it, streaming past my window out of the plane's tanks. I

stared helplessly at it, aware that around me flight attendants were helping people get into crash position and comforting those who were hysterical.

8   Forcing my attention away from that spilling fuel, I looked at my fellow travelers. I was stunned by what I saw. Even the most stoic° looked grim and ashen—their faces were actually gray with terror. No one faces death without fear, I thought. Some were silent, some hysterical, but all were visibly frightened. As I scanned the faces around me, I wondered if there was anyone whose inner strength would provide peaceful calm at such a moment. I saw no such person.

9   I didn't see anyone, but then I heard something—a quiet, calm voice. A couple of rows to my left, a woman was speaking in an absolutely normal, conversational tone. There was no tremor or tension. It was a lovely, warm voice.

10   All around me, people cried. Many wailed° and screamed. A few of the men held onto their composure° by gripping armrests and clenching teeth, but fear enveloped them. Through the babble° of frightened, sobbing voices I strained my ears to catch that sweet, calm woman's voice again. I followed it to its source and saw it came from a mother who was talking, in the midst of all the chaos, to her child, who was sitting on her lap. The woman, in her mid-thirties and unremarkable in appearance, was looking full into the face of her daughter, who looked about 4. The child listened closely, sensing the importance of her mother's words. The mother's gaze held the child so fixed and intent that they both seem untouched by the sounds of grief and fear all around. It was as if a circle had been drawn around the two of them, and panic and grief could not cross the line.

11   A picture flashed into my mind of another little girl I'd seen on the news recently. She had survived a terrible plane crash. It seemed that she had lived because her mother had folded her own body around the little girl's in order to protect her. The mother did not survive. Newspapers had reported how the little girl had been treated by psychologists for weeks afterwards. They hoped to save her from feelings of guilt and unworthiness that often haunt survivors of tragedy. The child was told over and over again that it had not been her fault that her mommy had died. I hoped this situation would not end the same way.

12   I tried hard to hear what this mother was saying to her child. I felt compelled° to hear. Finally, I made out what this soft, sweet voice was saying in tones of such assurance. Over and over again, the mother said, "I love you so much. Do you know for sure that I love you more than anything?"

13   "Yes, Mommy," the little girl said.

14   "And remember, no matter what happens, that I love you always. And that you are a good girl. Sometimes things happen that are not your fault. You are still a good girl, and my love will always be with you."

15   And with that, the mother strapped the seat belt over both of them, wrapped her body over the little girl's, and prepared to crash.

16   For no earthly reason, our landing gear held and our touchdown was not the tragedy it seemed destined to be. It was over in seconds. We filed out of the plane, once again calm business people going about our day, already planning our alternate routes to Atlanta.

17   But I took something away from the plane that day. I knew that none of the tough professionals on that plane, myself included, could have broken through our own terror to speak in an unwavering° voice like that woman's. She had done what seemed to the rest of us emotionally and physically impossible. Was she born with a far greater share of courage than the rest

of us? I doubt it. I think what I witnessed that day was evidence that a parent's love for a child is the source of a strength that can't be measured. While facing her own death, this mother was able to reach deep into herself, far past the fear she must have felt, to focus wholly on the welfare of her child. Calmly and surely, she spent what could have been her last seconds on earth promising her child that she would always be safe in her mother's love.

That mom showed me what a real hero looks like. For those few minutes, I was in the presence of a love that is truly stronger than the fear of death: the love of a parent for a child.   18

Phonics Questions

Use phonics clues you learned from this and the previous chapter to answer the following questions. Circle the letter of your choice for each question.

1. In the word *six*, used in the sentence below, the **x** sounds like
   a. **ks.**
   b. **gz.**
   c. **z.**

   "I learned it on a flight I took six years ago. . . . " (Paragraph 1)

2. In the word *years*, used in the sentence below, the **y** is a
   a. consonant.
   b. vowel.

   "I learned it on a flight I took six years ago. . . . " (Paragraph 1)

3. Which word from the sentence below has a **y** that sounds like long **e**?
   a. *only*
   b. *my*
   c. *eyes*

   "I learned it on a flight I took six years ago, and only now can I speak of it without tears filling my eyes." (Paragraph 1)

4. Which word from the sentence below has a silent consonant and a consonant blend?
   a. *magazine*
   b. *became*
   c. *apparent*

   "But I put down my magazine as it became apparent this was not going to be a calm flight." (Paragraph 3)

5. In the word *plane*, used in the sentence below,
   a. the vowels have their short vowel sounds.
   b. the **a** is long and the **e** is short.
   c. the **a** is long and the **e** is silent.

   "The plane began dipping wildly, one wing lunging downward." (Paragraph 4)

6. The word *crash*, used in the sentence below, has
   a. two consonant blends.
   b. two consonant digraphs.
   c. a consonant blend and a consonant digraph.

   "In other words, we were about to crash." (Paragraph 6)

7. In the word *clenching*, used in the sentence below,
   a. the first **c** is hard, and the second is soft.
   b. the first **c** is soft, and the second is hard.
   c. the first **c** is hard, and the second is part of a consonant digraph.

   "A few of the men held onto their composure by gripping armrests and clenching teeth, but fear enveloped them." (Paragraph 10)

8. The **s** in the word *mother's*, used in the sentence below,
   a. has its usual sound, as in *salt*.
   b. sounds like **z**.

   "The child listened closely, sensing the importance of her mother's words." (Paragraph 10)

9. In the word *reach*, used in the sentence below, the vowel sound follows which rule?
   a. The silent-**e** rule
   b. The two-vowels-together rule
   c. The sounds of vowels followed by an **r**

   "While facing her own death, this mother was able to reach deep into herself. . . ." (Paragraph 17)

10. Which word from the sentence below follows the Silent-**e** Rule?
    a. *me*
    b. *real*
    c. *like*

    "That mom showed me what a real hero looks like." (Paragraph 18)

Discussion Questions

1. The author states that she learned of a "love that is stronger than terror." Do you think love is always stronger than terror? Or was the event the author describes just an unusual incident?

2. The pilot of the aircraft tells the passengers exactly what is happening, saying, for example, "we are not sure our landing gear will lock" and "we are dumping fuel from our fuel tanks. We want to have as little on board as possible in the event of a rough touchdown." Should the pilot have been so open with his passengers, who were then struck with fear, or should he have said nothing and concentrated on flying the plane? Why?

3. In your opinion, what is the strongest love that exists? The love of a parent for a child? What about love *for* a parent? Or for a spouse? Is all love the same?

Note: Writing assignments for this selection appear on page 540.

Check Your Performance			**VOWELS**
Activity	*Number Right*	*Points*	*Score*
Review Test 1 (5 items)	_____	× 2 =	_____
Review Test 2 (20 items)	_____	× 1.5 =	_____
Review Test 3 (25 items)	_____	× 1 =	_____
Review Test 4 (10 items)	_____	× 3.5 =	_____
		TOTAL SCORE =	_____%

Enter your total score into the **Reading Performance Chart: Review Tests** on the inside back cover.

VOWELS: Test 1

A. For each item below, write a word with the vowel sound shown. Choose from the words in the box; use each word once.

cute	grant	not	rope	skip
slide	stage	stun	tent	three

1. Short **a** sound: _____

2. Long **a** sound: _____

3. Short **e** sound: _____

4. Long **e** sound: _____

5. Short **i** sound: _____

6. Long **i** sound: _____

7. Short **o** sound: _____

8. Long **o** sound: _____

9. Short **u** sound: _____

10. Long **u** sound: _____

B. Here are the rules for long vowel sounds:

> *Silent* **e:** When a word or syllable ends with vowel-consonant-**e**, the vowel before the consonant is long and the final **e** is silent.
>
> *Two vowels together:* When two of certain vowels are together, the first vowel is long and the second is silent.
>
> *Final single vowel:* A single vowel at the end of a word or syllable (other than a silent **e**) usually has a long sound.

Beside each word, write the name of the rule that applies: Silent **e**, Two Vowels Together, or Final Single Vowel. In the second space, write a short explanation of the rule. Note the example.

Example

boat   *Two Vowels Together*   *The "o" is long, and the "a" is silent.*

11. hope   _____   _____

12. she   _____   _____

13. neat   _____   _____

(Continues on next page)

14. cane   _____   _____

15. goal   _____   _____

C. Here are the rules for **y** as a vowel:

Sounds of **y**

> ***Short*-i *sound*:** In the middle of a word or syllable, **y** usually sounds like short **i**.
>
> ***Long*-i *sound*:** At the end of a one-syllable word, **y** sounds like long **i**.
>
> ***Long*-e *sound*:** At the end of a word with more than one syllable, **y** sounds like long **e**.

Beside each word, identify the **y** sound by writing in one of the following:

     ĭ (short **i**)   ī (long **i**)   ē (long **e**).

In the second space, write a short explanation of the rule that applies. Note the example.

Example

     empty   __ē__   *At end of word with more than one syllable* _____

16. ply   _____   _____

17. happy   _____   _____

18. mystic   _____   _____

19. try   _____   _____

20. worry   _____   _____

VOWELS: Test 2

A. Beside each word, write its vowel sound.

- If the vowel is short, write **ă, ĕ, ĭ, ŏ,** or **ŭ**.
- If the vowel is long, write **ā, ē, ī, ō,** or **ū**.
- If the vowel is followed by **r**, write **r**.

1. bleed   _____   6 hot   _____

2. trick   _____   7. stay   _____

3. park   _____   8. write   _____

4. check   _____   9. cute   _____

5. stump   _____   10. fork   _____

B. Complete each sentence by filling in the word with a ***short*** vowel sound. Remember that a vowel followed by **r** is neither long nor short.

11. When a dog relaxes, usually its tail wags and its ears *(drape, droop, drop)*

    _____.

12. Many students find that a term paper takes as many as *(four, five, ten)*

    _____ hours longer than they expected.

13. The fifty-year-old maple tree in the back yard is full of *(sap, leaves, life)*

    _____.

14. On weekends, some people unwind by taking a long *(drive, run, hike)*

    _____ in the country.

15. A glass window pane and a(n) *(oak, steel, brick)* _____
    wall are made with the same main ingredient: sand.

(Continues on next page)

C. Here are the rules for long vowel sounds:

> *Silent* **e:** When a word or syllable ends with vowel-consonant-**e**, the vowel before the consonant is long and the final **e** is silent.
>
> *Two vowels together:* When two of certain vowels are together, the first vowel is long and the second is silent.
>
> *Final single vowel:* A single vowel at the end of a word or syllable (other than a silent **e**) usually has a long sound.

Use the rules to help you write the words below in the right spaces.

| hi | snake | soap |
| treat | wrote | |

Silent-e rule	*Two-vowels-together rule*	*Final vowel rule*
16. _____	18. _____	20. _____
17. _____	19. _____	

D. Use a check (✓) to indicate whether the **oo** in each word is long or short.

	Long **oo**	*Short* **oo**
21. room	_____	_____
22. crook	_____	_____
23. noon	_____	_____
24. stood	_____	_____
25. proof	_____	_____

VOWELS: Test 3

A. Circle each word in the box that contains a ***short*** vowel sound. The words appear either straight across or straight down. Then write each word under the correct heading.

Here are the words to look for:

add	bench	chin	flat	nun
plod	quilt	romp	smell	stuff

s	t	u	f	f	t	f	l	y
m	e	a	d	l	y	k	n	o
e	a	p	o	a	d	d	u	u
l	k	l	w	t	o	w	n	r
l	o	o	n	s	d	u	s	b
o	a	d	c	r	o	m	p	e
c	a	s	e	e	o	z	i	n
n	o	c	h	i	n	i	k	c
q	u	i	l	t	b	e	e	h

*Short **a***	*Short **e***	*Short **i***	*Short **o***	*Short **u***
1._____	3._____	5._____	7._____	9._____
2._____	4._____	6._____	8._____	10._____

B. Complete each sentence below by filling in the word that has a ***long*** vowel sound. (Remember that a vowel followed by **r** is neither long nor short.)

11. The tune-up on my car at Harry's Rapid Service Shop was *(fast, quick, speedy)* _____ but poorly done.

12. After being out in the cold, *(Jill, Jake, Jack)* _____ looked forward to a hot cup of cocoa.

(Continues on next page)

75

13. After a rain, children like to *(push, float, sink)* _____ paper boats in sidewalk puddles.

14. A college assignment that at first seems *(easy, dumb, effortless)* _____ can in fact be very challenging and useful.

15. If you *(put, install, place)* _____ a special radio signal in your car, the police can trace the car if it's stolen.

C. Use a check (✓) to indicate whether the **y** in each word sounds like ĭ, ī, or ē.

	Short **i**	*Long* **i**	*Long* **e**
16. holy	_____	_____	_____
17. spy	_____	_____	_____
18. symbol	_____	_____	_____
19. funny	_____	_____	_____
20. cry	_____	_____	_____

D. Find the five words with **oo** in the paragraph below. Write the words in the blank spaces at the left, and use a check (✓) to show whether each **oo** has a long or short sound.

If you are looking for a new apartment, remember that each place has drawbacks as well as pluses. For instance, the apartment may be in a great location or have a terrific view. But you must pay attention to details. Make sure that the bed you have will fit in the bedroom. Is the bath area large enough, or is it so small that you will have trouble finding space for toothpaste and shampoo? And make sure that you won't need to buy a set of tools to repair the place.

	Long **oo**	*Short* **oo**
21. _____	_____	_____
22. _____	_____	_____
23. _____	_____	_____
24. _____	_____	_____
25. _____	_____	_____

VOWELS: Test 4

A. Circle each word in the box that contains a ***long*** vowel sound. The words appear either straight across or straight down. Then write each word under the correct heading.

Here are the words to look for:

boat	cheese	claim	cute	glide
stain	sweet	toast	use	wise

s	s	w	e	e	t	g	w	c
s	f	e	w	k	r	l	i	h
t	o	n	v	y	w	i	s	e
a	p	t	c	a	n	d	k	e
i	b	p	l	q	n	e	v	s
n	o	n	a	n	u	s	e	e
q	a	c	i	l	i	t	x	n
r	t	o	m	o	c	u	t	e
y	d	t	o	a	s	t	o	n

*Long **a***	*Long **e***	*Long **i***	*Long **o***	*Long **u***
1._____	3._____	5._____	7._____	9._____
2._____	4._____	6._____	8._____	10._____

B. Complete each sentence below by filling in the word that has a ***short*** vowel sound. (Remember that a vowel followed by **r** is neither long nor short.)

11. If you water your plants too much or too little, they are likely to *(die, wilt, droop)* _____.

12. Enrique was not looking forward to spending two weeks with his aunt in *(New York, Montana, Ohio)* _____.

(Continues on next page)

13. Heart disease accounts for one *(half, third, fourth)* _____
    of all American deaths each year.

14. I turned to tell my *(wife, date, sister)* _____ that I thought
    the play was boring, but she was already asleep.

15. People who visit California seldom get lost—all they have to remember is
    that if they keep driving *(north, west, east)* _____, they will
    reach the ocean.

C. Here are the rules for long vowel sounds:

> *Silent* **e:** When a word or syllable ends with vowel-consonant-**e**, the vowel
> before the consonant is long and the final **e** is silent.
>
> *Two vowels together:* When two of certain vowels are together, the first
> vowel is long and the second is silent.
>
> *Final single vowel:* A single vowel at the end of a word or syllable (other
> than a silent **e**) usually has a long sound.

Beside each word, write the name of the rule that applies: Silent **e**, Two Vowels
Together, or Final Single Vowel.

16. beef   _____   21. grime   _____

17. shape   _____   22. we   _____

18. no   _____   23. slope   _____

19. bail   _____   24. train   _____

20. cream   _____   25. loaf   _____

VOWELS: Test 5

A. Complete each sentence by writing in the word with a ***short*** vowel sound. Remember that a vowel followed by **r** is neither long nor short.

1. Sharri's *(apple, peach, lime)* _____ tree bore so much fruit that she gave much of it away.

2. Now a democracy, Australia was once ruled by a *(king, queen, czar)* _____.

3. Amad keeps a spare key *(below, near, under)* _____ a big rock by his back door.

4. A triathlon consists of three *(parts, events, sports)* _____: a swim, a bike ride, and a run.

5. Despite the best efforts of firefighters, the fire continued to *(burn, ignite, blaze)* _____.

B. Complete each sentence by writing in the word that has a ***long*** vowel sound. Remember that a vowel followed by **r** is neither long nor short.

Then, using the rules for long vowel sounds below, circle the letter of the rule the word follows: Silent **e**, Two Vowels Together, or Final Single Vowel.

Here are the rules for long vowel sounds:

***Silent* e:** When a word or syllable ends with vowel-consonant-**e**, the vowel before the consonant is long and the final **e** is silent.

Two vowels together: When two of certain vowels are together, the first vowel is long and the second is silent.

Final single vowel: A single vowel at the end of a word or syllable (other than a silent **e**) usually has a long sound.

---

6. Although gorillas look as if they can *(maim, kill, crush)* _____ anything they want, they are actually very gentle creatures.

7. The word you chose follows this rule:
   a. Silent **e**   b. Two Vowels Together   c. Final Single Vowel

(Continues on next page)

8. The way Mimi remembers a phone number is to repeat it *(six, nine, ten)* _____ times.

9. The word you chose follows this rule:
   a. Silent **e**   b. Two Vowels Together   c. Final Single Vowel

10. When it started raining hard, Guadalupe began to *(race, dash, run)* _____ across the parking lot to her car.

11. The word you chose follows this rule:
    a. Silent **e**   b. Two Vowels Together   c. Final Single Vowel

12. Scientists continue to *(goad, prod, urge)* _____ us to eat breakfast, as it is considered the most important meal of the day.

13. The word you chose follows this rule:
    a. Silent **e**   b. Two Vowels Together   c. Final Single Vowel

14. A man at the toy store was showing how to use a new *(ball, yo-yo, truck)* _____.

15. The word you chose follows this rule:
    a. Silent **e**   b. Two Vowels Together   c. Final Single Vowel

C. Complete the following sentence by filling in the word that has a **y** which sounds like a short **i**.

16. Many scientists believe that tales of the hairy humanlike creature called Bigfoot are just *(myths, fantasy, yarns)* _____.

D. Complete each sentence with the word that has a **y** which sounds like a long **i**.

17. Willy's *(tricky, sly, sneaky)* _____ ways got him into trouble with his family and friends.

18. The weather report called for continued *(cloudy, dry, foggy)* _____ conditions.

E. Complete each sentence with the word that has a **y** which sounds like a long **e**.

19. When Juan asked for the keys to the car, his father answered, "*(Yes, Maybe, Surely)* _____."

20. Ever since my little brother got a toy drum, he wants to *(carry, play, try)* _____ it all day long.

VOWELS: Test 6

A. Fill in each blank with the word that has a ***short*** vowel sound.

Most owls nest in trees and come out at night to (1. *eat, fly, hunt*) _____. An exception is the burrowing owl. This (2. *little,*

tiny, wee) _____ owl is only about (3. *six, eight, nine*) _____ inches high. As its name suggests, it nests underground. This owl hunts during the day and can be seen sitting on fence posts near its (4. *home, mate, nest*) _____. Once common throughout the Southwest, the burrowing owl is in danger of extinction, mostly because of (5. *huge, large, vast*) _____ development projects.

B. In the following paragraph, ten words are boldfaced. Each word fits under one of the headings below. Write the words in the appropriate spaces.

Where would **we** be without the **fish** in the sea? Half of the world's population depends on fish as its **main** source of food. **Yet** there are danger signs that the oceans are being overfished. Four of the richest fishing areas of the **world** include the west **coast** of Australia, the **west** coast of South America, the Mediterranean Sea, and the **east** coast of Asia. In the past **five** years, the fish catch in each of **these** areas has declined significantly.

Silent-e rule	*Two-vowels-together rule*	*Final vowel rule*
6. _____	8. _____	11. _____
7. _____	9. _____	
	10. _____	

Short vowel rule	*Vowel followed by* **r**
12. _____	15. _____
13. _____	
14. _____	

(Continues on next page)

C. Find the five words with **oo** in the paragraph below. Write the words in the blank spaces on the left, and use a check (✓) to show whether each **oo** has a long or short sound.

> The hot summer day was too much for Salvatore. Rather than stay around the house and watch TV all day, he thought it might be nice to take the family on a picnic. "We'll pick up some food on the way, and relax by a babbling brook." Salvatore's wife, Diana, loved the idea. The last thing they wanted to do was cook in a hot kitchen. And the kids liked the idea, as well. Sal Jr. figured it was a great opportunity to play touch football. And Darlene saw herself sitting beneath a large oak tree, reading a mystery novel.

		Long **oo**	*Short* **oo**
16.	_____	_____	_____
17.	_____	_____	_____
18.	_____	_____	_____
19.	_____	_____	_____
20.	_____	_____	_____

3
Phonics III: Syllables

To pronounce long words that are unfamiliar to you, you should first separate them into parts called *syllables*. You can then focus on pronouncing each syllable and go on to read the entire word.

This chapter first reminds you what a syllable is. Then it provides five rules that will help you break words into syllables. Using these rules and remembering the phonics from the first two chapters will help you to pronounce many difficult words you come across as you read.

SYLLABLES

A **syllable** is a word or part of a word that has one vowel sound. This vowel sound is spoken together with any consonant sounds in the syllable.

For example, the word *rip* has just one vowel sound; thus it has only one syllable. The sounds of **r**, short **i**, and **p** are all spoken together. The word *fast* also has only one vowel sound. The sounds of **f**, short **a**, and the consonant blend **st** are all spoken together.

A word with more than one syllable is pronounced in parts. For example, *sunscreen* is pronounced in two parts, each with its own vowel sound: *sun* and *screen*. The vowel sound in the first syllable is short **u**, so the sounds of **s**, short **u**, and **n** are all spoken together. The second syllable starts with the consonant blend **scr**, then has a long **e** vowel sound, then the single consonant **n**. By separating a word into its syllables, you can use phonics rules to pronounce each syllable correctly. Then you can put the syllables together for the right pronunciation of the word.

Some one-, two-, and three-syllable words are listed below. Say each word to yourself. Notice the single vowel sound in each syllable. Also note any consonant sounds that are spoken with the vowel.

One-syllable words	Two-syllable words	Three-syllable words
go	kindness	happily
I	golden	Superman
fun	moral	upbringing
stand	confess	president
Fred	happy	syllable

Now, in the blank spaces below and under the correct headings, write these words:

brother	clock	dishonest
grandparent	lunch	market

One-syllable words	Two-syllable words	Three-syllable words
_____	_____	_____
_____	_____	_____

You should have added *clock* and *lunch* to the one-syllable list, *brother* and *market* to the two-syllable list, and *grandparent* and *dishonest* to the three-syllable list.

Words with More Than One Vowel in a Syllable

In the lists above, each syllable contains just one vowel with one vowel sound. However, some words and syllables have *two* vowels but only *one* vowel sound. They include the following:

1   Words with a silent final *e*

Here are some words in which the final **e** is silent.

    Eve   rose   same   tune   write

Each word has two vowels but only one vowel sound. In each case, the final **e** is silent. Since each word has only one vowel *sound,* each is a one-syllable word. (As you learned in Chapter 2, when a word ends with vowel-consonant-**e**, the vowel before the consonant is long and the final **e** is silent.)

2   Words with two vowels together in which one vowel is silent

Here are some examples of words with this pattern:

pair	play	heat	breed	pie
soap	toe			

Each word has two vowels together but only one vowel sound. In each case, the second vowel is silent. Since each word has only one vowel *sound*, each is a one-syllable word. (As you learned in Chapter 2, when two of certain vowels are together, the first one is long, and the second is silent.)

➤ *Practice 1*

Fill in the blank spaces below. Note the examples.

	Number of vowels	*Number of vowel sounds*	*Number of syllables*
Examples:			
silent	2	2	2
ride	2	1	1
1. boat	_____	_____	_____
2. doe	_____	_____	_____
3. cane	_____	_____	_____
4. heel	_____	_____	_____
5. among	_____	_____	_____
6. chair	_____	_____	_____
7. however	_____	_____	_____
8. least	_____	_____	_____
9. freezing	_____	_____	_____
10. amuse	_____	_____	_____

FIVE RULES FOR DIVIDING WORDS INTO SYLLABLES

You have learned that each syllable has one vowel sound. That knowledge and the following rules will help you divide words into syllables. There are exceptions, but the rules can be followed much of the time.

Dividing Between Two Consonants

> *Rule 1:* **When two consonants come between two vowels, divide between the consonants.**

This rule is also known as the VC/CV (vowel-consonant/consonant-vowel) pattern. Here are examples of words divided according to rule 1:

> donkey: don-key   happen: hap-pen   silver: sil-ver

To break each word into syllables, divide between the consonants: between **n** and **k** in *donkey,* between **p** and **p** in *happen,* and between **l** and **v** in *silver.*

According to the VC/CV rule, where would you divide the following words? Draw a line between the syllables.

> hostage   import   tunnel

The correct divisions for these words are *hos-tage, im-port,* and *tun-nel.*

Pronunciation tip: A vowel before two consonants usually has a short sound. For example, the **o** in *hostage,* the **i** in *import,* and the **u** in *tunnel* each have a short sound. (As you learned in Chapter 2, when a word or syllable has one vowel followed by one or more consonants, the vowel is usually short.)

➤ *Practice 2*

Break the following words into syllables by dividing between two consonants (VC/CV). Note the example.

> **Example:** arrest   _____ *ar-rest* _____

1. candy   _____

2. napkin   _____

3. harbor   _____

4. trumpet   _____

5. muffin   _____

Dividing Between Three Consonants

At times a word will have three consonants in a row, as in these examples:

applaud   monster   surprise

In such cases, you usually divide between the first consonant and the second two, as shown below:

ap-plaud   mon-ster   sur-prise

The second and third consonants form a **consonant blend**—two or more consonants that keep their sounds but are spoken together.

➤ *Practice 3*

Break each of the following words into syllables by dividing between a consonant and a consonant blend. Note the example.

    Example: displace   *dis-place*

    1. central   _____

    2. address   _____

    3. complete   _____

    4. attract   _____

    5. obscure   _____

Dividing Before a Single Consonant

Rule 2: **When a single consonant comes between two vowel sounds, divide before the consonant.**

This rule is also known as the V/CV (vowel/consonant-vowel) pattern. Here are examples of words that are divided according to rule 2:

even: e-ven   minus: mi-nus   pony: po-ny

To break each word into syllables, divide before the single consonant: between the **e** and **v** in *even*, between the **i** and **n** in *minus*, and between the **o** and **n** in *pony*.

According to the V/CV rule, where would you divide the following words? Draw a line between the syllables.

baby   female   moment

The correct divisions for these words are *ba-by, fe-male,* and *mo-ment.*

Pronunciation tip: A vowel before a single consonant division often has a long sound. For example, the **a** in *baby,* the first **e** in *female,* and the **o** in *moment* each have a long sound. (As you learned in Chapter 2, when a single vowel other than silent **e** ends a word or syllable, the vowel is usually long.)

➤ *Practice 4*

Break each of the following words into syllables by dividing before the single consonant (V/CV). Note the example.

> **Example:** cater _____ *ca-ter* _____
>
> 1. bonus _____
>
> 2. item _____
>
> 3. final _____
>
> 4. major _____
>
> 5. unit _____

Dividing Before a Consonant + *le*

> ***Rule 3:*** **If a word ends in a consonant followed by *le*, the consonant and *le* form the last syllable.**

The words below are divided according to this rule.

handle: han-dle   cable: ca-ble   simple: sim-ple

According to the consonant + **le** rule, where would you divide the following words? Draw a line between the syllables.

ankle   circle   middle

The correct divisions for these words are *an-kle, cir-cle*, and *mid-dle.*

➤ *Practice 5*

Break the following words into syllables by dividing before the consonant + **le** . Note the example.

Example: table _____ *ta-ble*

1. idle _____

2. ripple _____

3. purple _____

4. title _____

5. gargle _____

Dividing After Prefixes and Before Suffixes

Rule 4: **Prefixes and suffixes are usually separate syllables.**

Prefixes are word parts that are added to the beginnings of words. Here are some common prefixes:

ad-	com-	con-	de-	dis-	ex-
in-	non-	pre-	re-	sub-	un-

Suffixes are word parts that are added to the ends of words. Here are some common suffixes:

-able	-en	-er	-ful	-ing	-ist
-less	-ly	-ment	-ness	-sion	-tion

Below are examples of words divided according to rule 4.

prefix: pre-fix   unfair: un-fair   player: play-er   statement: state-ment

The divisions above are made after the prefixes (*pre-* and *un-*) and before the suffixes (*-er* and *-ment).*

According to the rule for prefixes and suffixes, where would you divide the following words? Draw a line between the syllables.

holding   compete   cheapen   racist

The correct divisions for these words are *hold-ing, com-pete, cheap-en,* and *rac-ist.*

➤ *Practice 6*

Break the following words into syllables by dividing after a prefix or before a suffix. Note the example.

> **Example:** preview _____ *pre-view* _____
>
> 1. mission _____
>
> 2. advice _____
>
> 3. unbend _____
>
> 4. playful _____
>
> 5. export _____
>
> 6. nation _____
>
> 7. mindless _____
>
> 8. consist _____
>
> 9. react _____
>
> 10. disease _____

The Suffix *-ed*

The suffix *-ed* is a separate syllable only when it follows **d** or **t**, as in the following examples.

>   ended: end-ed   molded: mold-ed   dented: dent-ed   quilted: quilt-ed

Otherwise, *-ed* is not a separate syllable. It is the end of a syllable.

>   played: played   happened: hap-pened   wondered: won-dered

In *played*, *-ed* does not follow **d** or **t**, so it is not a separate syllable; *played* is a one-syllable word. In *happened* and *wondered*, *-ed* also does not follow a **d** or **t**. So in each of those words, it is the end of a syllable, not a separate syllable.

➤ *Practice 7*

Indicate with a check (✓) whether the *-ed* in each word is a separate syllable or not. Note the example.

	Separate syllable	*Not a separate syllable*
Example: pleased	_____	___✓___

(In *pleased*, *-ed* does not follow **d** or **t**, so it is not a separate syllable.)

	Separate syllable	Not a separate syllable
1. parted	_____	_____
2. boxed	_____	_____
3. lived	_____	_____
4. minded	_____	_____
5. rested	_____	_____

Dividing Between the Words in a Compound Word

> *Rule 5:* **Compound words are always divided between the words they contain.**

A **compound word** is a combination of two words. When compound words are broken into syllables, they are always divided between the words they contain. Here are examples:

    bloodstream: blood-stream   goldfish: gold-fish   ringside: ring-side

    According to the rule for compound words, where would you divide the following words? Draw a line between the syllables.

    breakfast   railroad   redhead

The correct divisions for these words are *break-fast, rail-road,* and *red-head.*

➤ *Practice 8*

Break the following words into syllables by dividing between the words they contain. Note the example.

    Example: southeast   _____*south-east*_____

    1. notebook   _____

    2. raincoat   _____

    3. popcorn   _____

    4. workshop   _____

    5. seashell   _____

A Final Note

Although there are exceptions to the rules in this chapter, the rules will usually help you divide a word into syllables. Then, to sound out each syllable, you can apply the phonics principles you learned in Chapters 1 and 2.

If you are in doubt about how to pronounce a word, you can turn to the dictionary. In Chapter 4, "Dictionary Use," you will learn how to use dictionary symbols to pronounce words.

CHAPTER SUMMARY

In this chapter, you learned the following:

- A **syllable** is a word or part of a word that has one vowel sound. So to figure out the number of syllables in a word, count the number of vowel *sounds*. Some vowels are silent, including the following:

  Silent **e**: ros**e**

  The second letter of certain vowel pairs: p**a**ir, pl**a**y, he**a**t, bre**e**d, pi**e**, so**a**p, to**e**

- Five rules can help you divide words into syllables:

  Rule 1 (VC/CV): When two consonants come between two vowels, divide between the consonants: si**l-v**er.

  If a word has three consonants in a row, divide between the first consonant and the consonant blend: mo**n-st**er.

  Rule 2 (V/CV): When a single consonant comes between two vowel sounds, divide before the consonant: po-**n**y.

  Rule 3: If a word ends in a consonant followed by **le**, the consonant and **le** form the last syllable: han-**dle**.

  Rule 4: Prefixes and suffixes are usually separate syllables: **un**-fair, play-**er**.

  Rule 5: Compound words are always divided between the words they contain: **gold-fish**.

➤ *Review Test 1*

To review what you have learned in this chapter, answer each of the following questions. Fill in the blank, or circle the letter of the correct answer.

1. _____ TRUE OR FALSE? A syllable is a word or part of a word that contains only one vowel sound.

2. When two consonants come between two vowels, divide
   a. before the two consonants.
   b. between the two consonants.
   c. after the two consonants.

3. When a single consonant comes between two vowel sounds,
   a. divide before the consonant.
   b. divide after the consonant.
   c. both vowel sounds will usually be long.

4. _____ TRUE OR FALSE? Prefixes and suffixes are usually separate syllables.

5. _____ TRUE OR FALSE? Compound words are divided between the words they contain.

➤ Review Test 2

A. Using the rules shown in the box, divide the following words into syllables. For each word, also write the number of the rule that applies. The first one has been done for you.

> **Rule 1. Divide between two consonants.**
> **Rule 2. Divide before a single consonant.**

	Syllable division	*Rule number*
1. pencil	*pen-cil*	*1*
2. system		
3. focus		
4. comment		
5. music		
6. maintain		
7. lecture		
8. vacate		
9. silent		
10. immune		

B. Using the rules shown in the box, divide the words below into syllables. For each word, also write the number of the rule that applies. The first one has been done for you.

Rule 3. Divide before a consonant followed by *le*.
Rule 4. Divide after prefixes and before suffixes.
Rule 5. Divide between the words in a compound word.

	Syllable division	*Rule number*
11. footstep	*foot-step*	5
12. payment	_____	_____
13. sample	_____	_____
14. sailboat	_____	_____
15. trouble	_____	_____
16. joyful	_____	_____
17. bottle	_____	_____
18. sometimes	_____	_____
19. toothpaste	_____	_____
20. unpaid	_____	_____

➤ *Review Test 3*

A. Each word below has three syllables. Using the rules shown in the box, divide the words into syllables. For each syllable break, write the number of the rule that applies. The first one has been done for you.

Rule 1. Divide between two consonants.
Rule 2. Divide before a single consonant.

	Syllable division	*Rule numbers*	
1. festival	*fes-ti-val*	1	2
2. contradict	_____	_____	_____

	Syllable division	*Rule numbers*	
3. important	_____	_____	_____
4. frequency	_____	_____	_____
5. magnitude	_____	_____	_____
6. circumstance	_____	_____	_____
7. attorney	_____	_____	_____
8. romantic	_____	_____	_____
9. illegal	_____	_____	_____
10. privacy	_____	_____	_____

B. Each word below has three syllables. Using the rules shown in the box, divide the words into syllables. For each syllable break, write the number of the rule that applies. The first one has been done for you.

Rule 3. Divide before a consonant followed by *le*.
Rule 4. Divide after prefixes and before suffixes.
Rule 5. Divide between the words in a compound word.

	Syllable division	*Rule numbers*	
11. seasickness	*sea-sick-ness*	5	4
12. replacement	_____	_____	_____
13. disable	_____	_____	_____
14. resettle	_____	_____	_____
15. delightful	_____	_____	_____
16. breathtaking	_____	_____	_____
17. nonsmoker	_____	_____	_____
18. invention	_____	_____	_____
19. loudspeaker	_____	_____	_____
20. preventing	_____	_____	_____

➤ *Review Test 4*

Here is a chance to apply your understanding of syllables to a full-length reading. This selection explains that strong social ties appear to be good preventive medicine. How do we know that family and friends keep us healthier? And why would a strong social life make for a strong body? Vicky Chan offers some interesting evidence. After reading this selection, answer the questions that follow about syllables and other phonics topics.

Words to Watch

Following are some words in the reading that do not have strong context support. Each word is followed by the number of the paragraph in which it appears and its meaning there. These words are indicated in the reading by a small circle (°).

> *subjects* (2): people being studied in an experiment
> *confirms* (4): supports
> *tend* (5): are likely
> *responsive* (5): reacting easily
> *abrupt* (9): sudden
> *literally* (11): actually

FRIENDSHIP AND LIVING LONGER

Vicky Chan

1   Do you want to be healthier and live longer? Spend time with your friends. That is the prescription given by several medical studies. These surveys show that people with strong social ties—to friends, family, and loved ones, even to pets—live longer and enjoy better health than lonely people.

2   One study in California, for example, followed 7,000 people over a period of nine years. The subjects° were asked to describe their social ties. Some said that they were isolated from others. These subjects had death rates two or three times higher than people with families and friends.

3   The stronger the social ties to others, the study found, the lower the death rate. This pattern held true for men and women, young and old, rich and poor. The race of the subject did not change the result. It also applied to people with different lifestyles. Cigarette smokers who had friends lived longer than friendless smokers. Joggers involved with other people lived longer than joggers who lived isolated lives.

4   Another study confirms° this result. The University of Michigan looked at 2,754 adults in Tecumseh, Michigan. The researchers carefully

measured their subjects' health at the beginning of the study. The lonely, isolated people started out as healthy as the others. But over ten years, they were two to four times as likely to die.

5 Other findings also show the health value of personal ties. Married men and women tend° to live longer than single, divorced, or widowed people of the same age. In nursing homes, patients became more aware and responsive° when they played with cats and dogs. Pet owners are more likely to survive heart attacks than people without pets.

6 Another kind of proof that social ties support good health comes from Japan. Most Japanese people live hectic lives in cities as crowded, noisy, and polluted as ours. Such a way of life seems unhealthy. Yet the Japanese are among the healthiest and longest-lived people in the world. One reason may be their diet. Another reason, though, is their way of life. Japanese have strong ties to family and coworkers. These ties are rarely broken. For example, companies tend to move coworkers as a group, rather than one at a time. Thus the work groups remain the same.

7 Studies of Japanese-Americans support the importance of the role of Japanese social life in preserving their health. Japanese-Americans who live in strongly Japanese neighborhoods and have mainly Japanese friends tend to live longer than those who do not. Both groups eat mostly American-style food, and many in both groups smoke and drink. Thus it appears to be the strong social ties of Japanese communities that keep their members healthy.

8 Why is it more healthy to have friends and loved ones? We don't know, exactly. But it is probably a combination of several explanations. In part, people with strong social ties may simply have more to live for. They have loved ones or family who share their lives. They have friends who call them and ask them how they're doing. They have get-togethers to look forward to.

9 Social contacts also provide us with a buffer against the shocks of life. At some point, each of us moves, changes a job, or loses a loved one. Such abrupt° changes tend to cause increases in the rates of many diseases. These include heart disease, cancer, strokes, and mental illnesses. Accidents are also more likely to happen to people whose lives have suddenly changed. Friends, loved ones, even a loyal dog can help us to get through the otherwise very rough changes that we must deal with in life.

10 Finally, friends and loved ones can affect our health in still another way. If we are smokers, they may help us to quit. If we overeat, they may urge us to cut back. They can remind us to go for medical checkups. And if we have fears or sadnesses bottled up inside us, friends can help us face and overcome them. By caring for us, in other words, friends and family help us to care for ourselves.

11 Close human ties make life not only fuller, but also longer. Caring for others, and being cared for by them, is literally° a more healthy way to live.

Phonics Questions

Use phonics clues you learned from chapters 1–3 to answer the following questions. Circle the letter of your choice for each question.

1. The word *change*, used in the sentence below, contains a
   a. soft **c** sound.
   b. hard **c** sound.
   c. consonant digraph.

   "The race of the subject did not change the result." (Paragraph 3)

2. The word *another*, used in the sentence below, contains
   a. a consonant digraph.
   b. a consonant blend.
   c. both a digraph and a blend.

   "Another study confirms this result." (Paragraph 4)

3. The word *years*, used in the sentence below, contains a
   a. short vowel sound.
   b. long vowel sound.

   "But over ten years, they were over two to four times as likely to die." (Paragraph 4)

4. The word *remain,* used in the sentence below, contains
   a. two short vowel sounds.
   b. two long vowel sounds.
   c. one short vowel sound and one long vowel sound.

   "Thus the work groups remain the same." (Paragraph 6)

5. The **y** in the word *why*, used in the sentence below, sounds like a
   a. short **i**.
   b. long **i**.
   c. long **e**.

   "Why is it more healthy to have friends and loved ones?" (Paragraph 8)

6. The word *family*, used in the sentence below, contains
   a. one syllable.
   b. two syllables.
   c. three syllables.

   "They have loved ones or family who share their lives." (Paragraph 8)

7. The word *forward*, used in the sentence below, is broken into syllables as follows:
   a. forw-ard.
   b. for-ward.
   c. fo-rw-ard.

   "They have get-togethers to look forward to." (Paragraph 8)

8. The word *provide*, used in the sentence below, is broken into syllables as follows:
   a. pro-vide.
   b. prov-ide.
   c. pro-vi-de.

   "Social contacts also provide us with a buffer against the shocks of life." (Paragraph 9)

9. The word *suddenly*, used in the sentence below, is broken into syllables as follows:
   a. sudden-ly.
   b. sudd-en-ly.
   c. sud-den-ly.

   "Accidents are also more likely to happen to people whose lives have suddenly changed." (Paragraph 9)

10. The word *overcome*, used in the sentence below, is broken in syllables as follows:
    a. ov-er-come.
    b. o-ver-come.
    c. over-come.

    "And if we have fears or sadnesses bottled up inside us, friends can help us face and overcome them." (Paragraph 10)

Discussion Questions

1. Do you agree that "social contacts . . . provide us with a buffer against the shocks of life"? If so, what do you think are some of the ways these contacts keep us from feeling pain? Give an example.

2. How can people who have trouble making friends cope with crisis? In what ways could they form social ties?

3. Why do you think playing with cats and dogs helps people in nursing homes? Is there something the animals do for patients that doctors and nurses cannot?

Note: Writing assignments for this selection appear on pages 540–541.

Name _____

Section _____ Date_____

SCORE: (Number correct) _____ × 5 = _____%

SYLLABLES: Test 1

A. Using the rules shown in the box, divide the following words into syllables. For each word, also write the number of the rule that applies. Note the example.

> **Rule 1. Divide between two consonants.**
> **Rule 2. Divide before a single consonant.**

	Syllable division	*Rule number*
Example: climate	cli-mate	2
1. forward	_____	_____
2. occur	_____	_____
3. motive	_____	_____
4. welcome	_____	_____
5. unite	_____	_____
6. soda	_____	_____

B. Using the rules shown in the box, divide the words below into syllables. For each word, also write the number of the rule that applies. Note the example.

> **Rule 3. Divide before a consonant followed by *le*.**
> **Rule 4. Divide after prefixes and before suffixes.**
> **Rule 5. Divide between the words in a compound word.**

	Syllable division	*Rule number*
Example: moonlight	moon-light	5
7. cripple	_____	_____
8. gladly	_____	_____
9. hallway	_____	_____
10. distrust	_____	_____
11. puzzle	_____	_____
12. cloudburst	_____	_____
13. goodness	_____	_____

(Continues on next page)

C. Complete each sentence by underlining the compound word. Then, in the space provided, divide the compound word into syllables.

14. Kenny's first stop in registering for classes was _____ the school (*fieldhouse, library, gymnasium*).

15. Studies show that single men are more likely _____ than married men to have an emotional (*disorder, breakdown, collapse*).

16. Jogging is considered good exercise, but _____ running on the (*grass, pavement, sidewalk*) can be hard on the feet.

17. A tidal wave begins with a (*landslide,* _____ *movement, shaking*) on the ocean floor.

D. Three words below have a prefix or suffix. In the spaces provided, write those words, dividing them into syllables.

    badly   delayed   kneepad
    movement   statue   pilot

18. _____ 19. _____ 20. _____

SYLLABLES: Test 2

A. Using the rules shown in the box, divide the following words into syllables. For each syllable break, write the number of the rule that applies. Note the example.

Rule 1. Divide between two consonants.
Rule 2. Divide before a single consonant.

	Syllable division	Rule numbers	
Example: abandon	*a-ban-don*	2	1
1. entertain			
2. diplomat			
3. absolute			
4. hibernate			
5. alcohol			
6. terminal			

B. Using the rules shown in the box, divide the following words into syllables. For each syllable break, write the number of the rule that applies. Note the example.

Rule 3. Divide before a consonant followed by *le*.
Rule 4. Divide after prefixes and before suffixes.
Rule 5. Divide between the words in a compound word.

	Syllable division	Rule numbers	
Example: subtitle	*sub-ti-tle*	4	3
7. unfriendly			
8. outfielder			
9. previewing			
10. rattlesnake			
11. newlywed			
12. grandmother			
13. puzzlement			

(Continues on next page)

C. Complete each sentence by underlining the word with a prefix, a suffix, or both. Then, in the space provided, divide the underlined word into syllables.

14. I saw enough of the (*preview, plotline, story*) _____ to know that I didn't want to see the movie.

15. The letter had been (*proofread, refolded, torn*) _____ and put back into the envelope.

16. Dr. Nomo is a (*splendid, skillful, well-known*) _____ surgeon.

17. Only when we pay for college (*credit,* _____ *instruction, coursework*) do we appreciate high school's cost-free education.

D. Three words below are compound words. In the spaces provided, write those words, dividing them into syllables.

daybreak   hundred   magnet
pasture   pathway   schoolroom

18. _____   19. _____   20. _____

SYLLABLES: Test 3

A. Using the rules shown in the box, divide the following words into syllables. Then write the numbers of the two rules that apply. For each word, first use any of rules 3–5 that apply before using rule 1 or rule 2.

> **Rule 1. Divide between two consonants.**
> **Rule 2. Divide before a single consonant.**
> **Rule 3. Divide before a consonant followed by *le*.**
> **Rule 4. Divide after prefixes and before suffixes.**
> **Rule 5. Divide between the words in a compound word.**

	Syllable division	*Rule numbers*	
1. tomato	_____	_____	_____
2. incubate	_____	_____	_____
3. disconnect	_____	_____	_____
4. sincerely	_____	_____	_____
5. researcher	_____	_____	_____
6. anklebone	_____	_____	_____
7. solution	_____	_____	_____
8. belonging	_____	_____	_____
9. housekeeping	_____	_____	_____
10. photograph	_____	_____	_____

B. Complete each sentence by underlining the compound word. Then, in the space provided, divide the word into syllables.

11. When I'm hungry, I know I can find a snack   _____
in the (*cupboard, refrigerator, pantry*).

12. Roosevelt Grier was a three-hundred-pound   _____
football player with an unusual hobby for a
professional athlete: (*needlepoint, sewing, checkers*).

13. People in southern California fear the (*earthquakes,* _____
tornadoes, temperatures) that are common in the area.

(Continues on next page)

14. Though she was an excellent athlete, Darlene was   _____
a(n) (*commonplace, ordinary, terrible*) student.

15. One of the most dangerous jobs is that of a (*soldier,*   _____
firefighter, skier).

C. Each word below has three syllables. Using the rules you have learned in this chapter, circle the letter of the correct way to divide each word into syllables.

Note: For each word, first use any of rules 3–5 that apply before using rule 1 or rule 2.

16. unable   a. un-a-ble   b. un-ab-le   c. u-na-ble

17. equipment   a. equ-ip-ment   b. e-qui-pment   c. e-quip-ment

18. conviction   a. con-vic-tion   b. conv-ict-ion   c. con-vi-ction

19. candlelight   a. cand-le-light   b. can-dle-light   c. cand-lel-ight

20. remorseful   a. rem-orse-ful   b. re-morse-ful   c. re-mor-seful

SYLLABLES: Test 4

A. Using the rules shown in the box, divide the following words into syllables. Then write the numbers of the two rules that apply. For each word, first use any of rules 3–5 that apply before using rule 1 or rule 2.

> **Rule 1. Divide between two consonants.**
> **Rule 2. Divide before a single consonant.**
> **Rule 3. Divide before a consonant followed by *le*.**
> **Rule 4. Divide after prefixes and before suffixes.**
> **Rule 5. Divide between the words in a compound word.**

	Syllable division	*Rule numbers*
1. outstanding		
2. rearrange		
3. settlement		
4. incorrect		
5. following		
6. glassmaker		
7. electron		
8. expensive		
9. handlebar		
10. pillowcase		

B. Underline the five words that end in -**le**. Then in the spaces below, divide those words into syllables.

> See if you can solve this riddle. In a terrible car accident, a father is killed and his young son seriously hurt. The boy is rushed to the hospital, where the surgeon on duty takes one look at the horrible sight and says, "I'm unable to operate on this boy. He's my son." How is this possible? The answer, of course, is this: The surgeon is the boy's mother.

11. _____   14. _____

12. _____   15. _____

13. _____   *(Continues on next page)*

107

C. Complete each sentence by underlining the word that has *both* a prefix and a suffix. Then, in the space provided, divide the word into syllables.

Note: For each word, first use rules 3–5 before applying rule 1 or rule 2.

16. After (*adjusting, changing, following*) your diet and workout schedule, you are likely to feel and look much healthier.   _____

17. As a student, try to believe in yourself. For instance, do not have a (*disbelieving, doubtful, questioning*) look on your face if your professor tells you that you have earned an A for your project.   _____

18. Raoul is a (*mechanic, designer, principal*).   _____

19. One characteristic of a good dog is its (*devotion, attachment, loyalty*) to its master.   _____

20. Experts say that most car accidents are (*awful, dangerous, preventable*).   _____

D. Each word below has three or four syllables. Using the rules you have learned in this chapter, circle the letter of the correct way to divide each word into syllables.

Note: For each word, first use rules 3–5 before applying rule 1 or rule 2.

21. determined   a. de-ter-min-ed   b. de-ter-mined   c. det-erm-in-ed

22. nondrinker   a. non-drin-ker   b. nond-rin-ker   c. non-drink-er

23. subtraction   a. subt-rac-tion   b. sub-tract-ion   c. sub-trac-tion

24. prepayment   a. pre-pay-ment   b. prep-ay-ment   c. pre-paym-ent

25. favorable   a. fav-or-ab-le   b. fa-vor-a-ble   c. fa-vor-ab-le

✴ SYLLABLES: Test 5

A. Each word below has three syllables. Using the rules shown in the box, divide each word into syllables. Then write the number of the rule that applies to each division.

Note: For each word, first use any of rules 3–5 that apply before applying rule 1 or rule 2.

Rule 1. Divide between two consonants.
Rule 2. Divide before a single consonant.
Rule 3. Divide before a consonant followed by *le*.
Rule 4. Divide after prefixes and before suffixes.
Rule 5. Divide between the words in a compound word.

	Syllable division	*Rule numbers*	
1. nonrural	_____	_____	_____
2. cheeseburger	_____	_____	_____
3. unlawful	_____	_____	_____
4. sunbonnet	_____	_____	_____
5. mountaintop	_____	_____	_____
6. flamethrower	_____	_____	_____
7. motorbike	_____	_____	_____
8. belittle	_____	_____	_____
9. opening	_____	_____	_____
10. chairperson	_____	_____	_____

(Continues on next page)

B. Complete the passage by filling in each blank with the word that has *both* a prefix and a suffix. Then, in the spaces provided below, divide the words you chose into syllables, using Rule 4.

> In a famous story, a man named Rip Van Winkle goes to sleep and wakes up forty years later to (11. *find, discover, observe*) _____ a world that has changed (12. *completely, wholly, totally*) _____. A man named Sergei Krikalev is a modern-day, real-life Rip Van Winkle. Krikalev spent ten months in space, going around the Earth. He went into orbit as an astronaut from the USSR—the Soviet Union. While he was in space, the Soviet Union was broken up. So when he returned to Earth from his (13. *lengthy, exhausting, tiring*) _____ trip, Krikalev came back as an astronaut from a different country—Russia. Also, while Krikalev was in space, there was a (14. *changing, renaming, moving*) _____ of his hometown Leningrad to St. Petersburg. The financial system changed: Socialism was replaced by free-market capitalism. And because of the breakup, Krikalev actually returned to live in a foreign country—the former Soviet state of Kazakhstan.

11. _____   13. _____

12. _____   14. _____

C. Six words below have three syllables. In the space provided, write each word, dividing it into syllables.

Note: For each word, first use any of rules 3–5 that apply before applying rule 1 or rule 2.

> If you work at a computer terminal all day and complain of neck aches and backaches, a new exercise may help you. To relieve tension, you should do the following. First, lay your arms flat on the desk. Next, rest your head on your arms. Then straighten the curve in your lower back. Stay in place for twenty seconds. Finally, lift your head. You should feel an improvement right away. Repeat this routine as needed.

15. _____   18. _____

16. _____   19. _____

17. _____   20. _____

SYLLABLES: Test 6

A. Each word below has three syllables. Using the rules shown in the box, divide each word into syllables. Then write the number of the rule that applies to each division.

Note: For each word, first use any of rules 3–5 that apply before applying rule 1 or rule 2.

Rule 1. Divide between two consonants.
Rule 2. Divide before a single consonant.
Rule 3. Divide before a consonant followed by *le*.
Rule 4. Divide after prefixes and before suffixes.
Rule 5. Divide between the words in a compound word.

		Syllable division	*Rule numbers*
1.	rebuttal	_____	_____ _____
2.	kettledrum	_____	_____ _____
3.	Eskimo	_____	_____ _____
4.	revolver	_____	_____ _____
5.	cannibal	_____	_____ _____
6.	marketplace	_____	_____ _____
7.	conviction	_____	_____ _____
8.	jamboree	_____	_____ _____
9.	vacancy	_____	_____ _____
10.	cardholder	_____	_____ _____

(Continues on next page)

B. Complete the passage by filling in each blank with the word that has *both* a prefix and a suffix. Then, in the spaces provided below, divide the words you chose into syllables, using Rule 4.

> When people vacation, one of the most popular destinations is the island chain of Hawaii. The warm sun and gentle trade winds can melt away one's stress. Some people swear the islands are the perfect (11. *medicine, prescription, choice*) _____ for an ideal vacation. But where do the residents of Hawaii go for a (12. *relaxing, special, pleasant*) _____ time? There are several places Hawaiians go to get away from it all. One of their favored destinations may seem (13. *questionable, unlikely, strange*) _____—Las Vegas, Nevada, which has a dry, dusty climate, (14. *totally, completely, altogether*) _____ different from Hawaii's moist tropical environment. Yet many Hawaiians enjoy activities in Las Vegas, such as shows and gambling. However, the Hawaiians' favorite vacation spot is one familiar to most Americans: Disneyland.

11. _____   13. _____

12. _____   14. _____

C. Six words below have three syllables. In the space provided, write each word, dividing it into syllables .

Note: For each word, first use any of rules 3–5 that apply before applying rule 1 or rule 2.

> A revealing survey about patients' feelings toward their doctors was recently released. The results may seem surprising. Only 31 percent of patients felt that their doctors spent enough time with them. Also, 42 percent thought that their physicians were not clear when explaining their health problems. A full 63 percent felt that doctors make too much money. And 69 percent said that they had started to lose confidence in doctors.

15. _____   18. _____

16. _____   19. _____

17. _____   20. _____

4
Dictionary Use

The dictionary contains a lot of useful information. But if you have trouble looking up words, that information won't do you much good. So this chapter gives you some helpful hints on how to look up words in the dictionary. Then the chapter helps you makes sense of the information that a dictionary provides for each word.

OWNING YOUR OWN DICTIONARIES

You can benefit greatly from owning two dictionaries. The first dictionary you should own is a paperback you can carry with you. Any of the following would be an excellent choice:

American Heritage Dictionary, Paperback Edition
Random House Dictionary, Paperback Edition
Webster's New World Dictionary, Paperback Edition

The second dictionary you should own is a desk-sized hardcover edition which should be kept in the room where you study. All the above dictionaries come in hardbound versions containing a good deal more information than the paperback editions. For instance, a desk-sized dictionary defines far more words than a paperback dictionary, and there are more definitions per word. While desk-sized dictionaries cost more, they are worth the investment, as they are a valuable study aid.

Dictionaries are often updated to reflect changes in the language. New words come into use, and old words take on new meanings. So you should not use a dictionary which has been lying around the house for a number of years. Instead, invest in a new one. You will find that it is money well spent.

FINDING A WORD IN THE DICTIONARY

Using Guidewords to Find a Word

The two words on top of each dictionary page are called **guidewords**. Shown below is a page in the *American Heritage Dictionary,* Third Edition, Paperback.

| breather / bridle | 108 |

To inhale and exhale air. **2.** To be alive; live. See Syns at **be. 3.** To pause to rest. **4.** To utter quietly; whisper. —**idiom. breathe down (someone's) neck.** To threaten or annoy by proximity or close pursuit. [ME *brethen.*] —**breath′a•ble** *adj.*
breath•er (brē′thər) *n.* **1.** One that breathes. **2.** *Informal.* A short rest period.
breath•tak•ing (brĕth′tā′kĭng) *adj.* Inspiring awe. —**breath′tak′ing•ly** *adv.*
Brecht (brĕkt, brĕκнt), **Bertolt.** 1898–1956. German poet and playwright. —**Brecht′i•an** *adj.*
Breck•in•ridge (brĕk′ĭn-rĭj′), **John Cabell.** 1821–75. U.S. Vice President (1857–61).
breech (brēch) *n.* **1.** The buttocks. **2. breech•es** (brĭch′ĭz). **a.** Knee-length trousers. **b.** *Informal.* Trousers. **3.** The part of a firearm behind the barrel. [< OE *brēc,* trousers.]
breech•cloth (brēch′klŏth′, -klôth′) *n.* A loincloth.
breed (brēd) *v.* **bred** (brĕd), **breed•ing. 1.a.** To produce (offspring). **b.** To reproduce. **2.** To bring about; engender. **3.** To raise or mate animals. **4.** To rear or train; bring up. —*n.* **1.** A genetic strain, esp. one developed and maintained by controlled propagation. **2.** A kind; sort. [< OE *brēdan.*]
breed•er (brē′dər) *n.* **1.** One who breeds animals or plants. **2.** A source or cause.
breeder reactor *n.* A nuclear reactor that produces as well as consumes fissionable material.
breed•ing (brē′dĭng) *n.* **1.** One's line of descent; ancestry. **2.** Training in the proper forms of social and personal conduct.
breeze (brēz) *n.* **1.** A light gentle wind. **2.** *Informal.* Something, such as a task, that is easy to do. —*v.* **breezed, breez•ing.** *Informal.* To progress swiftly and effortlessly. [Perh. < OSp. *briza,* northeast wind.] —**breez′i•ly** *adv.* —**breez′i•ness** *n.* —**breez′y** *adj.*
  Syns: *breeze, cinch, pushover, snap, walkaway, walkover n.*
breeze•way (brēz′wā′) *n.* A roofed, open-sided passageway connecting two structures, such as a house and garage.
Bre•men (brĕm′ən). A city of NW Germany SW of Hamburg. Pop. 530,520.
Bren•ner Pass (brĕn′ər). An Alpine pass, 1,371 m (4,495 ft), connecting Innsbruck, Austria, with Bolzano, Italy.
Bre•scia (brĕsh′ə). A city of N Italy E of Milan. Pop. 206,460.
Brest (brĕst). A city of SW Belorussia on the Bug R.. Pop. 222,000.
breth•ren (brĕth′rən) *n.* A pl. of **brother** 2.
Bret•on (brĕt′n) *n.* **1.** A native or inhabitant of Brittany. **2.** The Celtic language of Brittany. —**Bret′on** *adj.*
Breu•ghel (broi′gəl). See **Brueghel.**
breve (brēv, brĕv) *n.* **1.** A symbol (˘) placed over a vowel to show that it has a short sound. **2.** *Mus.* A note equivalent to two whole notes. [< Lat. *brevis,* short.]
bre•vi•ar•y (brē′vē-ĕr′ē, brĕv′ē-) *n.*, *pl.* **-ies.** A book containing the hymns, offices, and prayers for the canonical hours. [< Lat. *breviārium,* summary < *brevis,* short.]
brev•i•ty (brĕv′ĭ-tē) *n.* **1.** Briefness of duration. **2.** Concise expression; terseness. [< Lat. *brevis,* short.]
brew (broō) *v.* **1.** To make (ale or beer) from malt and hops by infusion, boiling, and fermentation. **2.** To make (a beverage) by boiling or steeping. **3.** To be imminent: *Trouble's brewing.* [< OE *brēowan.*] —**brew** *n.* —**brew′er** *n.* —**brew′er•y** *n.*
Brezh•nev (brĕzh′nĕf), **Leonid Ilyich.** 1906–82. Soviet political leader.
Bri•an Bo•ru (brī′ən bə-roō′). 926–1014. Irish king (1002–14).
bri•ar¹ also **bri•er** (brī′ər) *n.* **1.** A Mediterranean shrub whose woody roots are used to make tobacco pipes. **2.** A pipe made from this root. [< OFr. *bruyere,* heath.]
bri•ar² (brī′ər) *n.* Var. of **brier¹.**
bribe (brīb) *n.* Something, such as money or a favor, offered or given to induce or influence a person to act dishonestly. —*v.* **bribed, brib•ing. 1.** To give, offer, or promise a bribe (to). **2.** To gain influence over or corrupt by a bribe. [< OFr., alms.] —**brib′a•ble** *adj.* —**brib′er•y** *n.*
bric-a-brac (brĭk′ə-brăk′) *n.* Small objects usu. displayed as ornaments. [Fr. *bric-à-brac.*]
brick (brĭk) *n.*, *pl.* **bricks** or **brick. 1.** A molded rectangular block of clay baked until hard and used as a building and paving material. **2.** An object shaped like a brick: *a brick of cheese.* —*v.* To construct, line, or pave with bricks. [< MDu. *bricke.*]
brick•bat (brĭk′băt′) *n.* **1.** A piece of brick, esp. when thrown. **2.** A critical remark.
brick•lay•er (brĭk′lā′ər) *n.* A person skilled in building with bricks. —**brick′lay′ing** *n.*
bri•dal (brīd′l) *n.* A wedding. [< OE *brȳdealo.*] —**bri′dal** *adj.*
bride (brīd) *n.* A woman recently married or about to be married. [< OE *brȳd.*]
bride•groom (brīd′groōm′, -groŏm′) *n.* A man who is about to be married or has recently been married. [< OE *brȳdguma* : *brȳd,* bride; see BRIDE + *guma,* man; see **dhghem-**.]
brides•maid (brīdz′mād′) *n.* A woman who attends the bride at a wedding.
bridge¹ (brĭj) *n.* **1.** A structure spanning and providing passage over an obstacle. **2.** The upper bony ridge of the human nose. **3.** A fixed or removable replacement for missing natural teeth. **4.** *Mus.* A thin, upright piece of wood in some stringed instruments that supports the strings above the sounding board. **5.** A crosswise platform or enclosed area above the main deck of a ship from which the ship is controlled. —*v.* **bridged, bridg•ing. 1.** To build a bridge over. **2.** To cross by or as if by a bridge. [< OE *brycg.* See **bhrū-**.] —**bridge′a•ble** *adj.*
bridge² (brĭj) *n.* Any of several card games usu. for four people, derived from whist. [Poss. < Russ. *birich,* a call.]
bridge•head (brĭj′hĕd′) *n.* A forward position seized by advancing troops in enemy territory as a foothold for further advance.
Bridge•port (brĭj′pôrt′, -pōrt′). A city of SW CT on Long Island Sound SW of New Haven. Pop. 141,686.
Bridge•town (brĭj′toun′). The cap. of Barbados, in the West Indies. Pop. 7,466.
bridge•work (brĭj′wûrk′) *n.* A dental bridge or bridges used to replace missing teeth.
bri•dle (brīd′l) *n.* **1.** The harness fitted about a horse's head, used to restrain or guide. **2.** A curb or check. —*v.* **-dled, -dling. 1.** To put

In the excerpt above, *breather* and *bridle* are guidewords. *Breather* is the first word that will be defined on this page, and *bridle* is the last word defined on the page. All the other words on the page fall alphabetically between the first and second guideword.

To see if you understand guidewords, circle the two words below which would appear on the same page as *breather* and *bridle:*

break   brevity   brilliant   bridge

The word *break* comes earlier in the alphabet than the guideword *breather,* so we know that it will not appear on the page. And *brilliant* comes later in the alphabet than the guideword *bridle,* so it will not appear on the page. The other two words, *brevity* and *bridge,* do come alphabetically between *breather* and *bridle.* They are the two words you should have circled.

➤ *Practice 1*

A. Below are five pairs of dictionary guidewords. Each pair is followed by a series of other words. Circle the two words in each series which would be found on the same page as the guidewords.

   1. **bluff / bob**

     black   blush   boil   boat   bonnet

   2. **dock / dogcatcher**

     dizzy   dogfish   dodo   dogfight   dogcart

   3. **likelihood / limp**

     lilac   lighthouse   line   limousine   likeable

   4. **radish / raise**

     radio   rainwater   raisin   racetrack   ragtime

   5. **web-footed / weird**

     weave   weightlifting   webbing   wedding   welcome

B. Tell on which dictionary page each italicized word below would be found by circling the letter of the correct guidewords.

   6. *Drill* would be found on the dictionary page with which guidewords?
     a. **drama / dredge**
     b. **dredge / drippings**
     c. **drive / drowsy**

   7. *Everglade* would be found on the dictionary page with which guidewords?
     a. **evacuate / every**
     b. **everybody / example**
     c. **export / extent**

8. *Jelly* would be found on the dictionary page with which guidewords?
   a. **Jackson / Janus**
   b. **Japan / Jefferson**
   c. **Jefferson City / jetty**

9. *Potpie* would be found on the dictionary page with which guidewords?
   a. **possible / postulate**
   b. **posture / pouch**
   c. **poultice / practical**

10. *Tzar* would be found on the dictionary page with which guidewords?
    a. **tutelage / twist**
    b. **twit / typography**
    c. **tyrannical / ulna**

Using Spelling Hints to Find a Word

Do you know how to find a word in the dictionary if you are unsure of its spelling? What you should do first is sound out the word. To sound out a word, apply the phonics principles you learned in Chapters 1 and 2. Pronouncing the word correctly will help you come closer to spelling it correctly. Write down, as best as you can, the word you want to look up. Then look up the word on the basis of how you think it is spelled. Here are some hints that will help you find a word when your first guess doesn't work:

Hints for Finding Words

Hint 1: Look at the consonants in the word. If you used single consonants, try doubling them. If you wrote double consonants, try removing one of them.

Hint 2: Remember that vowels often sound the same. Try an **i** in place of an **a**, an **i** in place of an **e**, and so on. For example, if you can't find a word you think starts with **hi**, try looking under **hy**.

Hint 3: Try substituting a letter or group of letters from the pairs or groups below. For example, if a word isn't spelled with a **c**, it may be spelled with a **k**; if it isn't spelled with an **f**, try **v** or **ph**.

c / k	c / s	f / v / ph	g / j	qu / kw / k	s / c / z
sch / sc / sk	sh / ch	shun / tion / sion		w / wh	able / ible
ai / ay	al / el / le	ancy / ency	ate / ite	au / aw	ea / ee
er / or	ie / ei	ou / ow	oo / u	y / i / e	

➤ *Practice 2*

Use your dictionary for this practice. Apply your knowledge of guidewords as well as the spelling hints in the box on the previous page to help you find the correct spelling of each of the following words. Write each correct spelling in the answer space.

1. revize _____

2. kiddnap _____

3. karry _____

4. jiant _____

5. realy _____

6. skoolteecher _____

7. pleeze _____

8. comming _____

9. beleive _____

10. tunnal _____

LEARNING FROM DICTIONARY ENTRIES

Each word that is defined in the dictionary is called an entry word. Entry words are in **boldface** print. Here is an example of a dictionary entry:

Sample Dictionary Entry

> **in•spire** (ĭn-spīr′) *v.* **-spired, -spiring. 1.** To fill with noble or reverent emotion; exalt. **2.** To stimulate to creativity or action. **3.** To elicit or create in another. **4.** To inhale. [< Lat. *īnspīrāre.*] —**in•spir′er** *n.*

All of the following information may be provided in a dictionary entry:

1 Spelling and Syllables

2 Pronunciation Symbols and Accent Marks

3 Parts of Speech

4 Irregular Forms of Words

5 Definitions and Special Labels

6 Word Origins

7 Synonyms

The rest of the chapter will look at each kind of information. The entries used are taken from the paperback version of the *American Heritage Dictionary,* Third Edition (abbreviated *AHD* from this point on).

1 SPELLING AND SYLLABLES

A dictionary entry first shows you the correct spelling and syllable breakdown of a word. Dots separate the word into syllables. As you learned in Chapter 3, each syllable is a separate sound that includes one vowel sound and any connected consonant sounds. The following word has three vowel sounds and three syllables.

> **de•tach•ment**

How many syllables does each of these entry words have?

> **ru•mor**   **ex•plic•it**   **stim•u•late**   **launch**

The dots tell you that *rumor* has two syllables and that *explicit* and *stimulate* have three syllables each. *Launch*, on the other hand, has no dots and only one syllable.

➤ Practice 3

Use your dictionary to separate the following words into syllables. Put a large dot between the syllables. Then write the number of syllables in each word. An example is provided.

> **Example:** c o n•f o r•m i•t y   ___4___ syllables
>
> 1. h i c c u p   _____ syllables
>
> 2. m i n i m a l   _____ syllables
>
> 3. d i s p o s a l   _____ syllables
>
> 4. i n s e n s i t i v e   _____ syllables
>
> 5. c o m m u n i c a t i o n   _____ syllables

2 PRONUNCIATION SYMBOLS AND ACCENT MARKS

After the entry word, additional information appears in parentheses, as you see in the following entry for *colorblind*.

> **col•or•blind** (kŭl′ər-blīnd′) *adj.* **1.** Partially or totally unable to distinguish certain colors. **2.** Not subject to racial prejudices.

The information in parentheses shows you how to pronounce the word. It includes two kinds of symbols: pronunciation symbols and accent marks. Following is an explanation of each kind.

Pronunciation Symbols

Pronunciation symbols tell you how to pronounce the letters in a word. The sounds of the consonants and vowels are shown in a pronunciation key at the beginning of the dictionary. Here is a pronunciation key (drawn from the *AHD*'s key) for the vowels and a few other sounds that often confuse dictionary users.

Pronunciation Key

ă pat	ā pay	â care	ä father	ě pet	ē bee	ĭ pit
ī pie, by	î pier	ŏ pot	ō toe	ô paw, for		oi noise
o͝o took	o͞o boot	ou out	th thin	*th* this		ŭ cut
û urge	yo͞o abuse	zh vision	ə about, item, edible, gallop, circus			

To use the above key, match the symbol (ă, ā, and so on) with the letter or letters in **bold print** in the short word that follows the symbol. For instance, ă sounds like the **a** in *pat*. You can pronounce the first *o* in *colorblind* by first finding the matching symbol within parentheses. Note that the matching symbol is ŭ. Then look for that symbol in the Pronunciation Key. It shows you that ŭ has the sound of **u** in the short word *cut*. You can also use the Pronunciation Key to pronounce the **i** in *colorblind* (ī). It shows you that ī is pronounced like the **i** in *pie* and the **y** in *by*.

The second vowel sound in *colorblind* is indicated by the symbol ə. That symbol, which looks like an upside-down **e,** is called the **schwa.** The pronunciation key tells you that the schwa has a weak, unstressed sound that usually sounds like "uh" (as in "**a**bout" and "gall**o**p") or "ih" (as in "**i**tem," "ed**i**ble," and "circ**u**s").

➤ *Practice 4*

Use your dictionary and the pronunciation key above to answer the following questions.

1. In the word *contest*, the **o** is pronounced like the **o** in what common word? _____

2. In the word *finger*, the **i** is pronounced like the **i** in what common word? _____

3. In the word *trust*, the **u** is pronounced like the **u** in what common word? _____

4. In the word *rapid*, the **a** is pronounced like the **a** in what common word? _____

5. In the word *shelf*, the **e** is pronounced like the **e** in what common word? _____

Accent Marks

The mark ′ that comes after the first syllable in the word *colorblind* (kŭl′ər-blīnd′) is called an **accent mark**. It tells you that you should put more stress on the first syllable of *colorblind*.

Words of one syllable have no accent mark. Longer words may have more than one accent mark, since they sometimes have emphasis on more than one syllable. When there is more than one accent mark, the darker mark shows which syllable gets the stronger accent. For example, in the word *colorblind*, the first syllable has a darker accent mark, so it receives more stress than the last syllable, which has a lighter accent. The second syllable, however, is unstressed.

➤ *Practice 5*

Use your dictionary to separate the following words into syllables. Put dots between the syllables. Then show how the word is pronounced by writing the word in pronunciation symbols. Include the accent mark or marks. An example is provided for you.

       Example: j u m • b l e   jŭm′bəl _____

    1. m a g n e t   _____

    2. j a n i t o r   _____

    3. e n c o u r a g e   _____

    4. s p e c u l a t e   _____

    5. t r o u b l e m a k e r   _____

3   PARTS OF SPEECH

Every word is at least one part of speech (noun, verb, and so on). Parts of speech are shown in a dictionary entry as abbreviations in *italicized* print. Look for the italicized abbreviations in the entry below.

> **pil•low** (pĭl′ō) *n.* **1.** A cloth case stuffed with soft material and used to cushion the head, esp. during sleep. **2.** A decorative cushion. — *v.* To serve as a pillow for. [< Lat. *pulvīnus.*] —**pil′low•y** *adj.*

The italicized abbreviations *n.* and *v.* show that this word can be two parts of speech: *noun* and *verb*. Following the abbreviation *n.* are the two noun definitions for *pillow*. The noun definitions are followed by a dash and then a *v.*, showing that the next definition will be a verb definition for *pillow*.

At the end of the entry is the abbreviation *adj.* It tells us that *pillowy* is the adjective form of the entry word.

Here is how parts of speech are abbreviated in the *AHD*:

n. — noun	*v.* — verb
pron. — pronoun	*conj.* — conjunction
adj. — adjective	*prep.* — preposition
adv. — adverb	*interj.* — interjection

➤ Practice 6

Use your dictionary to list parts of speech for each of the following words. Each word can be more than one part of speech—the number you should fill in is shown in each case. Use the abbreviations given above.

Parts of speech

1. go   a. _____   b. _____

2. head   a. _____   b. _____   c. _____

3. just   a. _____   b. _____

4. plus   a. _____   b. _____   c. _____

5. quiet   a. _____   b. _____   c. _____

4   IRREGULAR FORMS AND SPELLINGS

After the part of speech, the dictionary shows any irregular forms, difficult spellings, and comparison words that apply to the entry word. First, the dictionary shows any irregular plurals. Here's an example.

goose (go͞os) *n., pl.* **geese** (gēs).

The noun plural of *goose* is irregular. For most noun plurals, we add an *s* (*pencil—pencils*). However, for *goose,* the noun plural is not *gooses,* it's *geese.*

After the part of speech, the dictionary will also show any irregular verb parts, as in the example below.

draw (drô) *v.* **drew** (dro͞o), **drawn** (drôn), **draw•ing**.

If we followed normal rules with *draw,* the past tense, for instance, would be *drawed. Draw,* however, is an irregular verb, so the dictionary shows us its verb forms, including its past tense, *drew.*

Also shown after the part of speech are plurals and verb forms that may present spelling problems. The entry will show, for instance, how to spell the plural of a noun that ends in *y* (as for *bunny*) or the *-ing* form of a verb ending in **e** (as for *dare*).

> **bun•ny** (bŭn′ē) *n., pl.* **-nies.**
>
> **dare** (dār) *v.* **dared, dar•ing.**

Finally, comparative forms of adjectives and adverbs are also given at this point in an entry, both irregular forms (as for *good*) and regular forms (as for *high*).

> **good** (good) *adj.* **bet•ter** (bĕt′ər), **best** (bĕst).
>
> **high** (hī) *adj.* **-er, -est.**

➤ *Practice 7*

Each of the following words has at least one irregular form or spelling. Using your dictionary, write any irregular forms or special spellings provided for each word. An example is provided for you.

Example: hero   _____*heroes*_____

1. hide   _____

2. one-up   _____

3. skinny   _____

4. bad   _____

5. party   _____

5   DEFINITIONS AND SPECIAL LABELS

Definitions

A word often has more than one meaning. When it does, the definitions may be numbered in the dictionary. These meanings are divided according to part of speech. For example, look at the dictionary entry that follows. Then in the space below, lists the parts of speech for the entry word *sport* and the number of definitions for each part of speech. Then read the explanation.

sport (spôrt) *n.* **1.** An activity usu. involving physical exertion and having a set form and body of rules; game. **2.** An active pastime; diversion. **3.** Light mockery. **4.** One known for the manner of one's acceptance or defeat or criticism: *a bad sport.* **5.** *Informal.* One who lives a jolly, extravagant life. **6.** *Biol.* A mutation. —*v.* **1.** To play or frolic. **2.** To joke or trifle. **3.** To display or show off. —*adj.* Also **sports.** Of or appropriate for sport: *sport fishing.* [<OFr. *desport,* pleasure.] —**sport′i·ness** *n.* —**sport′y** *adj.*

In the spaces below, state which parts of speech are provided for *sport,* and how many definitions are given for each part of speech:

_____

_____

Explanation:

The italicized abbreviations show that *sport* can be three parts of speech: noun, verb, and adjective. *Sport* has six noun definitions, three verb definitions, and one adjective definition.

Definitions are listed in the *AHD* according to how commonly each is used. In other words, the first definition is the most common one, the second definition is the second most common one, and so forth.

Special Labels

There are two types of special labels: usage labels and field labels. (*Note:* These special labels appear in most dictionaries, but not in all of them.)

Usage Labels

Unless otherwise indicated, the definitions in an entry are "Standard English." This means that the definition is considered acceptable in speech and writing in both formal and informal situations. Any definition that is not Standard English will have a **usage label**, such as the fifth noun meaning for *sport.* The label *Informal* is written before that definition, which tells us that this use of *sport* is not considered proper for formal speech and writing. Following are several common usage labels:

- *Informal.* Considered acceptable only for informal speech or writing.
- *Slang.* A type of casual, playful language in which terms usually have short lives. Considered improper in formal conversation or writing. An example is the third noun definition given in the *AHD* for *chick*: "A young woman."

• *Non-Standard*. Usage considered unacceptable, either formally or informally. An example is *ain't*: "Am not."

• *Offensive*. Considered insulting. An example is the first noun definition given in the *AHD* for *midget*: "An unusually small or short person."

Field Labels

A **field label** tells if a word has a special meaning within a certain field. An example is the sixth noun definition of *sport*, which is labeled *Biol*. This means that the definition which follows applies only to the field of biology. Other such labels are *Phil* for *philosophy* and *Psych* for *psychology*.

➤ *Practice 8*

A. Below are three words and some of their definitions. A sentence using each word is also given. Write the number of the definition that best fits each sentence.

1. **conceive**   **1.** To become pregnant (with).
                   2. To think; imagine.

Which definition of *conceive* fits the following sentence? _____

It's hard to *conceive* of being five stories tall, but if you look out a fifth-floor window, you'll be able to imagine how some dinosaurs viewed the world.

2. **suspect**:   **1.** To regard as likely or probable.
                   2. To distrust or doubt.
                   3. To think of as guilty without proof.

Which definition of *suspect* fits the following sentence? _____

I *suspect* the exam is going to be all essay questions.

3. **pessimist**: **1.** One who takes the gloomiest possible view of a situation.
                   2. One who believes that this is the worst of all possible worlds.
                   3. One who believes that the evil in the world outweighs the good.

Which definition of *pessimist* fits the following sentence? _____

Don is too much of a *pessimist* to study for tests; he assumes he'll do poorly no matter how hard he tries.

B. Refer to the dictionary excerpt on page 114 to answer the following questions.

4. Which of the following words has an entry that includes a usage label? In the space provided, write the usage label and the definition.

a. *breather*

b. *breed*

c. *bribe*

The usage label and definition: _____

5. Which of the following words has an entry that includes a field label? In the space provided, write the field label and the definition.

a. *breeze*

b. *brew*

c. *bridge*

The field label and definition: _____

_____

_____

6 WORD ORIGINS

Most dictionaries will give you an idea about where words came from and what a word meant when it was created. For instance, the entry for the word *gorgeous* says this:

> **gor•geous** (gôr′jəs) *adj.* **1.** Dazzlingly brilliant or magnificent: *a gorgeous gown.* **2.** *Informal.* Wonderful; delightful. [< OFr. *gorrias,* elegant.] — **gor′geous ly** *adv.* — **gor′geous ness** *n.*

A list of abbreviations near the front of the dictionary explains that "OFr," stands for "Old French." The information in brackets tells us that *gorgeous* came from the Old French word *gorrias,* which meant "elegant."

➤ *Practice 9*

Using the dictionary excerpt on page 114, tell what language each of the following words comes from and what the word means in that language.

Note: Page vii of the *AHD* explains what language each abbreviation stands for.

Word	Language	Original meaning
1. breech	_____	_____
2. breeze	_____	_____
3. brevity	_____	_____

7 SYNONYMS

A **synonym** is a word whose meaning is similar to that of another word. For instance, two synonyms for the word *fast* are *quick* and *speedy*.

Some dictionary entries end with synonyms. For example, the entry below ends with a list of synonyms for the verb form of *slant*.

> **slant** (slănt) *v.* **1.** To slope or cause to slope. **2.** To present in a way that conforms with a particular bias. — *n.* **1.** A sloping plane, direction, or course. **2.** A particular bias. [< ME *slenten.*] —**slant′ing ly** *adv.* —**slant′-wise′** *adv. & adj.*
>
>   *Syns: slant, incline, lean, slope, tilt, tip v.*

If you want to see how the synonyms might differ in meaning, you can look them up in the dictionary.

More information on synonyms and **antonyms** (words with opposite meanings) can be found in a thesaurus, which is a collection of synonyms and some antonyms. A thesaurus can improve your writing by helping you find the precise word needed to express your thoughts. A thesaurus works much like a dictionary. You look up a word, but instead of the definitions provided by a dictionary, you get a list of synonyms for the word. Here are three good thesauruses:

> *The New American Roget's College Thesaurus in Dictionary Form*
> *The Random House Thesaurus*
> *Webster's Collegiate Thesaurus*

➤ *Practice 10*

Use the dictionary excerpt on page 114 to answer the following questions.

1. For which word are synonyms listed? _____

2. What are the synonyms listed for this word? _____

   _____

3. Only one of the definitions of this word applies to the synonyms. Write out

   that definition: _____

   _____

CHAPTER SUMMARY

In this chapter, you learned the following:

- It is important to own two dictionaries. One should be a paperback dictionary you can carry with you. The second should be a desk-sized dictionary you use at home.

- You can find a word in the dictionary with the help of guidewords, the two words at the top of each dictionary page. The first guideword is the first word on the page, and the second is the last word on the page. All the other words on the page fall alphabetically between those two words.

- The hints on page 116 can also help you find a word in the dictionary by helping you figure out how to spell the word.

- A dictionary entry for a word may provide the following information.

  — How the word is spelled and broken into syllables

  — How the word is correctly pronounced, including where it is accented if it has more than one syllable

  — Part (or parts) of speech

  — Any irregular forms, special spellings, and comparative forms

  — Definitions and any usage and field labels that may apply

  — The word's origin

  — Synonyms and antonyms

➤ *Review Test 1*

To review what you've learned in this chapter, answer each of the following questions by circling the letter of the correct answer.

1. Guidewords can help you
   a. pronounce a word in the dictionary.
   b. find a word in a dictionary.
   c. define a word in a dictionary.

2. You can learn to pronounce a word by using pronunciation symbols and
   a. part of speech.
   b. special labels.
   c. the pronunciation key.

3. A dark accent mark shows
   a. which syllable has the strongest stress.
   b. which syllable has the weakest stress.
   c. that the word has only one syllable.

4. A label such as *Biol.* or *Math.* means that the definition that follows
   a. is informal.
   b. applies to a specialized field.
   c. is no longer used for the entry word.

5. A thesaurus lists
   a. definitions.
   b. synonyms.
   c. word origins.

➤ *Review Test 2*

A. Below are three pairs of dictionary guidewords followed by a series of other words. Circle the two words in each series which would be found on the same page as the guidewords.

1–2. **airmail / alarm**

   Akron   algebra   alive   aim   airman

3–4. **Crete / Croatia**

   creek   crib   critter   crest   crossbar

5–6. **indisposed / indulge**

   indifferent   indicate   industry   individual   indoors

B. Tell on which dictionary page each italicized word below would be found by circling the letter of the correct guidewords.

7. *Refer* would be found on the dictionary page with which guidewords?
   a. **redress / referendum**
   b. **refill / regalia**
   c. **recreation / red pepper**

8. *Snowflake* would be found on the dictionary page with which guidewords?
   a. **Smith / snap**
   b. **snap bean / snow blindness**
   c. **snowbound / sobriety**

9. *Halo* would be found on the dictionary page with which guidewords?
   a. **habit-forming / hail**
   b. **half-life / halyard**
   c. **ham / handball**

C. Use your dictionary and the hints on page 116 to find the correct spelling of the following words.

10. toppic   _____   13. bycicle   _____

11. kwiz   _____   14. writting   _____

12. sirprize   _____   15. vizitor   _____

D. Use the pronunciation key on page 119 to answer the following questions.

16. In **fumble** (fŭm′bəl), the **u** is pronounced   _____
    like the **u** in what common word?

17. In **cable** (kā′bəl), the **a** is pronounced   _____
    like the **a** in what common word?

18. In **reside** (rĭ-zīd′), the first **e** is pronounced _____
    like the **i** in what common word?

19. In **reside** (rĭ-zīd′), the **i** is pronounced   _____
    like the **i** in what common word?

20. In **presume** (prĭ-zo͞om′), the **u** is pronounced   _____
    like the **oo** in what common word?

➤ *Review Test 3*

Use your dictionary to do all of the following.

A. Place dots between the syllables in the following words. Then write the correct pronunciation symbols, including the accent mark or marks.

1. p r i o r   _____

2. i n s u r e   _____

3. e n g a g e   _____

4. l e g i b l e   _____

5. s o c i a l i z e _____

B. List the parts of speech for each of the following words.

6. glow   *Two parts of speech*: _____

7. major   *Three parts of speech*: _____

C. Write the plural spelling for the following words.

8. factory   *Plural spelling*: _____

9. mouse   *Plural spelling*: _____

D. Write the dictionary definition of *lemon* that fits in the following sentence.

Don't sell me the car if you know it's a lemon.

10. Definition of *lemon* that fits:

_____

➤ *Review Test 4*

Here is a chance to apply your understanding of dictionary use to a full-length selection. This is a true story about Malcolm X, an African American civil rights leader in the 1950s and 1960s. In this excerpt from his autobiography, Malcolm X (with his coauthor, Alex Haley) explains how he used his time in jail to become "truly free." Read the selection and then answer the phonics and dictionary questions that follow.

Words to Watch

Following are some words in the reading that do not have strong context support. Each word is followed by the number of the paragraph in which it appears and its meaning there. These words are indicated in the reading by a small circle (°).

acquire (1): get
painstaking (5): very careful
ragged (5): uneven
burrowing (6): digging
succeeding (7): following
word-base (8): vocabulary
bunk (8): bed
wedge (8): a tool shaped like a triangle, used to separate two objects

DISCOVERING WORDS

Malcolm X with Alex Haley

1   It was because of my letters [which Malcolm X wrote to people outside while he was in jail] that I happened to stumble upon starting to acquire° some kind of a homemade education.

2   I became increasingly frustrated at not being able to express what I wanted to convey in letters that I wrote. . . . And every book I picked up had few sentences which didn't contain anywhere from one to nearly all the words that might as well have been in Chinese. When I skipped those words, of course, I really ended up with little idea of what the book said. . . .

3   I saw that the best thing I could do was get hold of a dictionary—to study, to learn some words. I requested a dictionary along with some tablets and pencils from the Norfolk Prison Colony school.

4   I spent two days just riffling uncertainly through the dictionary's pages. I'd never realized so many words existed! I didn't know *which* words I needed to learn. Finally, just to start some kind of action, I began copying.

5   In my slow, painstaking°, ragged° handwriting, I copied into my tablet everything printed on that first page, down to the punctuation marks. I believe it took me a day. Then, aloud, I read back to myself everything I'd written on the tablet. Over and over, aloud, to myself, I read my own handwriting.

6   I woke up the next morning, thinking about those words—immensely proud to realize that not only had I written so much at one time, but I'd written words that I never knew were in the world. Moreover, with a little effort, I also could remember what many of these words meant. I reviewed the words whose meanings I didn't remember. Funny thing, from the dictionary's first page right now, that *aardvark* springs to my mind. The dictionary had a picture of it, a long-tailed, long-eared, burrowing° African mammal, which lives off termites caught by sticking out its tongue as an anteater does for ants.

7   I was so fascinated that I went on—I copied the dictionary's next page. And the same experience came when I studied that. With every succeeding° page, I also learned of people and places and events from history. Actually, the dictionary is like a miniature encyclopedia. Finally, the dictionary's A section had filled a whole tablet—and I went on into the B's. That was the way I started copying what eventually became the entire dictionary. It went a lot faster after so much practice helped me to pick up handwriting speed.

8   I suppose it was inevitable that as my word-base° broadened, I could for the first time pick up a book and read and now begin to understand what the book was saying. Anyone who has read a great deal can imagine the new

world that opened. Let me tell you something: From then until I left the prison, in every free moment I had, if I was not reading in the library, I was reading on my bunk°. You couldn't have gotten me out of books with a wedge°. Months passed without my even thinking about being imprisoned. In fact, up to then, I never had been so truly free in my life.

Phonics and Dictionary Questions

Answer the questions that follow the two dictionary entries, both for words taken from the selection. The pronunciation key on page 119 will help you answer the pronunciation questions.

stum•ble (stŭm′bəl) *v.* **-bled, -bling. 1. a.** To trip and almost fall. **b.** To proceed unsteadily; flounder. See Syns at **blunder. c.** To act or speak falteringly or clumsily. **2.** To make a mistake. **3.** To come upon accidentally. [< ME *stumblen.*] —**stum′ble** *n.*

1. *Stumble* would be found on the dictionary page with which guidewords?
   a. **strongbox / study**
   b. **sulk / sunburst**
   c. **stuff / suave**
   d. **Stockton / store**

2. *Stumble* is divided into syllables according to which rule?
   a. Dividing Before a Single Consonant
   b. Dividing Before a Consonant + *le*
   c. Diving After Prefixes and Before Suffixes
   d. Dividing Between the Words in a Compound Word

3. The **u** in *stumble* sounds like the **u** in
   a. *cut.*
   b. *urge.*
   c. *abuse.*
   d *circus.*

4. The part of speech of *stumble* is
   a. adjective.
   b. adverb.
   c. pronoun.
   d. verb.

5. Which definition of *stumble* fits the sentence below?
   a. Definition 1a
   b. Definition 2
   c. Definition 3

   "It was because of my letters that I happened to stumble upon starting to acquire some kind of a homemade education." (Paragraph 1)

con•vey (kən-vā′) *v.* **1.** To carry; transport. **2.** To transmit. **3.** To communicate; impart. **4.** *Law.* To transfer ownership of or title to. [< Med. Lat. *conviare*, to escort.] — **con•vey′a•ble** *adj.* — **con•vey′er, con•vey′or** *n.*

6. *Convey* would be found on the dictionary page with which guidewords?
   a. **controlled substance / conveyor**
   b. **contort / control**
   c. **coordination / cord**
   d. **cordage / corner**

7. *Convey* is divided into syllables according to which rule?
   a. Dividing Between Two Consonants
   b. Dividing Before a Consonant +*le*
   c. Diving After Prefixes and Before Suffixes
   d. Dividing Between the Words in a Compound Word

8. The **o** in *convey* sounds like
   a. the **o** in *pot.*
   b. the **o** in *toe.*
   c. the **o** in *for.*
   d. the schwa in *gallop.*

9. The part of speech of *convey* is
   a. adjective.
   b. adverb.
   c. noun.
   d. verb.

10. Which definition of *convey* fits the sentence below?
    a. Definition 1
    b. Definition 2
    c. Definition 3

    "I became increasingly frustrated at not being able to express what I wanted to convey in letters that I wrote." (Paragraph 2)

Discussion Questions

1. At the end of the selection, Malcolm X says that even though he was still in jail, he "never had been so truly free" in his life. What does he mean by that? What is it that makes you feel free?

2. Malcolm X decided to improve his vocabulary in order to express himself better in letters. What was it that made you decide to continue your education? What do you hope to do with the knowledge you are gaining?

3. Malcolm X used a dictionary to learn and study new words. What other ways are there to learn new words? Which of them have you used, and how well did they work for you?

Note: Writing assignments for this selection appear on page 541.

Check Your Performance			DICTIONARY USE
Activity	*Number Right*	*Points*	*Score*
Review Test 1 (5 items)	_____	× 2 =	_____
Review Test 2 (20 items)	_____	× 1.5 =	_____
Review Test 3 (10 items)	_____	× 3 =	_____
Review Test 4 (10 items)	_____	× 3 =	_____
	TOTAL SCORE	=	_____ %

Enter your total score into the **Reading Performance Chart: Review Tests** on the inside back cover.

DICTIONARY USE: Test 1

A. Below are two pairs of dictionary guidewords followed by other words. Circle the two words in each series which would be found on the same page as the guidewords.

1–2. coverage / crab

    cow   cornice   cool-headed   crack   cozy

3–4. festive / fiberboard

    feud   fight   fiend   fiberglass   few

B. Tell on which dictionary page each italicized word below would be found by circling the letter of the correct guidewords.

5. *Jargon* would be found on the dictionary page with which guidewords?
   a. **Jackson / Janus**
   b. **Japan / Jefferson**
   c. **Jefferson City / jetty**

6. *Seal* would be found on the dictionary page with which guidewords?
   a. **seagoing / season ticket**
   b. **seat / secretary**
   c. **seedling / self-assured**

C. Answer the questions below about the following dictionary entry for *cite*.

cite (sīt) *v.* **cit•ed, cit•ing. 1.** To quote as an authority or example. **2.** To mention as support, illustration, or proof. **3.** To commend officially for meritorious action, esp. in military service. **4.** To summon before a court of law.

7. The part of speech of *cite* is
   a. verb.
   b. noun.
   c. adjective.

8. The past tense of *cite* has
   a. one syllable.
   b. two syllables.
   c. three syllables.

(Continues on next page)

9. The definition of *cite* that fits the sentence below is
   a. definition 1.
   b. definition 2.
   c. definition 3.
   d. definition 4.

   The judge himself is on trial; he was cited for taking bribes from local union officials.

10. The definition of *cite* that fits the sentence below is
    a. definition 1.
    b. definition 2.
    c. definition 3.
    d. definition 4.

    To back up my point that homemakers work hard, I cited a study which shows that most spend over fifty hours a week on household chores.

D. Use your dictionary and the hints on page 116 to find the correct spelling of the following words.

11. hury _____   14. eazy _____

12. sertain _____   15. bote _____

13. procead _____   16. beleive _____

E. Use the following pronunciation key to answer the questions below.

Pronunciation Key

ă pat	ā pay	â care	ä father	ě pet	ē bee	ĭ pit
ī pie, by	î pier	ŏ pot	ō toe	ô paw, for		oi noise
ŏŏ took	ōō boot	ou out	th thin	*th* this		ŭ cut
û urge	yōō abuse	zh vision	ə about, item, edible, gallop, circus			

17. In **elbow** (ĕl'-bō'), the **e** is pronounced like the **e** in what common word? _____

18. In **elbow** (ĕl'-bō'), the **o** is pronounced like the **o** in what common word? _____

19. In **nurture** (nûr'-chər), the first **u** is pronounced like the **u** in what common word? _____

20. In **nurture** (nûr'-chər), the second **u** is pronounced like the **u** in what common word? _____

DICTIONARY USE: Test 2

Use your dictionary as needed to answer the questions below.

A. Put dots between the syllables in each word. Then write out the word with the correct pronunciation symbols, including accent marks.

1. c r e d i t   _____

2. l e g a l   _____

3. p l e a s a n t _____

4. n e e d l e   _____

5. t w i l i g h t _____

B. List the parts of speech for the following words.

6. bend   _____

7. plain   _____

8. minor   _____

C. Write the irregular plural forms for the following words.

9. tooth   _____

10. life   _____

11. party   _____

D. Write the dictionary definitions of *crook* that fit the following sentences.

12. A well-known television preacher turned out to be a crook.

_____

13. Holding the umbrella by the crook of its handle, Hector swung it back and forth as he walked down the street, paying no attention to the rain.

_____

(Continues on next page)

E. Answer the questions below about the following dictionary entry for *input*.

in•put (in′po͝ot) *n.* **1.** Something put in. **2.** Energy, work, or power put into a system or machine. **3.** *Comp. Sci.* Information put into a data-processing system. **4.** *Informal.* **a.** Contribution of information, comments, or viewpoints to a common effort. **b.** Information in general. —**in′put′** *v.*

14. *The usage label and definitions:* _____

_____

15 *The field label and definition:* _____

_____

F. Use your dictionary as needed to answer the questions below.

16. A *coyote* is
    a. a small wolf-like predator.   c. native to South America.
    b. a large dog-like predator.   d. found all over the world.

17. *Mecca* is a city in
    a. Germany.   c. West Saudi Arabia.
    b. East Africa.   d. New South Wales, Australia.

18. A *filament* may be found in
    a. a decayed tooth.   c. a car tire.
    b. a light bulb.   d. a ditch.

19. If something is *potable*, you can
    a. carry it.   c. smoke it.
    b. drink it.   d. trade it.

20. *Fill in the blank:* Where does the plant known as Spanish moss grow?

    _____.

DICTIONARY USE: Test 3

A. Below are two pairs of dictionary guidewords followed by other words. Circle the two words in each series which would be found on the same page as the guidewords.

1–2. **divinity / docile**

distance	do	divine	dizzy	dock

3–4. **gate / gear**

garter	gather	gave	gearshift	general

B. On which dictionary page would each italicized word below be found?

5. *Thick* would be found on the dictionary page with which guidewords?
   a. **Thoreau / throat**
   b. **therein / thin**
   c. **texture / theater**

6. *Reunion* would be found on the dictionary page with which guidewords?
   a. **retina / reveille**
   b. **revel / revolution**
   c. **restaurant / reticent**

C. Answer the questions below about the following dictionary entry for *baby*.

ba•by (bā′bē) *n.*, *pl.* **-bies. 1. a.** A very young child; infant. **b.** The youngest member of a family or group. **c.** A very young animal. **2.** One who behaves in an infantile way. **3.** *Slang.* A girl or young woman. **4.** *Slang.* An object of personal concern: *The project is your baby.* — *v.* **-bied, -by•ing.** To treat overindulgently; pamper.

7. *Baby* is accented on
   a. its first syllable.
   b. its second syllable.
   c. both syllables.

8. *Fill in the blank*: The plural of *baby* is _____.

9. The definition of *baby* that applies to the sentence below is
   a. definition 1c.   c. definition 3.
   b. definition 2.   d. definition 4.

   "You're such a baby," complained Rhonda. "You always want your own way."

(Continues on next page)

10. The definition of *baby* that fits the sentence below is
    a. definition 1b.   c. definition 3.
    b. definition 2.   d. definition 4.

    It's hard to believe that Elena, the baby in our family, just became a teenager.

D. Use your dictionary and the hints on pages 116 to find the correct spelling of the following words.

11. reciept   _____   14. klean   _____

12. writting _____   15. wispor _____

13. dicide   _____   16. actshun _____

E. Use the following pronunciation key to answer the questions below.

Pronunciation Key

ă pat	ā pay	â care	ä father	ĕ pet	ē bee	ĭ pit
ī pie, by	î pier	ŏ pot	ō toe	ô paw, for		oi noise
ŏŏ took	ōō boot	ou out	th thin	*th* this		ŭ cut
û urge	yōō abuse	zh vision	ə about, item, edible, gallop, circus			

17. In *dignity* (dĭg′nĭ-tē), the **y** is pronounced like   _____
    the **ee** in what common word?

18. In *dignity* (dĭg′nĭ-tē), the **i**'s are pronounced like _____
    the **i** in what common word?

19. In *firetrap* (fīr′trăp′), the **i** is pronounced like   _____
    the **i** in what common word?

20. In *firetrap* (fīr′trăp′), the **a** is pronounced like   _____
    the **a** in what common word?

DICTIONARY USE: Test 4

Use your dictionary as needed to answer the questions below.

A. Put dots between the syllables in each word. Then write out the word with the correct pronunciation symbols, including accent marks.

1. e x e r c i s e _____   4. s u s p e n s e _____

2. i n q u i r e _____   5. w e l c o m e _____

3. m o d i f y _____

B. List the parts of speech for the following words.

6. loose   _____

7. glow   _____

8. total   _____

C. Write the irregular plural forms for the following words.

9. knife   _____

10. hero   _____

11. city   _____

D. Write the dictionary definitions of *quick* that fit the following sentences:

12. You are not going to learn a new language quickly.

_____

13. My boss has a quick temper.

_____

(Continues on next page)

141

E. Answer the following questions about special labels.

14. Which of the following words has an entry that includes a usage label? In the space provided, write the usage label and the definition.
    a. *soundtrack*
    b. *southpaw*
    c. *space bar*

    The usage label and definition: _____

    _____

15. Which of the following words has an entry that includes a field label? In the space provided, write the field label and the definition.
    a. *touchdown*
    b. *touchstone*
    c. *trademark*

    The field label and definition: _____

    _____

16. Which of the following is a seabird?
    a. A puffer   c. A pullet
    b. A puffin   d. A pulley

17. The *leeward* side of an island is
    a. facing the wind.   c. the highest part of the island.
    b. away from the wind.   d. the lowest part of the island.

18. Which of the following is the name of a Native American people?
    a. Papaya   c. Papago
    b. Papeete   d. Pandora

19. If an ocean tide *ebbs*, it
    a. gets higher.   c. stands still.
    b. recedes.   d. disappears.

20. Which of the following words has a *slang* usage label in its entry?
    a. *miser*   c. *rogue*
    b. *rascal*   d. *cheapskate*

DICTIONARY USE: Test 5

A. Below are two pairs of dictionary guidewords followed by other words. Circle the two words in each series which would be found on the same page as the guidewords.

1–2. **devil / diabolical**

    determine   devise   dextrose   diaper   digital

3–4. **index / indispensable**

    indignation   indorse   indicate   indeed   in-depth

B. On which dictionary page would each italicized word below be found?

5. *Myth* would be found on the dictionary page with which guidewords?
    a. **mush / mutate**   b. **mutation / myrrh**   c. **myrtle / Nagasaki**

6. *Tortoise* would be found on the dictionary page with which guidewords?
    a. **torso / touchy**   b. **tough / toxin**   c. **toy / traffic**

C. Answer the questions below about the following dictionary entry for *instant*.

in•stant (ĭn′stənt) *n.* **1.** A very brief space of time; moment. **2.** A particular point in time. — *adj.* **1.** Immediate. **2.** Imperative; urgent: *an instant need.* **3.** Designed or processed for quick preparation: *instant coffee.*

7. *Instant* has how many syllables?
    a. One
    b. Two
    c. Three

8. *Instant* is accented on
    a. its first syllable.
    b. its second syllable.
    c. both syllables.

9. *Fill in the blank:* The parts of speech of *instant* are _____.

10. The definition of *instant* that applies to the sentence below is
    a. definition *n* 1.   c. definition *adj* 1.
    b. definition *n* 2.   d. definition *adj* 2.

For just an instant, Alphonse thought he would be bumped from his flight.

(Continues on next page)

11. The definition of *instant* that fits the sentence below is
    - a. definition *n* 2.
    - b. definition *adj* 1.
    - c. definition *adj* 2.
    - d. definition *adj* 3.

    Just at the instant we were sitting down for dinner, both the telephone and the doorbell rang.

D. Use your dictionary and the hints on page 116 to find the correct spelling of the following words.

12. fullfil   _____   15. froun   _____

13. freind   _____   16. capible   _____

14. ordurly   _____   17. lable   _____

E. Use the pronunciation key below to answer the following questions.

Pronunciation Key

ă pat	ā pay	â care	ä father	ĕ pet	ē bee	ĭ pit
ī pie, by	î pier	ŏ pot	ō toe	ô paw, for		oi noise
ŏŏ took	ōō boot	ou out	th thin	*th* this		ŭ cut
û urge	yōō abuse	zh vision	ə about, item, edible, gallop, circus			

18. In *koala* (kō-ä′lə), the first **a** is pronounced like the **a** in what common word?   _____

19. In *mechanics* (mĭ-kăn′ĭks), the **e** is pronounced like the **i** in what common word?   _____

20. In *onyx* (ŏn′ĭks), the **y** is pronounced like the **i** in what common word?   _____

DICTIONARY USE: Test 6 ✗

Use your dictionary as needed to answer the questions below.

A. Put dots between the syllables in each word. Then write out the word with the correct pronunciation symbols, including accent marks.

    1. d e b a u c h   _____

    2. h o r t i c u l t u r e   _____

    3. o p p o s i t e   _____

    4. r e s o l u t i o n   _____

    5. s t r a i g h t a w a y   _____

B. List the parts of speech for the following words.

    6. draft   _____

    7. neck   _____

    8. prime   _____

C. Write the irregular forms for the following words.

    9. chewy   _____

    10. crisis   _____

    11. hit   _____

D. Write the dictionary definitions of *hitch* that fit the following sentences.

    12. When my car broke down on the freeway, I had to hitch a ride.

    _____

    13. Stefan spent four years in the Army but decided not to sign up for another hitch.

    _____

(Continues on next page)

E. Answer the following questions about special labels.

14. Which of the following words has a usage label? In the space provided, write the usage label and the definition.
    a. plunder
    b. pole vault
    c. pooch

    The usage label and definition: _____

    _____

15. Which of the following words has a field label? In the space provided, write the field label and the definition.
    a. annex
    b. article
    c. awesome

    The field label and definition: _____

    _____

    _____

16. Which of the following illustrates the word *homonym*?
    a. light / dark   c. bar / bark
    b. bear / bare   d. night / might

17. The word *quasar* would most likely appear
    a. on a map of southwestern Asia.   c. in an astronomy textbook.
    b. in a computer manual.   d. in a South American cookbook.

18. *Ravenous* would most likely describe
    a. a black bird.   c. someone who hasn't eaten all day.
    b. a deep valley.   d. someone who is very attractive.

19. If someone calls you a "*piker*," he or she
    a. thinks you are stingy.   c. believes you like motorcycles.
    b. thinks you look like a fish. d. has called you a pig.

20. *Fill in the blanks:* The word *dinosaur* comes from the Greek words for

    _____ and _____.

5

Vocabulary in Context

Do you know the meaning of the word *queries?* How about the word *tedious?* Or the word *transmit?*

You may be having trouble coming up with the meanings of these words. However, you will be more likely to know what they mean when you see them in complete sentences. Read each sentence below and see if you can understand the meaning of the word in italics. Circle the letter of the meaning you think is correct. Then read the explanation.

Dan was nervous about answering Detective Miller's *queries.* Why was he asking so many questions, anyway?

Queries are

a. statements of fact.   b. questions.   c. charges.

Most of my history teacher's lectures were *tedious,* but the one about what really happened on Paul Revere's famous ride was very interesting.

Tedious means

a. interesting.   b. long.   c. boring.

Mosquitoes transmit sleeping sickness through biting.

Transmit means

a. spread.   b. enjoy.   c. cure.

Explanation:

To decide on the right meanings, you used context clues. **Context** means the words surrounding an unfamiliar word. With the help of context clues, you may have guessed that *queries* means "questions," that *tedious* means "boring," and that *transmit* means "spread."

Context clues can help you figure out what unfamiliar words mean. Using context clues will help you in three ways:

1 It will save you time, since you won't have to stop and look up every important new word you read. However, you should still keep a dictionary handy. Sometimes there will be no context clues.

2 It will improve your understanding of what you read, since you will know more of the meanings of more of the words.

3 It will improve your "working vocabulary"—words you recognize as you read and will eventually be able to use when you speak and write.

TYPES OF CONTEXT CLUES

Here are four common types of context clues:

1 Examples

2 Synonyms

3 Antonyms

4 General Sense of the Sentence or Passage

Each of these clues will be explained in this chapter. Sentences will be provided to help you understand how each type of clue works. In addition, practice exercises will help you recognize and use context clues and add new words to your vocabulary.

1   Examples

An unfamiliar word may be followed by examples that reveal what the word means. The examples often follow signal words: *for example, including, for instance, such as, like, e.g.* (which means "for example"), and others.

To see how this type of clue works, read the sentences below. A difficult or unfamiliar word is in italics. Examples then follow and serve as context clues. The examples are in **boldfaced** type and follow signal words such as those above. The examples will help you to figure out the meanings of the words in italics. Circle the letter of the meaning of each word in italics. Then read the explanations that follow.

1. *Assets* such as **good health**, **a loving family**, and **a job you enjoy** make life rewarding.

   Assets are

   a. things of value.   b. rewards on the job.   c. helpful people.

2. A coyote's *prey* includes **squirrels**, **rabbits**, and **mice**.

   Prey means

   a. friends.   b. victims.   c. replacement.

3. The car had *defects* such as **a dented fender** and **torn seats**, but I didn't care. I had wanted a Corvette sports car for years, and I was going to buy it.

   Defects are

   a. faults.   b. out-of-date features.   c. attractive features.

Explanations:

1. The correct answer is *a*. The examples given—good health, a loving family, and a job you enjoy—show that *asset*s are "things of value."

2. The correct answer is *b*. The examples—squirrels, rabbits, and mice—reveal that *prey* are "victims."

3. The correct answer is *a*. The examples—dented fender and torn seats—show that *defects* are "faults."

➤ *Practice 1*

Read each item below and then do two things:

> **1** Underline the examples that suggest the meaning of the word in italics.
> **2** Circle the letter of the meaning of the word in italics.

1. There are some amazing things to see at Hearst Castle in central California. For instance, there is an indoor swimming pool whose *dimensions* are a length of 100 feet, a width of 15 feet, and a depth of 10 feet.

   Dimensions are

   a. costs.   b. benefits.   c. measurements.

2. The *notables* at the charity event included actor Tom Cruise, tennis star Patrick Rafter, and singer Janet Jackson.

   Notables means

   a. average people.   b. people worthy of notice.   c. movie stars.

3. The San Diego Zoo has not only such common animals as lions and tigers, but also *exotic* ones like giant pandas, snow leopards, and koala bears.

   Exotic means

   a. unusual.   b. small.   c. ordinary.

4. Newspaper reporters have been fired for writing *fictitious* articles that included quotations which were never said and events which never occurred.

   Fictitious means

   a. true.   b. unknown.   c. not real.

5. We often communicate what we mean by *gestures* such as the thumbs-up sign, hands on the hips, and a shrug of the shoulders.

   Gestures are

   a. hand signals.   b. good feelings.   c. motions of the body.

6. I don't enjoy *treacherous* activities like mountain climbing and deep-sea diving. I'd rather just float in a swimming pool.

   Treacherous means

   a. lazy.   b. safe.   c. dangerous.

7. Behavior such as belching in public and talking loudly in a movie theater is considered *obnoxious* by most people.

   Obnoxious means

   a. very unpleasant.   b. acceptable.   c. funny.

8. For better health and a longer life, doctors recommend *wholesome* habits, including exercising daily and eating nutritious foods.

   Wholesome means

   a. boring.   b. skillful.   c. healthy.

9. The student on your left has a bad cough. The student on your right sighs out loud. The student behind you kicks your chair. Why is it that you tend to notice such *distractions* only during an important test?

   Distractions are things that

   a. are friendly.   b. take away   c. increase your
                          your attention.   ability to perform.

10. Cat lovers appreciate cats' many *endearing* traits, such as purring, licking their owners' hands, and rubbing against their owners' legs.

    Endearing means

    a. exact.   b. stressful.   c. lovable.

2 Synonyms

Synonyms are words that mean the same or almost the same as another word. For example, the words *watch, look, see,* and *observe* are synonyms—they all mean about the same thing.

Synonyms serve as context clues by providing the meaning of an unknown word that is nearby. Each sentence below contains a synonym for the word in italics. Underline the synonym in each sentence, and then read the explanations that follow.

1. Jack was a *mediocre* student. He was also just an average baseball player.

2. It is hard to believe that my millionaire cousin was once *indigent,* so poor that he walked the streets without knowing where his next meal would come from.

3. Most companies have a *regulation* allowing new mothers to take three months off from work. Some firms also have a rule allowing fathers the same time off.

Explanations:

In each sentence, the synonym probably helped you understand the meaning of the word in italics:

1. Someone who is *mediocre* at something is "average."

2. Someone who is *indigent* is "poor."

3. A *regulation* is a "rule."

➤ *Practice 2*

In each item, underline the synonym for the word in italics. The synonym may be one or more words.

1. Luke is one of the best *patrons* of Ruby's Diner. He's a steady customer, not only because he likes the food there, but also because Ruby is his aunt.

2. While your *vocation* is important, experts advise that you treat it for what it is—a job, not your entire life.

3. Calcium *fortifies* bone and also strengthens teeth.

4. The *absurd* idea that people from outer space live among us is as ridiculous as the belief that the Earth is flat.

5. Judges are supposed to be *impartial,* but the judge in Rodolfo's trial didn't seem fair to me.

6. In the boxing match, the referee *intervened* only twice. And each time he came between the boxers, they quickly broke apart and started boxing again.

7. Some people hate to admit an error. My boss, for instance, will never *concede* that he might be wrong.

8. Students are often *apprehensive* of final exams, but with proper studying, they don't have to be fearful.

9. You may be *reluctant* to give a speech now, but the more speaking practice you get, the less unwilling you will be.

10. The belief that you can drink and then drive safely is a *fallacy;* unfortunately, many people hold that false belief.

3 Antonyms

Antonyms are words with opposite meanings. For example, *summer* is the opposite of *winter,* and *soft* is the opposite of *hard.* Antonyms serve as context clues by providing the opposite meaning of an unfamiliar word. Antonyms are often signaled by words such as *unlike, but, however, instead of, in contrast,* or *on the other hand.*

Each sentence below has an antonym as a context clue. Read each sentence and do two things:

1 Underline the antonym for the word in italics. Each antonym may be one or more words.
2 Circle the letter of the meaning of the word in italics.

Then read the explanations that follow.

1. *Adverse* weather conditions forced us to stay inside for most of our vacation. The day the weather finally turned nice, we had to leave.

Adverse means

a. nice.   b. bad.   c. summer.

2. I thought it was difficult to *ascend* the mountain, but I discovered that to climb down it was even worse.

   Ascend means

   a. climb up.   b. walk around.   c. climb down.

3. After years of *defying* my parents, I decided that life might be better if I tried agreeing with them once in a while.

   Defying means

   a. avoiding.   b. obeying.   c. opposing.

Explanations:

1. The correct answer is *b*. *Adverse* weather conditions are the opposite of "nice" ones—they are "bad."

2. The correct answer is *a*. To *ascend* is the opposite of to "climb down"—when you ascend, you "climb up."

3. The right answer is *c*. *Defying* one's parents is the opposite of "agreeing with" them. When you defy people, you oppose what they say.

➤ *Practice 3*

Antonyms provide context clues in the sentences below. Read each item, and do two things:

   1 Underline the antonym for the word or words in italics. Each antonym may be one or more words.
   2 Circle the letter of the meaning of the word or words in italics.

1. Your science project is much more *elaborate* than mine. In fact, mine looks very simple compared with yours.

   Elaborate means

   a. plain.   b. large.   c. complicated.

2. Gordon's family worried that he would remain an *obscure* author all his life. However, he believed that someday he would be famous.

   Obscure means

   a. unknown.   b. well-known.   c. good.

3. The attorney introduced facts she felt were *relevant* to the case. But the judge said the facts were unrelated to the trial.

   Relevant means

   a. legal.   b. related.   c. known.

4. When providing directions, give the steps *in sequence.* If they are out of order, those trying to follow the directions will become confused.

   In sequence means

   a. all at once.   b. in order.   c. in a confusing way.

5. Many executives will assign *trivial* projects to new employees. They will give the serious projects to experienced workers whom they trust.

   Trivial means

   a. important.   b. stupid.   c. unimportant.

6. The patient's pain was *acute* yesterday, but today it is mild.

   Acute means

   a. weak.   b. sharp.   c. old.

7. Why did we lose the game? Was it our lack of preparation, or was it the other team's winning *strategy?*

   Strategy means

   a. reason.   b. place.   c. plan.

8. Our English teacher *commended* Maria on the outstanding work she was doing. Then he criticized the rest of class for doing so poorly.

   Commended means

   a. blamed.   b. graded.   c. praised.

9. Students often prefer a *lenient* teacher to a strict one, but they may learn more from the strict teacher.

   Lenient means

   a. not strict.   b. not kind.   c. not having knowledge.

10. *Passive* citizens sit back and do little for society; active citizens vote, express their views, and do something for others.

    Passive means

    a. rich.   b. inactive.   c. peaceful.

4 General Sense of the Sentence or Passage

Often, the context of a new word contains no examples, synonyms, or antonyms. Then how can you figure out the correct meaning of the word? What you must do is read carefully, use your own experience with the situation being described, and look for helpful general clues.

In each sentence below, look for general clues to the meaning of the word in italics. Then circle the letter of your choice. Finally, read the explanations that follow.

1. Leilani lived in Hawaii for fifteen years, so it is hard for her friends to *conceive of* why she moved to Alaska.

   Conceive of means

   a. plan.   b. remember.   c. imagine.

2. At the animal shelter, Rita fell in love with a poodle, but Dan couldn't resist a collie. So they felt that there was no *alternative* but to keep both animals.

   An *alternative* is a

   a. choice.   b. reason.   c. mystery.

3. As a *consequence* of his bad report card, my brother could not watch TV until his teachers said he was improving.

   A *consequence* is a

   a. right.   b. result.   c. chance.

Explanations:

1. The correct answer is *c*. To *conceive of* something means to "imagine" something. Leilani's friends could not imagine why she would move from Hawaii to Alaska.

2. The right answer is *a*. An *alternative* is a "choice." Rita and Dan felt they had no choice but to take both dogs home.

3. The correct answer is *b*. A *consequence* is a "result." The result of the brother's bad report card was not being able to watch TV until his teachers reported that he had improved.

➤ *Practice 4*

Figure out the meaning of the word in italics by reading carefully and using your experience to get a general understanding of the situation being described. Then circle the letter of the meaning of the word.

1. Jesse was surprised when his speech *elicited* laughs from the audience. He was perfectly serious about his topic.

   Elicited means

   a. brought out.   b. hid.   c. copied.

2. Elena was glad she had *ample* time to collect her thoughts for the afternoon's midterm. Then she discovered that her watch was incorrect— she was actually late for the test!

   Ample means

   a. no.   b. plenty of.   c. little.

3. My brother felt it would be *futile* to try to make the basketball team. The other players were all at least eight inches taller than he.

   Futile means

   a. easy.   b. useless.   c. expensive.

4. The *impact* of the crash was so great that you couldn't tell the make of either car. Each was totally destroyed.

   Impact means

   a. force.   b. time.   c. place.

5. The young eagle was clearly a *novice* at flying. As he tried to land, he got himself all tangled in a thornbush.

   A *novice* is a

   a. bird.   b. success.   c. beginner.

6. It was *apparent* to everyone that Marcy's science project was the best in the class. Even Professor Santiago said it was one of the best he had ever seen.

   Apparent means

   a. clear.   b. confusing.   c. disturbing.

7. I have never met anyone as *obstinate* as my math teacher. Once he makes up his mind, he won't change it for anything.

   Obstinate means

   a. stubborn.   b. agreeable.   c. serious.

8. At a party given by a company for its clients, employees are expected to *mingle with* the guests so they feel comfortable.

Mingle with means

a. bother.   b. mix with.   c. sell things to.

9. From 1964 to 1975, the University of California–Los Angeles *dominated* men's basketball, winning ten national championships.

Dominated means

a. praised.   b. kept away from.   c. had the most important place in.

10. Big band music was popular during the 1940s. It then disappeared from the music scene, but it was *revived* during the late 1990s.

Revived means

a. lost.   b. brought back.   c. destroyed.

A NOTE ON TEXTBOOK DEFINITIONS

When you are reading textbooks, you don't always have to use context clues or the dictionary to find definitions. Textbook authors usually give formal definitions and explanations of important terms. Often one or more examples are also given.

Here is a passage from a college text in business. The term to be defined is set off in boldfaced type, and a definition and example follow. Read the passage and then read the explanation below.

> Short-range plans tend to be specific. One part of a short-range plan, **procedures**, tells employees exactly what steps to take in a given situation. A factory's procedures, for instance, may require moving raw materials from the receiving platform to the beginning of the assembly line.

The passage above defines the word *procedures*—the "part of a short-range plan" that "tells employees exactly what steps to take in a given situation." The words "for instance" signal that the author is also illustrating the new word. In this case, the author gives an example of a factory's procedures.

A focus on definitions and examples will help as you study a chapter and take notes on it. You will read more about textbook definitions and examples in Chapter 10 of this book.

CHAPTER SUMMARY

In this chapter, you learned the following:

- You can often figure out word meanings by watching for four types of context clues:

  Examples of a new word. The examples may be introduced by signal words: *for example, including, for instance, such as, like.*

  A **synonym** of a new word. The meaning of a new word may be provided by a nearby synonym, another word with the same or a similar meaning.

  An **antonym** of a new word. The meaning of a new word may be provided by a nearby antonym, a word with the opposite meaning. Antonyms may be signaled by words and phrases such as *unlike, but, however, instead, in contrast,* and *on the other hand.*

  A **general sense of the sentence or passage**. Often the general context of a passage reveals the meaning of a difficult or unfamiliar word. In such cases, you can figure out a word's meaning through careful reading and using your experience.

- Textbook authors provide definitions with examples for important new terms. Learning those definitions is an important part of studying a chapter.

➤ *Review Test 1*

To review what you have learned in this chapter, answer each of the following questions. Fill in the blank or circle the letter of the correct answer.

1. The context of a word is
   a. its meaning.   b. its opposite.   c. the words around it.

2. Which type of context clue is introduced by signal words such as *however, but,* and *on the other hand?*
   a. example   b. synonym   c. antonym

3. In the sentence below, which type of context clue suggests the meaning of the word in italics?
   a. example   b. synonym   c. antonym

   Since I was brought up in a city environment, I am comfortable with *urban* life.

4. In the sentences below, which type of context clue suggests the meaning of the word in italics?

    a. example   b. synonym   c. antonym

      Don't allow *despair* to get you down. Keep hope strongly in mind.

5. Fill in the blank: Often when textbook authors introduce a new word, they provide you with the word's _____ and follow it with examples that help make the meaning of the word clear.

➤ Review Test 2

Using context clues, circle the letter of the best meaning for each word or phrase in italics.

1. After standing empty for fifteen years, the old mansion had *deteriorated.* The wood was decaying, the plaster was peeling, and most of the windows had broken.

   Deteriorate means

   a. become older.   b. become worse.   c. become empty.

2. Successful students have learned that if they *adhere to* a schedule, they accomplish more. When they don't stick to a set routine, they get less done.

   Adhere to means

   a. follow faithfully.   b. avoid.   c. buy.

3. When Yasmin asked Alex whether he wanted to go camping or visit her brother, he said he was *indifferent*—it didn't matter to him where they went on their vacation.

   Indifferent means

   a. not the same.   b. unable to decide.   c. having no preference.

4. At an accident scene, the police must determine whose version of the accident *distorts* the event and whose tells it just as it happened.

   Distorts means

   a. explains.   b. describes falsely.   c. forgets.

5. If you are pushed and your books are knocked to the floor, you may find it hard to *refrain* from yelling at the person who caused the accident.

   Refrain means

   a. continue.   b. hold back.   c. take.

6. Olga always comes up with quick *retorts* to people's comments, but I can never think of a clever answer until it's too late.

   A *retort* is a

   a. clever reply.   b. dumb remark.   c. kind response.

7. Experts say exercise makes the appetite *diminish*. So wanting to lose weight provides another good reason to exercise.

   Diminish means

   a. grow larger.   b. get smarter.   c. get smaller.

8. Antonio made a *pretense* of writing the answers to the essay test, but he was just scribbling. He hadn't studied for the test at all.

   Pretense means

   a. intelligent attempt.   b. false show.   c. slow effort.

9. Lately there has been a *mania* for a certain type of stuffed animal. Some people are so excited about these toy animals that they will pay anything to own them.

   Mania means

   a. great enthusiasm.   b. dislike.   c. confusion over.

10. Twins separated early in life often lead *parallel* lives. For instance, many study the same subjects, get similar jobs, and marry the same kind of person.

    Parallel means

    a. vastly different.   b. matching.   c. boring.

➤ Review Test 3

A. Using context clues for help, circle the letter of the best meaning for each word or phrase in italics.

   1. Cheryl felt that the honor *bestowed on* her for working with the homeless could have been given to many others who had also worked hard.

      Bestowed on means

      a. given to.   b. removed from.   c. created by.

2. Juan looked forward to being *isolated* at his uncle's mountain cabin. He had been in the crowded city too long.

   Isolated means

   a. snowed in.   b. alone.   c. waited on.

3. My report was longer than what the instructor wanted, so I had to *delete* information.

   Delete means

   a. add.   b. invent.   c. remove.

4. Roland was so *miserly* that he refused to give his sons spending money. Also, to save electricity, he made them study by the light of one dim lamp.

   Miserly means

   a. stingy.   b. old.   c. sad.

5. Many communities have a wildlife *refuge* that is home to injured wild animals that have been rescued by concerned people.

   Refuge means a

   a. busy place.   b. meeting place.   c. safe place.

B. Using context clues, circle the letter of the meaning for each word in italics. Read the entire paragraph before choosing your answers.

   Marta was looking forward to her trip to Miami. Although she had not seen her aunt for ten years, Marta's memories of this special woman were *vivid*. Marta could still see Aunt Cristina gathering Marta's brothers and sisters and entertaining them with stories about life in the old country. Such memories usually filled Marta with great *nostalgia,* but now they only made her more excited about her upcoming trip.

6. *Vivid* means
   a. clear.   b. weak.   c. fearful.

7. *Nostalgia* is a
   a. need for a new   b. belief in something   c. desire for something
       experience.   unnatural.   from the past.

C. Using context clues, circle the letter of the meaning of each word in italics. Read the entire paragraph before choosing your answers.

> The marbled cellar spider is spreading throughout the United States. This two-inch spider is similar to the common long-legged spider known as "daddy longlegs," but more *adaptable*. It can set up its web just about anywhere, including houses, garages, flowers, and trees. And it has an *immense* appetite. It will eat just about anything that falls into its web, including other spiders. The marbled cellar spider will not harm humans. In fact, it is a very *beneficial* insect, since it eats mosquitoes, flies, and the young of the poisonous black widow spider.

8. *Adaptable* means
   a. able to adjust.   b. distant.   c. likable.

9. *Immense* means
   a. bad.   b. very large.   c. very small.

10. *Beneficial* means
   a. plain.   b. trusting.   c. helpful.

➤ Review Test 4

Here is a chance to apply the skill of understanding vocabulary in context to a full-length selection. Leo Buscaglia gained world-wide fame as a lecturer for the Public Broadcasting network and as the author of inspirational books including *Living, Loving, and Learning* and *The Fall of Freddie the Leaf*. In this essay, Buscaglia writes of the man who laid the foundation for his own lively curiosity and love of learning—the uneducated Italian factory worker whom Buscaglia knew as Papa. When you finish the selection, answer the questions that follow.

Words to Watch

Following are some words in the reading that do not have strong context support. Each word is followed by the number of the paragraph in which it appears and its meaning there. These words are indicated in the reading by a small circle (°).

> *fathom* (1): fully understand
> *protestations* (2): objections
> *elders* (3): senior citizens
> *insular* (3): isolated, set apart
> *complacency* (4): self-satisfaction
> *ritual* (5): something done regularly

paternal (5): fatherly
inevitable (6): not able to be avoided
pungent (7): sharply spicy
animated (8): lively
dialect (8): a regional variety of a language
profound (8): intellectually deep
unsettling (12): upsetting
reverential (19): deeply respectful
retrospect (22): review of the past
dynamic (22): powerful

PAPA

Leo Buscaglia

1   Papa had a natural wisdom. He wasn't educated in the formal sense. When he was growing up at the turn of the century in a very small village in rural northern Italy, education was for the rich. Papa was the son of a dirt-poor farmer. He used to tell us that he never remembered a single day of his life when he wasn't working. The concept of doing nothing was never a part of his life. In fact, he couldn't fathom° it. How could one do nothing?

2   He was taken from school when he was in the fifth grade, over the protestations° of his teacher and the village priest, both of whom saw him as a young person with great potential for formal learning. Papa went to work in a factory in a nearby village, the very same village where, years later, he met Mama.

3   For Papa, the world became his school. He was interested in everything. He read all the books, magazines, and newspapers he could lay his hands on. He loved to gather with people and listen to the town elders° and learn about "the world beyond" this tiny, insular° region that was home to generations of Buscaglias before him. Papa's great respect for learning and his sense of wonder about the outside world were carried across the sea with him and later passed on to his family. He was determined that none of his children would be denied an education if he could help it.

4   Papa believed that the greatest sin of which we were capable was to go to bed at night as ignorant as we had been when we awakened that day. The credo was repeated so often that none of us could fail to be affected by it. "There is so much to learn," he'd remind us. "Though we're born stupid, only the stupid remain that way." To ensure that none of his children ever fell into the trap of complacency°, he insisted that we learn at least one new thing each day. He felt that there could be no fact too insignificant, that each bit of learning made us more of a

person and insured us against boredom and stagnation.

5   So Papa devised a ritual°. Since dinnertime was family time and everyone came to dinner unless they were dying of malaria, it seemed the perfect forum for sharing what new things we had learned that day. Of course, as children we thought this was perfectly crazy. There was no doubt, when we compared such paternal° concerns with other children's fathers, Papa was weird.

6   It would never have occurred to us to deny Papa a request. So when my brother and sisters and I congregated in the bathroom to clean up for dinner, the inevitable° question was "What did you learn today?" If the answer was "Nothing," we didn't dare sit at the table without first finding a fact in our much-used encyclopedia. "The population of Nepal is . . . ," etc.

7   Now, thoroughly clean and armed with our fact for the day, we were ready for dinner. I can still see the table piled high with mountains of food. So large were the mounds of pasta that as a boy I was often unable to see my sister sitting across from me. (The pungent° aromas were such that, over a half century later, even in memory they cause me to salivate.)

8   Dinner was a noisy time of clattering dishes and endless activity. It was also a time to review the activities of the day. Our animated° conversations were always conducted in Piedmontese dialect° since Mama didn't speak English. The events we recounted, no matter how insignificant, were never taken lightly. Mama and

Papa always listened carefully and were ready with some comment, often profound° and analytical, always right to the point.

9   "That was a smart thing to do." "*Stupido,* how could you be so dumb?" "*Cose sia,* you deserved it." "*E allora,* no one is perfect." "*Testa dura* ('hardhead'), you should have known better. Didn't we teach you anything?" "Oh, that's nice." One dialogue ended and immediately another began. Silent moments were rare at our table.

10   Then came the grand finale to every meal, the moment we dreaded most—the time to share the day's new learning. The mental imprint of those sessions still runs before me like a familiar film clip, vital and vivid.

11   Papa, at the head of the table, would push his chair back slightly, a gesture that signified the end of the eating and suggested that there would be a new activity. He would pour a small glass of red wine, light up a thin, potent Italian cigar, inhale deeply, exhale, then take stock of his family.

12   For some reason this always had a slightly unsettling° effect on us as we stared back at Papa, waiting for him to say something. Every so often he would explain why he did this. He told us that if he didn't take the time to look at us, we would soon be grown and he would have missed us. So he'd stare at us, one after the other.

13   Finally, his attention would settle upon one of us. "Felice," he would say to me, "tell me what you learned today."

14   "I learned the population of Nepal is . . ."

15 Silence.

16 It always amazed me, and reinforced my belief that Papa was a little crazy, that nothing I ever said was considered too trivial for him. First, he'd think about what was said as if the salvation of the world depended on it.

17 "The population of Nepal. Hmmm. Well."

18 He would look down the table at Mama, who would be ritualistically fixing her favorite fruit in a bit of leftover wine. "Mama, did you know that?"

19 Mama's responses were always astonishing and seemed to lighten the otherwise reverential° atmosphere. "Nepal," she'd say. "Nepal? Not only don't I know the population of Nepal, I don't know where in God's world it is!" Of course, this was only playing into Papa's hands.

20 "Felice," he'd say. "Get the atlas so we can show Mama where Nepal is." And the search began. The whole family went on a search for Nepal. This same experience was repeated until each family member had a turn. No dinner at our house ever ended without having been enlightened by at least a half dozen such facts.

21 As children, we thought very little about these educational wonders and even less about how we were being enriched. We couldn't have cared less. We were too impatient to have dinner end so we could join our less-educated friends in a rip-roaring game of kick the can.

22 In retrospect°, after years of studying how people learn, I realize what a dynamic° educational technique Papa was offering us, reinforcing the value of continual learning. Without being aware of it, our family was growing together, sharing experiences, and participating in one another's education. Papa was, without knowing it, giving us an education in the most real sense.

23 By looking at us, listening to us, hearing us, respecting our opinions, affirming our value, giving us a sense of dignity, he was unquestionably our most influential teacher.

Phonics and Dictionary Questions

1. Which word from the sentence below has a **c** with a soft **c** sound?
   a. *century*
   b. *education*
   c. *rich*

   "When he was growing up at the turn of the century in a very small village in rural northern Italy, education was for the rich." (Paragraph 1)

2. Which word from the sentence below has a long vowel sound?
   a. *he*
   b. *all*
   c. *and*

   "He read all the books, magazines, and newspapers he could lay his hands on." (Paragraph 3)

3. The word *paternal,* used in the sentence below, would be found on a dictionary page with which guide words?
   a. **park / parsec**
   b. **pasty / patient**
   c. **patina / pause**
   d. **pave / p.d.**

   ". . . when we compared such paternal concerns with other children's fathers, Papa was weird." (Paragraph 5)

4. The word *clattering,* used in the sentence below, is broken into syllables as follows:
   a. clat-ter-ing
   b. clatt-ering
   c. clat-te-ring

   "Dinner was a noisy time of clattering dishes and endless activity." (Paragraph 8)

5. As indicated in your dictionary, Nepal, used in the sentence below, is located in
   a. Europe.
   b. southwest United States.
   c. Asia.
   d. South America.

   "Not only don't I know the population of Nepal, I don't know where in God's world it is!" (Paragraph 19)

Vocabulary Questions

Use context clues to help you choose the meaning of the italicized words in the questions below. Circle the letter of your answer choice for each question.

6. In the sentences below, the word *formal* means
   a. playful.
   b. standard.
   c. necessary.
   d. relaxing.

   "He wasn't educated in a formal sense. When he was growing up at the turn of the century . . . , education was for the rich." (Paragraph 1)

7. In the sentences below, the word *credo* means
   a. question.
   b. belief.
   c. delay.
   d. punishment.

   "The credo was repeated so often that none of us could fail to be affected by it. 'There is so much to learn,' he'd remind us. 'Though we're born stupid, only the stupid remain that way.'" (Paragraph 4)

8. In the sentence below, the word *insignificant* means
   a. new.
   b. unimportant.
   c. pleasing.
   d. expensive.

   "He felt that there could be no fact too insignificant, that each bit of learning made us more of a person." (Paragraph 4)

9. In the sentences below, the word *devised* means
   a. disliked.
   b. ended.
   c. invented.
   d. forgot.

   "So Papa devised a ritual. Since dinnertime was family time and everyone came to dinner . . . , it seemed the perfect forum for sharing what new things we had learned that day." (Paragraph 5)

10. In the sentence below, the word *congregated* means
   a. gathered.
   b. behaved.
   c. happened.
   d. remained silent.

   "So, when my brother and sisters and I congregated in the bathroom to clean up for dinner, the inevitable question was 'What did you learn today?' " (Paragraph 6)

Discussion Questions

1. As the children prepared for dinner, they would not "dare sit at the table without first finding a fact." Were the children greatly frightened of their father or deeply respectful? What do you think are the differences between fear and respect?

2. What does the reading suggest about the advantages or disadvantages of a family eating dinner together?

3. The author states, "Without being aware of it, our family was growing together, sharing experiences, and participating in one another's education" (paragraph 22). What are some other activities that would encourage families to grow together and encourage learning?

Note: Writing assignments for this selection appear on page 542.

Check Your Performance	VOCABULARY IN CONTEXT		
Activity	*Number Right*	*Points*	*Score*
Review Test 1 (5 items)	_____	× 2 =	_____
Review Test 2 (10 items)	_____	× 3 =	_____
Review Test 3 (10 items)	_____	× 3 =	_____
Review Test 4 (10 items)	_____	× 3 =	_____
	TOTAL SCORE	=	_____ %

Enter your total score into the **Reading Performance Chart: Review Tests** on the inside back cover.

VOCABULARY IN CONTEXT: Test 1

A. Read each item below and then do two things:

    1 Underline the **examples** that suggest the meaning of the word in italics.
    2 Circle the letter of the meaning of the word in italics.

  1. The students showed all the signs of *apathy,* including scribbling instead of taking notes, constantly looking at the clock, and writing messages to one another.

    Apathy means

    a. lack of interest.   b. curiosity.   c. attention.

  2. Many healthy elderly people are *vigorous* enough to enjoy such activities as swimming, jogging and biking.

    Vigorous means

    a. having difficulty learning.   b. having energy.   c. childlike.

  3. *Data* about the moon's surface include information gained from photos and soil samples.

    Data means

    a. questions.   b. facts.   c. reasons.

B. In each item, underline the **synonym** for the word in italics. The synonym may be one or more words.

  4. It is not *appropriate* to wear cut-off jeans to most job interviews. Nor is it suitable to smoke during an interview.

  5. When people are angry with each other, a *frank* discussion can be helpful. An honest exchange of ideas can lead to an understanding of the other person's point of view.

  6. The *ultimate* reward for working hard at school is earning a degree. Similarly, the greatest reward for working hard on the job is a big promotion.

(Continues on next page)

C. Antonyms provide context clues in the sentences below. Read each item and do two things:

 1 Underline the **antonym** for the word in italics. Each antonym may be one or more words.
 2 Circle the letter of the meaning of the word in italics.

7. College students often complain that a course is either overly *complex* or too simple.

   Complex means

   a. interesting.   b. dull.   c. difficult.

8. Although Juan's efforts to get back together with Margarita were truly *earnest,* she thought he was being dishonest.

   Earnest means

   a. successful.   b. pleasing.   c. honest.

D. Use the **general sense of each sentence** to figure out the meaning of each word in italics. Then circle the letter of the meaning.

9. Some people have a *phobia* about heights. They can't look down from the top of a tall building without feeling as if they are about to fall.

   A *phobia* is a

   a. humorous situation.   b. fear.   c. pleasant experience.

10. Tidal waves sometimes *accelerate* until they reach a speed of 450 miles an hour.

    Accelerate means

    a. slow down.   b. speed up.   c. bend.

VOCABULARY IN CONTEXT: Test 2

A. Read each item below and then do two things:

    1 Underline the **examples** that suggest the meaning of the word in italics.
    2 Circle the letter of the meaning of the word in italics.

  1. *Remote* areas such as the deserts of Arizona and the wilderness of Alaska appeal to people who want to get away for a while.

    Remote means

    a. populated.   b. fancy.   c. out-of-the-way.

  2. *Traits*—including height, eye color, and hair color—are passed on from generation to generation.

    Traits are

    a. features.   b. materials.   c. rights.

  3. *Awkward* movements are common for infants learning to walk. Sometimes they will fall backward; at other times they will move sideways instead of going forward.

    Awkward means

    a. correct.   b. clumsy.   c. expected.

B. In each item, underline the **synonym** for the word or words in italics. The synonym may be one or more words.

  4. Stress is difficult to *cope with.* Some people manage stress by exercising, others by mental toughness.

  5. One goal of prisons is to *reform* inmates. If more prisoners are changed for the better, fewer will return to prison.

  6. Television has *altered* the course of history. It changed life by making the world much smaller.

(Continues on next page)

C. Antonyms provide context clues in the sentences below. Read each item and do two things:

> **1** Underline the **antonym** for the word in italics. Each antonym may be one or more words.
>
> **2** Circle the letter of the meaning of the word in italics.

7. Soap opera is a made-for-TV *illusion.* Yet many fans of one show were so convinced of its reality that they sent gifts when a character got married.

Illusion means

a. stupidity.   b. appearance of reality.   c. fun.

8. It is important to keep *alert* in class. If you are sleepy, you may miss a key point.

Alert means

a. notes.   b. quiet.   c. wide-awake.

D. Use the **general sense of each sentence** to figure out the meaning of each word in italics. Then circle the letter of the meaning.

9. Certain foreign officials in this country have *immunity from* our laws; they can't be arrested even for murder.

Immunity from means

a. freedom from.   b. punishment for.   c. fear of.

10. With just a few pieces of clothing, a good designer can put together a *versatile* wardrobe. By matching just the right clothes and jewelry, one can have casual, work, and dressy outfits.

Versatile means

a. expensive.   b. large.   c. all-purpose.

VOCABULARY IN CONTEXT: Test 3

Using context clues, circle the letter of the meaning of each word in italics.

1. No one likes a *chronic* complainer like Simon, who criticizes everything all the time.

   Chronic means

   a. rare.   b. constant.   c. messy.

2. In a hospital emergency room, it is common to see such *gruesome* sights as burned skin and bleeding wounds.

   Gruesome means

   a. horrible.   b. common.   c. false.

3. "Your paper should be more *coherent,*" my English teacher wrote. "In places, it is poorly organized and lacking in logic."

   Coherent means

   a. disorganized.   b. detailed.   c. organized and logical.

4. Would weeds make a good *supplement* to your diet? There is evidence that a daily addition of certain weeds would give you all you need of vitamins A and C.

   A *supplement* is

   a. a substitute.   b. an addition.   c. a flavoring.

5. Sometimes people with *contrary* qualities are attracted to each other. For example, a shy person may go out with someone who likes to party a lot.

   Contrary means

   a. similar.   b. unusual.   c. opposite.

6. To *prolong* your life, you should consider getting married. Married people tend to live longer than people who stay single.

   Prolong means

   a. make shorter.   b. make longer.   c. make duller.

(Continues on next page)

7. Common *transactions* include buying food and clothing, going to the bank, and getting gas for the car.

   Transactions are

   a. reasons.   b. pieces of business.   c. thrills.

8. Many cities have decided to *initiate* a recycling program so that their old newspapers, bottles, and cans will be reused instead of dumped.

   Initiate means

   a. cancel.   b. apologize for.   c. start.

9. There is a special chair that eases the *ordeal* of giving birth. Most women who use the chair say they feel less pain and give birth more quickly than when lying down.

   An *ordeal* is

   a. a difficult   b. an enjoyable   c. a very short
      experience.   experience.   experience.

10. On a warm summer day, you may say, "It is my opinion that the level of heat has gone beyond what I am able to consider comfortable." A *concise* way to say the same thing is "I'm hot."

    Concise means

    a. different.   b. confusing.   c. brief and clear.

VOCABULARY IN CONTEXT: Test 4

Using context clues, circle the letter of the meaning of each word in italics.

1. Watching television seems to be as *vital* to some people as food and air.

   Vital means

   a. difficult.   b. necessary.   c. unimportant.

2. When an Asian volcano blew up in 1883, the sound was *audible* three thousand miles away.

   Audible means

   a. able to be seen.   b. able to be heard.   c. able to be felt.

3. A headache can be so *severe* that it keeps a person from being able to work.

   Severe means

   a. serious.   b. new.   c. mild.

4. One usually *rational* football fan became so crazy when his favorite team lost the Super Bowl that he shot the TV.

   Rational means

   a. insane.   b. very popular.   c. reasonable.

5. It was said that no *obstacle*—whether extreme heat, snow, or rocky land— could keep the Pony Express from delivering the mail on time. Once, when a rider fell off and was killed, the horse went on to deliver the mail alone.

   Obstacle means

   a. something that gets   b. temperature.   c. animal.
      in the way.

6. Ice is harder than most people think; its hardness is *comparable to* that of concrete.

   Comparable to means

   a. as thick as.   b. similar to.   c. different from.

(Continues on next page)

7. My sister is such an *inept* cook that she never needs to call the family to supper. We just come to the table when the smoke alarm goes off.

Inept means

a. excellent.   b. slow.   c. unskilled.

8. When my friend asked, "Do you feel all right?" she *implied* that I did not look well.

Implied means

a. suggested.   b. asked.   c. forgot.

9. The small record store had large jazz and rock sections, but not much in the *category* of country music.

Category means

a. goal.   b. feeling.   c. group.

10. My father died when I was a baby, but Mom told me so many stories about him that I feel I know him. For example, one *anecdote* was about how he cried with joy when I was born.

Anecdote means

a. a story.   b. an untrue story.   c. a funny story.

VOCABULARY IN CONTEXT: Test 5

A. Using context clues, circle the letter of the meaning of each word in italics.

1. My plants did poorly in the living room, but they have *thrived* in the sunny kitchen window.

   Thrived means

   a. needed more care.   b. grown weaker.   c. grown very well.

2. Police officers report that criminals are often not very *candid*. Criminals will say anything to convince the police that they are not guilty.

   Candid means

   a. pleasing.   b. happy.   c. honest.

3. People who *encounter* a wild animal in the woods should stay calm and try to back away as soon as possible.

   Encounter means

   a. admire.   b. meet.   c. get away from.

4. A complicated lecture can be *illuminated* with logical examples and clear-cut explanations.

   Illuminated means

   a. made clear.   b. practiced.   c. confused.

5. Many elected officials *advocate* a clean environment. It is up to citizens to see if these officials actually vote for bills that will make our air, streams, and lakes cleaner.

   Advocate means

   a. support.   b. oppose.   c. need.

(Continues on next page)

B. Using context clues, circle the letter of the meaning of each word in italics.

Traveling to foreign countries can be fun and educational. Returning home can be the worst part. Travelers *disembarking from* an airplane or ship often must *endure* long lines at the customs counter. A new electronic *device* may change all that. Some customs officials are now *utilizing* a new machine—a combination document-reader and hand scanner. A traveler inserts a passport into the machine, then puts his or her hand on the scanner. The scanner compares the palm print with a photocopy of the palm on the passport. If the person's palm print *correlates with* the one on the passport, he or she is cleared to leave. The process takes less than one minute.

6. *Disembarking from* means
   a. getting on.   b. getting off.   c. looking down from.

7. *Endure* means
   a. put up with.   b. want.   c. avoid.

8. *Device* means
   a. announcement.   b. invention.   c. problem.

9. *Utilizing* means
   a. ignoring.   b. using.   c. preventing.

10. *Correlates with* means
    a. matches.   b. challenges.   c. amuses.

VOCABULARY IN CONTEXT: Test 6

A. Using context clues, circle the letter of the meaning of each word in italics.

1. It is hard to be *impartial* when you listen to two people arguing. Usually you want to take one person's side.

   Impartial means

   a. interested.　　b. friendly.　　c. not favoring one side over another.

2. Many students begin college because they see only two *options:* either go to college and get a good-paying job or work for minimum wages the rest of their life.

   Options means

   a. choices.　　b. wishes.　　c. habits.

3. I *procrastinated* so long in getting a baby sitter for New Year's Eve that by the time I called, all of our sitters were busy for that night.

   Procrastinated means

   a. worked.　　b. changed.　　c. delayed.

4. Recently Sabrina had a choice of studying for a final or going out for pizza with her friends. She chose to study, and that turned out to be a *prudent* decision. She got an A on the exam, while her friends all got D's.

   Prudent means

   a. generous.　　b. wise.　　c. unfortunate.

5. If a prisoner shows no *remorse* for committing a crime, the judge is likely to sentence him or her to the longest possible prison term.

   Remorse means

   a. regret.　　b. pleasure.　　c. purpose.

(Continues on next page)

B.   Read the entire paragraph below. Then, using context clues, circle the letter of the meaning of each word in italics.

In several *locales* around the country, the United States Postal Service has set up a special room where postal clerks have an *extraordinary* job: they open and read your mail. This room is called the "Dead Letter Office." Reading people's mail is permitted because the clerks are trying to find out where the mail is supposed to go or who sent it. Millions of letters each year are sent with incorrect addresses, no return addresses, or both. Others are written in a scribble that must be *deciphered* or in a foreign language that must be translated. Some envelopes are completely blank. Specially trained clerks spend their time opening letters and packages to discover whether or not they can be sent to the intended *recipient* or returned to the sender. Estimates are that only 30 percent of the mail that ends up at the Dead Letter Office *ultimately* finds it way to the sender or receiver.

6. *Locales* means
   a. targets.   b. places.   c. boxes.

7. *Extraordinary* means
   a. common.   b. very unusual.   c. dangerous.

8. *Deciphered* means
   a. easy.   b. ignored.   c. figured out.

9. A *recipient* is a
   a. letter carrier.   b. receiver.   c. writer.

10. *Ultimately* means
    a. in the end.   b. illegally.   c. sadly.

6
Main Ideas

The most helpful reading skill is the ability to find an author's **main idea**, the main point that the author is trying to make. This chapter will help you develop that ability.

As you read a paragraph or a passage, ask this question: "What is the main point the author is trying to make?" Very often the main point is stated in one general sentence, called the **topic sentence**. So a good way to find the point is to try to locate a general statement. If that statement is supported by most or all of the other material in the paragraph, you have found the main idea.

For example, try to find the main idea in the following paragraph.

> [1]Americans love to send greeting cards. [2]For instance, over 4 million birthday cards are sent out in this country every day. [3]Around Valentine's Day last year, over 900 million cards were mailed. [4]And close to 3 billion holiday greeting cards were sent out during the Christmas season.

Below are four statements from the passage. Choose the one that is a general statement supported by the other material in the paragraph. Write the letter of your choice in the space provided. Then read the explanation that follows.

Four statements from the passage:

a. Americans love to send greeting cards.
b. Over 4 million birthday cards are sent out in this country every day.
c. Around Valentine's Day last year, over 900 million cards were mailed.
d. Close to 3 billion holiday greeting cards were sent out during the Christmas season.

The general statement that expresses the main idea of the passage is _____ .

Explanation:

a. "Americans love to send greeting cards" is the most general idea in the paragraph. "Greeting cards" is broad enough to include the three specific types of cards named in the paragraph—birthday, Valentine's Day, and Christmas cards. Sentence 1 is therefore the sentence that states the main idea. So you should have written *a* in the blank space.

b. The number of birthday cards sent by Americans is just one specific detail in the paragraph. This statement is not general enough to cover the details about other types of greeting cards.

c. The fact that Americans sent millions of Valentine's Day cards is another specific detail. It is too narrow to include the other types of greeting cards.

d. The number of Christmas cards sent is a final specific detail. Sentence 4 is also too narrow to include the other types of greeting cards.

The Main Idea as an "Umbrella"

Think of the main idea as an "umbrella" that "covers" all of the other ideas in the paragraph. The main idea is a general idea. Under it fits all or most of the other material in the paragraph. This other material consists of specific ideas that support the main idea—examples, reasons, facts, and other evidence. The diagram below shows this relationship.

AMERICANS LOVE TO SEND
GREETING CARDS

4 million birthday cards are sent out daily.
900 million cards are sent around Valentine's Day.
3 billion cards are sent at Christmas.

GENERAL VERSUS SPECIFIC IDEAS

The **main idea** in a paragraph is the *general idea* that is supported by all or most of the *specific ideas*. To improve your skill at finding main ideas, it is helpful to practice separating general from specific ideas.

We often separate general and specific ideas without thinking about it. For example, you may do this in choosing your school classes. You may think, "I need credits in science. Should I take biology or chemistry?" In this case, *science* is the general idea, and *biology* and *chemistry* are the specific ideas. A general idea (science) includes specific ideas (biology and chemistry).

Or you may go home from school or work and think, "I'll get some fish for dinner." You may then consider flounder, salmon, and tuna. In this example, *fish* is the general idea; *flounder, salmon,* and *tuna* are the specific ideas.

In other words, **general ideas** are broad, and **specific ideas** are narrower. Try the following:

Countries is a general term. Write the names of three specific countries below.

_____   _____   _____

Fruit is a general term. Write the names of three kinds of fruits below.

_____   _____   _____

Answers to the above exercise will vary, but for the first item you should have written three specific country names, such as *United States, Mexico,* and *Japan.* For the second item, the specific names of any three fruits would be correct, including *apple, orange,* and *banana.*

The practices that follow will give you experience in recognizing general and specific ideas.

➣ *Practice 1*

Each group of words below has one general idea and four specific ideas. The general idea includes all the specific ideas. Underline the general idea in each group.

Before beginning, look at the example.

Example   anger   love   fear   <u>emotion</u>   envy

(*Emotion* is the general idea because it includes *anger, love, fear,* and *envy,* which are specific kinds of emotions.)

1. parrot   kitten   goldfish   hamster   pet

2. square   circle   triangle   shape   diamond

3. up	down	sideways	direction	north
4. soda	beer	orange juice	beverage	water
5. high-risk job	astronaut	firefighter	policeman	miner
6. sleeping bag	sheet	pillow	blanket	bedding
7. "hello"	greeting	a wave	"hi"	open arms
8. screech	noise	crash	off-key music	sirens
9. jump	command	stop	move	sit down
10. jail	hanging	suspension	fine	punishment

➤ *Practice 2*

In each item below, one idea is general and one is specific. The general idea includes the specific ideas. In the spaces provided, write two more specific ideas that are covered by the general idea.

Before beginning, look at the example.

Example   *General idea:* containers
   Specific ideas: box, _____envelope_____, _____bottle_____

(*Containers* is the general idea; *box* is a specific kind of container. *Envelope* and *bottle* are also specific kinds of containers.)

1. *General idea:* movie stars
   Specific ideas: Tom Cruise, _____, _____

2. *General idea:* wild animals
   Specific ideas: gorilla, _____, _____

3. *General idea:* office machines
   Specific ideas: copier, _____, _____

4. *General idea:* desserts
   Specific ideas: ice cream, _____, _____

5. *General idea:* U.S. cities
   Specific ideas: Los Angeles, _____, _____

6. *General idea:* holidays
   Specific ideas: Thanksgiving, _____, _____

7. *General idea:* planets
   Specific ideas: Earth, _____, _____

8. *General idea:* relatives
   Specific ideas: uncle, _____, _____

9. *General idea:* kitchen appliances
   Specific ideas: toaster, _____, _____

10. *General idea:* vegetable
    Specific ideas: spinach, _____, _____

➤ *Practice 3*

In each item below, one idea is general and the other is specific. The general idea includes the specific one. Do two things:

1   Underline the general idea in each pair of words.
2   Write in one more specific idea that is covered by the general idea.

Before beginning, look at the example.

Example   purple   <u>color</u>   _____ *red* _____

(*Color* is the general idea because it includes *purple,* which is a specific color. Another specific color is the one written in the blank space: *red.*)

1. bird   eagle   _____

2. furniture   table   _____

3. bus   vehicle   _____

4. sunshine   weather   _____

5. pretzels   snack   _____

6. pen   writing tool   _____

7. tango   dance   _____

8. insect   bee   _____

9. lipstick   cosmetics   _____

10. job   salesclerk   _____

FINDING THE MAIN IDEA

Finding the main idea in a paragraph can be done in two steps: First, find the topic. Second, find the topic sentence.

Step 1: Finding the Topic of the Paragraph

The **topic** of a paragraph is the subject that the paragraph is about. To find the topic, ask yourself this simple question:

In general, who or what is this paragraph about?

Your answer to this question will be the paragraph's topic.

For example, read the paragraph below. As you do so, ask yourself, "In general, who or what is this paragraph about?" Then circle the letter of what you think is the topic, and read the explanation. Finally, do the practice exercise that follows.

Several remedies for too much sun can be made in your own kitchen. For instance, you can soothe a case of sunburn by spreading plain yogurt over the burned area for ten minutes. Or you can sit in cool bath water to which you have added a cup of vinegar or baking soda. If your eyes have been irritated by the sun, cover them for five minutes with chilled tea bags or cotton soaked in milk.

The topic of the paragraph is
a. using yogurt to soothe sunburn.
b. remedies for too much sun.
c. remedies.

Explanation:

a. "Using yogurt to soothe sunburn" is too specific to be the topic of the paragraph. It does not cover the other remedies, such as the one using tea bags.

b. "Remedies for too much sun" is general enough to include all of the other ideas in the paragraph. This is the topic of the paragraph.

c. "Remedies" is too general—it includes remedies other than those for sunburn.

➢ *Practice 4*

Circle the letter of the topic of each paragraph below. Make sure your choice is not too general or too specific by asking yourself these questions:

- Does your choice cover much more than what is in the paragraph? If so, it cannot be the topic, because it is too general.

- Does your choice leave out important ideas included in the paragraph? If so, it cannot be the topic, because it is too specific.

1. People who are addicted to shopping have low self-esteem and a high need for excitement. There seem to be two types of addicted shoppers. One is the daily shopper, who cannot miss a single day at the stores. The other is the binge buyer, who goes shopping weekly to buy huge numbers of things.

   The topic is
   a. addicts.
   b. shopping addicts.
   c. the daily shopper.

2. Headaches have two main causes. Research shows that most headaches result from muscle tension. And the most common reason for that muscle tension is continuing stress. Headaches can also be caused by changes in the supply of blood to the head. Such changes are often reactions to pollen and food chemicals.

   The topic is
   a. headaches.
   b. pain.
   c. muscle tension as a cause of headaches.

3. Every human body has electricity. But the electricity in Pauline Shaw's body is so great that she is destructive. This Englishwoman has destroyed irons, toasters, radios, and other appliances. She has also ruined over two hundred light bulbs. One scientist at Oxford University says that Shaw can produce an electric charge as high as eighty thousand volts. He believes that a rare allergy to some foods is at fault. Shaw's system breaks down these foods in a way that affects her body's electricity.

   The topic is
   a. Pauline Shaw's effect on light bulbs.
   b. Pauline Shaw's life.
   c. the electricity in Pauline Shaw's body.

4. Your visit to the hospital can be a helpful experience for a patient. Comfort a patient who is ill and afraid by giving him or her a warm pat or by holding his or her hand. People often wonder what they should say to patients, but it is good to remember that patients often need someone to listen to them. So be a caring listener. And remember not to stay too long—people who are seriously ill tire easily.

The topic is
a. your visit to a patient in the hospital.
b. your visit to friends.
c. listening to a hospital patient you visit.

5. Researchers who do surveys depend on what people tell them. People who are surveyed, however, sometimes lie. In one survey, for instance, people were asked if they used seat belts. Later, researchers checked to see how many people really did use their seat belts. It turned out that almost 40 percent of those who said they buckled up did not. Also, researchers once asked people about their smoking habits. Then they tested these people's saliva for a chemical that is found in the mouths of smokers. The tests showed that 6 percent of the women and 8 percent of the men had lied about smoking.

The topic is
a. researchers.
b. people who are surveyed.
c. people who are surveyed about smoking.

Step 2: Finding the Topic Sentence of the Paragraph

Finding the topic of a paragraph prepares you to find the main idea of the paragraph. Once you have found the topic, ask yourself this question:

What is the author's main point about the topic?

The answer will be the main idea. Authors often state that main point, or main idea, in a sentence called the **topic sentence**. That sentence will make a general statement about the topic which will be supported by the rest of the paragraph.

For instance, here is the paragraph on sunburn remedies that you have already read. Read it again, remembering that "remedies for too much sun" is the topic. As you read, choose the sentence that gives you the main point about "remedies for too much sun." Write the number of that sentence in the space provided and then read the explanation. Finally, do the practice exercise that follows.

¹Several remedies for too much sun can be made in your own kitchen. ²For instance, you can soothe a case of sunburn by spreading plain yogurt over the burned area for ten minutes. ³Or you can sit in cool bath water to which you have added a cup of vinegar or baking soda. ⁴If your eyes have been irritated by the sun, cover them for five minutes with chilled tea bags or cotton soaked in milk.

The number of the sentence that states the main point about "remedies for too much sun" is _____.

Explanation:

To find the sentence that states the main idea, you should have asked this question: "What is the author's main point about remedies for too much sun?" Sentences 2–4 give specific remedies. But sentence 1 is more general—it states that several remedies for sunburn can be made in your kitchen. All the details support this idea, describing a series of remedies that can be made in the kitchen. So sentence 1 is the correct answer. It is the topic sentence—the umbrella statement that covers the other ideas in the paragraph.

➤ Practice 5

After reading each of the following paragraphs, do the following:

    1 First, find the topic of the paragraph. Circle the letter of the correct choice.

    2 Then find the sentence in which the author states the main idea about that topic. Circle the letter of the correct choice.

A. ¹Work-sharing can benefit both employees and employers. ²In work-sharing, a full-time job is divided into part-time jobs shared by two or more workers. ³Working mothers, students, and people just returning to work find these positions very practical. ⁴Employers like work-sharing too. ⁵In a two-year work-sharing project, workers had a mere 13 percent turnover rate; the usual turnover rate is 40 percent. ⁶In addition, workers' productivity was greater than expected.

  1. The topic is
    a. work.
    b. work-sharing.
    c. students using work-sharing.

  2. The main idea is stated in sentence
    a. 1.
    b. 3.
    c. 6.

B. ¹The older part of the population of the United States is growing. ²In 1960, 0.05 percent of the population was over 85 years old. ³Today that figure is over 2 percent. ⁴Researchers at Duke University project that by the year 2040, 12.5 percent of Americans will be 85 years of age or older. ⁵This translates to over 42 million people.

3. The topic is
   a. the year 2040.
   b. people over 85 years old in 1960.
   c. the older part of the U.S. population.

4. The main idea is stated in sentence
   a. 1.
   b. 2.
   c. 5.

C. ¹As you speak with someone, you can gather clues as to whether he or she understands you. ²Then you can adjust what you say accordingly. ³But when you write, you must try to predict the reader's reactions without such clues. ⁴You also have to give stronger evidence in writing than in conversation. ⁵A friend may accept an unsupported statement such as "My boss is awful." ⁶But in most writing, the reader would expect you to back up such a statement with proof. ⁷Obviously, effective writing requires more attention to detail than everyday conversation.

5. The topic is
   a. proof.
   b. conversation.
   c. effective writing versus conversation.

6. The main idea is stated in sentence
   a. 1.
   b. 5.
   c. 7.

D. ¹From birth on, male and female children are often treated and viewed differently. ²First, boys get a blue blanket and girls get pink. ³Also, although more male than female babies fall ill, studies say parents are more likely to consider a baby strong if it is male. ⁴Similarly, parents urge boys to take part in rough-and-tumble play. ⁵But parents prefer that girls watch and talk rather than be physically active. ⁶When questioned, most parents say they want their sons to be successful and independent, and they want their daughters to be loving and well-behaved.

7. The topic is
   a. males and females.
   b. male and female children.
   c. childhood illness.

8. The main idea is stated in sentence
   a. 1.
   b. 2.
   c. 6.

E. ¹An enlarged heart can be a sign that the heart is having trouble pumping blood. ²This could be caused by a bad heart valve or by high blood pressure. ³An enlarged heart could also be caused by a high level of exercise. ⁴Athletes such as long-distance runners frequently have larger-than-average hearts. ⁵However, their hearts operate at a high rate of efficiency. ⁶An enlarged heart, then, can be a sign of bad health or good health.

9. The topic is
   a. pumping blood.
   b. athletes and their hearts.
   c. an enlarged heart.

10. The main idea is stated in sentence
    a. 1.
    b. 4.
    c. 6.

Final Notes

1 In selections made up of many paragraphs, such as articles and textbook chapters, the topic is often expressed as a title. So if you are reading a psychology text and you see "Chapter 4: Interpreting Dreams," you have a good idea of what the chapter will be about. In a similar way, the title of a journal or magazine article often tells you what the article will be about. An article titled "Where Whales Migrate During Winter" lets you know that you will be reading about where whales go during winter months.

2 In selections made up of many paragraphs, the overall main idea is called the **central point**. From now on, when you read longer selections in this text, you will be given practice in finding the central point, as well as in finding the main ideas of paragraphs within the reading.

Chapter 7 will help you see how authors use supporting details to develop and explain their main ideas.

CHAPTER SUMMARY

In this chapter, you learned the following:

- A **general idea** includes **specific ideas**.

  General idea: country
  Specific ideas: United States, Mexico, Japan

- The **topic** is the subject of a paragraph. To find the topic of a paragraph, ask this question:

  In general, who or what is this paragraph about?

- The **topic sentence** states the main idea about the topic of a paragraph. To find the topic sentence, ask this question:

  What is the author's main point about the topic?

➤ *Review Test 1*

To review what you've learned in this chapter, answer each of the following questions by filling in the blank or circling the letter of the correct answer.

1. Supporting details are always more *(general or specific?)* _____ than the main idea.

2. The umbrella statement that covers all of the material in a paragraph is the
   a. topic.   b. topic sentence.   c. central point.

3. _____ TRUE OR FALSE? To find the main idea of a paragraph, you may find it helpful to first look for the topic.

4. When the main idea is stated in one sentence of a paragraph, that sentence is called the
   a. topic.   b. topic sentence.   c. central point.

5. For selections made up of many paragraphs, the author's overall main point is called the
   a. central topic.   b. central point.   c. topic sentence.

➤ *Review Test 2*

A. Each group of words below consists of one general idea and four specific ideas. The general idea includes all the specific ideas. Underline the general idea in each group.

1. uncle	grandmother	relative	cousin	sister
2. vanilla	flavor	chocolate	strawberry	butterscotch
3. poker	hide and seek	baseball	Monopoly	game
4. paper plates	potato salad	ants	picnic	lemonade
5. sandals	boots	sneakers	footwear	high heels

B. In each item below, one idea is general and one is specific. In the spaces provided, write two more specific ideas that are covered by the general idea.

6–7. *General idea:* precious stones
      Specific ideas: diamond, _____, _____

8–9. *General idea:* winter clothing
      Specific ideas: wool scarf, _____, _____

10–11. *General idea:* means of transportation
       Specific ideas: train, _____, _____

12–13. *General idea:* TV news shows
       Specific ideas: Dateline NBC, _____, _____

14–15. *General idea:* musical instruments with strings
       Specific ideas: guitar, _____, _____

C. In each pair below, one idea is general and the other is specific. The general idea includes the specific one. Do two things:

    1 Underline the idea in each pair that you think is more general.
    2 Write in one more specific idea that is covered by the general idea.

16–17. sneezing	cold symptom	_____
18–19. tongue	mouth	_____
20–21. magazine	*Time*	_____
22–23. infancy	life stage	_____
24–25. length	inch	_____

➤ *Review Test 3*

A. Circle the letter of the topic of each paragraph below. Make sure your choice is not too general or too specific by asking yourself these questions:

- Does your choice cover much more than what is in the paragraph? If so, it cannot be the topic, because it is too general.

- Does your choice leave out important ideas included in the paragraph? If so, it cannot be the topic, because it is too specific.

1. People riding a bicycle through busy city streets should follow several guidelines, according to experts. One such guideline is to wear a helmet to prevent head injury in case the rider falls. Another guideline is to stay off the sidewalk. Also, riders should obey traffic rules, including respecting one-way signs.

   The topic is
   a. transportation safety.
   b. wearing a biker's helmet.
   c. people riding a bicycle on busy city streets.

2. Despite all the criticism it gets, television has its good points. First of all, it is educational. From live documentaries to taped nature programs, it teaches in a colorful and interesting way. In addition, TV is relaxing and entertaining. After a stressful day, it is sometimes restful just to put your feet up and enjoy a favorite program or a good movie.

   The topic is
   a. television.
   b. television as entertainment.
   c. the educational side of TV.

3. The crocodile and a small bird called the plover have a surprisingly friendly relationship. A crocodile's jaws are strong, and its teeth are razor-sharp. Yet the plover dares to step inside the croc's mouth. You see, after eating, the crocodile opens its mouth. This allows its "living toothbrush" to step in and clean uneaten food from its teeth. In return for this service, the plover gets a free meal.

   The topic is
   a. the crocodile's habits.
   b. the crocodile and the plover.
   c. friendly relationships between animals.

4. It's well known that trees provide shade, beauty, and protection from the wind. However, trees also have two lesser-known benefits. First, trees clean the air. Their leaves actually filter out pollution in the air. One large sugar maple, for example, can remove as much pollution as is put into the air by cars burning a thousand gallons of gas. The second lesser-known benefit of trees is that they reduce stress. Experiments show that people relax more when shown scenes with trees than when shown city scenes without natural greenery.

The topic is
a. nature.
b. trees.
c. anti-stress benefits of trees.

B. After reading each of the following paragraphs, do the following:

  1 First, find the topic of the paragraph. Circle the letter of the correct choice.

  2 Then find the sentence in which the author states the main idea about that topic. Circle the letter of the correct choice.

[1]Some people think an only child is lucky because of the material goods and attention he or she receives. [2]But only children have their problems too. [3]For one thing, they have no privacy. [4]Parents always feel entitled to know everything that's going on in an only child's life. [5]Also, only children miss the companionship of brothers and sisters. [6]They can be lonely, and they may have trouble making friends later in life because they never learned to get along with a brother or sister.

5. The topic is
   a. only children.
   b. children.
   c. the loneliness of only children.

6. The main idea is stated in sentence
   a. 1.
   b. 2.
   c. 6.

[1]Researchers in the food industry are studying the influence of diet on health. [2]According to these researchers, certain foods may protect against certain diseases. [3]For instance, some fish oils contain a substance that may lower blood pressure. [4]Also, broccoli and Brussels sprouts have a chemical

that may help fight some types of cancer. [5]Carrots have chemicals that may protect against strokes and heart attacks. [6]And something in garlic and onions appears to reduce cholesterol.

7. The topic is
   a. certain vegetables.
   b. certain healthful foods.
   c. some fish oils.

8. The main idea is stated in sentence
   a. 1.
   b. 2.
   c. 3.

   [1]Speech experts recommend various tactics for dealing with children who stutter. [2]First, experts say you should speak to those children slowly. [3]This will allow them time to process what they are hearing. [4]Second, don't talk too much. [5]Too much talk may actually overstimulate children so that their mouths can't keep up with their brains. [6]Third, allow a couple of seconds between the time the child speaks and the time you begin your response. [7]This will tell the child that what he or she has to say is important to you. [8]Finally, don't ask a stuttering child to recite or read a long story out loud. [9]Reducing anxiety will lessen the stuttering.

9. The topic is
   a. speech.
   b. dealing with children who stutter.
   c. speaking slowly to stuttering children.

10. The main idea is stated in sentence
   a. 1.
   b. 2.
   c. 8.

➤ Review Test 4

Here is a chance to apply your understanding of main ideas to a full-length reading. First read the following selection. It provides information on a key classroom skill that can make a very big difference in how well you learn and what grades you get. Then answer the questions that follow on topics, main ideas, and the central point. There are also phonics, dictionary, and vocabulary questions to help you continue working on skills from previous chapters.

Words to Watch

Following are some words in the reading that do not have strong context support. Each word is followed by the number of the paragraph in which it appears and its meaning there. These words are indicated in the reading by a small circle (°).

> *deaden* (3): dull
> *glazed* (3): glassy
> *launching pad* (7): starting point
> *groping* (8): reaching
> *cement* (18): fix firmly

CLASSROOM NOTETAKING

Clarissa White

1   How would you feel if you were forced to spend 1800 hours—the equivalent of 75 days in a row—sitting in a hard-backed chair, eyes wide open, listening to the sound of someone else's voice? You wouldn't be allowed to sleep, eat, or smoke. You couldn't leave the room. To make matters worse, you'd be expected to remember every important point the speaker made, and you'd be punished for forgetting. And, to top it off, you'd have to pay thousands of dollars for the experience.

2   Sound like the torture scene from the latest spy thriller? Actually, it's nothing of the kind. It's what all college students do who take a full load of five courses for four years. Those 1800 hours are the time they'll spend in the lecture room.

3   Unfortunately, many students do regard these hours as torture, and they do all sorts of things to deaden° the pain. Some of them sit through class with glazed° eyes, minds wandering to the athletic field or the movie theater. Others hide in the back of the room, sneaking glances at the newspaper or the book they're being tested on in their next class. Still others reduce the pain to zero: they simply don't come to class. These students do not realize that if they don't listen in class—and take notes—they're missing out on one of the most important aspects of their education.

WHY TAKE LECTURE NOTES?

4   One reason you should take lecture notes is that lectures add to what you read in textbooks. Lecturers combine the material and approaches of many texts, saving you the trouble of researching an entire field. They keep up to date with their subjects and can include the latest studies or discoveries in their presentations; they needn't wait for the next edition of the book to come

out. They can provide additional examples or simplify difficult concepts, making it easier for you to master tricky material. And the best lecturers combine knowledge with expert showmanship. Both informative and entertaining speakers, they can make any subject, from ancient civilizations to computers, leap vividly to life.

5   True, you say, but isn't it good enough just to listen to these wonderful people without writing down what they say? Actually, it isn't, which leads us to another reason for taking lecture notes. Studies have shown that after two weeks, you'll forget 80 percent of it. And you didn't come to the lecture room just to be entertained. You came to learn. The only way to keep the material in your head is to get it down in permanent form—in the form of lecture notes.

HOW TO TAKE LECTURE NOTES

6   There are three steps to mastering the art of taking good lecture notes: the preparation, the notetaking process itself, and the post-lecture review.

Preparation

7   First, mentally prepare yourself to take good notes. Examine your attitude. Remember, you're not going to the lecture room to be bored, tortured, or entertained; you're going there to learn. Also, examine the material the lecture will cover. Read the textbook chapter in advance. If your instructor's lecture usually follows the organization of the textbook, you'll be familiar with the material and won't have to spend half the lecture wondering what it's about or how to spell a key term. If, however, your instructor merely uses the textbook as a launching pad° and devotes most of the lecture to supplementary material, at least you'll have the background to follow what is being said.

8   Second, prepare yourself physically. Get a good night's sleep, and get to class—on time. Even better, get to class early, so you can get a good seat near the front of the room. You'll hear better there and be less tempted to let your mind wander. You'll also have time to open your notebook to a new page, find your pen, and write the date, course, and topic of the lecture at the top. This way, you won't still be groping° under your chair or flipping through pages when the instructor begins to speak.

Process

9   When you take class notes, always use 8½″ x 11″ paper, preferably in a looseleaf notebook so you can insert handouts. Write on only one side of the paper. Later, you might want to spread all your notes out in front of you. Have a pen to write with rather than a pencil, which moves more slowly across a page and is not as legible.

10   Be prepared to do a good deal of writing in class. A good rule of thumb for taking notes is "When in doubt, write it down." After class, you will

have time to go over your notes and make decisions about what is important enough to study and what is not. But in the midst of a lecture, you don't always have time to decide what is really important and what is quite secondary. You don't want to miss getting down a valuable idea that the instructor does not repeat later.

11   Be sure to always write down what the instructor puts on the board. If he or she takes the time to write something on the board, it is generally safe to assume that such material is important. And don't fall into the trap that some students fall into. They write down what is on the board but nothing more. They just sit and listen while the instructor explains all the connections between those words that have been chalked on the board. Everything may be perfectly clear to a student then, but several days later, chances are that all the connecting material will be forgotten. If you write down the explanations in class, it will be much easier for you to make sense of the material and to study it later.

12   As much as possible, organize your notes by starting main points at the margin. Indent secondary points under the main points and indent examples even further. Skip lines between main sections. Wherever possible, number the points. If the instructor explains three reasons for poverty, or four results of the greenhouse effect, make sure you number each of those reasons or results. The numbers help organize the material and make it easier for you to study and remember it.

13   Here are some other hints for taking good classroom notes:

- If you miss something, don't panic. 14 Leave space for it in your notes and keep going. Later, get the missing information from a classmate or your textbook.

- Be alert for signals that something is 15 an important point ("A major cause of anxiety is . . ."), a new topic ("Another problem of urban living is . . ."), the beginning of an enumeration ("There are seven warning signals . . ."), or a summary ("In conclusion . . ."). These signals will help you organize your note-taking. If your instructor says, "The point I am trying to make is . . . ," be sure you *get the point*—in your notes.

- Use abbreviations in order to save 16 time. Put a key for abbreviated words in the top margin of your notes. For instance, in a business class, *com* could stand for *communication; info* for *information*. In a psychology class, *beh* could stand for *behavior; mot* for *motivation*. You can also abbreviate certain common words, using a "*+*" for *and,* a "*w/*" for *with,* and an "*ex*" for *example.*

- Finally, don't ignore the very 17 beginning and end of class. Often, instructors devote the first five minutes of their lectures to a review of material already covered or a preview of the day's lecture. The last five minutes of a lecture can contain a clear summary of the class—or ten more major points the instructor simply *has* to make before the bell rings. Don't spend the first five minutes of class getting your materials out and the last five minutes putting them away. If you do, you'll probably miss something important.

Post-Lecture Review

18   Taking good notes lets you bring the lecture home with you. The real learning takes place after class. As soon as you have time, sit down and reread your notes. Fill in anything unclear or missing while it's still fresh in your mind. Then, in the left-hand column of each page, write a few key words and phrases that summarize the points of the lecture. Cover your notes, and, using only these key words, try to reconstruct as much of the lecture as you can. This review will cement° the major points in your memory—and will save significant time when you study for the exam.

To sum all this up, be prepared to   19 go into class and be not just an active listener but an active notetaker as well. Being in class and taking good notes while you are there are the most valuable steps you can take to succeed in college.

Word Skills Questions

Phonics

1. The word *textbooks*, used in the sentence below, is broken into syllables according to which rule?
   a. Dividing Before a Single Consonant
   b. Dividing After Prefixes and Before Suffixes
   c. Dividing Between the Words in a Compound Word

   ". . . lectures add to what you read in textbooks." (Paragraph 4)

Dictionary Use

Use the following dictionary entry to answer questions 2–3.

sec•ond•ar•y (sĕk′ən-dĕr′ē) *adj.* **1a.** Of the second rank; not primary. **b.** Inferior; minor. **2.** Derived from what is original: *a secondary source.* **3.** Of or relating to education between elementary school and college.

2. The **y** at the end of *secondary*
   a. is silent.
   b. has the long **e** sound.
   c. has the short **e** sound.

3. Which definition of *secondary* fits the sentence at the top of the next page?
   a. Definition 1a
   b. Definition 2
   c. Definition 3

"But in the midst of a lecture, you don't always have time to decide what is really important and what is quite secondary." (Paragraph 10)

Vocabulary in Context

Use context clues in the reading to help you decide on the best meaning for each italicized word. Then circle the letter of your choice.

4. In the sentence below, the word *showmanship* means
   a. dramatic skill.
   b. handwriting.
   c. research ability.
   d. popularity.

   "And the best lecturers combine knowledge with expert showmanship. . . . they can make any subject, from ancient civilizations to computers, leap vividly to life." (Paragraph 4)

5. In the sentence below, the word *supplementary* means
   a. textbook.
   b. unimportant.
   c. additional.
   d. boring.

   "If, however, your instructor merely uses the textbook as a launching pad and devotes most of the lecture to supplementary material, at least you'll have the background to follow what is being said." (Paragraph 7)

6. In the sentence below, the word *enumeration* means a
   a. new topic.
   b. signal.
   c. list.
   d. question.

   "Be alert for signals that something is . . . the beginning of an enumeration ('There are seven warning signals . . . ')" (Paragraph 15)

Reading Comprehension Questions

Central Point

7. Which subject is the topic of the entire selection?
   a. Students
   b. Success in school
   c. College lectures
   d. Taking lecture notes

8. Which sentence expresses the selection's central point (the main idea of the entire reading)?
   a. Students can learn more from lectures than from reading textbooks.
   b. Taking lecture notes is an important skill involving three main steps.
   c. College lectures are more than just entertainment.
   d. There are various ways to achieve success in school.

Main Ideas

9. The main idea of paragraph 4 is stated in its
    a. first sentence.   c. third sentence.
    b. second sentence.   d. last sentence.

10. Which sentence expresses the main idea of paragraph 18?
    a. Notetaking allows you to bring a copy of the lecture home with you.
    b. Always fill in the blanks in your notes as soon as class ends.
    c. Completing and reviewing lecture notes soon after class will help you remember the material.
    d. Reread your notes soon after class.

Discussion Questions

1. Of all the advice in this selection, what three points will probably be the most helpful for you to use? Tell why.

2. Besides knowing how to take lecture notes, what other study skills do you think are important for students to know and practice? For example, what skills are useful when reading, studying material, or taking a test?

3. According to the reading, part of a student's preparation for classroom notetaking should be to examine his or her attitude (paragraph 7). Why do you think the author feels examining one's attitude is so important?

Note: Writing assignments for this selection appear on pages 542–543.

Check Your Performance   **MAIN IDEAS**

Activity	Number Right	Points	Score
Review Test 1 (5 items)	_____	× 2 =	_____
Review Test 2 (25 items)	_____	× 2 =	_____
Review Test 3 (10 items)	_____	× 2 =	_____
Review Test 4 (10 items)	_____	× 2 =	_____
		TOTAL SCORE =	_____%

MAIN IDEAS: Test 1

A. Each group of words below consists of one general idea and four specific ideas. The general idea includes all the specific ideas. Underline the general idea in each group.

1. jazz	blues	rap	music	rock
2. telephone	dishwasher	personal computer	household machine	dryer
3. fry	boil	cook	bake	steam
4. insurance	burglar alarm	guard dog	protection	suntan lotion
5. murder	crime	stealing	speeding	kidnapping

B. In each item below, one idea is general and one is specific. In the spaces provided, write two more specific ideas that are covered by the general idea.

6–7. *General idea:* pop singer
Specific ideas: Gloria Estefan, _____, _____

8–9. *General idea:* flowers
Specific ideas: tulip, _____, _____

10–11. *General idea:* tools
Specific ideas: saw, _____, _____

12–13. *General idea:* floor coverings
Specific ideas: carpet, _____, _____

14–15. *General idea:* TV or radio talk show
Specific ideas: The Tonight Show, _____, _____

(Continues on next page)

C. In each pair below, one idea is general and the other is specific. The general idea includes the specific one. Do two things:

> **1** Underline the general idea in each pair.
> **2** Write in one more specific idea that is covered by the general idea.

16–17. Mexican food	taco	_____
18–19. comics section	newspaper	_____
20–21. Miami	city	_____
22–23. weapon	knife	_____
24–25. iron	metal	_____

MAIN IDEAS: Test 2

A. Each group of words below consists of one general idea and four specific ideas. The general idea includes all the specific ideas. Underline the general idea in each group.

1. bonnet   turban   hat   baseball cap   helmet

2. granola   oatmeal   raisin bran   cereal   bran flakes

3. mortgage   credit-card bill   debt   child support   car loan

4. burned toast   minor problem   boring date   flat tire   a cold

5. microwave ovens   take-out food   high-speed trains   timesavers   express mail

B. In each item below, one idea is general and one is specific. In the spaces provided, write two more specific ideas that are covered by the general idea.

6–7. *General idea:* trees
   Specific ideas: maple, _____, _____

8–9. *General idea:* ways to communicate
   Specific ideas: telephone, _____, _____

10–11. *General idea:* relaxing activities
   Specific ideas: sunbathing, _____, _____

12–13. *General idea:* ways to pay
   Specific ideas: check, _____, _____

14–15. *General idea:* sports with a ball
   Specific ideas: basketball, _____, _____

(Continues on next page)

C. In each pair below, one idea is general and the other is specific. The general idea includes the specific one. Do two things:

     1 Underline the general idea in each pair.
     2 Write in one more specific idea that is covered by the general idea.

16–17.	monster	Dracula	_____
18–19.	nylon	fabric	_____
20–21.	poker	card game	_____
22–23.	good-luck charm	four-leaf clover	_____
24–25.	household chore	washing floors	_____

MAIN IDEAS: Test 3

A. In each pair below, one idea is general and the other is specific. The general idea includes the specific one. Do two things:

> **1** Underline the general idea in each pair.
> **2** Write in one more specific idea that is covered by the general idea.

1–2. elected official   president   _____

3–4. tea   hot beverage   _____

5–6. reading material   newsmagazine   _____

B. Circle the letter of the topic of each paragraph below. Make sure your choice is not too general or too specific by asking yourself these questions:

- Does your choice cover much more than what is in the paragraph? If so, it cannot be the topic, because it is too general.

- Does your choice leave out important ideas included in the paragraph? If so, it cannot be the topic, because it is too specific.

7. The United States accepts almost two million legal immigrants each year. California is the top destination. It accepts almost 40 percent. Texas is next, accepting 12 percent. These two states are followed by New York, Florida, and Illinois as favorite destinations.

   The topic is
   a. immigration.
   b. legal immigrants in California.
   c. legal immigrants to the United States.

8. Herding dogs share certain characteristics that make them excellent watchdogs. They are large dogs. Among the purebreds classified as herding dogs by the American Kennel Club are collies, sheepdogs, and German shepherds. Also, herding dogs are bred to work closely with humans. They are fast learners, are eager to please, and like to dominate situations.

   The topic is
   a. herding dogs.
   b. dogs.
   c. collies, sheepdogs, and German shepherds.

(Continues on next page)

9. People who favor laws against handguns have several reasons. They argue, for example, that handguns make it easier to kill people. Other weapons, such as knives, may cause less damage. Also, people who own guns could leave a loaded handgun within reach of a small child. Children do not know the difference between a toy gun and the real thing. Finally, half of all the guns used in crimes have been stolen. This means that criminals get many of their weapons from people who bought guns to protect themselves.

The topic is
a. various types of weapons.
b. arguments for laws against handguns.
c. one way criminals get handguns.

10. Although people dream of being celebrities, fame has serious disadvantages. First, the famous are expected to look perfect all the time. There's always someone ready to photograph a celebrity looking dumpy in old clothes. The famous also give up their privacy. Their divorces and other problems end up on the evening news and in headlines. Even worse, famous people are often in danger. They get threatening letters and are sometimes attacked.

The topic is
a. the dangers of fame.
b. the disadvantages of fame.
c. the advantages and disadvantages of fame.

MAIN IDEAS: Test 4

A. In each pair below, one idea is general and the other is specific. The general idea includes the specific one. Do two things:

> **1** Underline the general idea in each pair.
> **2** Write in one more specific idea that is covered by the general idea.

1–2. organization   4-H Clubs   _____

3–4. catcher   baseball player   _____

5–6. body of water   ocean   _____

B. Circle the letter of the topic of each paragraph below. Make sure your choice is not too general or too specific by asking yourself these questions:

- Does your choice cover much more than what is in the paragraph? If so, it cannot be the topic, because it is too general.

- Does your choice leave out important ideas included in the paragraph? If so, it cannot be the topic, because it is too specific.

7. Losers in presidential elections often fade away after one attempt at the White House. But some unsuccessful presidential nominees try more than once. Richard Nixon was defeated by John F. Kennedy in 1962 yet was successful eight years later. Adlai Stevenson lost to Dwight Eisenhower in 1954 and then tried again in 1958. He was unsuccessful again. But Henry Clay and William Jennings Bryan can top that. Each was nominated three times and lost each time.

The topic is
a. some unsuccessful presidential nominees.
b. Richard Nixon and John F. Kennedy.
c. nominees for the presidency.

(Continues on next page)

8. Flea markets and garage sales appeal to people for a couple of reasons. First, of course, a used item costs less than a new one. Many people on a budget have wonderful wardrobes they have assembled with good used clothing. Second, many who shop at flea markets and garage sales are collectors. There are people who collect old hats, 1950s toasters, toaster covers, salt and pepper shakers, comic books, and just about anything else you can think of.

The topic is
a. collecting old hats.
b. flea markets and garage sales.
c. places to shop.

9. Secondhand smoke—smoke from someone else's cigar or cigarette—can cause breathing illnesses and even lung cancer. According to the government, there are at least three ways to avoid the dangers of secondhand smoke. First, don't allow smoking at all in your home. Second, if someone smokes outdoors, it should not be in areas where nonsmokers pass by. Third, in restaurants that allow smoking, ask to be seated as far away from the smoking area as possible.

The topic is
a. smoking.
b. the smoking area in restaurants.
c. secondhand smoke.

10. Many employees steal small items from their workplaces. The most common stolen goods are office supplies. People who would never steal a pen from a supermarket shelf think nothing of taking one home from work. Also, many office workers consider personal use of the office copying machine a benefit of the job. And then there are specialists. One famous story concerns an appliance plant worker. He regularly helped himself to parts from the assembly line. Eventually, he had enough to build his own refrigerator.

The topic is
a. crime.
b. theft by employees.
c. theft of office supplies by employees.

MAIN IDEAS: Test 5

Circle the letter of the topic of each of the following paragraphs. Then find the sentence in which the author states the main idea about the topic, and circle the letter of that sentence.

[1]Businesses leaving the United States do so for various reasons. [2]Lower cost for plants and labor is a major reason. [3]Being purchased by a foreign company is another reason for a business to leave the United States. [4]Some companies feel that the taxes in the United States are too high. [5]Also, a host country might be offering special benefits.

1. The topic is
   a. businesses that leave the United States.
   b. business in the United States.
   c. taxes in different countries.

2. The main idea is stated in sentence
   a. 1.   b. 2.   c. 4.

[1]Gasoline is the most common product made from petroleum. [2]However, about three thousand products other than gasoline are also made from petroleum. [3]Some of the others are bubble gum, crayons, floor polish, and house paint. [4]Eyeglasses and loudspeakers also contain petroleum.

3. The topic is
   a. gasoline.
   b. eyeglasses and loudspeakers.
   c. products other than gasoline made from petroleum.

4. The main idea is stated in sentence
   a. 1.   b. 2.   c. 4.

(Continues on next page)

[1]Motion sickness is caused by mixed messages sent by the eyes and ears to the brain. [2]When a vehicle is moving, the body moves up and down. [3]The eyes usually sense this and send the brain a message that everything is OK. [4]But the ears may not be so sure, and they can send the brain a worry message. [5]The brain relays these messages to the rest of the body. [6]When the messages reach the stomach, sickness results.

5. The topic is
   a. the stomach.
   b. motion sickness.
   c. a moving vehicle.

6. The main idea is stated in sentence
   a. 1.   b. 2.   c. 6.

[1]Toxic chemicals are often found around the house. [2]However, harmful household chemicals can be replaced with safe alternatives. [3]For instance, baking soda can be used in place of harsh oven cleaners and stain removers. [4]Instead of a chemical cleaner, a mixture of vinegar and water can be used to clean windows and glass. [5]Vinegar and salt can remove mildew. [6]And skim milk can be used to polish linoleum floors.

7. The topic is
   a. skim milk.
   b. concern for the environment.
   c. alternatives to harmful household chemicals.

8. The main idea is stated in sentence
   a. 1.   b. 2.   c. 3.

[1]Twenty years ago, most dentists advised patients not to chew gum. [2]It was thought that chewing gum would increase tooth decay. [3]Ten years ago, chewing gum became more accepted by dentists. [4]Today, there is evidence that chewing gum can actually assist in the fight against tooth decay. [5]As a result, more dentists are recommending that their patients chew gum daily. [6]Over the years, then, dentists' advice on chewing gum has changed greatly.

9. The topic is
   a. health.
   b. health advice.
   c. dentists' advice on chewing gum.

10. The main idea is stated in sentence
    a. 1.   b. 2.   c. 6.

MAIN IDEAS: Test 6

Circle the letter of the topic of each of the following paragraphs. Then find the sentence in which the author states the main idea about the topic, and circle the letter of that sentence.

[1]Fairy tales are often thought to be charming, lovely stories for children. [2]Yet the original versions of some familiar fairy tales are shockingly violent. [3]"Cinderella" is the story of a handsome prince who searched for Cinderella with a glass slipper worn by Cinderella at a ball. [4]In the original version, Cinderella's sisters cut off their toes to make the slipper fit. [5]"Little Red Riding Hood" is another familiar fairy tale that has become less shocking. [6]In the original version, a wicked queen sent a hunter to kill Riding Hood and bring back her heart and lungs.

1. The topic is
   a. fairy tales.
   b. original versions of some fairy tales.
   c. "Little Red Riding Hood."

2. The main idea is stated in sentence
   a. 1.   b. 2.   c. 6.

[1]The Environmental Protection Agency (EPA) estimates that American cars use over 200 million gallons of motor oil per year. [2]Only 10 percent of this is recycled. [3]The rest is dumped. [4]It eventually makes its way into streams, rivers, lakes, and oceans. [5]The amount of motor oil dumped is ten times more than the worst oil spill this country has ever known. [6]Recycling the motor oil your car uses, then, is a very good way to help the environment.

3. The topic is
   a. motor oil.
   b. dumped motor oil.
   c. recycling.

4. The main idea is stated in sentence
   a. 1.   b. 2.   c. 6.

[1]The average amount of body fat in individuals differs according to gender and athletic ability. [2]In general, between 15 to 18 percent of men's body weight is fat. [3]In contrast, women have between 23 to 27 percent of their weight as fat. [4]Athletes of both sexes generally have less body fat. [5]Among the best male athletes, less than 10 percent of their total weight is fat. [6]Among women athletes, generally between 12 to 15 percent of their weight is fat.

(Continues on next page)

5. The topic is
   a. body fat.
   b. body fat of athletes.
   c. the best male athletes.

6. The main idea is stated in sentence
   a. 1.   b. 2.   c. 4.

[1]Children who don't read during summer vacation will lose six months of their reading level by September. [2]There are several things parents can do to help children maintain their reading level during summer vacation. [3]First, turn the TV off when it is not being watched. [4]Second, set up a daily reading time for children. [5]Third, be a role model by reading novels, magazines, or newspapers. [6]Leave them around the house so that children will see reading materials around. [7]Fourth, show an interest in what your child is reading by asking questions or by taking turns reading out loud. [8]Also remember that writing and reading go together. [9]Leave notes for your child that require a written response. [10]Buy a notebook for children in which they can record their daily activities and thoughts.

7. The topic is
   a. reading.
   b. helping children maintain their reading level during summer vacation.
   c. being a good role model for reading during summer vacation.

8. The main idea is stated in sentence
   a. 1.   b. 2.   c. 3.

[1]Biologists recently discovered that the common field mouse has a surprisingly complicated social structure. [2]Among California field mice, for instance, males and females stay with each other for as long as they both live. [3]In addition, a chemical produced by the female encourages the male to take care of the young. [4]Finally, older siblings take care of younger ones. [5]When the female gives birth to one litter, she immediately gets pregnant again, and another litter is born soon thereafter. [6]Those born in the first litter take care of the next generation.

9. The topic is
   a. biology.
   b. the common field mouse.
   c. field-mouse siblings.

10. The main idea is stated in sentence
    a. 1.   b. 2.   c. 6.

7

Supporting Details

Chapter 6 introduced you to the most important reading skill—finding the main idea. To master this skill, you must understand another key reading skill—locating supporting details. These details provide the added information that is needed for you to fully comprehend a main idea. In this chapter you will develop your ability to recognize both main ideas *and* their supporting details.

WHAT ARE SUPPORTING DETAILS?

Supporting details are reasons, examples, facts, steps, or other kinds of evidence that develop and support a main idea. The information that details give helps us understand main ideas. For example, look at this main idea from Chapter 6:

Americans love to send greeting cards.

To explain this statement, the author went on to provide evidence—specific details that show the truth of the main idea. Here, again, is the full paragraph:

[1]Americans love to send greeting cards. [2]For instance, over 4 million birthday cards are sent out in this country every day. [3]Around Valentine's Day last year, over 900 million cards were mailed. [4]And close to 3 billion holiday greeting cards were sent out during the Christmas season.

Sentences 2–4 give facts to show that the main idea is true. Those facts are the supporting details of the paragraph.

The group of items below includes a main idea and two supporting details. Remember that the main idea is more general than the supporting details. In the space provided, label each item with one of the following:

MI—for the **main idea**
SD—for a **supporting detail**

Then read the explanation that follows.

_____ a. TV has begun to deal with sex in a more realistic way.

_____ b. Couples on TV now openly discuss topics such as birth control.

_____ c. Bedroom scenes are now being shown in detail on some TV shows.

Explanation:

Sentences *b* and *c* describe specific realistic ways in which sex is dealt with on TV. In contrast, sentence *a* is not specific—it makes the general point that TV has started to deal with sex in a more true-to-life way. Item *a* thus gives the main idea (MI). Items *b* and *c* give examples of that main idea. Each is a specific supporting detail (SD) for the main idea.

➤ Practice 1

Each group of items below includes a main idea and two supporting details. In the space provided, label each item with one of the following:

MI—for the **main idea**
SD—for a **supporting detail**

Group 1

_____ a. Eating buttercups can cause indigestion.

_____ b. If eaten, certain common garden plants can make people ill.

_____ c. Lilies of the valley can cause an irregular heartbeat.

Group 2

_____ a. For twenty years, *Sesame Street* has taught children a great deal.

_____ b. Countless children have learned letters and numbers from *Sesame Street*.

_____ c. The show has also covered such important topics as love, death, and marriage.

Group 3

_____ a. The word *trombone* comes from the French words for "pull" and "push."

_____ b. In Latin, *violin* means "to skip like a calf."

_____ c. The names of many musical instruments come from the way they are played.

Group 4

_____ a. According to experts, new technology will allow people to live longer and healthier lives in the twenty-first century.

_____ b. Specialists predict that the world will be a very different place in the twenty-first century.

_____ c. In the twenty-first century, say experts, new means of transportation will make our jets look old-fashioned.

MAJOR AND MINOR SUPPORTING DETAILS

There are two types of supporting details: major and minor. Major details explain and develop the main idea. In turn, minor details help fill out and make clear the major details. For instance, look at the following main idea.

Main idea:

A recent poll found Americans' four most popular hobbies.

How much do we learn from that general sentence? Not much. If the author named the four hobbies, we would have a better understanding of the general idea. Those four activities would then be the major supporting details of the paragraph. Below is the same main idea with the four major details.

Main idea with major details:

A recent poll found Americans' four most popular hobbies. The number-one hobby enjoyed by Americans is reading. The second most popular hobby is photography. The third most popular hobby is gardening. Finally, the fourth most popular hobby is collecting things.

Now there is some meat on the bare bones of the main idea. The author has provided major details (the four most popular hobbies) to support the main idea. Together, the main idea and the major supporting details form the basic framework of a paragraph.

These major details are often more fully explained, and that's where minor supporting details come in. Major details provide added information about the main idea. In the same way, minor details provide added information about the major details. The paragraph on hobbies can be filled out even more with some minor details, as the paragraph below shows.

Main idea with major and minor details:

A recent poll found Americans' four most popular hobbies. The number-one hobby enjoyed by Americans is reading. Fiction is favored by most, followed by biographies. The second most popular hobby is photography. Americans like taking pictures of just about anything, including family members and wildlife. The third most popular hobby is gardening. Many gardeners enjoy raising vegetables and planting flower gardens. Finally, the fourth most popular hobby is collecting things. Items collected include stamps, the most popular, and beer cans, which rank second.

Just as the major details expanded on the main idea, the minor details have further explained the major details. Now the main idea has even more meaning for us.

PREPARING OUTLINES

One way to see the relationship between a passage's main idea and the details that support it is to prepare an outline. An outline separates the main idea from the major details, and the major details from the minor details.

Here is one way to create an outline: After you read a passage, write down the main idea. Then number and list the major details. If the minor details are important, list them under the major details they support. Give each minor detail a letter—*a, b*, and so on. Using this method, you could outline the paragraph about hobbies as follows:

Main idea: A recent poll found Americans' four most popular hobbies.

Major detail: 1. Reading
Minor details: a. Most popular: fiction
                        b. Second most popular: biographies
Major detail: 2. Photography
Minor details: a. Photos of family members
                        b. Photos of wildlife
Major detail: 3. Gardening
Minor details: a. Raising vegetables
                        b. Planting flower gardens
Major detail: 4. Collecting things
Minor details: a. Most popular: stamps
                        b. Second most popular: beer cans

Now at a glance we can see the relationship between the main idea, the major supporting details, and the minor supporting details. The main idea is the most general idea. Major details are more general than the minor details. For instance, the topic "gardening" is more general than the topic "raising vegetables"—raising vegetables is a specific type of gardening.

Below is a paragraph that contains a main idea, major details, and minor details. The main idea is boldfaced. Read the paragraph and try to determine which ideas are major details and which are minor details. You may find it helpful to mark the major details with a check (✓) or a number (*1, 2, . . .*). Then complete the outline that follows. Finally, read the explanation.

In our busy lives, there are three ways we manage to save time. First, we use modern inventions that help us do more in less time. For instance, we use a microwave oven to cook a baked potato instead of baking it in the oven. Or we grate large amounts of vegetables with a food processor instead of by hand. We also save time by doing more than one thing at a time. For example, a student may finish writing a paper while eating breakfast. Or we may take a shower and brush our teeth at the same time. Finally, of course, we may simply rush. We may save time simply by gulping a meal or running to catch a bus.

Main idea: There are three ways we manage to save time.

Major detail: 1. _____

_____

Minor details: a. _____

_____

b. We grate large amounts of vegetables with a food processor instead of by hand.

Major detail: 2. We do more than one thing at a time.

Minor details: a. _____

_____

b. _____

_____

Major detail: 3. _____

Minor details: a. We may gulp a meal.

b. _____

Explanation:

The main idea of the paragraph is in the first sentence. It is a general idea that is explained and illustrated in the rest of the paragraph.

The major details are the "three ways we manage to save time": 1) "First, we use modern inventions that help us do more in less time," 2) "We also save time by doing more than one thing at a time," and 3) "Finally, of course, we may simply rush."

The minor details are examples of each of the major details. For the first major detail, the minor details are "we use a microwave oven to cook a baked potato instead of baking it in the oven" and "we grate large amounts of vegetables with a food processor instead of by hand."

For the second major detail, the minor details are "a student may finish writing a paper while eating breakfast" and "we may take a shower and brush our teeth at the same time."

The minor details that support the third major detail are "We may gulp a meal" and "We may run to catch a bus."

As you can see, outlining a passage will help you understand and see clearly the relationship between a main idea and its supporting details. Outlines start with a main idea (or a heading that summarizes the main idea). The major details follow. Sometimes there will be a level of minor details as well.

Here are some tips that will help you prepare outlines.

Tips for Outlining: Recognizing Major and Minor Details

1. *Look for opening phrases with list words.* An opening phrase is part of many topic sentences. The opening phrase tells you that a list of major details is coming. For example, a paragraph may begin like this: "Air pollution can be reduced in several ways." The words "several ways" suggest that what follows will be a list of ways to reduce air pollution. Each way will be a major detail.

Here are some typical opening phrases that tell you that a list of major details will follow. Such phrases are often called "list words."

Opening Phrases with List Words

several kinds of	a series of
four causes of	a few reasons for
three characteristics of	two advantages of
two effects	a number of steps involved in
a few causes	

Opening phrases like those in the box provide a good idea of what the major details will be. For example, look again at the first sentence of the paragraph about popular hobbies:

A recent poll found Americans' four most popular hobbies.

Here the opening phrase "four most popular hobbies" suggests that those hobbies will be the major details of the paragraph. That phrase also tells how many major details there will be: "four."

Now look back at the paragraph about saving time (on page 219). Write here the opening phrase that tells us what the major details will be:

_____

The opening phrase in the paragraph about saving time is "three ways we manage to save time." That phrase suggests that the paragraph will list "ways we manage to save time." The phrase also tells us how many major details to watch for: "three."

2. Look for words that introduce major details.   Certain words and phrases often introduce major details. They are called "addition words" because they show that an idea is one of a series—the author is *adding* one or more ideas to another. The addition word *first,* for example, often introduces the first idea in a list of major details. (You will read more about addition words in Chapter 9, on pages 294–295.) Below are some common addition words:

Addition Words

first	first of all	in addition	final
one	also	next	finally
second	another	moreover	last of all
third	furthermore		

In a paragraph that begins,"There are three main causes of heart disease," the major details may be introduced with addition words: "The *first* cause is . . . ," "The *next* leading cause is . . . " and "The *final* cause is . . . "

Now look again at the paragraph about saving time (on page 219), and note the addition words used to introduce the major details. In the second sentence, the word *first* introduces the first major detail.

- Which word introduces the second major supporting detail?

   _____

- Which word introduces the final major supporting detail?

   _____

The second major detail is introduced by the addition word *also*: "We also save time by doing more than one thing at a time." The third major detail is introduced by the addition word *finally*: "Finally, of course, we may simply rush."

3. Look for words that introduce a minor detail. Minor details do not introduce new points—they are intended to make major details more clear. They usually follow a major detail and make it clearer in some way, often by illustrating it. In such cases, the minor details may be introduced by example words. Here are some common example words:

Example Words

for instance	such as	like
for example	including	

Now look yet again at the paragraph about saving time.

- Which words introduce the first minor detail about modern inventions, in the third sentence? _____

- Which words introduce the first minor detail about "doing more than one thing at a time," in the sixth sentence? _____

The minor detail in the third sentence is introduced with the example words *for instance*. The minor detail in the sixth sentence is introduced with the example words *for example*.

➤ Practice 2

Read each passage below, and complete the outline by filling in the missing supporting details. Then answer the questions that follow each outline. The first outline includes only major details. The second includes both major and minor details.

You may find it helpful to mark the major details with a check (✓) or a number (*1, 2, . . .*).

1. While we lack the instincts of animals, humans do share several powerful motives. One is the drive to achieve. This desire is what urges us to set athletic records or to try out for the starring role in a play. Another human motive is the urge to use power. People with a strong power drive may join a campus activity in order to become its leader. The desire to associate with other people is a third powerful motive. This motive moves people to join organizations, work on committees, socialize, and marry.

Main idea: Humans share several powerful motives.

Major detail: 1. _____

Major detail: 2. The urge to use power

Major detail: 3. _____

- Which phrase in the main idea suggests that a list is coming?

  _____

- Which word introduces each of the following:

  The first major detail? _____

  The second major detail? _____

  The last major detail? _____

2. In high school, almost every student belongs to one of three subcultures. One subculture is the delinquent group, the least popular of the subcultures. Members of this group dislike authority figures and hate school in general. The next step up the ladder of popularity is the academic subculture. These students are known for their high regard for education. They also have the reputation of being hard-working. Last of all, the most popular group is the fun subculture. Members of this group are interested in such things as social status and material goods like clothes and cars.

Main idea: In high school, almost every student belongs to one of three subcultures.

Major detail: 1. The least popular: _____

Minor details: a. _____

                b. Hate school in general

Major detail: 2. The next in popularity: the academic subculture

Minor details: a. _____

                b. Known as hard-working

Major detail: 3. _____

Minor details   a. Interested in social status

                b. _____

- Which phrase in the main idea suggests that a list is coming?

  _____

• Which word or words introduces each of the following:

The first major detail? _____

The second major detail? _____

The third major detail? _____

PREPARING MAPS

Students sometimes find it helpful to use maps rather than outlines. A **map** is a diagram that uses shapes such as circles or boxes to show the relationship between the main idea and its supporting details. When a map is used, the main idea is often expressed as a heading, like a newspaper headline, rather than in a complete sentence.

Below, again, is the paragraph on saving time followed by a map of that paragraph. Note that lines connect the major details to the main idea and minor details to the major ones. Fill in the one missing major detail, and then read the explanation.

In our busy lives, there are three ways we manage to save time. First, we use modern inventions that help us do more in less time. For instance, we use a microwave oven to cook a baked potato instead of baking it in the oven. Or we grate large amounts of vegetables with a food processor instead of by hand. We also save time by doing more than one thing at a time. For example, a student may finish writing a paper while eating breakfast. Or we may take a shower and brush our teeth at the same time. Finally, of course, we may simply rush. We may save time simply by gulping a meal or running to catch a bus.

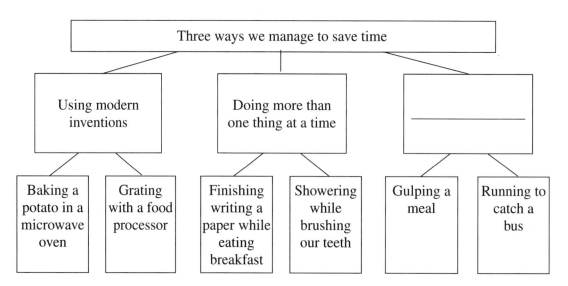

Explanation:

The first two major details are "Using modern inventions" and "Doing more than one thing at a time." You should have filled in "Rushing" for the third major detail. Each major detail is connected to two minor details.

➤ *Practice 3*

A. Fill in the details needed to complete the map of the following passage. The main idea heading is on top.

You may find it helpful to mark major details with a check (✓) or a number (*1, 2, . . .*).

An "official language" is the language used to conduct state business. There are a few especially popular official languages. Spanish, for instance, is the official language in twenty countries throughout the world. A second common official language is French, the official language of twenty-seven countries. The leader is English, which is the official language of forty-four countries.

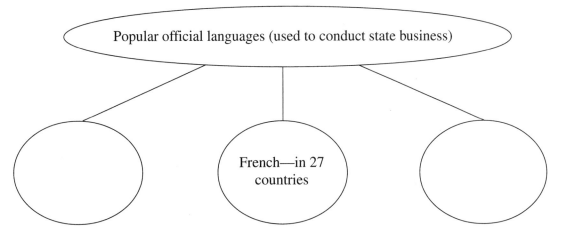

B. After reading the passage, complete the heading of the map below it. Then fill in the details needed to complete the map.

You may find it helpful to mark major details with a check (✓) or a number (*1, 2, . . .*).

Here are a few simple suggestions that study experts recommend you follow in order to do better on tests. First, experts say that slow and steady preparation for exams is best: Focus on new material; however, review once a week. Another helpful method is to arrive early for a test. It's calming to have a few minutes to sit down in the classroom and collect your thoughts. Third, follow successful test-taking strategies. Answer the easier questions first; then go back and tackle the hard ones. Also, for essay tests, make a brief outline before beginning to write.

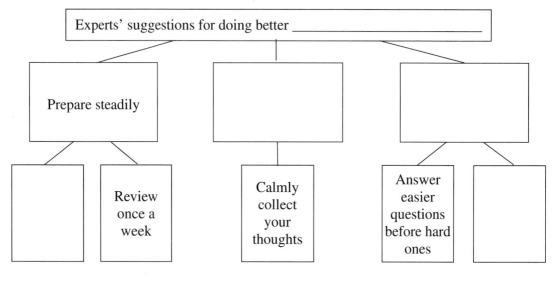

- Which word or words introduce each of the following:

  The first major detail? _____

  The second major detail? _____

  The third major detail? _____

READING CAREFULLY

As you have seen, the major details support the main idea, and the minor details expand on the major ones. Keeping these relationships in mind will make you a more careful reader.

Use the paragraph below to practice applying your knowledge of supporting details. First read the paragraph. Note that the topic sentence is set off in boldface. Then answer the questions that follow—they focus on major and minor details. Finally, read the explanation.

You may find it helpful to mark major details with a check (✓) or a number (*1, 2, . . .*).

[1]Are you stressed? [2]Do you ever feel you need to relax—and fast? [3]**Here are two relaxation methods you can use in just a few minutes.** [4]One method involves slowly inhaling and exhaling. [5]As you inhale, mentally check for stress in the muscle groups in your body: face, neck, shoulders, arms, belly, legs, and feet. [6]As you exhale, relax those muscles

that are tense. [7]A second method uses mental images. [8]First, close your eyes. [9]Then imagine a lovely, relaxing scene, such as the beach. [10]Spend a few minutes noticing every detail of the scene. [11]If you are imagining the beach, for instance, see the water, hear the waves, and feel the warm sun.

1. As the topic sentence suggests, the major details of this paragraph are
   a. breathing methods.
   b. muscle groups.
   c. relaxation methods.

2. The paragraph lists
   a. one major detail.
   b. two major details.
   c. three major details.

3. What are the brief relaxation methods mentioned?
   a. 1) inhaling, 2) exhaling, and 3) images
   b. 1) inhaling and exhaling and 2) using mental images
   c. 1) closing your eyes and 2) imagining a relaxing scene

4. In doing the inhaling-exhaling method, what should you do when exhaling?
   a. Mentally check muscle groups
   b. Relax tense muscles
   c. Imagine a relaxing scene

5. *Fill in the blank*: In using mental images, the first step is to _____

   _____.

Explanations:

1. As clearly stated in the topic sentence, the paragraph lists relaxation methods. So the answer to question 1 is *c.*

2. As indicated by the list words "two relaxation methods," the answer is *b.* The first relaxation method is introduced in sentence 4; it is introduced by the addition word *one.* The second method is introduced in sentence 7; it is signaled by the addition word *second.*

3. The two methods listed (the two major details) are the inhaling-exhaling method and using mental imagery. So the answer to question 3 is *b.*

4. The answer to this question is *b*—when inhaling, one should relax tense muscles. To find the answer to this question, see sentence 6.

5. The answer to question 5 is "close your eyes." For the answer to this question, see sentence 8.

If you missed any of these questions, reread the paragraph and try to see why you were wrong. Then go on to the following practice.

➤ Practice 4

Answer the questions that follow each paragraph. The topic sentence of each paragraph is set off in boldface.

A. Science fiction writer Arthur C. Clarke correctly predicted when a rocket would first go to the moon. **Clarke has also made many interesting predictions that have yet to come true.** One of these predictions is that we'll have cars without wheels. He feels cars will be made that can float on air instead of rolling on the ground. He has also predicted that there will be settlements on the moon. They will exist under air-conditioned domes, where food will be grown. Materials for the buildings in these settlements will be mined from the moon itself, he says.

1. The main idea suggests that this paragraph will list certain
   a. writings.
   b. times.
   c. predictions.

2. The major details of this paragraph are
   a. 1) predictions, 2) cars, and 3) settlements on the moon.
   b. 1) cars without wheels and 2) settlements on the moon.
   c. 1) food grown under domes and 2) building materials mined on the moon.

3. The first major detail is introduced by the *addition* word
   a. *one.*
   b. *these.*
   c. *also.*

4. *Fill in the blank*: Clarke feels cars will one day move by _____

   _____.

5. *Fill in the blank*: Clarke predicts that people will live on the moon under

   _____.

B.   Prescription drugs can be just as dangerous as illegal drugs if used carelessly. **Several guidelines can help consumers avoid the dangers of prescribed drugs.** One guideline is for patients to become aware of a drug's possible side effects. Unexpected side effects, such as dizziness, can be frightening and even dangerous. Second, the patient should find out if it is safe to take the medicine along with other drugs he or she is using. Some combinations of drugs can be deadly. Finally, people should always store a medicine in its own labeled bottle. Accidental mix-ups of drugs can have tragic results.

6. As the topic sentence suggests, this paragraph lists
    a. various prescription drugs.
    b. guidelines for avoiding the dangers of prescription drugs.
    c. side effects of prescription drugs.

7. *Fill in the blank:* The first major detail is signaled by the addition word

    _____.

8. *Fill in the blank:* The second major detail is signaled by the addition word

    _____.

9. *Fill in the blank:* The third major detail is signaled by the addition word

    _____.

10. Circle the letter of the best outline of the paragraph.

     A. Dangers of prescribed drugs
        1. Frightening and dangerous side effects
        2. Dizziness can be frightening and dangerous
        3. Tragic results of accidental mix-ups of drugs.

     B. Guidelines that can help consumers avoid the dangers of prescription drugs
        1. Become aware of a drug's possible side effects.
        2. Find out if it is safe to take the medicine with other drugs being used.
        3. Store medicine in its own labeled bottle.

     C. Prescription drugs
        1. Dangerous drugs
        2. Side effects
        3. Combinations

CHAPTER SUMMARY

In this chapter, you learned the following:

- Supporting details are ideas that develop and support a main idea.

- There are two types of supporting details: major and minor.

  —Major details are the chief points that support a main idea. Major details are often introduced by a phrase telling you that a list of major details will follow.

  —Minor details are facts, examples, or reasons that explain the major details.

- Outlines and maps can help you to organize what you have read.

- Reading carefully—watching for main ideas and their major and minor supporting details—will help you concentrate on and master the materials you are reading.

➤ *Review Test 1*

To review what you learned in this chapter, answer each of the following questions. Fill in the blank or circle the correct answer.

1. _____ TRUE OR FALSE? Major supporting details are more general than minor supporting details.

2. Opening phrases can tell us
   a. that a list of some type will follow.
   b. how many major details will follow.
   c. both of the above.

3. An addition word can tell us
   a. how many major details to expect.
   b. that a new major detail is being introduced.
   c. both of the above.

4. A diagram that uses shapes such as circles to organize material is called a

   _____.

5. Label each part of the outline form on the next page with one of the following:
   - Main idea
   - Major supporting detail
   - Minor supporting detail

1. _____

    a. _____

    b. _____

2. _____

    a. _____

    b. _____

➤ Review Test 2

A. (1–6.) Each group of items below includes a main idea and two major supporting details. In the space provided, label each item with one of the following:

        MI—for the **main idea**
        SD—for a **supporting detail**

Group 1

_____ a. Nurses walk the most, over five miles a day.

_____ b. One study found that occupations influence how much people walk.

_____ c. Dentists walk the least, under one mile each day.

Group 2

_____ a. Not sleeping on the back keeps some people from snoring.

_____ b. Wearing a chin strap that holds the mouth shut helps others.

_____ c. Various types of remedies have been developed for snoring.

B. (7–10.) Complete the outline of the following passage by filling in the missing major and minor details. Note that addition words signal the major details.

You may find it helpful to mark major details with a check (✓) or a number (*1, 2, . . .*).

Good speakers "talk" with their bodies in several ways. First, they use eye contact. Looking directly into people's eyes helps speakers build a warm bond with the audience. Eye contact can also tell speakers whether or not they are keeping the audience's interest. Facial expressions are another way speakers use their bodies. Shaking one's head can show dislike for an idea. A nod and a smile can show acceptance of a concept.

Finally, good speakers can use hand movements to accent what is being said. Upraised hands can show a positive emphasis to one's words. And a clenched fist can demonstrate anger.

Main idea: Good speakers "talk" with their bodies in several ways.

1. _____

   a. Looking directly into people's eyes helps speakers build a warm bond with the audience.

   b. Eye contact tells speakers if they are keeping the audience's interest.

2. They use facial expressions.

   a. Head shaking can show dislike for an idea.

   b. _____

     _____

3. _____

   _____

   a. _____

     _____

   b. A clenched fist can demonstrate anger toward something.

➤ Review Test 3

A. (1–5.) Complete the main idea heading. Then fill in the supporting details needed to complete a map of the following passage. Finally, answer the question that follows.

The topic sentence of the paragraph is set off in boldface.

More than two thousand human-made satellites orbit the earth. **There are various types of these human-made satellites, each with its own function.** One type is weather satellites. They are positioned around the globe to gather information for weather prediction. Another is spy satellites. Their function is to gather intelligence information. Astronomy satellites are a third type of satellite. Astronomy satellites gather information from deep space. The fourth type is communications satellites, which transmit television shows and telephone conversations.

Kinds and functions of _____

Weather satellites gather information for weather prediction.			

5. In the paragraph above, the major details are introduced by the addition words
   a. *two thousand, several, which.*
   b. *one, another, third, fourth.*
   c. *first, second, next, last.*

B. Answer the questions that follow the paragraph below. The topic sentence of the paragraph is set off in boldface.

> **In addition to fresh vegetables, gardening offers several health benefits**. One study found that gardeners have fewer heart attacks than others. The reasons seem to be that being around plants lowers blood pressure and helps people better resist stress. Another benefit of gardening is harder bones. For women, who are at risk of weak bones, this benefit is especially important. Experts feel that work such as pushing a wheelbarrow or lugging bags of manure slows bone loss. A third benefit of gardening is that it provides safe exercise.

6. In general, the major details of the paragraph are
   a. fresh vegetables.
   b. health benefits of gardening.
   c. reasons that gardeners have fewer heart attacks.

7. Which addition word introduces the first major detail? _____

8. Which addition word introduces the last major detail? _____

9. Specifically, the major details of this paragraph are
   a. 1) blood pressure and 2) resistance to stress.
   b. 1) the pleasures of fresh vegetables and 2) health benefits.
   c. 1) fewer heart attacks, 2) harder bones, and 3) safe exercise.

10. Experts feel that bones benefit from
   a. fewer heart attacks.
   b. low blood pressure.
   c. certain work.

➤ *Review Test 4*

Here is a chance to apply your understanding of supporting details to a textbook selection. Things that we do in life often involve right ways and wrong ways. As this informative selection from *The Human Side of Organizations,* by Michael W. Drafke and Stan Kossen (Addison-Wesley, 1998) tells us, there is a right way to conduct business during a meal. As you read, think about how these rules might help you with your career. To help you continue to strengthen your skills, the reading is followed by questions on what you've learned in this and previous chapters.

Words to Watch

Following are some words in the reading that do not have strong context support. Each word is followed by the number of the paragraph in which it appears and its meaning there. These words are indicated in the reading by a small circle (°).

> *graze* (4): feed
> *utensils* (4): tools, in this case those used for eating
> *vertically* (5): upright
> *bass fiddle* (5): a large musical string instrument that produces low tones
> *diagonally* (5): slanted; not at right angles
> *discreet* (6): wise; careful
> *gratuity* (6): tip
> *standing account* (6): an account that remains in force indefinitely, so one does not need to pay every time a transaction takes place
> *pretentious* (7): showy

BUSINESS DINING

Michael W. Drafke and Stan Kossen

1   In some industries and professions, business is conducted during meals. For the unprepared, this can be a tense affair. Variations occur, depending on the situation and location, but we will at least cover the basics here. Some general rules of etiquette will be discussed along with rules for ordering, eating and drinking, host and guest rules, and manners.

2   The first general rule of business dining is to remember that the food is not the central issue. The whole purpose for the business lunch is business. Second, business is properly discussed after everyone has placed an order. Don't appear overeager and begin talking shop until everyone has had a chance to look at the menu and order. Otherwise, you delay the meal,

and the pause after ordering is a natural time to change the subject to business. When you start to discuss business, do not speak so loudly that those at other tables hear you.

3   Ordering a business lunch or dinner has a set of rules all its own. To indicate that you are ready to order, close your menu and place it on the table. Because the main reason for the meal is to conduct business, order foods that will not interfere with the discussion and will be easy to eat. Do not order foods such as lobster, clams in the shells, or corn on the cob. Furthermore, guests should not order the most expensive item on the menu unless invited to do so by the host. Guests should also not order a first course unless others do. Because alcoholic drinks are often not a part of a business lunch, guests should wait to see what the host does, and if alcohol is ordered, it should be consumed in moderation (one, maybe two drinks). You should not drink at all, however, if you are trying to close a sale or deal.

4   Once the food begins to arrive, the trouble really begins for some people. First, if it is a buffet lunch, do not pile your plate high with food. Remember: the real purpose is to conduct business, not graze° like cattle. Buffet or not, the next step is to decide which silverware to use. The first major point here is to use silverware for virtually everything, even french fries and chicken. Next, in general, start using the utensils° on the outsides of the setting first. For example, if there is a salad with the meal, the salad fork is typically the leftmost utensil. If you drop a piece of silverware, leave it on the floor and quietly ask the waiter for a replacement.

5   Once you have the correct utensil, remember the basic rules. With soup move the spoon away from you while in the bowl and then toward you to eat the soup, eating silently from the side of the spoon. When cutting foods, hold the fork in your left hand at a forty-five-degree angle from the plate, cutting one or two pieces of food at a time. Do not hold the fork vertically° in your fist and saw your food as if playing the bass fiddle°. After cutting, there are two acceptable methods for bringing the food to your mouth. The more common method in the United States is to set the knife down (placing it across the top of the plate), switching the fork from the left hand to the right, and bringing the food to the mouth with the right hand. The fork must then be switched back to the left hand for additional cutting. The other method is to leave the fork in the left hand and bring the food to the mouth with it after cutting. Not everything is cut, however. Do not cut bread or rolls; instead, break off a piece, butter it if you wish, and eat it. To signal that you are finished eating, place your knife and fork diagonally° across the plate, and if coffee is served do not blow on it, simply let it sit until cool enough to drink.

6   There are rules of etiquette for both host and guest during business dining, starting with who pays. In general, the person issuing the invitation to lunch or dinner (or even

breakfast) pays the bill. During the ordering, the host should tell the wait staff to "allow my guest to order first." This also signals to the wait staff that you are the one to receive the bill. An even more discreet° method is for a host to arrive early enough to sign an open charge slip, instructing the staff to add a gratuity° (possibly even 20 percent in this case). With this method, when the meal and business are complete, the entire payment scene is avoided and you have given the impression of being important enough to have some type of standing account° with the establishment. Another subtle signal a host can provide is to mention items that "look good" on the menu. This gives the guest an indication of what the host is considering and a price range that is comfortable to all.

As a guest, etiquette calls for you not to order a first course or a dessert unless others do and to wait to eat until the host begins.

Finally, some general guidelines   7 for good manners. Do not place your elbows on the table while you eat. Say please and thank you often. Do not eat until everyone at your table has been served. If you must leave during a meal, place your napkin on your chair. Because it makes people uncomfortable, do not send food back unless it is completely unfit to eat. To send something back runs the risk of making you look pretentious° or insulting to your host. If the occasion arises for you to reciprocate with an invitation, you must do so at a restaurant of similar quality.

Word Skills Questions

Phonics

1. The word *basic* in the sentence below has
   a. a long **a** sound and is broken into syllables like this: ba-sic.
   b. a short **a** sound and is broken into syllables like this: bas-ic.

   " . . . remember the basic rules." (Paragraph 5)

Dictionary Use

Use the following entry to answer question 2.

et•i•quette (ĕt′ĭ-kĕt) *n.* The practices and forms prescribed by social convention or by authority.

2. Which of the following statements about the above entry word is correct?
   a. *Etiquette* has two syllables and two accent marks.
   b. *Etiquette* has three syllables and three long vowel sounds.
   c. *Etiquette* has three syllables and three short vowel sounds.

Vocabulary in Context

3. In the sentences below, the word *conducted* means
   - a. carried on.
   - b. remembered.
   - c. believed.
   - d. skipped.

   "In some industries and professions, business is conducted during meals. . . . The whole purpose for the business lunch is business." (Paragraphs 1–2)

4. In the sentence below, the words *talking shop* mean
   - a. eating.
   - b. talking too much.
   - c. discussing business.
   - d. discussing shopping.

   "Don't appear overeager and begin talking shop until everyone has had a chance to look at the menu and order . . . ." (Paragraph 2)

5. In the sentence below, the word *reciprocate* means
   - a. refuse.
   - b. miss.
   - c. leave a meal.
   - d. return the favor.

   "If the occasion arises for you to reciprocate with an invitation, you must do so at a restaurant of similar quality." (Paragraph 7)

Reading Comprehension Questions

Central Point and Main Ideas

6. Which sentence best expresses the central point of the selection?
   - a. There are important rules to follow when conducting business during meals.
   - b. Food is not the central issue during business dining.
   - c. There are important rules to follow when conducting business.
   - d. There are certain ways to use silverware during a business lunch.

7. The main idea of paragraph 3 is stated in its
   - a. first sentence.
   - b. second sentence.
   - c. next-to-last sentence.
   - d. last sentence.

Supporting Details

8. According to the author, at a business meal where there is a buffet,
   - a. silverware is not needed to eat all foods.
   - b. it is best to pile your plate full of food.
   - c. you should let the host go first.
   - d. you should not put too much food on your plate.

9. In general, the person who issues the invitation to a business meal
   a. orders first.
   b. is the one who pays.
   c. always expects an invitation to the next business meal.
   d. never orders dessert.

10. According to the selection, if you must leave during a meal, you should
    a. pay for your meal.
    b. place your napkin on your chair.
    c. say please and thank you.
    d. send your food back.

Discussion Questions

1. The author suggests that business people expect a certain type of behavior during business dining. Why is this important? Shouldn't we be accepted just as we are?

2. Should the rules of dining described in the reading be followed during meals with friends and family? Why or why not?

3. The author says that the person issuing an invitation to a business meal should instruct "the staff to add a gratuity (possibly even 20 percent in this case)." Tipping is generally expected in the United States, but in some countries, tipping is frowned upon. Do you think people should be tipped for the job they do? Why or why not?

Note: Writing assignments for this selection appear on page 543.

Check Your Performance			**SUPPORTING DETAILS**
Activity	*Number Right*	*Points*	*Score*
Review Test 1 (5 items)	_____	× 2 =	_____
Review Test 2 (10 items)	_____	× 3 =	_____
Review Test 3 (10 items)	_____	× 3 =	_____
Review Test 4 (10 items)	_____	× 3 =	_____
		TOTAL SCORE =	_____%

Enter your total score into the **Reading Performance Chart: Review Tests** on the inside back cover.

SUPPORTING DETAILS: Test 1

A. (1–6.) Each group of items below includes a main idea and two major supporting details. In the space provided, label each item with one of the following:

> **MI**—for the **main idea**
> **SD**—for a **supporting detail**

Group 1

_____ a. Staying in the sun too long can cause sunstroke.

_____ b. People develop skin cancer after years of working on their tans.

_____ c. Spending time in the sun can be dangerous.

Group 2

_____ a. There are far more deaths in automobile accidents than in airplane accidents.

_____ b. The fear of flying is not based in reality.

_____ c. Six times as many people die in train wrecks as in commercial airline crashes.

(Continues on next page)

B. (7–10.) In the spaces provided, complete the outline of the paragraph by filling in the two missing major details. Then answer the questions that follow the outline.

> Many people continue to work after "retiring." There are two main reasons many senior citizens continue to work. The first reason, of course, is for the money. Many senior citizens need to add to what they receive from Social Security and pensions. According to one survey, 32 percent of older workers fall into this category. The second reason many senior citizens continue to work is because they like to. A retired mechanic, for instance, loves his $4.75-an-hour job at a fast-food restaurant. And a teacher who had always wanted to be a doctor went into medicine after "retirement," as a nurse.

Main idea heading: Two main reasons why many senior citizens continue to work

1. _____

2. _____

9. Which addition word introduces the first major detail?

   _____

10. Which addition word introduces the second major detail?

   _____

SUPPORTING DETAILS: Test 2

A. (1–6.) Each group of items below includes a main idea and two major supporting details. In the space provided, label each item with one of the following:

> **MI**—for the **main idea**
> **SD**—for a **supporting detail**

Group 1

_____ a. Each year there are over 40,000 new books of various kinds published in the United States.

_____ b. The most popular field is sociology, which accounts for over 5,000 titles.

_____ c. Juvenile books are second, with over 4,500 new titles.

Group 2

_____ a. To make sure your application is easy to read, use a pen and print or write clearly.

_____ b. Come prepared to fill out the details of your educational and employment backgrounds.

_____ c. There are a few things to remember when filling out a job application.

(Continues on next page)

B. (7–10.) Fill in the major details needed to complete the map of the paragraph below. Then answer the question that follows the map.

We all know that pets can be fun. However, pets can also be good for our mental health. Studies show that a dog or cat creates a more relaxed home environment which can help to end family arguments. In addition, pets often serve as an emotional outlet for older men. The men share thoughts and feelings with the pets that they don't share with the rest of the family. Pets also ease life's stressful events, including the death of a loved one. It has even been proved that pets increase older people's will to live.

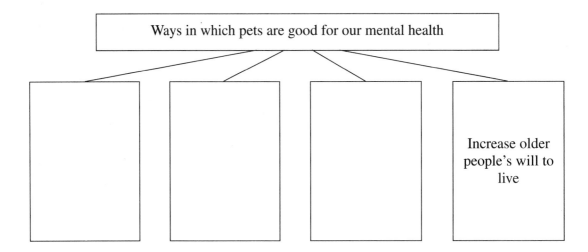

Ways in which pets are good for our mental health

Increase older people's will to live

10. *Fill in the blank:* One of the two addition words or phrases used to introduce major details is _____.

SUPPORTING DETAILS: Test 3

A. (1–4.) Fill in the major details needed to complete a map of the following passage. The main idea heading is on top.

A respectful parent guides and instructs more than he or she punishes. To be a respectful parent, there are several don'ts you should remember. First, don't yell a lot at children. Yelling will tell a child that the parent is out of control. Or it will result in a shouting match that causes a loss of respect. Second, don't make too many rules. Growing up is not boot camp. Too many rules will prevent children from understanding what is really important. Third, don't show disrespect to a child. This will create resentment. Fourth, don't order children around. They will not learn responsibility if they feel they have to do what you want at the instant you command it. Finally, don't neglect to acknowledge good behavior. Praise and hugs work wonders in promoting responsibility and respect.

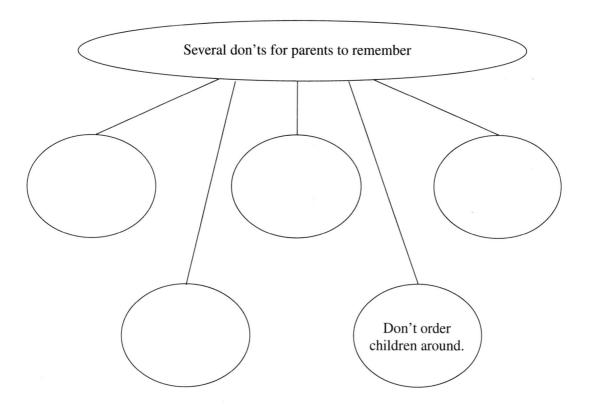

(Continues on next page)

B. (5–10.) Complete the outline of the following paragraph by filling in the missing major and minor details.

> Certain kinds of behavior by employees are likely to lead to dismissal. First is dishonesty. For example, if a boss thinks an employee is lying, that employee is not likely to be on the job long. Similarly, if a worker is believed to be stealing, he or she may not last long. A second type of unacceptable behavior is irresponsibility. For instance, most bosses dislike workers' taking too many breaks. Just as bad is an employee doing personal business during the workday. Finally, a poor attendance record can lead to dismissal. Employees cannot afford to be absent frequently. And on some jobs, an employee who is even fifteen minutes late will have some serious explaining to do.

Main idea heading: Certain kinds of behavior by employees likely to lead to dismissal

1. _____

    a. Lying

    b. _____

2. _____

    a. _____

    b. Doing personal business during the workday

3. Poor attendance

    a. _____

    b. _____

SUPPORTING DETAILS: Test 4

A. (1–5.) Complete the map of the following paragraph. First complete the main idea heading at the top, and then fill in the four major details.

Heart disease is the number one killer of Americans. The American Heart Association has identified the major causes of heart disease. Up until recently, it had listed three factors. Smoking was the number one cause. It was closely followed by high blood levels of cholesterol. The next most common cause of heart disease was high blood pressure. Recently a fourth cause was identified. Inactivity was added because evidence showed that people need to move to keep the heart stimulated.

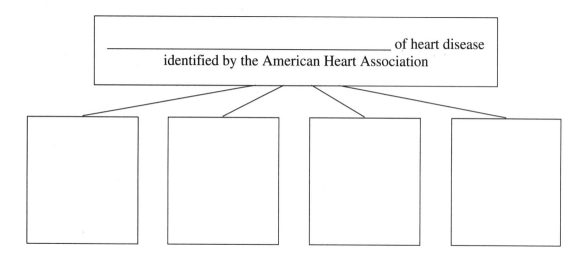

_____ of heart disease
identified by the American Heart Association

(Continues on next page)

B. (6–10.) Complete the outline of the following paragraph by filling in the missing major and minor details.

> Storytelling can be a good way to calm down a restless child. Here are some tips on how to keep a child interested in a story you are telling. First, use a fitting beginning. If the story is imaginary, you might start with "Once upon a time . . . ." If the story is true, you might begin with "Many years ago . . ." or "Before you were born . . . ." Second, have a setting for your story. For a fictional story, a phrase such as "in the forest" gives children a useful frame of reference. For a nonfiction story, even something like "at a mini-mart outside of town" gives children a frame of reference. Third, try to encourage the imagination by appealing to different senses. Describe how things look. For instance, you might mention colors that characters are wearing. Or imitate the sounds of parts of your story—for instance, a train whistle or a birdcall. When appropriate, also include descriptions of how things smelled and felt. Finally, don't worry if the child seems to be daydreaming as you tell the story—he or she may be imagining the story as you speak.

Main idea: Here are some tips on how to keep a child interested in a story you are telling.

1. Use a fitting beginning.

    a. _____

    _____

    b. If the story is true, begin with "Many years ago . . . " or "Before you were born . . . "

2. _____

    a. For a fictional story, a phrase such as "in the forest" gives children a useful frame of reference.

    b. _____

    _____

3. _____

    a. _____

    b. Imitate the sounds of parts of your story.

    c. When appropriate, also include descriptions of how things smelled and felt.

4. Don't worry if the child seems to be daydreaming as you tell the story—he or she may be imagining the story as you speak.

SUPPORTING DETAILS: Test 5

Read each paragraph below and then answer the questions that follow it. To help you focus on the details of each paragraph, the topic sentences have been boldfaced.

A. [1]**Parts of our environment affect the way we behave and feel.** [2]First, there is temperature. [3]Most of us prefer temperatures in the 70s. [4]When it is hotter than the 70s, we become less active and less alert. [5]Lighting also affects us. [6]In the classroom or on the job, bright light encourages work. [7]In contrast, the low lighting of a restaurant relaxes us and encourages informal conversation. [8]Last is color. [9]For example, red is felt as exciting, blue as calming, and yellow as cheerful.

1. As the topic sentence suggests, the major details of this paragraph are
   a. various temperatures.
   b. places where we work and relax.
   c. parts of our environment that affect our behavior and moods.

2. Specifically, the major details of this paragraph are
   a. cool, hot, and just-right temperatures.
   b. the classroom, the job, and the restaurant.
   c. temperature, lighting, and color.

3. The addition words that introduce the major details are
   a. *first, also,* and *last.*
   b. *most, when,* and *and.*
   c. *in contrast, for example,* and *as.*

4. According to the paragraph, most people become less alert
   a. in bright light.
   b. in temperatures over the 70s.
   c. in restaurants with low lighting.

5. The last sentence of the paragraph provides
   a. a major detail.
   b. minor details.
   c. both major and minor details.

(Continues on next page)

B.   [1]**Intelligence includes several basic mental abilities.** [2]One is language skill. [3]People strong in this ability do well on reading tests and have large vocabularies. [4]Another such ability is a quick memory. [5]People talented in this skill may learn the words to a popular song after hearing it only once or twice. [6]A third basic mental skill allows us to make sense of visual information. [7]People strong in this ability can quickly see similarities and differences between designs and pictures.

6. The major details of this paragraph are types of
   a. mental abilities.
   b. language abilities.
   c. similarities and differences.

7. *Fill in the blank:* The addition words that introduce the major details are

   one, another, and _____.

8. Circle the letter of the best outline of the paragraph.

   A. Intelligence
      1. Doing well on reading tests
      2. Having a large vocabulary
      3. Quickly learning the words to a popular song
      4. Seeing similarities and differences between designs and pictures

   B. Some basic mental abilities that make up intelligence
      1. Language skill
      2. A quick memory
      3. The ability to make sense of visual information

9. According to the paragraph, learning the words to a popular song quickly shows a strong
   a. language ability.
   b. memorizing ability.
   c. visual ability.

10. According to the paragraph, seeing quickly how designs and pictures are alike shows a strong
   a. language ability.
   b. memorizing ability.
   c. visual ability.

SUPPORTING DETAILS: Test 6

Read each paragraph below and then answer the questions that follow it. To help you focus on the details of each paragraph, the topic sentences have been boldfaced.

A. [1]**There are different ways to handle embarrassing moments.** [2]One way is to reduce the significance of the embarrassing moment. [3]For instance, if you don't make a big deal about spilling your coffee, other people probably won't. [4]Another way is to disown your behavior. [5]After the embarrassing moment, say something like "That's not the real me, you know." [6]And a third way to handle an embarrassing moment is to get help. [7]For example, if you spill food at a restaurant, don't try to clean it up yourself. [8]Have a friend or a waiter help you to clean up the mess.

1. The major supporting details for this paragraph are
   a. 1) embarrassing moments, 2) disowning yourself, and 3) spilling food at a restaurant.
   b. 1) reduce the significance of the event, 2) disown your behavior, and 3) get help.
   c. 1) don't make a big deal out of spilling your coffee; 2) say, "That's not the real me, you know"; and 3) let somebody else clean up a spill at a restaurant.

2. What word or words introduce the first major detail?
   a. *One*
   b. *For instance*
   c. *Another*

3. What word or words introduce the last major detail?
   a. *Another*
   b. *Third*
   c. *For example*

4. Sentence 3 provides a
   a. major detail.
   b. minor detail.

5. Sentence 4 provides a
   a. major detail.
   b. minor detail.

(Continues on next page)

B. ¹**The National Board of Medical Examiners recently released a number of alarming facts about doctors.** ²First, the amount of time doctors spend examining patients is down dramatically from previous years. ³Twenty years ago, doctors spent eleven minutes with patients. ⁴Today they take only seven minutes. ⁵Second, it was found that a large number of patients have been switching doctors. ⁶Within the past year, for instance, 25 percent of patients reported changing doctors. ⁷The most common reason given was that patients did not feel comfortable with the doctor they left. ⁸Finally, medical students' reasons for wanting to become a doctor were unexpected. ⁹The most common reason given was to make a good living. ¹⁰Working with people ranked third.

6. The opening phrase that describes the major supporting details is
   a. "The National Board of Medical Examiners."
   b. "a number of alarming facts about doctors."
   c. "the amount of time doctors spend examining patients."

7. The first major supporting detail is signaled by the word or words
   a. *a number of.*   b. *only.*   c. *first.*

8. The second major detail is introduced in sentence
   a. 3.   b. 5.   c. 6.

9. The third major detail is introduced in sentence
   a. 7.   b. 8.   c. 9.

10. Circle the letter of the outline that best reflects the paragraph.

    A. Main idea: The National Board of Medical Examiners recently released a number of alarming facts about doctors.
       1. Twenty years ago, doctors spent eleven minutes examining patients.
       2. Today, on the average, doctors spend seven minutes examining patients.
       3. Within the past year, 25 percent of patients reported changing doctors, in most cases because of discomfort with the doctor.
       4. The reasons medical students give for wanting to become a doctor were unexpected.

    B. Main idea: The National Board of Medical Examiners recently released a number of alarming facts about doctors.
       1. Doctors today spend less time examining patients than they did twenty years ago.
       2. A large number of patients have been switching doctors.
       3. Medical students rank making a good living as a more important reason to become a doctor than working with people.

8

Finding Main Ideas

Most of the topic sentences you have seen so far have been located in the first or second sentence of the paragraph. But the topic sentence may be located anywhere within a paragraph. And some paragraphs do not even have a topic sentence; in such cases, you have to figure out the main idea. This chapter describes common locations of topic sentences. It then provides practice in finding the topic sentence in a series of paragraphs. It also provides practice in finding unstated main ideas. By the end of the chapter, you should have a solid sense of how to find main ideas.

As you work through this chapter, keep in mind that a main idea is a general statement that covers most or all of the material in a paragraph.

TOPIC SENTENCE AT THE BEGINNING OF A PARAGRAPH

Topic Sentence
Supporting Detail
Supporting Detail
Supporting Detail
Supporting Detail

Authors often begin a paragraph with the main idea. The rest of the paragraph then supports the main idea with details. Here is an example, with the topic sentence boldfaced:

> **My desk is well organized.** I keep pencils and pens in the top left drawer. Typing and writing paper are in the middle left drawer. The bottom left side has all the other supplies I might need, from paper clips to staples.

The top of the desk is clear, except for a study light and a blotter. The right side of the desk has two drawers. The bottom one is a file drawer, where I keep my notes for each class. And in the top drawer? That's where I keep the nuts, raisins, and M&M's that I snack on while I work.

Explanation:

This paragraph follows a very common pattern: The first sentence is a general statement. The rest of the paragraph supports the general statement. The main idea—that the writer's desk is well organized—is in the first sentence. The rest of the sentences provide specific supporting details. They show us just how well organized the desk is.

TOPIC SENTENCE WITHIN A PARAGRAPH

Introductory Detail
Introductory Detail
Topic Sentence
Supporting Detail
Supporting Detail

When the topic sentence is within a paragraph, it often follows one or more introductory sentences. Those opening sentences lead up in some way to the main idea. They may introduce the topic of the paragraph, catch the reader's interest, relate the main idea to a previous paragraph, give background for the main idea, or ask a question. Below is an example of a paragraph with a topic sentence that is not first or last. See if you can find it. Write its number in the blank space. Then read the explanation.

[1]Do you know what to do if you have trouble sleeping? [2]In many cases, sleep problems can be avoided by following a few simple guidelines. [3]First, don't drink alcoholic beverages or drinks with caffeine close to bedtime. [4]Next, do not exercise within three hours of bedtime. [5]Finally, plan a sleep routine. [6]Every day, go to bed at the same time and get up at the same time.

Topic sentence: _____

Explanation:

The first sentence introduces the topic of sleep problems by asking a question. A question can never be a topic sentence. It is only asking something—it isn't making a statement. The second sentence states the author's main idea about that topic—that sleep problems can often be avoided by following a few simple guidelines. The rest of the paragraph lists the specific guidelines referred to only generally in the topic sentence.

A topic sentence within a paragraph is often the second sentence, as in the example above. But the topic sentence may come even later than the second sentence. See if you can find the topic sentence in the following paragraph. Then write its number in the space provided. Finally, read the explanation that follows.

> [1]Today we take worldwide communications for granted. [2]Through TV and radio, we learn almost instantly what happens throughout the world. [3]In Roman times, however, military leaders relied on a nonelectronic method to send important messages back to headquarters—pigeons. [4]Homing pigeons have a strong instinct to return home from just about anywhere. [5]The birds were kept in cages at the military camps. [6]When a message had to be sent, a soldier strapped it to the bird's leg. [7]The bird was then released, and it flew home, delivering the message.

Topic sentence: _____

Explanation:

At first, we might think sentence 1 states the main idea, since it is a general sentence that is supported by the point in sentence 2. But notice what happens in sentence 3. This sentence, also a general idea, takes the reader in a different direction (as shown by the signal word *however*). This sentence is then supported by details in sentences 4–7. Now it becomes clear that the first two sentences are leading up to the true main idea of the paragraph, stated in sentence 3. This is clear because sentences 4–7 all give specific details that explain the method referred to generally in sentence 3.

TOPIC SENTENCE AT THE END OF A PARAGRAPH

Supporting Detail
Supporting Detail
Supporting Detail
Supporting Detail
Topic Sentence

When the topic sentence ends a paragraph, the previous sentences build up to the main idea. Here is an example of a paragraph in which the topic sentence comes last. Read the paragraph and the explanation that follows.

[1]A recent study found that over 80 percent of mountain bikers reported being injured at least once. [2]Twenty-five percent needed to see a doctor. [3]In contrast, 50 percent of on-road, or street, bikers reported an injury, with 33 percent needing medical attention. [4]The study therefore concluded that while mountain bikers have more injuries, street bikers have more severe injuries.

Explanation:

When a topic sentence ends a paragraph, it often acts as a summary of the points made in the paragraph or as a conclusion, where all of the points lead up to a final, general point. In the paragraph above, sentences 1–3 provide information about different types of injuries to two kinds of bikers—mountain bikers and street bikers. The last sentence is a general conclusion that is supported by all the specific information that comes before it.

A topic sentence that is last in a paragraph may be signaled by words such as these: *in summary, to sum up, to conclude, concluded, in conclusion, thus, therefore, clearly,* and *obviously.*

➤ *Practice 1*

The topic sentence is in different locations in the following five paragraphs. Identify each topic sentence by filling in the correct sentence number in the blank space.

To find each topic sentence, do the following:

    a Identify the topic of the paragraph by asking yourself, "Who or what is the paragraph about?"

    b Find the general statement that tells you the author's main point about the topic.

    c Test your answer by asking yourself, "Is this general statement supported by all or most of the material in the paragraph?"

1. [1]Wood was once the only material used in a home's framework. [2]However, some homebuilders now have good reasons for using steel in constructing house frames. [3]First, wood is not always available. [4]Also, the cost of steel is often 20 percent less than that of wood. [5]Furthermore, unlike wood, steel is termite-proof. [6]Steel will not shrink, warp, or split. [7]Steel will not catch on fire, as wood will. [8]And steel is stronger and more durable than wood.

Topic sentence: _____

2. [1]Highway maintenance workers must be prepared to clean up just about any mess you can think of. [2]Once, twenty thousand gallons of molasses leaked from a tanker truck. [3]Highway workers spent hours scraping up the gooey mess. [4]Another time, a load of live chickens escaped from an overturned truck. [5]Workers ran all over trying to catch the birds. [6]Some escaped and are still living in bushes near the accident site. [7]One highway crew had to stop traffic to pick up a safe that someone had dropped. [8]A highway crew in California reported that in one month they picked up fifty mattresses, twenty ladders, fifteen chairs, ten refrigerators, and three bathtubs.

Topic sentence: _____

3. [1]There are at least eighty known spellings for Shakespeare's name. [2]Shakespeare himself spelled his name at least six different ways, including "Shakspere" and "Shakspeare." [3]In one legal document, he spelled his name two different ways. [4]He may never have spelled his name "Shakespeare." [5]While in previous centuries English spelling has often been inconsistent, it may never have been more so than in the time William Shakespeare lived.

Topic sentence: _____

4. [1]Does your child reject your suggestions about exercise? [2]The Council on Physical Education for Children has some ideas on how to get children to enjoy exercise. [3]First, have children play games like soccer, where everyone is involved. [4]Next, make sure equipment is the right size. [5]Smaller and more lightweight equipment will help young children develop skills. [6]Finally, avoid boring exercises such as jumping jacks and toe-touches.

Topic sentence: _____

5. [1]Our lives have been enriched by inventions we might never have known about without the determination of the products' inventors. [2]In 1939, for example, a professor built the first computer using "base 2," a series that was easy for a machine to identify. [3]He tried to sell his idea to IBM, but was turned down. [4]It took seven years before his idea was accepted and the first general-purpose computer was introduced. [5]Today, all computers use the system he devised. [6]Another example is the copy machine patented in 1939. [7]Its inventor tried to sell his idea to twenty different companies. [8]Because no one was interested then, the first commercial copy machine was not introduced until 1959.

Topic sentence: _____

PARAGRAPHS WITHOUT A TOPIC SENTENCE

Sometimes a paragraph does not have a topic sentence. In such cases, the author has decided to let the supporting details suggest the main idea. The main idea is unstated, or **implied**, and you must figure it out by deciding upon the point of the supporting details.

Asking two questions will help you to determine the author's main idea:

1 What is the topic, or subject, of the paragraph? In other words, what is the whole paragraph about?

2 What is the main point being made about the topic?

Here is an example of a paragraph that has no topic sentence. Ask the two questions above to help you identify the main idea of the paragraph. Circle the letter of the correct answer. Then read the explanation that follows.

> When you have a relationship with someone, it is almost certain that you will argue now and then. To keep an argument from causing hard feelings, listen to the other person's point of view. Don't just hear what you want to hear, but focus on what the person is saying. Also try to identify with his or her point of view as much as you can, remembering that a view other than your own may be valid. Another way to keep an argument from causing hard feelings is to concentrate on behavior that is annoying you, not on the other person's character. For example, say, "This bothers me a lot," not "Only a stupid idiot would act the way you do!" Finally, when the argument is over, put it behind you.

The unstated main idea is:

a. People often argue with each other.
b. When you have a relationships with someone, you should try not to argue with him or her.
c. There are guidelines you can follow to ensure that an argument does not cause hard feelings.
d. The most important point in knowing how to argue is to put an argument behind you once it is over.

Explanation:

If you answered the question "Who or what is the paragraph about?" you probably found the topic: arguing. The next question to ask is "What is the main point being made about arguing?" To answer that question, consider the supporting details: The details of the paragraph are not about how often people argue or the importance of trying not to argue; so answers *a* and *b* are wrong. The details of the paragraph are specific guidelines for keeping an argument from causing hard feelings: "listen to the other person's point of view," "try to identify with his or her point of view," "concentrate on behavior that is annoying you, not on the other person's character," and "when the argument is over, put it behind you." Therefore, answer *c* is correct—it makes a general statement that covers the specific guidelines listed. Answer *d* is wrong because it is too narrow: it is about only one of the guidelines.

The following exercise will give you practice in finding the implied main idea of a paragraph.

➤ *Practice 2*

In each of the paragraphs below, the main idea is unstated—there is no topic sentence. To find the main idea, ask the two questions shown below. Then circle the letter of the correct answer.

> **1** What is the topic, or subject, of the paragraph? In other words, what is the whole paragraph about?
>
> **2** What is the main point being made about the topic?

1. Two workers on the twenty-third floor of an office building saw a bird banging its head against the glass outside their office. They rescued the bird and took it to a nearby animal hospital. The vet explained that what happened was not unusual. The bird had eaten berries which had been on the vine long enough to ferment—the sugar had partially turned to alcohol. The bird, in other words, was drunk. The vet gave it time to sober up and then released it.

   The unstated main idea is:

   a. Two office workers learned through an interesting experience that birds get drunk.
   b. Workers in skyscrapers often rescue birds that bang on office windows.
   c. Birds often bang their heads on windows.
   d. A bird was taken by office workers to an animal hospital.

2. Because turnips were often eaten by the poor, other people often turned up their noses at them. Carrots were also once held in low esteem. They grew wild in ancient times and were used then for medicinal purposes. But they weren't considered fit for the table in Europe until the thirteenth century. Similarly, in the early seventeenth and eighteenth centuries, some

Europeans considered potatoes fit only for animals. Potatoes were thought to cause leprosy in humans.

The unstated main idea is:

a. Vegetables are a healthy addition to any diet.
b. In previous centuries, some Europeans thought potatoes were unhealthy for humans.
c. Through the centuries, people have had mistaken ideas about some vegetables.
d. While potatoes were once considered unhealthy, carrots were once used as medicine.

3. Some people avoid crossing the path of a black cat. The reason for this superstition is centuries old. People in the Middle Ages believed that witches were very dangerous creatures who could change themselves into black cats. Witches were also thought to be easily irritated. So if you wanted to avoid trouble, the safest thing to do was simply to avoid all black cats.

The unstated main idea is:

a. Some people avoid crossing the path of a black cat.
b. Superstitions have interesting historical backgrounds.
c. The superstition of avoiding the path of a black cat comes from beliefs people in the Middle Ages had about witches.
d. During the Middle Ages, people believed that witches were dangerous and could change themselves into black cats.

4. One way to fight garden pests without using chemical pesticides is to introduce other bugs to a garden. Insects such as ladybugs and dragonflies feed on other insects that harm crops. There are also several natural substances that repel insects. For example, citronella oil, which comes from a certain grass, keeps some insects away. Also, some people claim to discourage visits from ants by planting mint around the house.

The unstated main idea is:

a. Mint may discourage visits from ants.
b. Chemical pesticides in gardens can cause great harm.
c. Several natural substances can keep insects away from a garden.
d. Chemical pesticides can be replaced by various natural pest-control measures.

5. Children influence $132 billion in annual purchases. In addition, 62 percent of children visit supermarkets each week, and 50 percent participate in the choice of food or brand. Also, 50 percent of children say that they prefer a different salad dressing from their mothers. And a full 78 percent of them claim to influence their family's choice of cold cereal.

The unstated main idea is:

a. Mothers and children choose different salad dressings.
b. Appealing to children's tastes can be profitable for companies.
c. Parents should not allow their children to influence family purchases.
d. Children enjoy accompanying their parents on shopping trips.

FINDING MAIN IDEAS ON FOUR LEVELS OF DIFFICULTY

Finding the main idea is the most important of all reading skills. To give you practice in finding the main idea, the rest of this chapter presents a series of paragraphs. They are grouped into four levels of increasing difficulty. In the first three practices, the topic sentences appear at varying places. In the fourth practice, you are challenged to find implied main ideas. Don't skip any exercise! Doing the easier ones will prepare you for the more difficult ones.

As you work on these exercises, remember these guidelines for finding the main idea:

1 Identify the topic of the paragraph by asking yourself, "Who or what is the paragraph about?"

2 Find the general statement that tells you the author's main point about the topic.

3 Test your answer by asking yourself, "Is this general statement supported by all or most of the material in the paragraph?"

➤ *Practice: Level 1*

Write the number of each topic sentence in the space provided.

1. [1]The types of animals considered endangered or threatened are increasing. [2]In 1985, 329 species were listed by the U.S. Fish and Wildlife Service as being endangered or threatened. [3]This year, over 500 species are listed. [4]In addition, there are over 3,000 other species that officials have not had time to study. [5]Some of these may also qualify for the list.

Topic sentence: _____

2. ¹Hannibal Hamlin was one. ²George Dallas was another. ³Include the name of John Breckinridge. ⁴And you can add the names of Schuyler Colfax, Henry Wilson, and John Garner. ⁵What do all of these men have in common? ⁶Although few people know them by name, each of these men has been a vice president of the United States.

Topic sentence: _____

3. ¹Child abuse has many tragic results. ²A child who is abused often believes he or she is unworthy. ³This low self-esteem can lead to alcoholism, drug addiction, or even suicide. ⁴Of course in many cases, the abuse is physically harmful and even fatal. ⁵In addition, many abused children grow up to become abusers of their own children.

Topic sentence: _____

4. ¹There is much that people can do for their pets. ²But the opposite is also true—numerous studies have shown that owning a pet can improve a person's mental and physical well-being. ³A pet that a person feels attached to improves the owner's frame of mind. ⁴In addition, a pet gives a feeling of being needed to the person who takes care of it. ⁵Pets also give an unconditional love that makes coming home after a rotten day more bearable. ⁶Even being in the same room as a pet can lower one's blood pressure and heart rate.

Topic sentence: _____

5. ¹Lightning usually strikes outdoors. ²We've all heard about people who were struck by lightning while walking or working outside. ³However, lightning can be harmful inside as well as outside. ⁴It can come in through an open window or door and then bounce around a room until it finds a way outside again. ⁵Also, any electrical appliance which conducts electricity can act as a magnet for dangerous lightning. ⁶Lightning can even be conducted through telephone wires and electrocute a person talking on the phone.

Topic sentence: _____

➤ *Practice: Level 2*

Write the number of each topic sentence in the space provided.

1. ¹Several kinds of changes can warn that a teenager is considering suicide. ²Some changes are physical. ³The youngster may have no energy or may show a sudden gain or loss in weight. ⁴Other changes are emotional. ⁵There

can be sudden outbursts, usually for no apparent reason. ⁶Also, the youngster may stop communicating with the family or may even withdraw from people in general. ⁷The most dramatic signs of suicide are changes in old habits and interests. ⁸These signs often include new sleeping patterns and giving away favorite possessions.

Topic sentence: _____

2. ¹If asked, most people would say that ceramics are used for pottery and that plastic is used for toys. ²Those statements may be true today. ³In the near future, however, ceramics and plastics will be put to some very different uses. ⁴New methods have produced ceramics sturdy enough to be made into scissors and knives that never rust. ⁵The new ceramics can also be made into engines that run without a cooling system. ⁶The new plastics will be molded into bridges, fuel tanks, and high-fidelity loudspeakers.

Topic sentence: _____

3. ¹Marta is fourteen and lives in a village in San Salvador. ²In her family, as in most peasant families there, every day the women prepare tortillas, thin round pancakes made from mashed corn. ³In San Salvador, the tortillas are made in a few steps, the same way they were made hundreds of years ago. ⁴Marta collects the corn and puts it in a pot of water to soak. ⁵The next day, she puts the wet corn through a hand grinder. ⁶Her mother then puts the ground corn on a block of stone and mashes it back and forth many times until it is a pasty dough. ⁷This dough is then patted into tortillas, which are cooked on a flat griddle over an open fire. ⁸They are eaten with salt and a portion of beans.

Topic sentence: _____

4. ¹A tropical plant named kenaf (which rhymes with *giraffe*) grows to full maturity in only five months. ²In contrast, a pine tree requires sixty years to become fully grown. ³In addition, kenaf (similar in appearance to bamboo and sugar cane), has a tough outer fiber that is almost insect-proof. ⁴As a result, pesticides aren't needed in growing kenaf. ⁵Another plus for kenaf is that it yields two to four times as much raw pulp per acre as southern pine. ⁶For all these reasons, kenaf has been found to be a good raw material for various paper products, including newsprint and tissues.

Topic sentence: _____

5. ¹Parents have shown concern about the quality and safety of baby food. ²As a result of this parental concern, the leading baby food companies have

started a strict set of safety checks. ³First, representatives of the companies visit the farms where the produce is grown. ⁴The representatives make sure that levels of pesticides are the lowest possible. ⁵Next, they check every piece of incoming produce for chemicals and other impurities. ⁶Finally, spot checks of the finished products are done before they are shipped to the stores.

Topic sentence: _____

➤ Practice: Level 3

Write the number of each topic sentence in the space provided.

1. ¹Being a judge may be a lofty job, but judges often face the down-to-earth problem of fighting off sleepiness during a long trial. ²One reason is that arguments made by attorneys are usually routine. ³They are also often long and boring. ⁴Another reason is that judges are seated all during trials. ⁵This can slow the body down, especially after lunch. ⁶Also, courtrooms are usually stuffy. ⁷Air circulation is poor, there are no windows, and lighting is dim.

   Topic sentence: _____

2. ¹People complain about their doctors. ²"He rushes me through." ³"She doesn't explain what she's doing." ⁴However, instead of complaining, patients can do several things to become better managers of their own health. ⁵When visiting a doctor, patients should be prepared to describe their health problem fully and precisely. ⁶They should question the doctor when they don't understand what he or she is doing. ⁷They should make a habit of asking why certain procedures are recommended. ⁸They should ask exactly how, when, and why they are to take any medication. ⁹If a doctor reacts badly to a patient's questions, it may be time to find a new doctor.

   Topic sentence: _____

3. ¹Half of all Americans live within fifty miles of an ocean beach. ²No wonder there's hardly room for a beach towel—124 million people visit the seashore annually, and the number is growing as development booms. ³Unfortunately, all twenty-three coastal states lose two to four feet of beach a year to the ocean. ⁴More people and less beach should make for some very crowded seashores in the coming years.

   Topic sentence: _____

4. [1]We are all familiar with the United States flag, a field of white with red stripes and an upper quarter in blue with fifty white stars. [2]However, it has not always been this way—while the flag has always had the famous "stars and stripes," there have been many variations. [3]The original flag had thirteen stars and stripes, one star and one stripe to represent each original state. [4]When new states were added, more stars and stripes were added. [5]By 1818, there were twenty states, and Congress decided to add a star for each new state but to go back to thirteen stripes. [6]As late as the 1850s, there was a variety of different U.S. flags flying around the country and on ships. [7]One popular flag in 1857 had thirty-one small stars arranged to form one large star.

Topic sentence: _____

5. [1]Daylight-saving time usually ends on the last weekend of October. [2]This can be confusing, as not all states are on daylight-saving time. [3]But it is unlikely that any place has a harder time coping with time changes than Tuba City, Arizona. [4]The state of Arizona does not observe daylight-saving time. [5]But Tuba City is on a Navajo reservation, and the Navajo Nation does observe daylight saving. [6]The local school board, however, voted to return to standard time in early October. [7]Yet the school's maintenance staff has a contract that states it must follow the usual daylight-saving schedule. [8]Further, the Navajo Community College, next to the school, goes to standard time in early October. [9]The continuing education department, in the same building, stays on the usual daylight-saving schedule.

Topic sentence: _____

➤ *Practice: Level Four (Unstated Main Ideas)*

In each of the paragraphs below, the main idea is unstated, or implied—there is no topic sentence. Ask the two questions shown below to find the main idea of each paragraph. Circle the letter of the best statement of the main idea.

  1 What is the topic, or subject, of the paragraph? In other words, what is the whole paragraph about?

  2 What is the main point being made about the topic?

1. Switzerland is known for its chocolates. Ireland is famous for potatoes. Argentina is well known for its beef. Not only does Argentina raise cattle, but more beef is consumed per person in Argentina than any other country in the world. Japan is famous for raw fish dishes. Its sushi is admired around the world.

The unstated main idea is:

a. Certain countries can produce only particular foods.
b. Certain countries are associated with particular foods.
c. Beef is not eaten in Japan.
d. Italy is not famous for any particular kind of food.

2. To become president of the United States, a person must be at least thirty-five years of age. He or she must have lived in the United States for the last fourteen years. In addition, he or she must be a natural-born citizen of the country. A convicted felon cannot be president of the United States.

The unstated main idea is:

a. There is an age limit to becoming president.
b. There are specific rules about who can become an elected official of a country.
c. The requirements for becoming a president of the United States are too limiting.
d. There are certain requirements for becoming president of the United States.

3. The medical center at a large university recently released a list of the objects it had removed from people's ears one week. Ninety-eight separate objects were taken out of the ears of people of all ages. Less common items included beads and shotgun pellets. Food particles—including corn, candy, and cereal—were among the more common objects removed. The most common item removed was found in almost 50 percent of the people seen; it was a cockroach. Most of these roaches had crawled into the ears of sleeping people.

The unstated main idea is:

a. Cockroaches like to crawl into people's ears.
b. People get things stuck in their ears because they are not paying attention.
c. Children are more likely to have objects removed from their ears than anyone else.
d. One hospital has found that a surprising variety of things often get stuck in people's ears.

4. Polynesians once believed that a total eclipse of the sun occurred when the sun and moon made love. The stars were the offspring. Some North American Indian tribes believed that an eclipse signaled the death of a celestial body. Other tribes believed that coyotes which roamed the stars hunted during an eclipse. In China eclipses were so significant that three

thousand years ago two astronomers who failed to predict an eclipse were beheaded.

The unstated main idea is:

a. Natural events were not very well understood in earlier times.
b. Different cultures once had varying explanations for eclipses.
c. Eclipses of the sun were more frightening than eclipses of the moon.
d. In China three thousand years ago, eclipses were considered to be very significant.

5. In 1857, Egyptian businessmen tried to convince Congress that camels should be used in desert outposts in the West. The salesmen pointed out that a camel could carry up to a thousand pounds more than an elephant. They said a camel's energy was almost limitless. As proof, they had a camel race a horse across difficult land covering 110 miles. The horse won the race but died of fatigue shortly after. To show how much staying power the camel had, the salesmen had the camel run again the next day. The camel covered the same area at the same speed. The salesmen then pointed out how little water camels need. Camels barely sweat, and they regulate their body temperature depending on the heat. Congress was convinced and bought seventy-five camels for soldiers to use. However, the soldiers hated the beasts and turned them loose in the desert. Most disappeared, but there are still occasional sightings of camels in remote desert regions today.

The unstated main idea is:

a. Soldiers hated camels for various reasons.
b. Despite proof that camels could help soldiers in desert areas of the West, the camels did not work out.
c. Camels can carry more weight than elephants.
d. The camel's virtues come from its ability to get by on very little water and to regulate its own body temperature.

A Final Note: Paragraphs with Two Topic Sentences

A paragraph can have two topic sentences. An author will sometimes introduce a main idea at or near the beginning of a paragraph and then restate the idea, or make a similar general statement, at the end of the paragraph. The following paragraph is an example. Read it, and then read the explanation that follows.

[1]There are a number of ways to get young people involved in cutting down on the family food bill. [2]First, have your children go through newspapers to clip coupons. [3]They can also sort coupons into different categories and note expiration dates. [4]Next, have them help you compare

generic products and brand-name products. [5]Buy each, and have a taste test. [6]If kids can't taste a difference, point out how much you can save by buying the generic product. [7]Finally, give kids the responsibility of loading the shopping cart and calculating the savings their work has produced. [8]In these ways, children can take pride in making an impact on the family's food budget.

Explanation:

Sentences 2–7 detail some of the ways referred to in sentence 1, "ways to get young people involved in cutting down on the family food bill." The details in sentences 2–7 also support sentence 8 by showing how "children can take pride in making an impact on their family's food budget." So both sentences 1 and 8 cover all the details of the passage. Thus the paragraph has two topic sentences—one at the beginning and one at the end.

CHAPTER SUMMARY

In this chapter, you learned the following:

• The topic sentence of a paragraph can be located anywhere in a paragraph: beginning, middle, or end. (A paragraph can even have two topic sentences, one at or near the beginning, and one at the end.)

• To find a topic sentence, do the following:

1 Identify the topic of the paragraph by asking yourself, "Who or what is the paragraph about?"

2 Find the general statement that tells you the author's main point about the topic.

3 Test your answer by asking yourself, "Is this general statement supported by all or most of the material in the paragraph?"

• Some paragraphs do not have a topic sentence. To find an unstated main idea, ask yourself the following questions:

1 What is the topic, or subject, of the paragraph? In other words, what is the whole paragraph about?

2 What is the main point being made about the topic?

➤ *Review Test 1*

To review what you've learned in this chapter, answer each of the following questions. Fill in the blank or circle the letter of the correct answer.

1. The topic sentence of a paragraph states the
   a. supporting details.   b. introductory material.   c. main idea.

2. _____ TRUE OR FALSE? To find the topic sentence of a paragraph, look for a general statement.

3. _____ TRUE OR FALSE? The supporting details of a paragraph are more general than the main idea.

4. _____ TRUE OR FALSE? Every paragraph has a stated main idea.

5. When the main idea is stated in the last sentence of a paragraph, the topic sentence is likely to be
   a. a summary.   b. a conclusion.   c. either *a* or *b*.

➤ *Review Test 2*

The five paragraphs below are on the first and second levels of difficulty. Write the number of each topic sentence in the space provided.

1. ¹There have been more and more eucalyptus trees grown in the latter part of the 1900s. ²There are good reasons for the increase—in places where eucalyptus can be grown, it offers many advantages. ³First of all, the trees are fast-growing. ⁴Also, they are an excellent source of timber, firewood, and wood pulp used for paper. ⁵Fewer worker-hours are needed for management of eucalyptus than for almost any other tree. ⁶In addition, these trees serve as an excellent windbreak. ⁷Finally, a variety of wildlife thrives among eucalyptus.

   Topic sentence: _____

2. ¹Good college students do several things to keep up with their assignments. ²They read an assigned textbook chapter before class. ³They also go over notes from previous classes. ⁴In addition, they study weekly for each subject, knowing that this will make midterm and final examinations easier. ⁵And they prepare an essay, term paper, or speech well in advance of when it is due.

   Topic sentence: _____

3. ¹In 1948, a man named Edward Lowe was selling clay to businesses that needed something to soak up oil and grease. ²When a customer came in and asked for sand for his cat's litter box, Lowe gave him some clay instead. ³When the man returned for more, Lowe knew he was on to something. ⁴He made a couple of refinements and offered the product to customers. ⁵They came back for more as well. ⁶As a result of Lowe's efforts, the product we know as Kitty Litter was born.

Topic sentence: _____

4. ¹You can attract wildlife to your yard by following a few guidelines. ²First, plant shrubs around your yard. ³This will provide protection for animals and a place for birds to roost. ⁴Also, plant vegetation that the birds and animals like to eat. ⁵A local nursery can help you select the right vegetation. ⁶Third, leave some water for the wildlife to drink. ⁷Finally, keep dogs and cats away. ⁸Their presence will discourage wildlife from coming around.

Topic sentence: _____

5. ¹The word *home* may call forth warm images of peaceful family life. ²Unfortunately, the American home can be a violent place. ³Consider, first, that some parents punch and kick their children and even use weapons on them. ⁴Evidence suggests that almost four million children are abused by their parents each year. ⁵Second, husbands and wives hit, shoot, and stab each other. ⁶Almost two million people are abused by their spouses. ⁷Finally, some adults beat, tie up, and neglect the elderly. ⁸There may be over two million old people abused by their children and other caretakers.

Topic sentence: _____

► Review Test 3

A. The paragraphs below are on the third level of difficulty. Write the number of each topic sentence in the space provided.

1. [1]Have you ever thought that a week in bed would do you good? [2]Well, think again. [3]Several days of bed rest can actually do harm. [4]First, just as moving around keeps bones strong, lying in bed weakens them. [5]Also, when someone is in bed for several days, blood gathers in the upper body. [6]This causes the heart to function less well and leads to more risk of blood clots. [7]Lying down also changes the position of the lungs, making breathing more difficult.

   Topic sentence: _____

2. [1]On an island in the Indian Ocean, people honor the dead by treating them as if they were still alive. [2]Dead bodies are often removed from their tombs and dressed in new clothes. [3]Then, before being reburied, the bodies may be danced with, sung to, and given tours of their old neighborhoods. [4]Recently, a dead soccer player was treated to three games of soccer before being placed in the family tomb.

   Topic sentence: _____

3. [1]Some people say that victimless crimes should not be illegal. [2]However, the argument that some crimes have no victims is weak. [3]First, whoever commits a so-called victimless crime can do himself or herself harm. [4]For example, a drug user may overdose. [5]In addition, family members can be hurt. [6]Drug addicts may be unable to properly care for their children. [7]Finally, society can be harmed. [8]For instance, drug addicts often need costly treatment, paid for with our tax dollars.

   Topic sentence: _____

B. The paragraphs below are on the fourth level of difficulty. Each main idea is unstated—there is no topic sentence. Ask the two questions shown below to find the main idea of each paragraph. Then circle the letter of the choice that best states it.

   1 What is the topic, or subject, of the paragraph? In other words, what is the whole paragraph about?

   2 What is the main point being made about the topic?

4. Scientists check and recheck evidence before coming to conclusions. But sometimes careful research is not enough. In 1903, for example, n-rays were supposedly discovered. Many papers were published on such subjects as how bricks absorb n-rays and how loud noises interfere with n-rays. Several years later, scientists agreed that no such ray exists. In the 1970s, scientists believed that a new water called polywater had been invented. They feared that if any escaped a lab, all water would turn into polywater, ending life on earth. That danger passed when polywater was proved to be ordinary water with impurities.

The unstated main idea is:

a. Scientists always check their research carefully.
b. Mistakes that were made years ago are not made today.
c. We all learn from our mistakes.
d. Careful research has not stopped scientists from making mistakes.

5. As a prank, an eighth-grade class in Iowa made up the name "Jeff Schuman" for a fictitious classmate. They continued the gag into high school, nominating Jeff for student body president and homecoming king. One student entered Jeff in a national test on international affairs. The student filled out his own test and then filled out Jeff's test by randomly selecting answers. Not only did the imaginary student get a better score than the real student; the contest organizers sent the school a notification that Jeff Schuman had won third place. This made Jeff Schuman, who didn't exist, eligible for a scholarship.

The unstated main idea is:

a. Practical jokes always backfire.
b. Imaginary students often do better than real students.
c. A school prank produced surprising results.
d. Schools should not give national tests to students.

Review Test 4

Here is a chance to apply your understanding of finding main ideas to a full-length selection. This reading is written by a former community college student who has passionate opinions about what students really need to know as they begin their college careers. To help you continue to strengthen your skills, the reading is followed by questions on what you've learned in this and previous chapters.

Words to Watch

Following are some words in the reading that do not have strong context support. Each word is followed by the number of the paragraph in which it appears and its meaning there. These words are indicated in the reading by a small circle (°).

vocational (5): work-related
paralegal assistant (7): a person trained to assist a lawyer
persist (10): continue on
endured (13): carried on despite hardship
dismayed (14): discouraged
developmental (17): meant to improve skills in a subject
grim (24): gloomy
projected (25): gave the impression of
destinies (31): futures

LEARNING SURVIVAL SKILLS

Jean Coleman

1   For four years I was a student at a community college. I went to night school as a part-time student for three years, and I was able to be a full-time student for one year. My first course was a basic writing course because I needed a review of grammar and the basics of writing. I did well in that course and that set the tone for everything that followed.

2   It is now eleven years since I started college, and I have a good job with a Philadelphia accounting firm. When I was invited to write this article, the questions put to me were "What would you want to say to students who are just starting out in college? What advice would you give? What experiences would it help to share?" I thought a lot about what it took for me to be a successful student.

Here, then, are my secrets for survival in college and, really, for survival in life as well.

"BE REALISTIC."

3   The first advice that I'd give to beginning students is this: "Be realistic about how college will help you get a job." Some students believe that once they have college degrees the world will be waiting on their doorsteps, ready to give them wonderful jobs. But the chances are that unless they've planned, there will be *nobody* on their doorsteps.

4   I remember the way my teacher in a study skills course dramatized this point in class. He played a student who had just been handed a college degree. He opened up an imaginary

door, stepped through, and peered around in both directions outside. There was nobody to be seen. I understood the point he was making immediately. A college degree in itself isn't enough. We've got to prepare while we're in college to make sure our degree is a marketable one.

5   At that time I began to think seriously about (1) what I wanted to do in life and (2) whether there were jobs out there for what I wanted to do. I went to the counseling center and said, "I want to learn where the best job opportunities will be in the next ten years." The counselor referred me to a copy of the *Occupational Outlook Handbook* published by the United States government. The *Handbook* has good information on what kinds of jobs are available now and which career fields will need workers in the future. In the front of the book is a helpful section on job hunting. The counselor also gave me a vocational° interest test to see where my skills and interests lay.

6   The result of my personal career planning was that I eventually graduated from community college with a degree in accounting. I then got a job almost immediately, for I had chosen an excellent employment area. The firm that I work for paid my tuition as I went on to get my bachelor's degree. It is now paying for my work toward certification as a certified public accountant, and my salary increases regularly.

7   By way of contrast, I know a woman named Sheila who earned a bachelor's degree with honors in French. After graduation, she spent several unsuccessful months trying to find a job using her French degree. Sheila eventually wound up going to a specialized school where she trained for six months as a paralegal assistant°. She then got a job on the strength of that training—but her years of studying French were of no practical value in her career at all.

8   I'm not saying that college should serve only as a training ground for a job. People should take some courses just for the sake of learning and for expanding their minds in different directions. At the same time, unless they have an unlimited amount of money (and few of us are so lucky), they must be ready at some point to take career-oriented courses so that they can survive in the harsh world outside.

9   In my own case, I started college at the age of twenty-seven. I was divorced, had a six-year-old son to care for, and was working full time as a hotel night clerk. If I had had my preference, I would have taken a straight liberal arts curriculum. As it was, I did take some general-interest courses—in art, for example. But mainly I was getting ready for the solid job I desperately needed. I am saying, then, that students must be realistic. If they will need a job soon after graduation, they should be sure to study in an area where jobs are available.

"PERSIST."

10 The older I get, the more I see that life lays on us some hard experiences. There are times for each of us when simple survival becomes a deadly serious matter. We must then learn to persist°—to struggle through each day and wait for better times to come—as they always do.

11 I think of one of my closest friends, Neil. After graduating from high school with me, Neil spent two years working as a stock boy at a local department store in order to save money for college tuition. He then went to the guidance office at the small college in our town. Incredibly, the counselor there told him, "Your IQ is not high enough to do college work." Thankfully, Neil decided to go anyway and earned his degree in five years—with a year out to care for his father, who had had a stroke one day at work.

12 Neil then got a job as a manager of a regional beauty supply firm. He met a woman who owned a salon, got married, and soon had two children. Three years later he found out that his wife was having an affair. I'll never forget the day Neil came over and sat at my kitchen table and told me what he had learned. He always seemed so much in control, but that morning he lowered his head into his hands and cried. "What's the point?" he kept saying in a low voice over and over to himself.

13 But Neil has endured°. He divorced his wife, won custody of his children, and learned how to be a single parent. Recently, Neil and I got letters informing us of the twentieth reunion of our high-school graduating class. Included was a short questionnaire for us to fill out that ended with this item: "What has been your outstanding accomplishment since graduation?" Neil wrote, "My outstanding accomplishment is that I have survived." I have a feeling that many of our high-school classmates, twenty years out in the world, would have no trouble understanding the truth of his statement.

14 I can think of people who started college with me who had not yet learned, like Neil, the basic skill of endurance. Life hit some of them with unexpected low punches and knocked them to the floor. Stunned and dismayed°, they didn't fight back and eventually dropped out of school. I remember Yvonne, still a teenager, whose parents involved her in their ugly divorce battle. Yvonne started missing classes and gave up at midsemester. There was Alan, whose girlfriend broke off their relationship. Alan stopped coming to class, and by the end of the semester he was failing most of his courses. I also recall Nelson, whose old car kept breaking down. After Nelson put his last $200 into it, the breaks failed and needed to be replaced. Overwhelmed by his continuing car troubles, Nelson dropped out of school. And there was Rita, discouraged by her luck of the draw with teachers and courses. In sociology, she had a teacher who wasn't able to express ideas clearly.

She also had a mathematics teacher who talked too fast and seemed not to care at all about whether his students learned. To top it off, Rita's adviser had enrolled her in an economics course that put her to sleep. Rita told me she had expected college to be an exciting place, but instead she was getting busywork assignments and trying to cope with hostile or boring teachers. Rita decided to drop her mathematics course, and that must have set something in motion in her head, for she soon dropped her other courses as well.

15   In my experience, younger students seem more likely to drop out than do older students. I think some younger students are still in the process of learning that life slams people around without warning. I'm sure they feel that being knocked about is especially unfair because the work of college is hard enough without having to cope with other hardships.

16   In some situations, withdrawing from college may be the best response. But there are going to be times in college when students—young or old—must simply determine, "I am going to persist." They should remember that no matter how hard their lives may be, there are many other people out there who are quietly having great difficulties also. I think of Dennis, a boy in my introductory psychology class who lived mostly on peanut butter and discount store loaves of white bread for almost a semester in his freshman year. And I remember Estelle, who came to school because she needed a job to support her sons when her husband, who was dying of leukemia, would no longer be present. These are especially dramatic examples of the faith and hope that are sometimes necessary for us to persist.

"BE POSITIVE."

A lot of people are their own   17 worst enemies. They regard themselves as unlikely to succeed in college and often feel that there have been no accomplishments in their lives. In my first year of college especially, I saw people get down on themselves all too quickly. There were two students in my developmental° mathematics class who failed the first quiz and seemed to give up immediately. From that day on, they walked into the classroom carrying defeat on their shoulders the way other students carried textbooks under their arms. I'd look at them slouching in their seats, not even taking notes, and think, "What terrible things have gone on in their lives that they have quit already? They have so little faith in their ability to learn that they're not even trying." Both students hung on until about midsemester. When they disappeared for good, no one took much notice, for they had already disappeared in spirit after that first test.

They are not the only people in   18 whom I have seen the poison of self-doubt do its ugly work. I have seen others with surrender in their eyes and have wanted to shake them by the shoulders and say, "You are not dead. Be proud and pleased that you have brought yourself here to college. Many people would not have gotten so far. Be someone. Breathe. Hope. Act." Such people should refuse to use self-doubts as an excuse for not trying. They should roll up their sleeves and get to work. They should start taking notes in class and trying to learn. They should get a tutor, go to the learning center, see a counselor. If they honestly and fully try and still can't handle a course, only then should they drop it. Above all, they should not lapse into being "zombie students"—ones who have given up in their heads but persist in hanging on for months, going through hollow motions of trying.

19   Nothing but a little time is lost through being positive and giving school your best shot. On the other hand, people who let self-doubts limit their efforts may lose the opportunity to test their abilities to the fullest.

"GROW."

20   I don't think that people really have much choice about whether to grow in their lives. To not be open to growth is to die a little each day. Grow or die—it's as simple as that.

21   I have a friend, Jackie, who, when she's not working, can almost always be found at home or at her mother's. Jackie eats too much and watches TV too much. I sometimes think that when she swings open her apartment door in response to my knock, I'll be greeted by her familiar chubby body with an eight-inch-screen television set occupying the place where her head used to be.

22   Jackie seems quietly desperate. There is no growth or plan for growth in her life. I've said to her, "Go to school and study for a job you'll be excited about." She says, "It'll take me forever." Once Jackie said to me, "The favorite time of my life was when I was a teenager. I would lie on my bed listening to music and I would dream. I felt I had enormous power, and there seemed no way that life would stop me from realizing my biggest dreams. Now that power doesn't seem possible to me anymore."

23   I feel that Jackie must open some new windows in her life. If she does not, her spirit is going to die. There are many ways to open new windows, and college is one of them. For this reason, I think people who are already in school should stay long enough to give it a chance. No one should turn down lightly such an opportunity for growth.

"ENJOY."

24   I hope I'm not making the college experience sound too grim°. It's true that there are some hard, cold realities in life, and I think people need to plan for those realities. But I want to describe also a very important fact—that college is often a wonderful experience. There were some tough times when it would have been easy to just give up and quit, like the week when my son's babysitter broke her arm and my car's radiator blew up. If school had not been something I really enjoyed, I would not have made it.

25   To begin with, I realized soon after starting college that almost no

one there knew me. That might seem like a depressing thought, but that's not how it felt. I knew that people at college had not made up their minds about what kind of person Jean Coleman was. I imagined myself as shy, clumsy, and average. But in this new environment, I was free to present myself in any way I chose. I decided from my first week in school that my college classmates and instructors were going to see the new, improved Jean. I projected° a confidence I didn't always feel. I sat near the front in every class. I participated, even took the lead, in discussions. Instead of slipping away after class, I made a point to chat with my teachers and invite other students to have coffee with me. Soon I realized that my "act" had worked. People regarded me as a confident, outgoing woman. I liked a lot this new image of myself as a successful college student.

26   Another of the pleasures of college was the excitement of walking into a class for the first time. At that point, the course was still just a name in a catalog. The possibilities for it seemed endless. Maybe the course would be a magic one sweeping me off my feet. Maybe the instructor would be really gifted in opening students' minds to new thoughts. Maybe through this course I would discover potential in myself I never knew existed. I went into a new class ready to do everything I could— through my listening, participation, and preparation—to make it a success. And while some courses were more memorable than others, I rarely found

one that didn't have some real rewards to offer me.

27   I even enjoyed the physical preparation for a new class. I loved going to the bookstore and finding the textbooks I'd need. I liked to sit down with them, crack open their binding and smell their new-book scent. It was fun to leaf through a textbook and see what seemed like difficult, unfamiliar material, realizing that in a few weeks I'd have a better grasp of what I was seeing there. I made a habit of buying a new spiral-bound notebook for each of my classes, even if I had others that are only partially used. Writing the new course's name on the notebook cover and seeing those fresh, blank sheets waiting inside helped me feel organized and ready to tackle a new challenge. I was surprised by how many other students I saw scribbling their class notes on anything handy. I always wondered how they organized them to review later.

28   Surely one of the best parts of returning to school was the people I've met. Some of them became friends I hope I'll keep forever; others were passing acquaintances, but all of them have made my life richer. One of the best friends I made is a woman named Charlotte. She was my age, and she, like me, came back to school after her marriage broke up. I first met Charlotte in a basic accounting class, and she was scared to death. She was convinced that she could never keep up with the younger students and was sure she had made a big mistake returning to college. Since I often felt that way myself, Charlotte and I

decided to become study partners. I'll never forget one day about three weeks into the term when I found her standing in the hallway after class, staring as if into space. "Charlotte?" I said, and she turned to me and broke into a silly grin. "Jean, I get it!" she exclaimed, giving me a quick hug. "I just realized I was sitting there in class keeping up as well as anyone else. I can do this!" Seeing Charlotte's growing confidence helped me believe in my own ability to succeed.

29   I found that I was looked to as an "older, wiser woman" by many of my classmates. And while I didn't pretend to have all of the answers, I enjoyed listening to their concerns and helping them think about solutions. My advice to them probably wasn't much different from what other adults might have said—take college seriously, don't throw away the opportunities you have, don't assume that finding "the right person" is going to solve all the problems of life, start planning for a career now. But somehow they seemed to find listening to such advice easier when it came from me, a fellow student.

30   Getting to know my instructors was a pleasure, as well. I remember how I used to think about my high-school teachers—that they existed only between nine and three o'clock and that their lives involved nothing but teaching us chemistry or social studies. But I got to know many of my college instructors as real people and even as friends. I came to think of my instructors as my partners, working together with me to achieve my goals. They weren't perfect or all-knowing— they were just people, with their own sets of problems and shortcomings. But almost all were people who really cared about helping me get where I wanted to go.

IN CONCLUSION

31   Maybe I can put all I've said into a larger picture by describing briefly what my life is like now. I have many inner resources that I did not have when I was just divorced. I have a secure future with the accounting firm where I work. My son is doing OK in school. I have friends. I am successful and proud and happy. I have my fears and my loneliness and my problems and my pains, but essentially I know that I have made it. I have survived and done more than survive. I am tough, not fragile, and I can rebound if hard blows land. I feel passionately that all of us can control our own destinies°. I urge every beginning student to use well the chances that college provides. Students should plan for a realistic career, get themselves organized, learn to persist, be positive, and open themselves to growth. In such ways, they can help themselves find happiness and success in this dangerous but wonderful world of ours.

Word Skills Questions

Phonics

1. The word *expanding,* used in the sentence below, is broken into syllables according to which rule?
   a. Dividing Before a Single Consonant
   b. Dividing Before a Consonant + *le*
   c. Dividing After Prefixes and Before Suffixes
   d. Dividing Between the Words in a Compound Word

   "People should take some courses just for the sake of learning and for expanding their minds in different directions." (Paragraph 8)

Dictionary Use

Use the following dictionary entry to answer questions 2 and 3.

des•per•ate (dĕs′pər-ĭt) *adj.* **1.** Having lost all hope; despairing. **2.** Reckless or violent because of despair. **3.** Undertaken as a last resort. **4.** Nearly hopeless; critical. **5.** Extreme; great: *a desperate urge.* — **des•per•ate•ly** *adv.* — **des′per•a′-tion** (des′pə -rā′shən) *n.*

2. The word *desperate* has
   a. three syllables, and the first is accented.
   b. three parts of speech: adjective, adverb, and noun.
   c. two long vowel sounds.
   d. all of the above.

3. Which definition applies to the word *desperate* In the sentences below?
   a. Definition 1
   b. Definition 2
   c. Definition 3
   d. Definition 5

   "Jackie seems quietly desperate. There is no growth or plan for growth in her life." (Paragraph 22)

Vocabulary in Context

4. In the sentences below, the word *peered* means
   a. joked.
   b. looked.
   c. raced.
   d. hid.

   "He opened up an imaginary door, stepped through, peered in both directions outside. There was nobody to be seen." (Paragraph 4)

5. In the sentence below, the word *overwhelmed* means
   a. overlooked.
   b. strengthened.
   c. defeated.
   d. unconcerned.

   "Overwhelmed by his continuing car troubles, Nelson dropped out of school." (Paragraph 14)

Reading Comprehension Questions

Central Point and Main Ideas

6. Which sentence best expresses the central point of the selection?
   a. All people experience great problems in the course of their lives.
   b. Following certain guidelines will help you succeed in school and in life.
   c. Divorce can be the beginning of a new and better life.
   d. Certain survival skills can help you become a successful accountant.

7. Which sentence best expresses the main idea of paragraph 30?
   a. The author realized that her college instructors had private lives of their own.
   b. The author enjoyed working with and getting to know her college instructors.
   c. In high school, the author thought her teachers had no private lives.
   d. The author realized that most of her college instructors weren't perfect.

Supporting Details

8. The author suggests in paragraph 18 that successful students
   a. do not have self-doubts.
   b. are often "zombie students."
   c. keep trying despite self-doubts.
   d. concentrate on listening instead of taking notes.

9. The author saw herself as shy, clumsy, and average, but decided to
   a. project a confidence she didn't always feel.
   b sit in in the middle of the class so no one would notice her.
   c. get involved in school clubs.
   d. drop out of any classes that seemed worthless.

10. The author
    a. took a straight liberal arts curriculum.
    b. switched from being a French major to an accounting major.
    c. took accounting classes and ended up with a degree in art.
    d. took some general interest classes, but ended up with a degree in accounting.

Discussion Questions

1. The author's "secrets" for survival in college and in life are "be realistic," "persist," "be positive," "grow," and "enjoy." Which of these points do you feel are most important for you to remember, and why?

2. What does the author mean when she states, "A lot of people are their own worst enemies" (paragraph 17)? Have you found that self-doubts sometime keep you or people you know from trying harder? How can self-doubts be dealt with?

3. The author suggests that students should find out what jobs will be available in the future and then get a degree in a related field. What type of career do you think you'd be interested in, and why? What degree will help you enter that field?

Note: Writing assignments for this selection appear on page 543–544.

Check Your Performance			**FINDING MAIN IDEAS**
Activity	*Number Right*	*Points*	*Score*
Review Test 1 (5 items)	_____	× 2 =	_____
Review Test 2 (5 items)	_____	× 6 =	_____
Review Test 3 (5 items)	_____	× 6 =	_____
Review Test 4 (10 items)	_____	× 3 =	_____
		TOTAL SCORE =	_____ %

Enter your total score into the **Reading Performance Chart: Review Tests** on the inside back cover.

FINDING MAIN IDEAS: Test 1

The five paragraphs that follow are on the first level of difficulty. Write the number of each topic sentence in the space provided.

1. ¹In many homes, the refrigerator door is the family bulletin board. ²On it, people place things they don't want to lose. ³These may include the phone number of the local police or of a favorite baby sitter. ⁴Also kept there are reminders, including notes about social events. ⁵Finally, the refrigerator is a favorite spot to display things, such as a child's artwork.

   Topic sentence: _____

2. ¹Few things are more boring than standing in line. ²However, ways have been found to make some otherwise boring waits more bearable. ³Airlines now hire people to make sure customers don't waste time in the wrong lines. ⁴In some places, live entertainment cheers customers in long lines. ⁵It seems that being able to look at oneself also makes waiting easier. ⁶In large buildings, complaints about slow elevators decrease when mirrors are put up nearby.

   Topic sentence: _____

3. ¹The first frost in Montana occurs around September 15. ²Colorado gets its first frost about October 1. ³Oklahoma's first frost is near the end of October. ⁴Louisiana can expect a frost around the middle of November. ⁵And Florida can look for a frost about the middle of December. ⁶Clearly, the farther south you go, the later the first frost date is likely to be.

   Topic sentence: _____

4. ¹When parents decorate a child's room, they should not forget to do something with the ceiling. ²Hanging such things as banners, kites, or mobiles makes the room look more attractive. ³The hanging items can also be educational. ⁴Mobiles such as a model of the solar system or kites in the shape of eagles and owls can get youngsters interested in science.

   Topic sentence: _____

(Continues on next page)

5. ¹Have you ever wondered why we are attracted to certain people as friends and lovers? ²Several factors help explain our attraction to other people. ³One key is physical closeness. ⁴We are more likely to be interested in people we see often. ⁵What we think of as good looks are also important. ⁶We tend to like people whom we find attractive. ⁷We also are drawn to people with whom we share similar backgrounds, interests, and values.

Topic sentence: _____.

FINDING MAIN IDEAS: Test 2

The five paragraphs below are on the first and second levels of difficulty. Write the number of each topic sentence in the space provided.

1. ¹You may assume that television programs are similar around the world. ²However, TV programming varies from country to country. ³Some countries, such as Sweden and Zimbabwe, permit television to be broadcast only at certain times during the day. ⁴Other countries limit the number of hours that entertainment shows can be on the air. ⁵Poland, for example, insists that news shows be on the air for more time than entertainment shows. ⁶And some countries, including Argentina, ban advertising.

   Topic sentence: _____

2. ¹An ancient native American people in the desert of the Southwest dug wells in an unusual way. ²When the Cahuilla (ka-wee-la) Indians discovered a spring, they would build a passageway into the earth. ³They would then construct a stairway that wound down to the water. ⁴This may be why the Cahuilla word for "well" translates as "jug of water from the earth."

   Topic sentence: _____

3. ¹As people get older, their physical and mental capabilities decline. ²Yet research has shown that as people age, they are likely to feel happier. ³One poll found that two-thirds of people over 65 were happy with their lives. ⁴In contrast, only about half of the people between the ages of 18 and 49 said that they were pleased with their lives.

   Topic sentence: _____

4. ¹Some foreign students are uncomfortable with the casual relationship that exists between American teachers and students. ²In many countries, students treat teachers much more formally. ³In addition, foreign students have the language problem to deal with. ⁴Their English classes may not have prepared them to understand fast-paced conversations filled with slang expressions. ⁵Foreign students' social lives can be difficult as well. ⁶Having a background so different from that of other students can make it hard to find friends. ⁷Obviously, life in America can be hard on foreign students.

   Topic sentence: _____   *(Continues on next page)*

5. ¹William Henry Harrison had one of the most fascinating careers of all the presidents of the United States. ²He was the only president to study medicine. ³Before getting his degree, he left school and joined the Army, where he rose to the rank of general. ⁴He was elected president at age 68. ⁵Until Ronald Reagan, Harrison was the oldest man to be elected president. ⁶Harrison gave one of the longest inaugural addresses on record, close to two hours. ⁷Shortly after his speech, he caught pneumonia. ⁸Harrison died a little more than a month after taking office.

Topic sentence: _____

FINDING MAIN IDEAS: Test 3

The five paragraphs below are on the second level of difficulty. Write the number of each topic sentence in the space provided.

1. ¹Velcro is a fastening tape that was first seen as a replacement for the zipper. ²The ease in opening and closing Velcro has given it some interesting uses. ³For instance, astronauts have used it to keep objects—and themselves—from falling into space. ⁴They also have had small pieces of Velcro stuck inside their helmets so they could scratch an itchy nose. ⁵Today, the fabric is used to fasten the fireproof suits of race-car drivers. ⁶This allows a driver to jump out of a suit in seconds if necessary. ⁷Velcro is also used to join two parts of the artificial heart.

   Topic sentence: _____

2. ¹According to a medical journal, there are some important guidelines for having your ears or other body parts pierced. ²First, let a professional who uses sterile instruments perform the task. ³Second, do not pierce if you have a serious medical condition, including heart disease, a blood disorder, or diabetes. ⁴Also, for six weeks, do not wear rings that contain nickel or a gold alloy or that are gold-plated. ⁵Next, avoid the risk of infection by washing the pierced area twice a day with cotton dipped in rubbing alcohol. ⁶Finally, if the area becomes red, swollen, or sore, see a doctor immediately.

   Topic sentence: _____

3. ¹Every week, guns kill several hundred Americans. ²To cut down on these deaths, some say we should stop the sale of guns, or at least of the worst kinds of guns. ³Since so many people already own guns, others suggest we require a permit to carry one outside the home. ⁴Many gun owners call for yet another solution: tough penalties for those who use guns in crimes. ⁵These are just a few of the many ideas on how to reduce the dangers of guns in America.

   Topic sentence: _____

(Continues on next page)

4. [1]A single computer chip can hold a great deal of information. [2]For this reason as well as other reasons, veterinarians are implanting computer microchips under the skin of pets. [3]First, the chips can be used to recognize an animal that has been lost or stolen. [4]Second, they can be used to identify purebred animals that have come from breeders. [5]Breeders who guarantee that an animal is free from defects can identify the animal later in life. [6]And third, the animal's history can be kept on the chip. [7]This means that if a pet changes vets, the new doctor can see what treatments the animal has undergone.

Topic sentence: _____

5. [1]There are various ways to stay informed of important events in the world. [2]One is to read newspapers. [3]Good daily papers such as *The New York Times* and the *Los Angeles Times* are available in many cities across the country. [4]*USA Today* is sold nationally and provides state and national coverage. [5]Another way to stay informed is to subscribe to a weekly newsmagazine. [6]*Time* and *Newsweek* are the most popular. [7]A third way to keep informed is to watch TV news shows. [8]Each network broadcasts morning and evening news shows. [9]News reports of varying lengths can be found on cable channels at all times of the day. [10]CNN, for example, broadcasts news twenty-four hours a day.

Topic sentence: _____

FINDING MAIN IDEAS: Test 4

The five paragraphs below are on the second and third levels of difficulty. Write the number of each topic sentence in the space provided.

1. [1]Before much was known about germs, doctors unknowingly caused much illness and death by spreading germs. [2]Before the twentieth century, doctors did not wash their hands between tasks. [3]Doctors would finish one operation, then immediately start on another. [4]Then they would examine patients. [5]They never realized that they were carrying bacteria from one person to another. [6]In many cases, they seriously infected the very people they were trying to cure.

   Topic sentence: _____

2. [1]Instincts are animal behaviors that don't need to be learned. [2]One example of an instinct is the way birds build nests. [3]Birds don't stop to think about which type of nest to build. [4]All robins, for instance, build their nests the same way. [5]Also, ants don't think about how to get food. [6]Without lessons, they gather food as every other ant in the hill does. [7]A third example is that all cats lick themselves clean without learning to do so.

   Topic sentence: _____

3. [1]Husbands once had more power in a marriage. [2]They earned more, were better educated, and had jobs with more prestige. [3]But as women get better jobs and earn more, they gain power at home. [4]Another factor in the balance of power is whether or not both partners care about the marriage to the same degree. [5]If the husband, for example, cares more about staying married than the wife does, the wife will have more power. [6]That is because the husband will do more to please her. [7]Thus the power structure of marriage has become more complicated in recent years.

   Topic sentence: _____

(Continues on next page)

4. [1]What steps can you take if you turn an ankle or strain a muscle? [2]Many sports physicians recommend the "RICE" formula for sprains and strains: rest, ice, compression, and elevation. [3]First, rest the joint or muscle that hurts. [4]Second, apply ice to the injured area. [5]Ice may be used at regular times for two days. [6]A compression bandage, such as an Ace bandage, will also ease the pain. [7]Finally, elevating an injured ankle or knee will keep pressure off it and prevent further damage. [8]Of course, if the pain continues or if the injury swells, you should see a doctor at once.

Topic sentence: _____

5. [1]Since cattle spend most of their time eating, cattle ranchers have been looking for an inexpensive supplement to feed them. [2]Using discarded newspaper as a supplement for cattle might benefit both the ranchers and the environment. [3]Eating newspapers filled with hydrogen peroxide and hydrochloric acid will not hurt cattle. [4]While papers do not contain the vitamins and protein needed by cattle, they are high in fiber. [5]Cattle use fiber to produce energy. [6]With old newspapers selling for pennies a pound, cattle ranchers would be spending less money. [7]And any old newspapers fed to cattle would be recycled, instead of using precious landfill space.

Topic sentence: _____

FINDING MAIN IDEAS: Test 5

A. The paragraphs below are on the third level of difficulty. Write the number of each topic sentence in the space provided.

1. ¹There are six major problems that students bring into the high-school classroom, says the National Education Association. ²First, about a quarter of all students smoke marijuana regularly, and more than two-thirds use alcohol. ³Forty percent of today's fourteen-year-old girls will get pregnant in their teens, and 80 percent of these will drop out of high school. ⁴Also, 30 percent of all students now in high school will drop out. ⁵One out of three girls and one out of eight boys under eighteen years old have reported being sexually abused. ⁶Fifth, 15 percent of girls will suffer an eating disorder during part or all of their teenage years. ⁷Finally, suicide is the second most common cause of death among fifteen- through nineteen-year-olds.

   Topic sentence: _____

2. ¹In California, a "Victim's Bill of Rights" was passed recently. ²This law broadened the type of evidence that could be used in court. ³The idea was to keep criminals from going free because of legal loopholes. ⁴But defense lawyers soon learned that they, too, could use this law. ⁵In rape trials especially, the new law could be used to move part of the blame onto the victim. ⁶This was done by presenting evidence, not permitted before, that the victim was careless or sexually "loose." ⁷Therefore, a law intended to protect crime victims turned out to have just the opposite effect.

   Topic sentence: _____

3. ¹Our life stages—for example, birth, puberty, and death—may be set by biology. ²However, how we view life stages is shaped by society. ³During the Middle Ages, for example, children dressed—and were expected to act—like little adults. ⁴Adolescence became a separate stage of life only fairly recently, when a teenage subculture appeared. ⁵Before that, young people were "children" until about age 16. ⁶Then they went to work, married, and had their own children. ⁷Today, young adulthood has become a new stage of life, covering about ages 20 to 30. ⁸And now that people live longer and spend years in active retirement, older adulthood has also become a distinct life stage.

   Topic sentence: _____

(Continues on next page)

B. In each of the paragraphs below, the main idea is unstated—there is no topic sentence. Ask the two questions shown below to help you find the answer that best states the main idea of each paragraph. Then circle the letter of that answer.

> **1** What is the topic, or subject, of the paragraph? In other words, what is the whole paragraph about?
>
> **2** What is the main point being made about the topic?

4. In the 1600s, the word *spinster* referred to any female. Spinning thread or yarn for cloth was something every woman did at home. By 1700, *spinster* had become a legal term for an unmarried woman. Unmarried women had to work to survive, and spinning was their most common job. Before long, however, spinning was done in factories. *Spinster* then suggested someone who was "left over" or "dried up," just as the job of home spinning had dried up for women. Today, with so many women working and marrying later and later, most single women consider the word *spinster* an insult.

The unstated main idea is:

a. Marriage has changed a great deal over the centuries.
b. Factories eventually took over spinning.
c. The word *spinster* has had different meanings over the years.
d. In the 1600s, all women knew how to spin thread or yarn for cloth.

5. President Harry S. Truman ended the war in Korea by dropping an atomic bomb. Napoleon won the Battle of Waterloo. The Japanese bombed Pearl Harbor in 1943. General Douglas MacArthur was a leader of an anti-Communist drive in the 1950s. All of these statements have two things in common. First, they are wrong. Second, each has been found in a history textbook used by high-school students in the United States.

The unstated main idea is:

a. Many leaders did things they should not have done.
b. Incorrect statements have been found in American high-school history textbooks.
c. College history textbooks are probably more accurate than high-school history textbooks.
d. All textbooks contain inaccurate statements.

FINDING MAIN IDEAS: Test 6

A. The paragraphs below are on the third level of difficulty. Write the number of each topic sentence in the space provided.

1. [1]The distance we like to keep between ourselves and others depends on the other people, according to one researcher. [2]The space within about one foot from us is "intimate" space. [3]We share it willingly only with loved ones. [4]If forced to share it with strangers (in a crowded elevator, for instance), we feel uncomfortable. [5]Between one and four feet away is our "personal" space, which we share with friends. [6]This is about how far apart we sit at a restaurant, for example. [7]Between about four and ten feet away is "social" space. [8]This is the distance we keep from strangers at parties and other gatherings. [9]Finally, over ten feet away is "public" space, a distance at which we can pretty much ignore others.

   Topic sentence: _____

2. [1]A bullfighter usually kneels in front of the bull before a fight begins. [2]Audience members are amazed at his courage. [3]However, the truth is that by kneeling, the bullfighter tricks the bull into being gentle. [4]Among animals, when two males fight, one can signal that he gives up by taking a yielding position. [5]The animal drops to the ground and raises his backside. [6]This position tells the other male that he has won and thus reduces his instinct to fight. [7]For this reason, the bull thinks the kneeling bullfighter is giving up. [8]Therefore the bull does not attack.

   Topic sentence: _____

3. [1]The reason we shiver and get goosebumps when we are frightened has to do with our animal nature. [2]When animals see or hear something threatening, their fur stands on end. [3]This reaction makes them look larger and thus more dangerous to an enemy. [4]In addition, extra blood flows to their muscles, getting them ready for action. [5]Humans react in the same way. [6]When we sense danger, goosebumps appear where our fur would stand on end if we had any. [7]Also, the blood flow to our skin is reduced in favor of our muscles, making us feel cold. [8]Unlike other animals, we have no fur to warm us, so we shiver to get warm.

   Topic sentence: _____

(Continues on next page)

B. In each of the paragraphs below, the main idea is unstated—there is no topic sentence. Ask the two questions shown below to find the main idea of each paragraph. Then circle the letter of the answer choice that best states it.

> **1** What is the topic, or subject, of the paragraph? In other words, what is the whole paragraph about?
>
> **2** What is the main point being made about the topic?

4. For years, floods have caused extreme destruction in states along the Mississippi River. Before Europeans settled along its banks, the river responded to floods by widening. Workers changed that by building levees, mounds of earth or stone meant to hold back water. Also, engineers straightened the river. Both changes made the river move faster. Now, when floods come, the water has no place to go and presses against the levees. When the pressure becomes too great, the levees break, flooding towns. If the levees hold, there is a danger that the water will become higher than the levees, and this results in flooding as well.

   The unstated main idea is:

   a. Flooding is a real danger to towns that line the world's major rivers.
   b. Humans may be a major contributor to damaging flooding along the Mississippi River.
   c. On the whole, the Mississippi River is safer today than it ever has been.
   d. Straightening the path of a river makes it move faster.

5. Zoos used to be places where unhappy-looking animals paced back and forth in small cages. Gorillas were kept in square concrete cages with nothing to do. Lions were sometimes isolated in even smaller cages. Elephants were tied to a log in dimly lighted enclosures. Today many zoos have large "natural" areas for animals. In some zoos, for example, chimpanzees and gorillas live in large areas that look like rain forests. Huge animals such as elephants wander freely on "African plains" in the heart of New York City and San Diego. Zookeepers sometimes allow animals to work for their food in natural environments, as in the wild. In one zoo, for instance, honey is hidden in a fake anthill. Chimpanzees scoop the honey out with a stiff piece of hay, a process similar to how they "fish" for insects in Africa.

   The unstated main idea is:

   a. Today's zoos are much more expensive to build and maintain than zoos of the past.
   b. Many people who love animals feel that animals should never be locked up in zoos.
   c. Many of today's zoo exhibits are quite different from those of earlier zoos.
   d. While zoos once kept elephants in small dark exhibits, many today provide elephants with much bigger spaces.

9

Relationships I

The term "relationships" means the ways in which ideas are connected to each other. There are two common ways authors show relationships: by using transitions and patterns of organizations. Both are used to make ideas clearer.

This chapter explains transitions and patterns of organization and introduces two of five common types of relationships:

- Relationships of **addition**
- Relationships of **time**

Chapter 10 will present three additional types of relationships.

TRANSITIONS AND PATTERNS OF ORGANIZATION

Transitions are words or phrases that show a relationship between ideas. For instance, read the sentence below. The word in italics is a transition.

> A local bookstore hosts a weekly Scrabble game and *also* a monthly speed-reading tournament.

The word *also* signals a relationship of addition: A second event hosted by the bookstore is being added to the first one.

Also is one of many words and phrases that help writers to make their ideas clearer. Without transitions, the point a writer is trying to make might be hard to understand. For instance, read the following sentences:

> I quickly shut the back door. The mouse ran out.

The author's point is unclear. Did the mouse run out after the door was shut, or before? A transition is needed to make clear the order of the two events:

> I quickly shut the back door *after* the mouse ran out.

The time word *after* makes the relationship between the two events clear: *first* the mouse ran out, and *then* the door was shut. The transition has provided a bridge between the two ideas.

This chapter discusses two kinds of transitions:

- **Addition words**
- **Time words**

Patterns of organization are ways in which paragraphs and longer reading selections are organized. To help readers understand what they are reading, authors try to present main ideas and supporting details in clearly organized ways. Each pattern of organization typically relies on a particular type of transition. When you recognize the patterns, you will be able to make better sense of what you read. You will also be able to remember more of what you read.

This chapter discusses two major patterns of organization:

- **The list of items pattern**

  (Addition words are often used in this pattern of organization.)

- **The time order pattern**

  (Time words are often used in this pattern of organization.)

RELATIONSHIPS OF ADDITION

> *Transitions*: **Addition Words**
>
> *Pattern of organization*: **List of items**

Addition Words

Addition words show that an idea is being added to one already presented.

Read the following items, and circle the letter of the item that is clearer. Then read the explanation that follows.

    a. The sound on our TV is full of static. The picture keeps jumping in and out of focus.

    b. The sound on our TV is full of static. In addition, the picture keeps jumping in and out of focus.

Explanation:

You probably found that item *b* is easier to understand. The words *in addition* make the relationship between the sentences clear. The author is describing two separate problems with the TV. One problem is that the sound is full of static. An added problem is that the picture jumps in and out of focus. The author used an addition transition—*in addition*—to show how the two ideas are related.

Addition words tell us that writers are *adding* to their thoughts. They are presenting one or more ideas that continue along the same line of thought as a previous idea. Like all transitions, addition words help writers organize their information and present it clearly to readers. Here are some common addition words:

Addition Words

first	third	next	moreover
first of all	also	in addition	finally
one	another	additionally	last
second	other	furthermore	last of all
for one thing			

Examples

The following items contain addition words. Notice how these transitions introduce ideas that *add* to what has already been said.

A lively workout at the end of the day relaxes me. *Furthermore*, it makes my problems seem smaller.

A field of sunflowers is an undemanding crop. *First of all*, sunflowers require little fertilizer. *Second*, they don't need irrigation.

I hate my job because of the long hours. *Moreover*, my boss is often rude to me.

➣ Practice 1

Circle the addition word or phrase in each sentence below. Each transition can be found in the box above.

1. Biologists classify humans as mammals. Whales are also classified as mammals.

2. The Italian language has its roots in Latin. Other languages that developed from Latin include Spanish, French, and Portuguese.

3. The endangered timber rattlesnake is quite shy. In addition, it is a peaceful creature.

4. Paper and plastics are two products that many communities are asking people to recycle. Another is used motor oil.

5. The *Pocket Tipper* is a small folding guide that tells how much people should tip such service providers as waiters and parking attendants. Moreover, it lists the services that should be received from each service provider.

The List of Items Pattern

List of Items
Item 1
Item 2
Item 3

A **list of items** is a series of details such as reasons, examples, or facts that support a point. The items are listed in any order the author prefers. The list of items pattern often uses addition transitions, such as *also, another,* and *moreover.* Refer to the box of transitions on page 295 as needed to do the exercises in this chapter.

To get a sense of the list of items pattern, arrange the following group of sentences into the order signaled by the addition words. Write *1* in front of the sentence that should come first, *2* in front of the sentence that comes second, and *3* in front of the sentence that should be last. Then read the explanation that follows.

_____ In addition, a brisk walk is an excellent and inexpensive form of exercise.

_____ Walking can be a rewarding experience.

_____ For one thing, walking lets you see firsthand what's going on in your neighborhood.

Explanation:

The paragraph would begin with the main idea: "Walking can be a rewarding experience." The next two sentences go on to list two of the rewards of walking. The addition transitions *for one thing* and *in addition* introduce the points being listed and indicate their order. The paragraph should read as follows:

Walking can be a rewarding experience. *For one thing,* walking lets you see firsthand what's going on in your neighborhood. *In addition,* a brisk walk is an excellent and inexpensive form of exercise.

Textbook authors frequently organize material into lists of items, such as a list of kinds of businesses, effects of pollution, or benefits of exercise.

A List of Items Paragraph

The paragraph below is organized as a list of items. Finish the outline of the paragraph by completing the first item and filling in the last item. A main idea heading is provided for you; it tells what is being listed in the paragraph. When you're done, read the explanation that follows.

To locate the items (the major details of the paragraph), you may find it helpful to underline the addition words and number (*1, 2, . . .*) the items in the author's list.

A videotape called "How to Have a Moneymaking Garage Sale" lists three tips for success. First, it says to check with your insurance company to be sure that you are covered for unforeseen events such as accidents. Second, price your articles reasonably—clothes should sell for about 10 percent of their original value, and appliances for 20 percent. Finally, never publish a phone number in your advertisements. According to the videotape, this is a good security measure and will prevent nuisance calls.

Main idea heading: Tips for success in the videotape "How to Have a Moneymaking Garage Sale"

1. Check with your insurance company to be sure that _____

   _____

2. Price your articles reasonably.

3. _____

Explanation:

The main idea of the paragraph (the first sentence) tells us that the paragraph will list "tips for success" with a garage sale. Three tips are given: "check with your insurance company to be sure that you are covered for unforeseen events such as accidents," "price your articles reasonably," and "never publish a phone number in your advertisements." The addition words *first, second,* and *finally* introduce the three items listed.

➤ *Practice 2*

A. Below is a paragraph organized as a list of items. Complete the outline of the paragraph. The main idea heading has been started for you. It tells what is being listed.

> A recent study suggested that parents should be on the lookout for stress in their children. There are several signs of stress in young people. Unusual tiredness in a child is one sign. Another is temper tantrums. And a third is that the child forgets known facts; this may result from mental exhaustion.

Main idea heading: Several signs _____

1. _____

2. _____

3. _____

B. The paragraph below is organized as a list of items. Complete the map of the paragraph by finishing the main idea heading and filling in the missing items (that is, the missing major details).

> Most people think of pizza as junk food, but pizza contains healthful ingredients. First of all, the crust is rich in B vitamins, which keep the nervous system humming smoothly. Also, the tomato sauce is an excellent source of vitamin A, which is essential for good vision, among other things. And finally, the mozzarella cheese contains protein and calcium, each of which supports good health in many ways, including keeping bones strong.

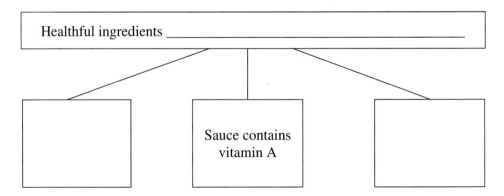

RELATIONSHIPS OF TIME

> *Transitions*: **Time words**
>
> *Pattern of organization*: **Time order**

Time Words

Time words tell *when* something happened in relation to another event.

Read the following items, and circle the letter of the item that is clearer. Then read the explanation that follows.

a. Mitch went for the job interview. He got a haircut and shaved off his mustache.

b. Mitch went for the job interview after he got a haircut and shaved off his mustache.

Explanation:

The first item isn't clear about *when* Mitch got a haircut and shaved off his mustache—before or after the interview. The word *after* in the second item makes the order of the two events clear. Mitch went for the job interview *after* he got a haircut and shaved. *After* and words like it are time words.

Time words help writers organize and make clear the order of events, stages, and steps in a process. Here are some common time words.

Time Words

first	next	as	while
second	before	now	during
then	after	until	when
since	soon	later	finally
recently	when	following	eventually

Examples

The following items contain time words. Notice how these transitions introduce ideas that show *when* something takes place.

Some teenagers were giggling loudly *during* the movie's love scenes.

After the accident, Roberto was questioned by the police.

In 1961, the Russian cosmonaut Yuri Gagarin became the first person to go into space. *Since* that date, more than four hundred people from over twenty-five countries have made the journey.

➤ *Practice 3*

Circle the time word or phrase in each sentence below. Each transition can be found in the box on the previous page.

1. You should let a cooked turkey sit for thirty minutes before carving it.

2. After serving as a United States Senator from Massachusetts, John Kennedy was elected president.

3. Here is a good technique to use to prepare for a test: Study hard for an hour or so. Then, take a break and relax.

4. Helena had difficulty learning to swim until she learned how to float.

5. Ken Kesey gained fame with his novel *One Flew Over the Cuckoo's Nest.* His next book, *Once a Great Notion*, was not as popular.

The Time Order Pattern

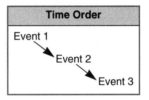

Authors usually present events in the order in which they happened. This results in the time order pattern of organization.

The **time order** pattern uses transitions that show time, such as *next, as,* and *during*. Other signals for this pattern are dates, times, and such words as *stages, series, steps*, and *process*. Refer to the box of transitions on page 299 as needed to do the exercises in this chapter.

To get a sense of the time order pattern, arrange the following group of sentences into an order that makes sense and that is suggested by the time words. Write *1* in front of the sentence that should come first, *2* in front of the sentence that comes second, and *3* and *4* in front of the two sentences that should come last. Then read the explanation which follows.

____ Finally, the chimp took the banana and ate it.

____ Eventually, the chimp grabbed the stick and poked it through the bars of the cage.

____ Next, the chimp dragged the banana within reach.

____ A psychologist placed a banana just outside a chimpanzee's cage and a stick inside the cage.

Explanation:

Helpful clues to the pattern of the above sentences are the time words *eventually, next,* and *finally*. The sentences should read as follows:

> A psychologist placed a banana just outside a chimpanzee's cage and a stick inside the cage. Eventually, the chimp grabbed the stick and poked it through the bars of the cage. Next, the chimp dragged the banana within reach. Finally, the chimp took the banana and ate it.

As a student, you will see time order used frequently. Textbooks in all fields describe events and processes, such as the events leading to the Battle of Bunker Hill, the process involved in making steel, or the stages of a frog's life. In addition, time order is often involved in any directions you have to follow.

A Time Order Paragraph

Below is a paragraph that organizes a series of events in time order. Complete the outline of the paragraph by listing the events in the order in which they happened. The main idea is provided for you. Also, two points have been filled in, and one has been started. When you're done, read the explanation that follows.

> The Model T, manufactured for about twenty years, was a great success for the Ford Motor Company and for mass production. In 1903, Henry Ford organized the company, which was profitable from the start. However, it became even more profitable when, in 1908, he introduced the Model T. That year, the company turned out 10,607 cars, each selling for $850. Ford gradually developed the principle of the assembly line, and by 1913, mass production made it possible for the company to produce more cars and lower the selling price. As a result, the Model T was the first car within reach of the average American. In 1916, the company produced 730,041 cars and sold them for $360 each. By the time production of the Model T stopped in 1927, a total of 15 million had been produced.

Main idea: The Model T, manufactured for about twenty years, was a great success for the Ford Motor Company and for mass production.

1. The Model T was introduced in 1908, when almost 11,000 were made and sold for $850 each.

2. By 1913, _____

   _____

3. In 1916, the company made over 730,000 Model T's, which were sold at less than half the original price.

4. _____

_____

Explanation:

The second point of the outline should have been finished with the second important point in the Model T's history. Here is one way of wording that point: "By 1913, mass production made it possible to produce more cars and lower the selling price." The last point of the outline could be worded like this: "By 1927, when production of the Model T stopped, 15 million had been made."

➤ *Practice 4*

A. The following passage describes steps in a process. Complete the outline below the paragraph. The main idea heading has been provided for you. Also, one step has been filled in, and a second has been started.

Do you have a noticeable stain or burn in your carpeting? It's easy to correct the problem. First, use a sharp utility knife to cut out the damaged area (but not the padding underneath). Then cut a patch the same size and shape from a leftover piece of carpet or a spot of carpeting that's not noticeable, such as under a radiator. Next, cut a piece of burlap the same size as the patch. Place the burlap where you cut out the damaged piece of carpet. Finally, glue the carpet patch to the burlap.

Main idea heading: Steps in eliminating a stain or burn in carpeting

1. Use a sharp utility knife to cut out the damaged area (but not the padding underneath).

2. _____

_____

3. Next, cut a piece of _____

_____

4. _____

_____

5. _____

_____

B. The following passage describes a sequence of events. Complete the map below the paragraph. The main idea is provided for you.

> The discovery and lure of gold led to rapid population growth in California. In January 1848, while building a sawmill along the American River, a carpenter and engineer named James Marshall saw gold flecks in the water. California then had a population of only about 14,000. By spring, many would-be miners were rushing to the area to look for the precious metal. Word about the gold gradually spread eastward, and by 1849, there were over 80,000 "forty-niners" in California hoping to strike it rich. By 1860, California's population had grown to 380,000.

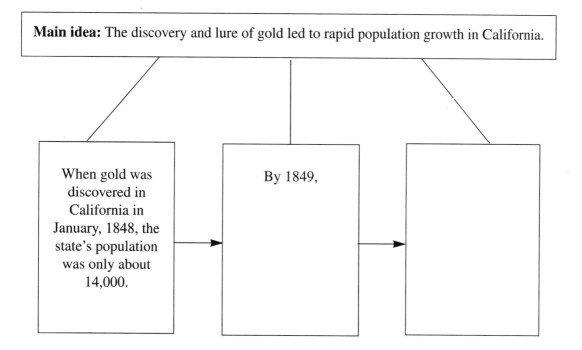

Main idea: The discovery and lure of gold led to rapid population growth in California.

When gold was discovered in California in January, 1848, the state's population was only about 14,000.

By 1849,

Two Final Points

1 A paragraph or passage may have just one pattern of organization, but often the patterns are mixed. For example, you may find that part of a passage uses a list pattern and another part of the same passage uses a time pattern.

2 Keep in mind that not all relationships between ideas are signaled by transitions. An author may present a list of items, for example, without using addition words. So as you read, watch for the relationships themselves, not just the transitions.

CHAPTER SUMMARY

In this chapter, you learned the following:

- "Relationships" are ways in which ideas are connected to each other.

- Authors connect ideas by using transitions and patterns of organization.

- Transitions are words or phrases that show relationships between ideas.

- Patterns of organization are ways in which the details in paragraphs and longer selections are organized.

- Two common relationships are addition and time. The pattern of organization that uses addition is called a list of items; it typically uses addition transitions. The pattern that uses time is called time order; it typically uses time transitions.

➤ *Review Test 1*

To review what you've learned in this chapter, complete each item by filling in the blank.

1. Transitions are words or phrases that signal (*parts of, relationships between, repeated*) _____ ideas.

2. Which type of transition tells us that an author is adding to an idea already mentioned? _____

3. A paragraph's pattern of organization is the way its (*supporting details, main ideas, topics*) _____ are organized.

4. Which pattern provides a series of events or stages? _____
   _____

> **Review Test 2**

A. Read each item below and circle the letter of the relationship that is signaled by the italicized word or phrase.

1. Thirty young athletes were killed in football games *during* the 1909 season.

   The transition signals
   a. addition.
   b. time.

2. Mark's family believes in volunteering. His mother delivers food to shut-ins, and his father works with the Boy Scouts. *In addition*, his older sister plays the piano at nursing homes.

   The transition signals
   a. addition.
   b. time.

3. An ideal apartment should be close to work and school. It should also be in a safe area. *Moreover*, it should be reasonably priced.

   The transition signals
   a. addition.
   b. time.

4. In the past, fingerprints were needed to positively identify a criminal. *Now*, the genetic code of a single cell is enough.

   The transition signals
   a. addition.
   b. time.

B. Read each passage and then answer the questions that follow.

   Recently, the city of Tracy, California, made out a $26,000 check to Thomas Russell, a tax collector in the city. However, the check was sent to the wrong Thomas Russell, an inmate in the Tracy County jail. When it was delivered, the inmate cashed the check, posted bond, and left jail. Officials soon discovered their mistake, tracked down the offender, and put him back in jail.

5. The main pattern of organization in this paragraph is
   a. list of items.
   b. time order.

6-7. Two of the transitions that signal major details of the paragraph are

   _____   _____.

Humans developed several physical features that characterize them as a species. One human feature is the ability to stand and walk upright. This posture, with the eyes at a high level, enables humans to see distant objects. Another distinctive human feature is their teeth and jaws. Human beings have smaller, more even teeth than other primates. A third human feature is the most important: a large brain. The human brain, for instance, is almost three times as large as the chimpanzee's.

8. The main pattern of organization in this paragraph is
   a. list of items.
   b. time order.

9–10. Two transitions that signal major details of the paragraph are

_____   _____.

> *Review Test 3*

A. Read each passage below and answer the questions that follow.

¹In 1848, famous lawman Wyatt Earp was born in Monmouth, Illinois. ²He led a typical law enforcer's life until he was involved in the controversial gunfight at the OK Corral in 1881. ³Ever since that fateful day when so many died, Earp could not escape the media spotlight. ⁴He was questioned wherever he went. ⁵Earp finally retired in California and died quietly in 1929 in Los Angeles.

1. The relationship of sentence 3 to sentence 2 is one of
   a. addition.
   b. time.

2. The relationship between the two parts of sentence 5 is one of
   a. addition.
   b. time.

3. The main pattern of organization of this paragraph is
   a. list of items.
   b. time order.

¹We communicate with each other for various reasons. ²One reason is to meet needs. ³Psychologists tell us that we are social animals; that is, we need other people just as we need food, water, and shelter. ⁴Two people

may converse happily for hours, gossiping and chatting about unimportant matters that neither remembers afterward. ⁵When they part, they may have exchanged little real information, but their communication met an important need—simply to talk with another human being. ⁶Another reason we communicate is to develop relationships. ⁷We get to know others through our communication with them. ⁸A third reason we communicate is to exchange information. ⁹We may be trying to decide how warmly to dress or whom to vote for in the next presidential election. ¹⁰All of us have countless exchanges that involve sending and receiving information.

4. The relationship of sentence 5 to sentence 4 is one of
   a. addition.
   b. time.

5. The relationship of sentence 8 to the sentences that come before it is one of
   a. addition.
   b. time.

6. The main pattern of organization in this paragraph is
   a. list of items.
   b. time order.

B. Read the paragraph below, and do the following:

   1 Circle the letter of the pattern of organization used in the paragraph.

   2 Complete the outline. The main idea has been started for you. Also, one point has been filled in, and a second has been started.

   A major expense in owning a car is insurance payments. There are several ways to lower the amount of your insurance premiums. First, take a higher deductible. A deductible is the amount of money you pay before your insurance kicks in. A higher deductible could reduce your payments by as much as 15 percent. Second, make sure your car is not the kind of car that is a target for thieves. Certain cars that are likely to be stolen have higher premiums. Third, buy a standard model car rather than one that is "souped up" for speed. Cars that appear to be purchased for speed have extremely high premiums. Finally, get an anti-theft device. Most insurance companies will lower your payments if one is installed in your car.

7. The pattern of organization in the above selection is
   a. list of items.
   b. time order.

8–10. Complete the outline of the selection.

Main idea heading: Ways to lower your insurance premiums

1. _____ .

2. Make sure your car is not _____

_____ .

3. Buy a standard model rather than one that is "souped up" for speed.

4. _____ .

➤ *Review Test 4*

Here is a chance to apply your understand of addition and time relationships to a full-length reading. The life of a migrant worker is rarely easy. For migrant worker Maria Cardenas, it was often a nightmare. Her childhood was an exhausting time of backbreaking labor, constant moves, and family violence. Remarkably, Maria continued to cling to her dreams of a better life. This selection tells the story of Maria's journey from the fields to the classroom.

To help you continue to strengthen your skills, the reading is followed by questions on what you've learned in this and previous chapters.

Words to Watch

Following are some words in the reading that do not have strong context support. Each word is followed by the number of the paragraph in which it appears and its meaning there. These words are indicated in the reading by a small circle (°).

blur (9): confused state
enraged (15): greatly angered
shattered (17): destroyed
abducted (18): taken away by force
taunted (22): cruelly teased
overwhelmed (24): overcame
briskly (24): in a lively manner
intimidated (24): fearful
GED (24): general equivalency diploma (equal to a high-school diploma)
eligible (27): qualified

MIGRANT CHILD TO COLLEGE WOMAN

Maria Cardenas

1　As I walk into the classroom, the teacher gazes at me with her piercing green eyes. I feel myself shrinking and burning up with guilt. I go straight to her desk and hand her the excuse slip. Just like all the other times, I say, "I was sick." I hate lying, but I have to. I don't want my parents to get in trouble.

2　I'm not a very good liar. She makes me hold out my hands, inspecting my dirty fingernails and calluses. She knows exactly where I've been the past several days. When you pick tomatoes and don't wear gloves, your hands get rough and stained from the plant oils. Soap doesn't wash that out.

3　In the background, I can hear the students giggling as she asks her usual questions: "What was wrong? Was your brother sick, too? Do you feel better today?" Of course I don't feel better. My whole body aches from those endless hot days spent harvesting crops from dawn to dusk. I was never absent by choice.

4　That year, in that school, I think my name was "Patricia Rodriguez," but I'm not sure. My brother and I used whatever name our mother told us to use each time we went to a new school. We understood that we had to be registered as the children of parents who were in the United States legally, in case Immigration ever checked up.

5　My parents had come to the States in the late '60s to work in the fields and earn money to feed their family. They paid eight hundred dollars to someone who smuggled them across the border, and they left us with our aunt and uncle in Mexico. My five-year-old brother, Joel, was the oldest. I was 4, and then came Teresa, age 3, and baby Bruno. The other kids in the neighborhood teased us, saying, "They won't come back for you." Three years later, our parents sent for us to join them in Texas. My little heart sang as we waved good-bye to those neighbor kids in Rio Verde. My father did love us!

6　My parents worked all the time in the fields. Few other options were open to them because they had little education. At first, our education was important to them. They were too scared to put us in school right away, but when I was 8 they did enroll us. I do remember that my first-grade report card said I was "Antonietta Gonzales." My father made sure we had everything we needed—tablets, crayons, ruler, and the little box to put your stuff in. He bragged to his friends about his children going to school. Now we could talk for our parents. We could translate their words for the grocer, the doctor, and the teachers. If Immigration came by, we could tell them we were citizens, and because we were speaking English, they wouldn't ask any more questions.

7　In the years to come, I often reminded myself that my father had not

forgotten us like the fathers of so many kids I knew. It became more important for me to remember that as it became harder to see that he loved us. He had hit my mother once in a while as I was growing up, but when his own mother died in Mexico in 1973, his behavior grew much worse. My uncles told me that my father, the youngest of the family, had often beaten his mother. Maybe it was the guilt he felt when she died, but for whatever reason, he started drinking heavily, abusing my mother emotionally and physically, and terrorizing us kids. The importance of our education faded away, and now my papa thought my brother and I should work more in the fields. We would work all the time—on school vacations, holidays, weekends, and every day after school. When there were lots of tomatoes to pick, I went to school only every other day.

8   If picking was slow, I stayed home after school and cooked for the family. I started as soon as I got home in the afternoon. I used the three large pots my mother owned: one for beans, one for rice or soup, and one for hot salsa. There were also the usual ten pounds of flour or maseca, ground corn meal, for the tortillas. I loved this cooking because I could eat as much as I wanted and see that the little kids got enough before the older family members finished everything. By this time there were three more children in our family, and we often went to bed hungry. (My best subject in school was lunch, and my plate was always clean.)

9   Other than lunchtime, my school life passed in a blur°. I remember a little about teachers showing us how to sound words out. I began to stumble through elementary readers. But then we'd move again, or I'd be sent to the fields.

10   Life was never easy in those days. Traveling with the harvest meant living wherever the bosses put us. We might be in little houses with one outdoor toilet for the whole camp. Other times the whole crew, all fifty or one hundred of us, were jammed into one big house. Working in the fields meant blistering sun, aching muscles, sliced fingers, bug bites, and my father yelling when we didn't pick fast enough to suit him.

11   But we were kids, so we found a way to have some fun. My brother and I would make a game of competing with each other and the other adults. I never did manage to pick more than Joel, but I came close. One time I picked 110 baskets of cucumbers to Joel's 115. We made thirty-five cents a basket.

12   Of course, we never saw any of that money. At the end of the week, whatever the whole family had earned was given to my father. Soon he stopped working altogether. He just watched us, chatted with the field bosses, and drank beer. He began to beat all of us kids as well as our mother. We didn't work fast enough for him. He wanted us to make more money. He called us names and threw stones and vegetables at us. The other workers did nothing to make him stop. I was always scared of my father, but I loved him even though he treated us so badly. I told myself that he loved us, but that alcohol ruled his life.

13   I knew what controlled my father's life, but I never thought about being in control of my own. I did as I was told, spoke in a whisper, and tried not to be noticed. Because we traveled with the harvest, my brothers and sisters and I attended three or four different schools in one year. When picking was good, I went to the fields instead of school. When the little kids got sick, I stayed home to watch them. When I did go to school, I didn't understand very much. We spoke only Spanish at home. I don't know how I got through elementary school, much less to high school, because I only knew how to add, subtract, and multiply. And let's just say I got "introduced" to English writing skills and grammar. School was a strange foreign place where I went when I could, sitting like a ghost in a corner alone. I could read enough to help my mother fill out forms in English. But enough to pick up a story and understand it? Never. When a teacher told the class "Read this book, and write a report," I just didn't do it. I knew she wasn't talking to me.

14   In 1978, my mother ran away after two weeks of terrible beatings. Joel and I found the dime under the big suitcase, where she had told us it would be. We were supposed to use it to call the police, but we were too scared. We stayed in the upstairs closet with our brothers and sisters. In the morning, I felt guilty and terrified. I didn't know whether our mother was alive or dead. Not knowing what else to do, I got dressed and went to school. I told the counselor what had happened, and she called the police. My father was arrested. He believed the police when they said they were taking him to jail for unpaid traffic tickets. Then the police located my mother and told her it was safe to come out of hiding. My father never lived with us again although he continued to stalk us. He would stand outside the house yelling at my mother, "You're gonna be a prostitute. Those kids are gonna be no-good drug addicts and criminals. They're gonna end up in jail."

15   My father's words enraged° me. I had always had a hunger for knowledge, always dreamed of a fancy job where I would go to work wearing nice clothes and carrying a briefcase. How dare he try to kill my dream! True, the idea of that dream ever coming true seemed unlikely. In school, if I asked about material I didn't understand, most of the teachers seemed annoyed. My mother would

warn me, "Please, don't ask so many questions."

16   But then, somehow, when I was 14, Mrs. Mercer noticed me. I don't remember how my conversations with this teacher started, but it led to her offering me a job in the Western clothing store she and her husband owned. I helped translate for the Spanish-speaking customers who shopped there. I worked only Saturdays, and I got paid a whole twenty-dollar bill. Proudly, I presented that money to my mother. The thought "I can actually do more than field work" began to make my dreams seem like possibilities. I began to believe I could be something more. The month of my sixteenth birthday, Mrs. Mercer recommended me for a cashier's job in the local supermarket. I worked there for six weeks, and on Friday, January 16, 1981, I was promoted to head cashier. I was on top of the world! I could not believe such good things were happening to me. I had a good job, and I was on my way to becoming my school's first Spanish-speaking graduate. I thought nothing could go wrong, ever again.

17   But that very night, my dreams were shattered° again—this time, I thought, permanently. The manager let me off at nine, two hours early. I didn't have a ride because my brother was not picking me up until 11:00 p.m. But I was in luck! I saw a man I knew, a friend of my brother's, someone I had worked with in the fields. He was a trusted family friend, so when he offered me a lift, I said, "Of course." Now I could go home and tell everybody about the promotion.

18   I never made it home or to my big promotion. The car doors were locked; I could not escape. I was abducted° and raped, and I found myself walking down the same abusive road as my mother. My dreams were crushed. I had failed. In my old-fashioned Mexican world, I was a "married woman," even if I wasn't. To go home again would have been to dishonor my family. When I found I was pregnant, there seemed to be only one path open to me. I married my abductor, dropped out of tenth grade, and moved with him to Oklahoma.

19   "My father was right," I thought. "I am a failure." But dreams die hard. My brother Joel was living in the same Oklahoma town as I was. He would see me around town, my face and body bruised from my husband's beatings. But unlike the workers in the fields who had silently watched our father's abuse, Joel spoke up. "You've got to go," he would urge me. "You don't have to take this. Go on, you can make it."

20   "No!" I would tell him. I was embarrassed to have anyone know what my life had become. I imagined returning to my mother, only to have her reprimand me, saying, "What's the matter with you that you can't even stay married?"

21   But Joel wouldn't give up. Finally he told me, "I don't care what you say. I am going to tell Mother what is going on."

22   And he did. He explained to our mother that I had been forced to go with that man, that I was being abused, and that I was coming home. She accepted what he told her. I took

my little girl and the clothes I could carry, threw everything into my car, and left Oklahoma for Florida. My husband taunted° me just as my father had my mother: "You'll be on food stamps! You can't amount to anything on your own!" But I proved him wrong. I worked days in the fields and nights as a cashier, getting off work at midnight and up early the next day to work again. I don't know how I did it, but I kept up the payments on my little car, I didn't go on food stamps, and I was happy.

23   But as Antonietta grew up and started school, I began to think my little triumphs were not enough. I was thrilled to see her learning to read, doing well in school. And when she would bring me her simple little books and trustingly say, "Read with me!" it filled me with joy. But I realized the day would come, and come soon, that I would be unable to read Antonietta's books. What would she think of me when I said, "I can't"? What would I think of myself?

24   Teaching myself to read became the most important goal in my life. I began with Antonietta's kindergarten books. I thought sometimes how people would laugh if they saw me, a grown woman, a mother, struggling through *The Cat in the Hat*. But with no one to watch me, I didn't care. Alone in my house, after my daughter was asleep, I read. I read everything we had in the house—Antonietta's books, cereal boxes, advertisements that came in the mail. I forced myself through them, stumbling again and again over unfamiliar words. Eventually I began to feel ready to try

Maria Cardenas poses with her husband Alfonso, after a day in the orange fields.

a real story, a grown-up story. But my fears nearly stopped me again. We lived near a library. Antonietta had asked again and again to go there. Finally I said "all right." We walked in, but panic overwhelmed° me. All those people, walking around so briskly°, knowing where to find the books they wanted and how to check them out! What was someone like me doing there? What if someone asked me what I wanted? Too intimidated° to even try, I insisted that we leave. I told Antonietta to use the library at her school. I struggled on in private, eventually earning my GED°.

25   The years passed, and I married a wonderful man who loved me and my daughter. He was proud that I had some real education, and he knew that I wanted more. But I couldn't imagine that going on in school was possible.

26   Then, in 1987, I was working for the Redlands Christian Migrant

Association. They provided services for migrant children. One day, in the office, I spotted something that made my heart jump. It was a book called *Dark Harvest.* It was filled with stories about migrant workers. Although my reading skills had improved, I had still never read a book. But this one was about people like me. I began reading it, slowly at first, then with more and more interest. Some of the people in it had gone back for a GED, just as I had! Even more—some had gone on to college and earned a degree in education. Now they were teaching. When I read that book, I realized that my dream wasn't crazy.

27   My husband and I took the steps to become legally admitted residents of the United States. Then, my husband found out about a federal program that helps seasonal farm workers go to college. I applied and found I was eligible°. When I took my diagnostic tests, my reading, English, and math levels turned out to be seventh-grade level. Not as bad as I thought! The recruiter asked if I would mind attending Adult Basic Education classes to raise my scores to the twelfth-grade level. Mind? I was thrilled! I loved to study, and in spite of a serious illness that kept me out of classes for weeks, my teacher thought I was ready to try the ABE exams early. Her encouragement gave my confidence a boost, and I found my scores had zoomed up to a 12.9 level.

28   Then, in the fall of 1994, I took the greatest step of my academic life. Proud and excited, I started classes at Edison Community College in Florida.

Of course, I was also terrified, trembling inside almost like that scared little girl who used to tiptoe up to the teacher's desk with her phony absence excuses. But I'm not a scared little kid anymore. My self-confidence is growing, even if it's growing slowly.

29   I laugh when I look back at that day I fled in terror from the library. My family and I might as well live there now. We walk in with me saying, "Now, we have other things to do today. Just half an hour." Three hours later, it's the kids saying to me, "Mom, are you ready *yet*?" But it's so exciting, knowing that I can learn about anything I want just by picking up a book! I've read dozens of how-to books, many of them about gardening, which has become my passion. I can't put down motivational books, like Ben Carson's *Gifted Hands* and *Think Big.* I love Barbara Kingsolver's novels. One of them, *The Bean Trees,* was about a young woman from a very poor area in Kentucky whose only goal, at first, was to finish school without having a child. I could understand her. But my favorite author is Maya Angelou. Right now, I'm re-reading her book *I Know Why The Caged Bird Sings.* She writes so honestly about the tragedy and poverty she's lived with. She was raped when she was little, and she had a child when she was very young. And now she's a leader, a wonderful writer and poet. When I see her—she read a poem at President Clinton's inauguration—I am very moved. And I can't talk about my life now without mentioning Kenneth and Mary Jo Walker, the president of Edison Community College and his

wife. They offered me a job in their home, but so much more than that: they have become my friends, my guardian angels. I am constantly borrowing books from them, and they give me so much encouragement that I tell them, "You have more faith in me than I do myself."

30   Sometimes I have to pinch myself to believe that my life today is real. I have a hard-working husband and three children, all of whom I love very much. My son Korak is 11. Whatever he studies in school—the Aztecs, the rainforest, Mozart—he wants to find more books in the library about it, to learn more deeply. Jasmine, my little girl, is 7, and is reading through the *Little House on the Prairie* books. Like me, the children have worked in the fields, but there is little resemblance between their lives and mine as a child.

They are in one school the whole year long. They work at their own pace, learning the value of work and of money—and they keep what they earn. Antonietta, who inspired me to begin reading, is 17 now. Although she's only a junior in high school, she's taking college calculus classes and planning to study pre-med in college, even though her teachers have encouraged her to become a journalist because of her skill in writing.

31   And guess what! My teachers compliment my writing too. When I enrolled in my developmental English class at Edison, my teacher, Johanna Seth, asked the class to write a narrative paragraph. A narrative, she explained, tells a story. As I thought about what story I could write, a picture of a scared little girl in a schoolroom popped into my head. I began writing:

With the help of her English teacher, Johanna Seth,
Maria uses a word processor to edit one of her papers.

32   *As I walk into the classroom, the teacher gazes at me with her piercing green eyes. I feel myself shrinking and burning up with guilt. I go straight to her desk and hand her the excuse slip. Just like all the other times, I say, "I was sick." I hate lying, but I have to. I don't want my parents to get in trouble.*

33   I finish my narrative about giving my phony excuses to my grade-school teachers and hand it in. I watch Mrs. Seth read it and, to my horror, she begins to cry. I know it must be because she is so disappointed, that what I have written is so far from what the assignment was meant to be that she doesn't know where to begin to correct it.

34   "Did you write this?" she asks me. Of course, she knows I wrote it, but she seems disbelieving. "You wrote this?" she asks again. Eventually I realize that she is not disappointed. Instead, she is telling me something incredible and wonderful. She is saying that my work is good, and that she is very happy with what I've given her. She is telling me that I can succeed here.

35   And now I know she's right. I'm graduating from Edison as a member of Phi Theta Kappa, the national academic honors society for junior colleges. I'll enroll in the fall at Florida Gulf Coast University to finish my degree in elementary education. I will spend the summer working, maybe picking crops once again. But in the fall, when my children return to school, so will I. I have a goal: to teach migrant children to speak English, to stand on their own two feet, to achieve their dreams. In helping them, I will be making my own dream come true.

Posing with Maria at graduation are President and Mrs. Walker and their daughter Keri; Maria's husband, Alfonso; and the children, Antoinetta, Korak, and Jasmine.

Word Skills Questions

Phonics

1. Which of the following words from the sentence below has two short vowel sounds?
   a. *trembling*
   b. *inside*
   c. *tiptoe*

   > "Of course, I was also terrified, trembling inside almost like that scared little girl who used to tiptoe up to the teacher's desk with her phony absence excuses." (Paragraph 28)

2. The **s** in the word *teacher's*, in the excerpt below, sounds like
   a. **s** as in *salt.*
   b. **z.**

   > "Of course, I was also terrified, trembling inside almost like that scared little girl who used to tiptoe up to the teacher's desk. . . ." (Paragraph 28)

Dictionary Use

Use the following dictionary entry to answer questions 3–5.

es•cape (ĭ-skāp′) *v.* **-caped, -cap•ing 1.** To break out (of). **2.** To avoid capture, danger, or harm. **3.** To succeed in avoiding. **4.** To elude: *Her name escapes me.* **5.** To leak or issue (from). *n.* **1.** The act or a means of escaping. **2.** A leakage. **3.** *Comp. Sci.* A key used esp. to interrupt a command or exit a program.

3. Which definition of *escape* has a field label?
a. Verb definition 1	c. Noun definition 1
b. Verb definition 4	d. Noun definition 3

4. *Escape* has
   a. two short vowel sounds, with the accent on the second syllable.
   b. three parts of speech, each with the same number of definitions.
   c. two syllables, with the accent on the second syllable.
   d. a usage label.

5. Which definition of *escape* fits the sentence below?
   a. Verb definition 1
   b. Verb definition 5
   c. Noun definition 2
   d. Noun definition 3

   > "The car doors were locked; I could not escape." (Paragraph 18)

Vocabulary in Context

6. In the sentence below, the word *briskly* means
   a. slowly.   c. in a lively manner.
   b. in confusion.   d. foolishly.

   "All those people, walking around so briskly, knowing where to find the books they wanted and how to check them out!" (Paragraph 24)

7. In the sentences below, the word *options* means
   a. opinions.   c. gifts.
   b. pleasures.   d. choices.

   "My parents worked all the time in the fields. Few other options were open to them because they had little education." (Paragraph 6)

8. In the sentence below, the word *reprimand* means
   a. scold.   c. compliment.
   b. ignore.   d. support.

   "I imagined returning to my mother, only to have her reprimand me, saying, 'What's the matter with you that you can't even stay married?'" (Paragraph 20)

9. In the sentences below, the word *intimidated* means
   a. thoughtful.   c. fearful.
   b. bored.   d. critical.

   "We lived near a library. . . . What if someone asked me what I wanted? Too intimidated to even try, I insisted that we leave." (Paragraph 24)

10. In the sentence below, the word *resemblance* means
   a. difference.   c. confusion.
   b. similarity.   d. pride.

   "Like me, the children have worked in the fields, but there is little resemblance between their lives and mine as a child." (Paragraph 30)

Reading Comprehension Questions

Central Point and Main Ideas

1. Which sentence best expresses the central point of the entire selection?
   a. Maria's goal is to graduate from college and teach migrant children to achieve their dreams.
   b. With hard work and courage, Maria was able to overcome great difficulties to build a wonderful family and go to college.

   c. Some books are filled with inspiration stories that can help us all.

   d. Maria showed us that certain skills are necessary if we want to succeed in college.

2. The topic sentence of paragraph 10 is its
   a. first sentence.
   b. second sentence.
   c. third sentence.
   d. last sentence.

3. Which sentence best expresses the main idea of paragraph 16?
   a. One of Maria's teachers offered Maria a job at a Western clothing store.
   b. One of Maria's teachers and her husband owned a Western clothing store.
   c. Thanks to a kind teacher and her own good work, Maria began to believe she could be more than a field worker.
   d. At the age of 16, Maria became a supermarket cashier and soon was promoted to head cashier.

4. Which sentence best expresses the main idea of paragraph 26?
   a. In 1987, Maria worked for the Redlands Christian Migrant Association.
   b. The book *Dark Harvest* convinced Maria that her dream for a better education wasn't crazy.
   c. The Redlands Christian Migrant Association provided services for migrant children.
   d. The book *Dark Harvest* contained stories about migrant workers, including some who had gone on to college and became teachers.

Supporting Details

5. Maria's father began to drink heavily and abuse his wife more than ever after
   a. he lost his job.
   b. his children began going to school.
   c. Immigration came to the house.
   d. his mother died.

6. After he began drinking a lot, Maria's father eventually
   a. stopped working.
   b. began to beat his children.
   c. threw things at his children.
   d. did all of the above.

7. After being raped, Maria
   a. ran away.
   b. dropped out of tenth grade and married the man who raped her.
   c. went to the police.
   d. did all of the above.

Relationships

8. The first word of the sentence below signals a relationship of
   a. addition.   b. time.

   "When the little kids got sick, I stayed home to watch them." (Paragraph 13)

9. The relationship of the second sentence below to the first is one of
   a. addition.   b. time.

   "Proud and excited, I started classes at Edison Community College in Florida. Of course, I was also terrified. . . . " (Paragraph 28)

10. The overall pattern of organization of this selection is
    a. list of items.   b. time order.

Discussion Questions

1. Maria's children work in the fields, as their mother had. In what ways are those children's lives different from Maria's life when she was a child working in the fields?

2. Why do you think Mrs. Seth cried upon reading the narrative about Maria giving phony excuses to her grade-school teachers? Why do you think Maria thought that Mrs. Seth was disappointed with what she had written?

3. What do you think Maria means when she says she wants to teach migrant children to "stand on their own two feet"?

Note: Writing assignments for this selection appear on pages 544–545.

Check Your Performance			RELATIONSHIPS I
Activity	*Number Right*	*Points*	*Score*
Review Test 1 (4 items)	_____	× 2.5 =	_____
Review Test 2 (10 items)	_____	× 3 =	_____
Review Test 3 (10 items)	_____	× 3 =	_____
Review Test 4 (20 items)	_____	× 1.5 =	_____
	TOTAL SCORE	=	_____%

Enter your total score into the **Reading Performance Chart: Review Tests** on the inside back cover.

RELATIONSHIPS I: Test 1

A. For each item below, circle the letter of the type of transition indicated by the italicized word.

1. *While* digging in his garden, Lonnie discovered an old tin box full of coins.

   The transition signals
   a. addition.
   b. time.

2. To avoid drunk drivers, some people stay off the road late at night. They *also* stay home on New Year's Eve.

   The transition signals
   a. addition.
   b. time.

3. Anita planned to become a flight attendant *until* she discovered that she got airsick.

   The transition signals
   a. addition.
   b. time.

4. Some desert plants, such as mesquite, grow long root systems that tap water deep in the ground. *Other* desert plants, such as cactuses, have shallow root systems and store water in their stems and leaves.

   The transition signals
   a. addition.
   b. time.

(Continues on next page)

B. Read each passage, and then answer the questions that follow.

Recently a man in Kansas caused a stir when he created and used a device to go hot-air ballooning. He strapped forty-two weather balloons to a lawn chair and then inflated the balloons. Sitting in the chair, he took off and climbed to sixteen thousand feet before shooting some of the balloons with a BB gun. He descended faster than he expected and finally crashed into some power lines. He was uninjured, but he spent the next few days in jail.

5. The main pattern of organization in this paragraph is
   a. list of items.
   b. time order.

6–7. Two transitions that signal major details of the paragraph are

   _____   _____.

According to experts, you can help your children become able people in several ways. One way is to encourage them to have close social relationships with the important people in their lives. A second way to help children become able is to give them help when they need it, rather than either giving help too soon or ignoring them. Third, speak to them. They will not pick up language from listening to radio or TV. Fourth, give children physical freedom to explore. Do not confine them regularly in a playpen, crib, jump seat, or small room.

8. The main pattern of organization in this paragraph is
   a. list of items.
   b. time order.

9–10. Two transitions that signal major details of the paragraph are

   _____   _____.

RELATIONSHIPS I: Test 2

A. For each item below, circle the letter of the type of relationship signaled by the italicized word or phrase.

1. *After* it started to rain, the weather reporter said showers were likely.

   The transition signals
   a. addition.
   b. time.

2. A computer word-processing program can help you correct your spelling errors. It can *also* help you fix your grammar problems.

   The transition signals
   a. addition.
   b. time.

3. *During* the 1960s, many American college students protested against the Vietnam war.

   The transition signals
   a. addition.
   b. time.

4. Oil spills in rivers and lakes cause great problems for wildlife. *Moreover,* the oil is a threat to our own water supply.

   The transition signals
   a. addition.
   b. time.

(Continues on next page)

B. Read each passage, and then answer the questions that follow.

The state of Hawaii offers more to visitors than sunshine and beaches. There are many natural wonders that are not soon forgotten. One such wonder is Waimea Canyon on the island of Kauai. The canyon is 3,600 feet deep, 10 miles long, and reddish in color. It is known as the "Grand Canyon of the Pacific." Another is Volcano National Park on the big island of Hawaii. Here an active volcano often spews lava hundreds of feet into the air. Finally, on the island of Maui, visitors can drive to the top of a mountain and hike into a crater that was actually used by astronauts as they trained to walk on the moon.

5. The pattern of organization in this paragraph is
   a. list of items.
   b. time order.

6–7. Two transitions that signal major details of the paragraph are

   _____   _____.

When the United States was founded, Ben Franklin wanted to name the wild turkey as the national bird. That did not happen. Following the naming of the bald eagle as the national bird, the wild turkey became nearly extinct, owing to overhunting and development. In 1950, it was estimated that only thirty thousand wild turkeys existed in the entire country. Since that time, conservationists have worked hard to ensure the survival of the bird. Now the number of wild turkeys in the United States is estimated at well over 1 million.

8. The pattern of organization in this paragraph is
   a. list of items.
   b. time order.

9–10. Two transitions that signal major details of the paragraph are

   _____   _____.

RELATIONSHIPS I: Test 3

A. Read each passage and answer the questions that follow.

[1]The United States Census Bureau reports that close to 40 percent of the country's citizens live in states other than where they were born. [2]Two main factors are involved. [3]One is economic. [4]People who are looking for work tend to move where the jobs are. [5]Another consideration is weather. [6]People seem to enjoy the warmer states. [7]This is especially true of senior citizens. [8]When given the chance to move from a snowy state to a sunny state, many older Americans will do so.

1. The relationship of sentence 5 to sentences 3 and 4 is one of
   a. addition.
   b. time.

2. The relationship between the two parts of sentence 8 (on both sides of the comma) is one of
   a. addition.
   b. time.

3. The main pattern of organization in this paragraph is
   a. list of items.
   b. time order.

[1]Nuclear weapons have been used in war only two times, both in Japan during World War II. [2]On August 6, 1945, the United States dropped the first atomic bomb on Hiroshima, Japan. [3]Over 140,000 people were killed. [4]Many were killed by the bomb itself. [5]Additional casualties occurred from the radiation that followed. [6]Three days later, the United States dropped an atomic bomb on the Japanese city of Nagasaki. [7]This bomb killed over 70,000 people. [8]Following the bombings, Japan surrendered unconditionally, and the war ended.

4. The relationship of sentence 5 to sentence 4 is one of
   a. addition.
   b. time.

5. The relationship of sentence 8 to the sentences that come before it is one of
   a. addition.
   b. time.

6. The main pattern of organization in this paragraph is
   a. list of items.
   b. time order.

(Continues on next page)

B. Fill in each blank with the appropriate transition from the box. Two transitions
will be left over. Then circle the letter of the paragraph's pattern of organization.

also	as	first of all
furthermore	since	

A steroid is a type of drug that is taken to improve muscles and
performance. A steroid can help an athlete compete in certain sports.
However, the medical profession has raised various concerns about steroid
use. (7)_____, a steroid can raise blood pressure.
It can (8)_____ lead to violent mood swings.
(9)_____, a steroid may lead to increased heart
disease and liver and kidney failure. The dangers of using steroids far
outweigh the benefits, and they are banned in most athletic contests.

10. The main pattern of organization of this passage is:
    a. list of items.
    b. time order.

RELATIONSHIPS I: Test 4

A. Read each passage and answer the questions that follow.

[1]We generally classify the people we have relationships with into three categories. [2]First are acquaintances. [3]These are people we know by name and talk to when the opportunity arises. [4]But our interactions with acquaintances tend to be limited in quality and quantity. [5]The second category of relationships is friends. [6]Friends are people with whom we have built personal relationships by choice. [7]The third category of relationships is close friends. [8]These are people with whom we share our deepest feelings.

1. The relationship of sentence 5 to the sentences that come before it is one of
   a. addition.
   b. time.

2. The relationship of sentence 7 to the sentences that come before it is one of
   a. addition.
   b. time.

3. The main pattern of organization in this paragraph is
   a. list of items.
   b. time order.

[1]A new species of ant was discovered in the office of the president of the World Wildlife Fund. [2]The president, Kathryn Fuller, came into her office one day and prepared for a long day of work. [3]She first went to water her plants. [4]She found a number of ants in one plant. [5]She did not recognize the ants as any species she had ever seen. [6]She then consulted a number of textbooks. [7]She also asked her staff if they knew what species the ants belonged to. [8]Later she called an expert, who studied the ants for several months. [9]The expert eventually agreed with Ms. Fuller that such ants had never before been seen by scientists and should be considered a new species.

4. The relationship of sentence 6 to the sentences before it is one of
   a. addition.
   b. time.

5. The relationship of sentence 8 to the sentence before it is one of
   a. addition.
   b. time.

6. The main pattern of organization in this paragraph is
   a. list of items.
   b. time order.

(Continues on next page)

B. Fill in each blank with the appropriate transition from the box. Two transitions will be left over. Then answer the question about pattern of organization.

before	following	then
until	when	

One of the most celebrated robberies of the century occurred in Great Britain in August of 1963. Fourteen robbers stopped a mail train that was traveling from Glasgow, Scotland to London, England. The robbers (7)_____ made off with over seven million dollars. (8)_____ the robbery, a national search for the criminals took place. Almost all were caught and sentenced to thirty years in prison. One, Ronald Biggs, escaped from jail in 1965 and made his way to Brazil. (9)_____ he was discovered there in 1974, British officials requested his return. Brazil refused, and Biggs is still living there.

10. The main pattern of organization of this passage is
    a. list of items.
    b. time order.

RELATIONSHIPS I: Test 5

Read each paragraph, and then answer the questions that follow.

An African-American cavalry unit called the Buffalo Soldiers was on duty patrolling the American frontier between 1866 and 1944. In about 1870, the unit was given its name by Native Americans who came to respect the soldiers' bravery. In 1898, the Buffalo Soldiers rode with Teddy Roosevelt into Cuba. In 1916, they chased the Mexican bandit Pancho Villa to his homeland. And they monitored the United States–Mexico border on horseback until 1944, when the brigade was disbanded.

1. The main pattern of organization is
   a. list of items.
   b. time order.

2. One transition that signals a major detail of the paragraph is

   _____.

3–5. Complete the outline of the selection.

   Main idea: An African-American cavalry unit called the Buffalo Soldiers patrolled the American frontier between 1866 and 1944.

   1. In about 1870, _____

      _____

   2. _____

      _____

   3. In 1916, they chased the bandit Pancho Villa to his homeland, Mexico.

   4. They monitored the United States–Mexico border _____

      _____

(Continues on next page)

Three bridges in the United States have proved terrifying to a number of drivers. One is the Chesapeake Bay Bridge in Maryland. It is over four miles long and at one point is two hundred feet above the water. It is a very narrow bridge with safety barriers that let drivers see the water below but not the land ahead. A second frightening bridge is in northern California. The Richmond Bridge is only three miles in length, but it rises, dips, and rises again. Some drivers have complained that they felt they were on a roller coaster. In addition, there is one span of this bridge where drivers can see no land but have a clear view of ships passing directly underneath the bridge. The ships appear to be so close that some drivers have believed the ships were about to hit the bridge. Finally, there is the Mackinaw Bridge in Michigan. This bridge is five miles long and 190 feet tall at its highest point. Some drivers are so panicked at driving across this bridge that the state allows its bridge officers to drive frightened drivers across the bridge at no cost.

6. The main pattern of organization is
   a. list of items.
   b. time order.

7–8. Two transitions that signal major details of the paragraph are

_____   _____.

9–10. Complete the map of the selection.

Main idea heading: Bridges that have proved _____

| The Chesapeake Bay Bridge in Maryland is very narrow and lets drivers see only the water below, not the land ahead. | The Richmond Bridge in northern California moves like a roller coaster and sometimes gives the impression that ships are about to hit it. | |

RELATIONSHIPS I: Test 6

Read each textbook passage, and then answer the questions that follow.

> Your chances of becoming a group leader are increased if you behave in certain ways during group discussions. First, be knowledgeable about the group work. Group members are more willing to follow someone who is well informed. Also, the more knowledge you have, the better you will be able to analyze what members of the group say. Second, work harder than anyone else in the group. Leadership is often a question of setting an example. Third, be willing to make decisions at key moments in a discussion. When leaders are unsure of themselves or unwilling to make decisions, the group may lose direction. Fourth, interact freely with others in the group. This does not mean that you should take over the discussion. It does mean sharing your ideas and feelings about the group's work. Finally, help the group work together smoothly. Effective leaders, for instance, make others in the group feel good. And they take care to give credit where it is due.

1. The main pattern of organization in the above selection is
   a. list of items.
   b. time order.

2. One transition that signals a major detail of the paragraph is

   _____.

3–5. Complete the outline of the selection.

   Main idea: Your chances of becoming a group leader are increased if you behave in certain ways during group discussions.

   1. _____

   2. _____

   3. Be willing to make decisions at key moments in a discussion.

   4. _____

   5. Help the group work together smoothly.

(Continues on next page)

Although the exact cause of childhood obesity is not known, there are a number of theories. One cause may be a child's genes. A study of 540 adopted adults found that their weight was more like that of their biological parents than their adoptive ones. A second cause is environment. Children tend to eat the same foods and develop the same habits as the people around them. Third, heavier children are less active. But are they less active because they are fat, or do they become fat because they are less active? So far, there is no final answer. But some support the conclusion that children become fat because they are less active. Finally, watching too much television may also be a factor. According to studies, every hour a day spent watching TV results in a 2 percent increase in the frequency of obesity. Children who watch a lot of TV tend to eat more snacks, especially the high-calorie snacks they see in ads. They are also less active than other children.

6. The main pattern of organization in the above selection is
   a. list of items.
   b. time order.

7. Two transitions that signal major details of the paragraph are

   _____   _____.

8–10. Complete the map of the selection.

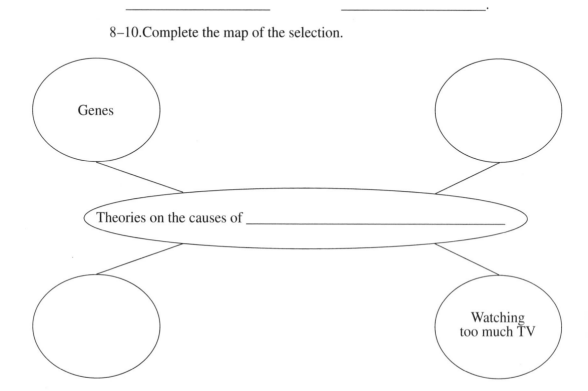

Genes

Theories on the causes of _____

Watching too much TV

10

Relationships II

Chapter 9 explains transitions and patterns of organization. It also presents two common types of relationships:

- Relationships of **addition**
- Relationships of **time**

This chapter looks at three other common types of relationships:

- Relationships of **comparison and contrast**
- Relationships of **cause and effect**
- Relationships of **definition and example**

RELATIONSHIPS OF COMPARISON AND CONTRAST

Transitions: Comparison and contrast words

Pattern of organization: Comparison-contrast

Comparison Words

Comparison words signal that one thing is *like* another in some way.

Read the following items, and circle the letter of the item you think is clearer. Then read the explanation that follows.

a. For many people, the first day on a new job is a scary experience. The first class in college can be a frightening experience.

b. For many people, the first day on a new job is a scary experience. Similarly, the first class in college can be a frightening experience.

Explanation:

In item *a*, it seems as if the second sentence is changing the subject. However, in item *b*, the word *similarly* makes the relationship between the sentences clear: Just as the first day on a new job can be frightening, so can being in a college class for the first time. *Similarly* is a transition word that signals a comparison between ideas.

Comparison words show you that the author is pointing out how two ideas are alike. The second idea will be *like* the first idea in some way. Here are some common comparison words:

Comparison Words

as	alike	similar	resembles
just as	likewise	similarly	resembled
like	same	similarities	
just like	in the same way	equally	

Contrast Words

Contrast words signal that ideas *differ* from each other. Contrast words are the opposite of comparison words.

Read the following items, and circle the letter of the item you think is clearer. Then read the explanation that follows.

a. The dog next door is lovable. She barks a lot at night.

b. The dog next door is lovable even though she barks a lot at night.

Explanation:

The first item suggests that one of the lovable things about the dog is that she barks at night. The transition *even though* in the second item shows a contrast: The dog is lovable *despite* the barking. *Even though* is a transition phrase that signals a contrast between two ideas. Here are some common contrast words:

Contrast Words

but	instead	still	difference
yet	in contrast	as opposed to	different
however	on the other hand	in spite of	differently
although	on the contrary	despite	differs
nevertheless	even though	rather than	unlike

Examples

The first two examples below contain comparison words. Notice how these transitions help show how things are *alike* in some way. The last two items contain contrast transitions. Notice how these words signal that one thing is *different* from another.

> Hakim always succeeded both academically and athletically. *Likewise,* his daughter Aliya is a scholar-athlete at Bentley High School.

> Most people can't stand the sound of brakes screeching. *Equally* annoying is hearing chalk squeak across a chalkboard.

> The test results I got in my lab experiment were *unlike* those reached by everyone else in the class.

> Alberto was angry when he didn't get a raise. His wife, *however,* took the news calmly.

➤ Practice 1

Circle the comparison or contrast word or phrase in each sentence below. Each transition can be found in one of the boxes on page 336. Then tell whether the relationship is one of comparison or contrast by circling the letter of your choice.

1. A frozen banana tastes just like banana ice cream.
   The circled word or phrase shows
   a. comparison.   b. contrast.

2. Even though the penguin can't fly, it can swim faster than any fish.
   The circled word or phrase shows
   a. comparison.   b. contrast.

3. Despite the long winters in Alaska, many people enjoy living there.
   The circled word or phrase shows
   a. comparison.   b. contrast.

4. Some cats will wait patiently to be fed. Others, however, will follow their owner around the house meowing when they are hungry.
   The circled word or phrase shows
   a. comparison.   b. contrast.

5. Grandma's favorite saying is, "Do unto others as you would have others do unto you."
   The circled word or phrase shows
   a. comparison.   b. contrast.

The Comparison-Contrast Pattern

The **comparison-contrast pattern** shows how two things are like each other, or how they are different, or both. When things are compared, you are shown how they are alike. When things are contrasted, you are shown how they differ. This pattern often uses comparison words (such as *like, similar to,* and *just as)* or contrast words (such as *unlike, however,* and *in contrast),* or both.

To get a sense of the comparison-contrast pattern, arrange the following group of sentences into an order that makes sense. Write *1* in front of the sentence that should come first, *2* in front of the sentence that comes second, and *3* in front of the sentence that should be last. Finally, read the explanation that follows.

_____ City and country dwellers give different reasons for living where they do.

_____ On the other hand, people who live in the country talk about a slower pace of life, clean air and water, and friendly neighbors.

_____ People who live in cities mention good-paying jobs and closeness to cultural events.

Explanation:

The first sentence states the main idea: "City and country dwellers give different reasons for living where they do." This sentence suggests that the reasons city dwellers give for where they live will contrast with those of country dwellers. The transitional phrase *on the other hand* signals that a contrast is being made. The paragraph should read as follows:

City and country dwellers give different reasons for living where they do. People who live in cities mention good-paying jobs and closeness to cultural events. On the other hand, people who live in the country talk about a slower pace of life, clean air and water, and friendly neighbors.

We often compare and contrast, even though we may not be aware of it. For example, a simple decision about what to do on a Saturday night requires us to compare and contrast possible choices. Do we want to go to the movies, or do we want to rent a video? Do we feel like having friends over or do we prefer being alone? Or should we study for the big test that is coming up?

A Comparison-Contrast Paragraph

Read the passage at the top of the next page and answer the questions that follow. Then read the explanation.

There are two different views of the value of computers in the classroom. Some people feel that computers will soon replace many of the teachers' duties. One writer states, "Computers make do-it-yourself education downright efficient. Your child can probably learn spelling or arithmetic or a foreign language faster on a computer" than from a teacher in a crowded classroom. However, others warn that too much technology may harm children. One psychologist warns that computers, as well as video games and TV, may weaken children's language skills.

1. Is this paragraph comparing, contrasting, or both? _____

2. What is being compared and/or contrasted?

_____

3. What are the two comparison or contrast words used in the paragraph?

_____   _____

Explanation:

The first sentence states the main idea. It tells us that the paragraph will contrast opinions on the value of computers in the classroom. The two contrast words used in the paragraph are *different* and *however.*

➣ *Practice 2*

A. The following passage uses the comparison-contrast pattern. Read the passage and answer the questions that follow.

As shown by state records, men and women can be equally bad drivers. On the female side is the Arkansas woman who needed 104 attempts before passing her driver's test. A similarly bad driver is the Texas man who received ten tickets, drove on the wrong side of the road four times, and was involved in four hit-and-run accidents. He accomplished all this in just one year.

1. Is this paragraph comparing, contrasting, or both? _____

2. What is being compared and/or contrasted?

_____

3. The two comparison or contrast words used in the paragraph are

_____   _____

B. The following passage uses the comparison-contrast pattern. Complete the map of the paragraph by completing the heading and filling in the missing supporting details.

Stepfamilies and "natural" families have interesting similarities and differences. Both types of families have a similar range of everyday values, and both types have backgrounds that tend to be alike as well. On the other hand, the stepfamily includes more people—ex-husbands, ex-wives, ex-in-laws, and various other relatives on both sides. In addition, the stepfamily has anger, guilt, and conflicts that "natural" families don't face. For example, stepchildren are likely to have bitter feelings toward their stepparents that don't surface in relationships between children and their natural parents.

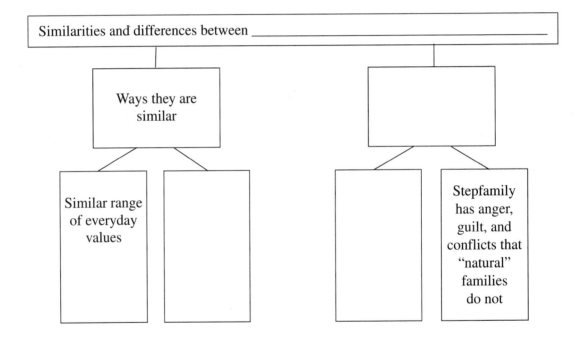

Similarities and differences between _____

Ways they are similar

Similar range of everyday values

Stepfamily has anger, guilt, and conflicts that "natural" families do not

RELATIONSHIPS OF CAUSE AND EFFECT

> *Transitions:* **Cause-effect words**
>
> *Pattern of organization:* **Cause-effect**

Cause and Effect Words

Cause and effect words signal the reason something occurred or the effects of something.

Read the following items, and circle the letter of the item you think is clearer. Then read the explanation that follows.

> a. The baby refused to eat her breakfast. I was in a bad mood all morning.
>
> b. The baby refused to eat her breakfast. As a result, I was in a bad mood all morning.

Explanation:

In the first item, we are not sure of the relationship between the two ideas. Were there two problems: the baby refusing to eat and the bad mood? Or did the first problem cause the second one? The transition phrase *as a result* shows that the baby's behavior caused the bad mood.

Cause and effect words show that the author is discussing one or more reasons or results. These words signal that one thing *causes* another to occur. Here are some common cause and effect words:

Cause and Effect Words

cause	due to	result	reason
effect	affect	as a result	lead to
because	therefore	resulting	so
because of	thus	resulted	so that
consequently	why		

Examples

The following examples contain cause and effect words. Notice how these transitions introduce a reason for something or the result of something.

> Students who work full-time sometimes nap before classes *because* they are tired after work.
>
> One *reason* for our lower electric bills is that we turned down the thermostat.

Home exercise machines have become big business *as a result of* people becoming more interested in keeping in good shape.

➤ *Practice 3*

Circle the cause and effect word or phrase in each sentence below. Each transition can be found in the box on page 341.

1. Drinking large amounts of carrot juice can cause a person's skin to turn orange.

2. Most baseball stadiums have lights so that day games which run late don't need to be called off.

3. The lifeguard at Baywatch Beach thought she spotted a shark. As a result, the beach was closed for the rest of the day.

4. Scientists in the Antarctic no longer wear fur because they have discovered that quilted, layered clothing keeps them warmer.

5. The contract offered by management did not satisfy union members. Therefore, they decided to go on strike.

The Cause and Effect Pattern

Paragraphs using the **cause and effect pattern** address questions such as "Why did this event happen?" or "What would be the result of doing this?" In other words, they discuss the causes and/or the effects of an event.

The cause and effect pattern often uses cause-effect words such as *because, as a result,* and *reason.*

To get a sense of the cause and effect pattern, arrange the following group of sentences into an order that makes sense. Write *1* in front of the sentence that should come first, the sentence with the main idea. Write *2* in front of the sentence that comes second and *3* in front of the sentence that should be last. Then read the explanation which follows.

____ It commonly results in great relaxation.

____ Meditation has been found to have a wide variety of effects.

____ It has also been found now and then to cause such negative effects as anxiety and even depression.

Explanation:

The paragraph would begin with the main idea: "Meditation has been found to have a wide variety of effects." The rest of the paragraph is made up of two examples of those effects. The transition words *effects, results,* and *cause* suggest the cause and effect pattern. In paragraph form, the sentences would read as follows:

> Meditation has been found to have a wide variety of effects. It commonly results in great relaxation. It has also been found now and then to cause such negative effects as anxiety and even depression.

Authors often discuss events with a cause and effect pattern. They don't just tell you *what* happened; they tell you *why* it happened as well. For example, a textbook account of the Boston Tea Party would be incomplete without giving its cause: The colonists threw 342 chests of a British tea into the water of Boston's harbor *because* the British company was allowed to sell the tea without paying taxes. An important part of any effort to understand events and processes includes learning about cause and effect relationships.

A Cause and Effect Paragraph

The following passage contains items that are either causes or effects. Read the paragraph and then look at the items below the paragraph. Write **C** in front of each item that is a cause and **E** in front of each item that is an effect. Then read the explanation.

> Researchers have learned that laughing can be good for you. Laughing relaxes the facial muscles, causing you to look and feel less tense. It also increases the oxygen in the brain, resulting in a lightheaded sense of well-being. In addition, laughing is a proven stress-reducer; thus it decreases your chances of getting stress-related illnesses.

____ Laughing

____ Looking and feeling less tense

____ Increase of oxygen in the brain and a lightheaded sense of well-being

____ Decreased chances of getting stress-related illnesses.

Explanation:

The paragraph explains three results of laughing. Laughing, then, is the cause. The other three items are what can happen when you laugh. They are the effects.

> *Practice 4*

A. Read the following comparison-contrast paragraph, and then look at the items below the paragraph. Write **C** in front of each item that is a cause and **E** in front of each item that is an effect.

> Changes at the end of the 1800s created more work for women. Workplaces put a greater emphasis on being efficient and clean. This emphasis was applied to housework as well. As a result, women spent more time dusting, cleaning, and scrubbing. The availability of a greater variety of foods also led to more work. Women thus spent more time on such food preparation as plucking feathers from chickens, roasting coffee beans, grinding whole spices and sugar, and cooking meals. By 1900, the typical housewife worked six hours a day on just two tasks: meal preparation and cleaning. And there were other household tasks as well, such as doing the laundry.

____ Greater emphasis on being efficient and clean

____ More time spent on dusting, cleaning, and scrubbing

____ A greater variety of foods available

____ More time spent on food preparation

B. The following passage uses the cause-effect pattern. Complete the map of the paragraph. First finish the main idea heading. Then fill in the missing supporting detail, and complete the incomplete supporting detail.

> Being unemployed can have harmful effects on health. In poor countries especially, unemployment may result in little or no medical care. The experience of unemployment itself can affect one's health. Studies have shown that anxiety and depression can result from the loss of a job. Abuse of alcohol and tranquilizers increase with unemployment, as well. One study showed that when unemployment rises, the death rate for heart disease also rises.

Harmful health effects of _____

| Especially in poor countries, little or no medical care | Anxiety and depression | | Greater chance of dying of _____ _____ |

RELATIONSHIPS OF EXAMPLE

> *Transitions:* **Example words**
>
> *Pattern of organization:* **Definition and example**

Example Words

Example words introduce one or more examples, or illustrations, of a general idea. Read the following items, and circle the letter of the item you think is clearer. Then read the explanation that follows.

> a. Young children often use private speech. For instance, they make sound effects as they play.
>
> b. Young children often use private speech. They make sound effects as they play.

Explanation:

The second item leads us to wonder if making sound effects during play is something different from private speech. The words *for instance* in the first item make it clear that making sound effects is one *example* of private speech.

Words such as *for instance* show that what follows is an example. Example words tell us that an author will provide one or more illustrations to make an idea clearer. Here are some common example transitions:

Example Words

example	to illustrate	including
for example	illustration	such as
once	instance	
one time	for instance	

Examples

The following sentences contain example transitions. Notice how these transitions signal that one or more examples will follow.

> Nine states got their names from rivers that flow through them. *For example,* Minnesota is named after the Minnesota River.
>
> Some Canadians, *including* Michael J. Fox and Peter Jennings, moved to the United States to seek fame and fortune.

If you want to buy an old house, beware of problems *such as* bad plumbing and a rotting roof.

➤ *Practice 5*

Circle the example word or phrase in each sentence below. Each transition can be found in the box on page 345.

1. Nita's parents speak Spanish when they don't want their children to understand them, such as when they are planning a birthday party.

2. Various health claims are being made for new foods. For instance, broccoli sprouts are said to protect against cancer.

3. English has borrowed words from other languages, including French, which gave us the words *quiche* and *fondue.*

4. President Abraham Lincoln was famous for his honesty. Once, when he worked at a store, he walked several miles to return change to a customer.

5. Governments own some businesses. For example, local governments often own parking structures and water systems.

The Definition and Example Pattern

The **definition and example pattern** includes just what its name suggests: a definition and one or more examples. If a textbook author uses a term that readers may not understand, the author may provide a definition. Then, to make sure the definition is clear, the author may give one or more examples. The definition and example pattern often uses example transitions, such as *for example* and *to illustrate.*

To get a sense of the definition and example pattern, arrange the following group of sentences into a paragraph that makes sense. Write *1* in front of the sentence that should come first, *2* in front of the sentence that comes second, and *3* in front of the sentence that should be last. Then read the explanation which follows.

____ Other common phobias include fears of snakes, water, and enclosed places.

____ One example is a fear of heights that is so extreme that one cannot drive over bridges without trembling.

____ A phobia is an irrational and extreme fear of some object or situation.

Explanation:

The paragraph begins with the definition of the term *phobia*. An example that is explained in some detail comes next, followed by a list of other examples. A total of four examples (fear of heights, snakes, water, and enclosed places) are used to illustrate the term *phobia*. The paragraph uses the example words *example* and *include*. It should read as follows:

A phobia is an irrational and extreme fear of some object or situation. One example is a fear of heights that is so extreme that one cannot drive over bridges without trembling. Other common phobias include fears of snakes, water, and enclosed places.

Textbook authors want to help readers understand important terms, whether the subject is psychology, business, or any other specialized field. For this reason, these authors often make sure to include definitions of key terms. The definitions may be general and abstract. Therefore, authors often present explanatory details and examples to help readers better understand each term.

A Definition and Example Paragraph

The following paragraph defines a term, gives additional information about it, and gives examples of it. Read the paragraph and then answer the questions. Finally, read the explanation that follows.

[1]Functional illiteracy is the inability to read and write at a level required for success in daily life. [2]The problem is wide-ranging. [3]For instance, it is estimated that one in five adults is unable to read warning labels on containers of harmful substances. [4]Other examples are the many adults who cannot read the headlines in a newspaper or fill out a job application. [5]Yet another illustration of this problem is the half of the adult population in this country that is unable to read a book written at an eighth-grade level.

1. What term is being defined? _____

2. Which sentence gives the definition? _____

3. Which sentence explains how common the problem is? _____

4. In which sentence does the first example appear? _____

5. How many examples are given in all? _____

Explanation:

The term being defined is "functional illiteracy." It is defined in the first sentence: "the inability to read and write at a level required for success in daily life." The second sentence tells us how common the problem is: "wide-ranging." The first example—the inability of many adults to read warning labels—is introduced in sentence 3. Three other illustrations are given in sentences 4–5 (the inability to read headlines, to fill out a job application, and to read a book written at an eighth-grade level), making a total of four examples. Note that three example transitions are used: *for instance, examples,* and *illustration.*

➤ Practice 6

A. The following passage uses the definition-example pattern. Read the passage and answer the questions that follow.

> [1]Some people have charisma, a special charm or appeal that draws other people to them. [2]People with charisma are not always the best-looking people, the smartest, or the best-dressed. [3]But they have sparkling personalities and the ability to make the people near them feel special. [4]The late President John F. Kennedy is one well-known example of a person with great charisma. [5]One admirer said of him, "When you spoke with him, he looked at you as though you were the most important person in the world." [6]Another person who illustrates charisma is Diana, the late Princess of Wales. [7]People who met her felt a particularly strong presence that they could not understand or explain, but that made them feel richer.

1. What term is being defined? _____

2. Which sentence gives the definition? _____

3. In which sentence does the first example begin? _____

4. How many examples are given in all? _____

B. The following passage has a definition-example pattern. Complete the map of the paragraph. First, write the definition in the heading. Then fill in the two missing supporting details—examples of the term that's defined.

> Regeneration is the ability some animals have to renew lost body parts. This ability can come in very handy when a limb is lost in an accident or in a fight. For instance, an octopus can regrow lost tentacles. The sea star is another example of an animal that can regenerate. Even one

leg of a sea star that includes part of the center of the body can regenerate a whole new body. Also, some lizards can regrow their tail. When such a lizard is caught by its tail, it releases the tail and runs away. A new tail is then grown.

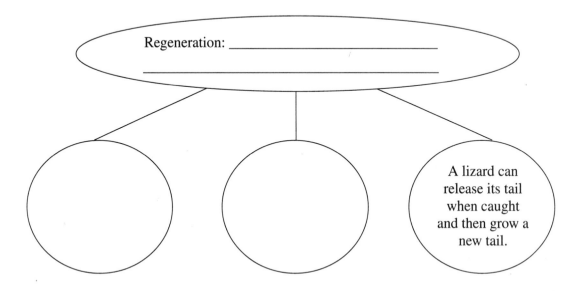

TOPIC SENTENCES AND PATTERNS OF ORGANIZATION

The topic sentence of a paragraph often suggests how the paragraph will be organized. For instance, here is the topic sentence of a paragraph you worked on earlier: "A videotape called 'How to Have a Moneymaking Garage Sale' lists several tips for success." This sentence strongly suggests that the paragraph will go on to list a number of tips. Even before finishing the paragraph, you can expect that it will be organized as a list of items (one of the two patterns discussed in Chapter 9).

Here are two more topic sentences. Write in the blank space the pattern of organization you think each one suggests. Then read the explanations that follow.

1. Building a cage for a rabbit involves several steps.

   Pattern of organization: _____

2. There are a number of differences between private colleges and public colleges.

   Pattern of organization: _____

Explanations:

The first sentence suggests that a series of steps for building a rabbit cage will follow. The paragraph is likely to be arranged in a time order.

The second sentence suggests that the paragraph will discuss the differences between public and private colleges. In all likelihood, the paragraph will have a contrast pattern—it will discuss the differences between the two types of colleges.

➤ Practice 7

In the space provided, write the letter of the pattern of organization that each topic sentence suggests. Choose from all the patterns discussed in Chapters 9 and 10:

a List of items
b Time order
c Comparison and contrast
d Cause and effect
e Definition and example

_____ 1. The loss of a job can be compared to the end of a marriage.

_____ 2. The National Restaurant Association recently put together a list of the most popular takeout foods in the nation.

_____ 3. Defense mechanisms are psychological methods people use to protect their self-esteem.

_____ 4. Smoking is on the decline in America because of government efforts to educate people about the unfavorable effects of the habit.

_____ 5. You can successfully plant a tree by following a few simple steps.

_____ 6. Large lawns have led to extreme demands on water systems.

_____ 7. Humans and chimpanzees are alike.

_____ 8. Some strong cleaning products are known to cause health problems.

_____ 9. Volcanoes have several characteristics.

_____ 10. Internal noise is thoughts and feelings that interfere with the communication process.

A Final Note

Paragraphs and longer passages are often made up of more than one pattern of organization. For instance, the paragraph in this chapter about the results of laughing uses a cause-effect pattern. But the results themselves—relaxed facial muscles, more oxygen in the brain, reduced stress—are presented as a list of items. As you apply what you've learned about patterns to your studies, use the patterns that make sense to you, the ones that help you to understand and take notes on the material.

CHAPTER SUMMARY

In this chapter you learned the following:

- Three common relationships are comparison and contrast, cause and effect, and definition and example.

- A comparison-contrast paragraph will be about how two things are like each other, or how they are different, or both. It typically uses comparison or contrast transitions, or both.

- A cause and effect paragraph will be a discussion of the reason or reasons for something or the effects of something. It typically uses cause-effect transitions.

- A definition and example paragraph provides a definition and one or more examples of the definition. It typically uses example transitions.

- The topic sentence often suggests how a paragraph will be organized.

➤ *Review Test 1*

To review what you've learned in this chapter, answer each of the following questions. Fill in the blank, or circle the letter of the correct answer.

1. _____ TRUE OR FALSE? When a passage provides a series of effects, it uses a comparison-contrast pattern of organization.

2. _____ TRUE OR FALSE? The pattern of organization that relies on example transitions is called cause and effect.

3. Which pattern of organization is often signaled by such transitions as *because, as a result,* and *since*?
   a. Comparison-contrast
   b. Cause and effect
   c. Definition and example

4. Which pattern of organization is often signaled by transitions such as *similarly* and *on the other hand*?
   a. Comparison-contrast
   b. Cause and effect
   c. Definition and example

➤ Review Test 2

A. Circle the letter that shows which type of transition is italicized.

1. A stereotype is an overly generalized image of members of a group. One common stereotype, *for instance,* is the image of all professors as being absent-minded.

   The transition signals
   a. comparison.
   b. contrast.
   c. cause and effect.
   d. an example.

2. The earliest known bird had a large bony tail that *resembled* a reptile's tail.

   The transition signals
   a. comparison.
   b. contrast.
   c. cause and effect.
   d. an example.

3. A professor of hearing sciences at Ohio University has discovered that people with certain speech problems lack feeling in their tongues. *Therefore,* they have trouble placing their tongues in the correct position for certain sounds.

   The transition signals
   a. comparison.
   b. contrast.
   c. cause and effect.
   d. an example.

4. In the Northern Hemisphere, the months of July through September are warmest. *However,* in the Southern Hemisphere, those are the coldest months.

   The transition signals
   a. comparison.
   b. contrast.
   c. cause and effect.
   d. an example.

B. Read each passage and then answer the questions that follow.

Glossy and flat paints have different advantages. A glossy paint is easier to keep clean than a flat paint. On the other hand, a flat paint covers flaws in the wall better than a glossy one. The cost of both paints is about the same. The choice of which is better depends on the buyer's needs and preferences.

5. The main pattern of organization for this paragraph is
   a. comparison-contrast.
   b. cause and effect.
   c. definition and example.

6–7. Two of the transitions that signal the paragraph's pattern of organization are

_____   _____.

The United States Postal Service has set up a special room in several locations around the country. This room is known as the "Dead-Letter Office." Here postal clerks open and read mail. Why do they open private mail? There are a couple of reasons. Millions of letters are sent each year with an incorrect address and no return address. These letters are opened so that clerks can find out where to return the mail. Other letters have envelopes that are completely blank. Consequently, postal clerks must also open these letters to try to discover where they should be sent. According to estimates, only 30 percent of the opened letters find their way to the sender or the person the letter was meant to reach.

8. The main pattern of organization in this paragraph is
   a. comparison-contrast.
   b. cause and effect.
   c. definition and example.

9–10. Two transitions that signal the paragraph's pattern of organization are

_____   _____.

➤ *Review Test 3*

A. Read each paragraph and answer the questions that follow.

[1]An embarrassing event led to a disastrous result for one diplomat. [2]He was representing his country at a formal dinner. [3]He got up from the dinner table and noticed that his fly was open. [4]He sat down and tried to zip up, but he got his tie caught in the zipper. [5]As he tried to undo the tie, he

knocked over a bottle of wine into the lap of the guest sitting next to him. [6]His actions caught the attention of the hostess. [7]She saw that she had to do something, so she reluctantly cut off the man's tie. [8]The diplomat had called attention to himself, something not allowed under diplomatic rules. [9]As a result, he was fired.

1. The relationship between the two parts of sentence 4 (on each side of the comma) is one of
   a. comparison.
   b. contrast.
   c. cause and effect.
   d. example.

2. The relationship between sentences 8 and 9 is one of
   a. comparison.
   b. contrast.
   c. cause and effect.
   d. example.

3. The main pattern of organization in this paragraph is
   a. comparison-contrast.
   b. cause and effect.
   c. definition and example.

[1]When is a person truly dead? [2]There are two main differing positions taken by doctors and scientists. [3]One is that a person should be declared legally dead when blood circulation and breathing have stopped. [4]Then organs that are still in good working order can be removed and donated to critically ill patients in need of a new liver, heart, or kidney. [5]However, there are those who say that death does not occur until the entire brain stops functioning. [6]These people admit that waiting for brain death means organs may stop working and not be in condition to be donated. [7]But they point out that some individuals have awakened months after going into a state that seems like death.

4. The relationship of sentence 5 to the two sentences before it is one of
   a. comparison.
   b. contrast.
   c. cause and effect.
   d. example.

5. The main pattern of organization in this paragraph is
   a. comparison-contrast.
   b. cause and effect.
   c. definition and example.

6. One transition that signals the paragraph's pattern of organization is

   _____.

B. Read the paragraph below. Then answer the question and complete the map that follows.

> A mutant is a plant or animal with a brand-new characteristic. For instance, one mutant that was born not too long ago is a two-headed calf. Another example is a recently hatched chicken with four legs. Some mutants turn out to be useful. For example, a small orange cauliflower was recently found in a field of normal white cauliflower. It was crossed with a regular-sized cauliflower to produce a new vegetable—a full-sized orange cauliflower.

7. The pattern of organization for this paragraph is
   a. comparison-contrast.
   b. cause-effect.
   c. definition-example.

8–10. Complete the map of the paragraph by completing the main idea heading and filling in the missing major details.

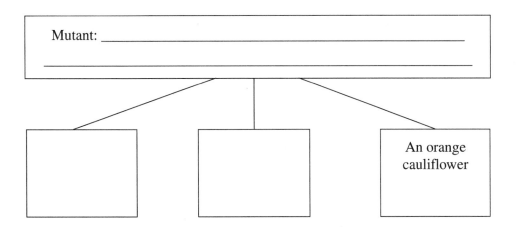

➤ *Review Test 4*

Here is a chance to apply your understanding of definition-example, comparison-contrast, and cause-effect relationships to a full-length selection. The reading tells what happens when the author finds a cat lying in the middle of the road and decides to move it off the road. When he finds that the cat is still alive, his day becomes a complicated one.

To help you continue to strengthen your skills, the reading is followed by questions on what you've learned in this and previous chapters.

Words to Watch

Following are some words in the reading that do not have strong context support. Each word is followed by the number of the paragraph in which it appears and its meaning there. These words are indicated in the reading by a small circle (°).

grimaced (2): made a twisted face
immobile (2): not moving
ligament (5): a band of tissue which connects bones or supports organs
tendon (5): a tissue which connects muscles to bones and other parts of the body
good Samaritan (6): someone who helps others unselfishly
kinked (7): twisted
resignation (9): acceptance without resistance
dejected (11): depressed
pathetic (11): pitiful

LIFE OVER DEATH

Bill Broderick

1   My reaction was as it always is when I see an animal lying in the roadway. My heart sank. And a lump formed in my throat at the thought of a life unfulfilled. I then resolved to move him off the road, to ensure that one of God's creations did not become a permanent part of the pavement. Some might ask what difference it makes. If it's already dead, why not just leave it there? My answer is that I believe in death with dignity, for people and for animals alike.

2   So I pulled my car over to the side of the road and walked back to where the cat lay motionless. Two cars passed over him, managing to avoid running him over. With no other cars in sight, I made my way to the lifeless form just as a jogger went by. The jogger grimaced° at the sight of the immobile° cat, blood dripping from

his mouth. "How'd it happen?" he asked. I replied that I didn't know; he probably got hit by some careless driver. I just wanted to get him off the road. I reached down for the cat and got the surprise of my life. The little creature lifted his head ever so slightly and uttered a pitiful, unforgettable little "meow." He was still alive.

3   What was I going to do now? I was already late for work. All I had intended to do was move the cat off the road. I didn't need this. But I knew I had no choice. I sighed deeply, then reached down and carefully cradled the cat in my hands. I asked the jogger to open my car trunk and remove the things from a small box. Then I gently placed the cat in the box. He was in shock, so he probably could not feel the pain from his obvious injuries. "Kinda funny lookin', isn't he?" asked the jogger. I was annoyed by his question, but I had to admit that he was right. This cat looked peculiar. Not ugly, mind you. But he seemed to have a comical look on his face, even at such a dreadful time.

4   "What are you gonna do with him?" the jogger asked. I told him I would take the cat to the local vet and let him decide what to do.

5   The vet was only five minutes away. My wife and I had been bringing our animals to him for several years, and I knew I could rely on him to do what was best for the cat. I brought the cat into the reception room and placed it on the counter. As this was an emergency, the vet was summoned right away. He examined the cat thoroughly, listing the injuries for his assistant to write down. "Broken jaw, that'll have to be set. Two teeth broken. A couple more loose. Possible internal injuries, but they don't look too bad. Uh-oh. This doesn't look good. He doesn't appear to have any movement in his right front leg. Possible break, definite ligament° and tendon° damage."

6   The vet completed his examination, then looked at me and asked what I wanted to do. I knew what he meant. Did I want to have the cat "put to sleep"? I became uneasy. I clumsily explained that I was hoping to get advice from him on what to do. Fair enough. The jaw would have to be wired shut for six weeks, and the cat would have to wear a cast on its leg for three months. There was no way of knowing if the damage to the leg was permanent. He could have the cast removed and still not be able to use the leg. The cost of all the surgery would be high, but I would get a 50 percent "good Samaritan°" discount if I went ahead with it.

7   Now I was really at a loss. If I went ahead with the surgery, I'd be paying for a cat which wasn't mine, whose owner I'd probably never find, and who might end up with the use of only three legs. And on top of it, this was one of the funniest-looking cats ever born. Black and white, spotted where it shouldn't be, kinked° tail, and a silly half-smile on its face. I chuckled at that and the entire situation.

8   "What do you want to do, Bill?" asked the vet.

*After surgery, Pokey had to wear a cast
on one leg for three months.*

9   I shrugged my shoulders in resignation°. "Dan, I'll choose life over death every time. Let's give it our best shot."

10   I called back later in the day and learned that the surgery had been successful. "You can pick up your cat tomorrow morning," I was told. My cat. I started to say that he was not my cat, but I knew otherwise.

11   The next morning, my wife and I drove to the vet and picked up the cat. He looked ghastly. His jaw was now bandaged, and a cast covered one leg entirely and wrapped around his midsection. We were dejected°. But, as we drove him home, we began thinking that perhaps this cat was not as pathetic° as he looked. As frightened as he must have been, as much pain as he must have felt, he sat calmly in my wife's lap. He purred and stared out the window with his curious half-smile.

12   When we got home, we introduced him to our two Siamese cats, who stared in disbelief at this strange creature. They sensed it might be a cat, but they had never seen one like this. It took him very little time to get used to his new surroundings. It took him longer to get used to the cast, which made even walking a chore. Surely he must have been embarrassed. After all, an animal normally able to glide around quietly should not make a resounding thump every time he moves.

13   In due time, the cast came off. To our relief, Pokey, as we now called him, had about 90 percent mobility in the leg. He got around okay, but he limped whenever he tried to move any faster than a slow walk.

14   All this occurred four years ago. Pokey is still with us today. In fact, he has become our most beloved cat. Because of his injury, he is strictly an indoor cat. This does not seem to bother him at all. It is hard to believe that any cat has ever enjoyed himself more. Maybe it's because he had been slowed after being hit by a car, or perhaps he just has a special individuality. He is never bored. At times he will race around the house like he is leading the Indy 500. Or he'll leap into the air at an imaginary

foe. Or he'll purr loudly at the foot of our bed, staring into space with that silly grin on his face. And he couldn't care less that he still looks funny.

15   It would have been easy to let Pokey lie in the middle of the road. And it would have been just as simple to have the vet put him to sleep. But when I think of all the pleasure this cat has given us, and of how much fun he has living with us, I know the right decision was made. And I'd do it again in a second. I'll take life over death every time.

Word Skills Questions

Phonics

1. The word *grimaced*, in the sentence below, has a
   a. hard **g** and a hard **c**.
   b. hard **g** and a soft **c**.
   c. soft **g** and a hard **c**.

   "The jogger grimaced at the sight of the immobile cat, blood dripping from his mouth." (Paragraph 2)

2. Which of the following words from the sentence below follows the syllable rule to "divide before a single consonant"?
   a. *because*
   b. *strictly*
   c. *indoor*

   "Because of his injury, he is strictly an indoor cat." (Paragraph 14)

Dictionary Use

Use the dictionary entry on the next page to answer questions 3–5.

in•di•vid•u•al•i•ty (ĭn′də-vĭj′o͞o-ăl′ĭ-tē) *n.* **1.** The combination of qualities that distinguish one individual from another. **2.** The quality of being individual.

3. *Individuality*, in the sentences below, would be found on a dictionary page with which guidewords?
   a. **imply / impressive**
   b. **index / indispensable**
   c. **indisposed / indulge**
   d. **indulgence / inexpressible**

   "It is hard to believe that any cat has ever enjoyed himself more. Maybe it's because he had been slowed after being hit by a car, or perhaps he just has a special individuality." (Paragraph 14)

4. *Individuality* has
   a. four syllables.
   b. five syllables.
   c. six syllables.
   d. seven syllables.

5. *Individuality* has one strong accent and
   a. one other accent.
   b. two other accents.
   c. three other accents.
   d. four other accents.

Vocabulary in Context

6. In the sentence below, the word *resolved* means
   a. forgot.
   b. hid.
   c. decided.
   d. drove.

> "I then resolved to move him off the road, to ensure that one of God's creations did not become a permanent part of the pavement." (Paragraph 1)

Pokey, now fully recovered, is the author's favorite cat.

7. In the sentences below, the word *summoned* means
   a. paid.
   b. called for.
   c. telephoned.
   d. ignored.

   "As this was an emergency, the vet was summoned right away. He examined the cat thoroughly. . . ." (Paragraph 5)

8. In the sentences below, the word *ghastly* means
   a. clever.
   b. appealing.
   c. terrible.
   d. marvelous.

   "He looked ghastly. His jaw was now bandaged, and a cast covered one leg entirely and wrapped around his midsection." (Paragraph 11)

9. In the sentences below, the word *disbelief* means
   a. uncertainty.
   b. time.
   c. pleasure.
   d. hatred.

   " . . . our two Siamese cats . . . stared in disbelief at this strange creature. They sensed it might be a cat, but they had never seen one like this." (Paragraph 12)

10. In the sentence below, the word *resounding* means
    a. soft.
    b. brave.
    c. relaxed.
    d. loud.

    "After all, an animal normally able to glide around quietly should not make a resounding thump every time he moves." (Paragraph 12)

Reading Comprehension Questions

Central Point and Main Ideas

1. Which sentence best expresses the central point of the selection?
   a. Drivers need to be alert to dangers on the road.
   b. Every life is valuable.
   c. Cats make great pets.
   d. Pokey is strictly an indoor cat because of his injury.

2. Which sentence best expresses the main idea of paragraphs 3 and 4?
   a. The author didn't know what to do.
   b. The author was willing to take responsibility for the cat.
   c. The author was annoyed at the jogger's questions.
   d. The cat was funny looking.

3. Which sentence best expresses the main idea of paragraph 6?
   a. The author was asked what he wanted to do with the cat.
   b. The vet didn't know what to do with the cat.
   c. The vet explained to the author what could be done for the cat and what it would cost.
   d. The author expected the vet to say that the cat should be "put to sleep."

4. Which sentence best expresses the main idea of paragraph 14?
   a. Pokey is beloved and enjoys life a great deal now.
   b. Pokey sometimes leaps into the air at imaginary enemies.
   c. Pokey must spend the rest of his life indoors.
   d. Pokey was injured four years ago.

Supporting Details

5. The author
   a. saw a car hit the cat.
   b. was very surprised that the cat was still alive.
   c. was surprised that the jogger came by.
   d. thought that the cat was ugly.

6. The author
   a. had heard about the vet.
   b. looked for the nearest vet.
   c. knew and trusted the vet.
   d. drove for hours till he found a vet.

7. For Pokey's surgery, the vet charged the author
   a. nothing.
   b. extra, because of the emergency circumstances.
   c. half the usual cost.
   d. the usual cost.

Relationships

8. The transition word *then*, in the sentence below, signals
   a. addition.
   b. time.
   c. comparison.
   d. contrast.

   "I sighed deeply, then reached down and carefully cradled the cat in my hands." (Paragraph 3)

9. The relationship between the two parts of the sentence below (before and after the comma) is one of
   a. addition.
   b. time.
   c. contrast.
   d. cause and effect.

   "The cost of all the surgery would be high, but I would get a . . . discount if I went ahead with it." (Paragraph 6)

10. The selection is organized as a
    a. series of events in the saving of one animal's life.
    b. list of animals that have been saved.
    c. discussion of the causes of harm to animals.
    d. definition of a term with a long example.

Discussion Questions

1. In the first paragraph, the author uses the expression "death with dignity." What do you think he means by that expression?

2. When the vet told the author that he could pick up his cat at the vet's office, the author began to protest but then stopped. Why do you think he decided the cat was really his?

3. Can and should something be done to make the world a better place for hurt and homeless animals like Pokey? Explain your answer.

Note: Writing assignments for this selection appear on page 545.

Check Your Performance			RELATIONSHIPS II
Activity	*Number Right*	*Points*	*Score*
Review Test 1 (4 items)	_____	× 2.5 =	_____
Review Test 2 (10 items)	_____	× 3 =	_____
Review Test 3 (10 items)	_____	× 3 =	_____
Review Test 4 (20 items)	_____	× 1.5 =	_____
		TOTAL SCORE =	_____ %

Enter your total score into the **Reading Performance Chart: Review Tests** on the inside back cover.

RELATIONSHIPS II: Test 1

A. In each item below, which type of relationship is signaled by the italicized transition?

1. *Just as* human infants suck their thumb, baby elephants suck their trunks.

   The transition signals
   a. comparison.
   b. contrast.
   c. cause and effect.
   d. an example (illustration).

2. The chef stuffed steel wool into the cracks of the restaurant *so that* mice could no longer get into the kitchen.

   The transition signals
   a. comparison.
   b. contrast.
   c. cause and effect.
   d. an example (illustration).

3. People can insure just about anything. *For instance,* the comedians Abbott and Costello once insured themselves against any member of the audience dying of laughter.

   The transition signals
   a. comparison.
   b. contrast.
   c. cause and effect.
   d. an example (illustration).

4. Movie audiences usually dislike film monsters. *However,* filmgoers in the 1930s pitied King Kong and even shed tears at his death.

   The transition signals
   a. comparison.
   b. contrast.
   c. cause and effect.
   d. an example (illustration).

(Continues on next page)

B. Read each paragraph and answer the questions that follow.

Teens and young adults lose hair for various reasons. As part of normal changes in the body, they can expect to lose about one hundred hairs per day. Medical problems may result in more hair loss. Under-nourishment may cause abnormal hair loss, so teens should be mindful of their diet. Fevers can also lead to more hair falling out than normal. Significant hair loss may also be due to allergic reactions to dyes or hair straighteners.

5. The main pattern of organization in this paragraph is
   a. comparison-contrast.
   b. cause-effect.
   c. definition-example.

6–7. Two transitions that signal the paragraph's pattern of organization are

_____   _____.

A "tell sign" is a nonverbal clue that indicates a person may be lying. For instance, if a person is making more obvious hand gestures than normal, he or she may not be telling the truth. Other illustrations are touching one's ear, scratching the neck, or tugging at the collar. These may indicate a subconscious effort to rub out an untrue statement. Another example of the tell sign is a continual shrugging of the shoulders, which may be an unconscious action meant to contradict what has been said.

8. The main pattern of organization in this paragraph is
   a. comparison-contrast.
   b. cause-effect.
   c. definition-example.

9–10. Two transitions that signal the paragraph's pattern of organization are

_____   _____.

RELATIONSHIPS II: Test 2

A. In each item below, which type of relationship is signaled by the italicized transition?

    1. The zookeeper put a large mirror in the peacock's cage. *As a result,* the bird spread its tail and showed off for the "other" peacock.

    The transition signals
    a. comparison.
    b. contrast.
    c. cause and effect.
    d. an example (illustration).

    2. Humberto's recent camping trip was a disaster. *For instance,* one morning he got scared by a skunk and fell into poison ivy.

    The transition signals
    a. comparison.
    b. contrast.
    c. cause and effect.
    d. an example (illustration).

    3. The first apartment we looked at was in a noisy neighborhood. The second was *just as* bad, with blaring traffic in every room.

    The transition signals
    a. comparison.
    b. contrast.
    c. cause and effect.
    d. an example (illustration).

    4. The savings rate of Americans *differs* from the savings rate in Japan.

    The transition signals
    a. comparison.
    b. contrast.
    c. cause and effect.
    d. an example (illustration).

(Continues on next page)

B. Read each paragraph and answer the questions that follow.

People are much more likely to cooperate with each other in small groups than in large groups. In small groups, each person feels more responsible for the group's success. In contrast, individuals in large groups feel weak ties to most others in the group, be it a large corporation or a large city. People in small groups are more likely to take no more than their share of available resources. A few families in a small neighborhood in Washington state took care to conserve water when the water supply got low. However, in large cities, many residents do not voluntarily conserve resources such as water.

5. The main pattern of organization in this paragraph is
   a. comparison-contrast.
   b. cause-effect.
   c. definition-example.

6–7. The two transitions that signal the paragraph's pattern of organization are

_____   _____ .

Why are white socks traditionally worn during sports from running to racquetball? The reason has to do with the tragic death of a president's son. Calvin Coolidge, president of the United States from 1923 to 1929, saw his son die after playing tennis. The son accidentally broke his skin as he played, and a dye in his sock entered his bloodstream. Poisons present in the dye are thought to have killed him. Because of the publicity from this tragedy, the public became convinced that only white socks should be worn during athletic events.

8. The main pattern of organization in this paragraph is
   a. comparison-contrast.
   b. cause-effect.
   c. definition-example.

9–10. Two transitions that signal the paragraph's pattern of organization are

_____   _____ .

RELATIONSHIPS II: Test 3

A. Read each passage and answer the questions that follow.

> [1]There are interesting differences between honeybees and bumble-bees. [2]First of all, they have contrasting living circumstances. [3]Honeybees live in large colonies and need a lot of space to build their hives. [4]However, bumblebees live in small underground colonies and require little territory to nest. [5]Honeybees and bumblebees also differ in their stinging behavior. [6]Honeybees will sting with little reason. [7]In contrast, bumblebees rarely sting, even if they are accidentally disturbed. [8]However, their sting is far more painful than that of a honeybee.

1. The relationship of sentence 4 to sentence 3 is one of
   a. comparison.
   b. contrast.
   c. cause and effect.
   d. illustration.

2. The main pattern of organization in this paragraph is
   a. comparison-contrast.
   b. cause-effect.
   c. definition-example.

3. One transition that signals the paragraph's main pattern of organization is

   _____.

> [1]During the Middle Ages, people in Europe hated and feared ordinary house cats, which they thought were used by witches to contact demons. [2]Unfortunately, this fear of cats resulted in many more deaths from the terrible illness bubonic plague than otherwise would have occurred. [3]Because of their fear, people drove cats away from their houses and villages. [4]Rats were thus totally free to breed there and spread disease. [5]Millions of people died from bubonic plague, which was carried by diseased rats. [6]If more cats had been allowed to stay, they could have killed many of these rats.

4. The relationship between the two parts of sentence 3 (on each side of the comma) is one of
   a. comparison.
   b. contrast.
   c. cause and effect.
   d. illustration.

(Continues on next page)

5. The main pattern of organization in this passage is
   a. comparison-contrast.
   b. cause and effect.
   c. definition and example.

6. One transition that signals the paragraph's pattern of organization is

   _____.

B. Read the following paragraph, and then fill in each blank with an appropriate transition from the box. Note that two transitions will be left over. Finally, answer the question that follows.

| because | different | for instance |
| in contrast | unlike | |

     American people and British people view burial in very (7)_____ ways. English churchyards are often maintained in a rather wild state, with plenty of wildflowers and weeds. However, American cemeteries have their lawns mowed and neatly trimmed. The way the two countries handle the casket also differs. The British don't try to protect the coffin, or the mourners, from close contact with raw earth. (8)_____ the British, Americans cover the dirt near a grave with plastic grass, and they lower the casket onto a protective wooden shell. Also, the British accept the fact that the dead and their caskets will decay. (9)_____, in America, embalming fluid makes the dead look alive, and casket catalogues emphasize that their products will last for years.

10. The main pattern of organization in this passage is
    a. comparison-contrast.
    b. cause and effect.
    c. definition and example.

RELATIONSHIPS II: Test 4

A. Read each passage and answer the questions that follow.

> [1]Marsupials are animals whose females raise their young in a pouch located on the abdomen. [2]The female shelters and feeds the young in this pouch. [3]Most marsupials are found in Australia. [4]For example, the kangaroo is an Australian marsupial. [5]Baby kangaroos crawl from the birth canal to the mother's pouch by themselves. [6]Another example of an Australian marsupial is the koala. [7]However, not all marsupials are located in Australia. [8]The opossum is a marsupial that is found in many countries, including the United States. [9]At birth young marsupials are blind, extremely small, and helpless. [10]For instance, opossum newborns are so tiny that more than a dozen could fit into a teaspoon.

1. The relationship of sentence 4 to sentence 3 is one of
   a. comparison.
   b. contrast.
   c. cause and effect.
   d. illustration.

2. The relationship of sentence 6 to sentence 3 is one of
   a. comparison.
   b. contrast.
   c. cause and effect.
   d. illustration.

3. The main pattern of organization in this passage is
   a. comparison-contrast.
   b. cause-effect.
   c. definition-example.

> [1]Officials in California recently released water from a dam down a river. [2]They did this because they wanted to improve the environment for wildlife. [3]Instead of helping wildlife, however, they harmed it. [4]Over five thousand salmon, trout, and catfish were killed. [5]Wildlife drinking from the river became sick, and many died. [6]The reason for this catastrophe was revealed in a federal study. [7]It showed that the water which was released carried more sediment and waste than officials had expected. [8]The fish and animals could not tolerate the pollutants that officials had failed to account for.

(Continues on next page)

4. The relationship between sentences 1 and 2 is one of
   a. comparison.
   b. contrast.
   c. cause and effect.
   d. illustration.

5. The relationship of sentence 3 to sentence 2 is one of
   a. comparison.
   b. contrast.
   c. cause and effect.
   d. illustration.

6. The main pattern of organization in this paragraph is
   a. comparison-contrast.
   b. cause-effect.
   c. definition-example.

B. Read the paragraph below, and then fill in each blank with the appropriate transition from the box. Note that two transitions will be left over. Finally, answer the question that follows.

differently	for instance	in contrast
resulting in	similar	

Some of the richest coral reefs in the world are found in two countries: Australia and the Philippine Islands. However, those two countries have cared for their reefs very (7)_____. The Great Barrier Reef off the east coast of Australia is in very good condition. The Australian government has taken great pains to protect the delicate ecosystem that attracts tourists from around the world. Although some fishing is allowed, strict laws are upheld to protect marine life and environment. (8)_____, in the Philippines, fishermen are being allowed to destroy coral reefs. The fishermen often catch fish by throwing explosives into the water. This kills the fish, but it also destroys the fragile coral reef. Scientists are trying to persuade the Philippine government to take precautions (9)_____ to those taken in Australia.

10. The main patten of organization in this passage is
    a. comparison-contrast.
    b. cause-effect.
    c. definition-example.

RELATIONSHIPS II: Test 5

A. Read the paragraph below. Then answer the questions and complete the outline that follows.

> A computer virus is an unwanted program that causes a problem of some sort with a computer. For instance, the Ping-Pong virus has a ball bouncing on the screen. The ball erases characters from the screen as it bounces. Another example is the Falling-Letter virus, which takes characters from the screen and drops them to the bottom of the monitor. DataCrime is a virus that reformats the computer's hard drive and adds unwanted material to it.

1. The main pattern of organization in this paragraph is
   a. comparison-contrast.
   b. cause-effect.
   c. definition-example.

2–3. The two transitions that signal major details of the paragraph are

   _____   _____ .

4–6. Finish the map of the paragraph by completing the heading and filling in the missing supporting details.

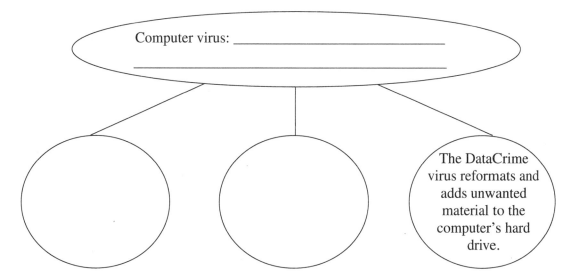

(Continues on next page)

B. Read the paragraph below. Then answer the question and complete the outline that follows.

> Many former runners have abandoned the aches and pains of jogging for the enjoyment of biking. The question for many is this: which kind of biking should I do? The choice for bikers is between mountain bikes and racing bikes, which differ considerably. Mountain bikes are meant to be used off roads. They are very durable, and they have wide tires, fifteen to twenty-four gears, and straight-across handlebars for upright riding. Racing bikes are meant to be ridden on streets. They are extremely light and built for speed, with comfort less of a concern. They have very narrow tires, ten to fourteen gears, and curved handlebars which are turned down so there is less wind resistance against the rider.

7. The main pattern of organization in this paragraph is
   a. comparison-contrast.
   b. cause-effect.
   c. definition-example.

8–10. Complete the outline of the paragraph by writing in the missing supporting details.

Main idea: There are important differences between two types of bikes.

1. Mountain bikes—for off-road biking

   a. Durable

   b. _____

   c. 15–24 gears

   d. Straight-across handlebars for upright riding

2. _____

   a. Light—built more for speed than comfort

   b. Very narrow tires

   c. _____

   d. Curved, turned-down handlebars for less wind resistance

RELATIONSHIPS II: Test 6

A. Read the paragraph below. Then answer the question and complete the outline that follows.

> Stress can lead to extreme behaviors. Some people react to stress by trying to escape from their problems through drug abuse. These people see drugs as a way to cope with problems. Aggression, including child abuse and other violence between family members, is another extreme behavior caused by stress. A person who acts aggressively tries to control people in order to get his or her own way. Stress may also lead someone to become so depressed that he or she attempts suicide. Sometimes people who become severely depressed think suicide is the only way to resolve a hopeless situation. Depressed people often feel a deep sense of loneliness that they assume will never change or go away.

1. The main pattern of organization in this paragraph is
   a. comparison-contrast.
   b. cause-effect.
   c. definition-example.

2–5. Complete the outline of the paragraph by finishing the main idea and then writing in the missing major supporting details.

Main idea: Stress can lead to _____.

1. _____

2. _____

    a. _____

    b. Other family violence

3. Suicidal depression

(Continues on next page)

B. Read the paragraph below. Then answer the question and complete the map that follows.

> Obsessive-compulsive behavior is a disorder in which people have repeated thoughts and actions they cannot control. One example involves an extreme fear of germs. After doing a routine action such as opening a book or eating a sandwich, one man would wash his hands for fifteen minutes. Another illustration of this disturbing disorder is a constant focus on money. One man was so consumed by the thought of becoming a millionaire at age 30 that he worked day and night. At age 29, he was working so hard that he collapsed and was taken to a hospital. At the hospital, he attempted to pull out his gold fillings and sell them to an attendant.

6. The main pattern of organization in this paragraph is
   a. comparison-contrast.
   b. cause-effect.
   c. definition-example.

7–10. Complete the map of the paragraph: Finish the heading and the two incomplete supporting details; also, fill in the missing supporting detail.

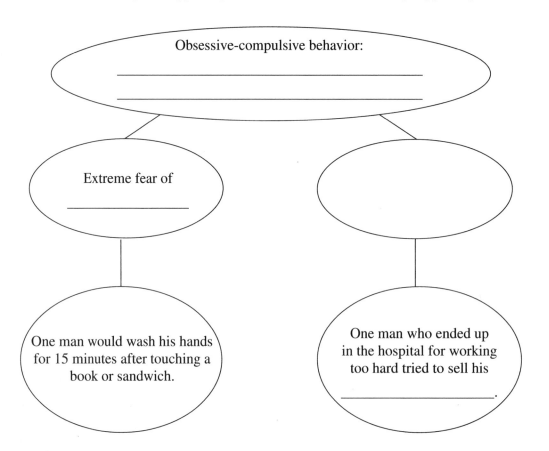

Obsessive-compulsive behavior: _____

_____

Extreme fear of

_____

One man would wash his hands for 15 minutes after touching a book or sandwich.

One man who ended up in the hospital for working too hard tried to sell his _____.

Part II

TEN READING SELECTIONS

1

Learning to Read: The Marvel Kretzmann Story

Mary Sherry

Preview

Here is a true story about a person with a learning disability—she was unable to read for almost twenty years. Being good at math, she was passed on from one grade to the next. Although she was able to get a good job after high school, her difficulties with reading made life difficult. Eventually, she decided it was better to face her problem and conquer it. This is Marvel Kretzmann's success story.

Words to Watch

poised (18): calm and confident
self-esteem (19): confidence
brush-up (21): review
IQ (22): abbreviation for "intelligence quotient," one measure of intelligence
memos (26): short written reminders
thesaurus (26): a book of synonyms
illiterate (30): unable to read or write
floored (31): shocked

1   Imagine a world where you can't read the street signs. You have to find your way by using only landmarks. When you see a sign or road map, you can't understand it, even though it is written in your own language. And when people give you oral directions, you cannot write quickly enough to take useful notes.

In this world, getting around isn't   2 your only challenge. You must struggle to read directions on packages of cake

mixes and cleaning products. Figuring out the doses of over-the-counter medicines actually gives you a head-ache. You keep faulty products rather than return them to the store because you cannot fill out a refund slip. The only jobs you dare apply for are those that do not require any reading or writing.

3   This was Marvel Kretzmann's world for almost twenty years. It was a very small world because she feared getting lost if she went beyond her place of work, familiar stores, and well-known routes to friends' and family's homes. She lived in daily fear that she would be asked to fill out a form or write something down for someone. Her world was a terrifying place.

4   Marvel's greatest fear of all was being found out. What if people *knew*

that she could barely read and couldn't write at all?

5   Marvel was in the fifth grade when it became clear to her that she was far behind her classmates in reading and writing, and that she would never be able to catch up.

6   "I remember hearing giggles in the classroom as soon as I was called on to read out loud. The kids knew what was going to happen, and so did I. Any word with an "s" sound in it was sure to make me stumble. As I hesitated, my teacher would say the words for me, over and over, urging me to repeat after her. But all I could hear was the laughing in the background.

7   "Finally, the teacher would give up and say, 'We'll move on.' Even though I felt relief, I also felt embarrassed. I was pulled out of class for extra work, but by that time—as I realize now—it was too late. I was already labeled by classmates and teachers as 'slow.'

8   "But I was pretty good in math. This helped me get passed from grade to grade. It also helped me to hide how serious my problem was from my parents. I didn't want to bring the problem to their attention. As a ten-year-old, I was more interested in having fun than working hard on reading and writing."

9   Marvel had two close friends who accepted her for what she was, and is today: kind, generous, and a lot of fun. They would take notes for her and coach her through courses, and they helped cover her disability.

10   But those friends couldn't be with her all the time. Marvel recalls how in the large junior and senior high

schools she attended, classmates soon caught on to her problem when the teacher asked students to take turns reading out loud. "Come on! Hurry up! She can't read!" she heard kids saying under their breath. Soon, rather than calling on students in order, up and down rows, teachers would skip around the class. That way, they wouldn't have to call on Marvel.

11   "In high school I learned to avoid classes that had writing assignments and heavy reading. I took the easiest courses I could. I kept quiet and tried not to be noticed. I never volunteered in class. I earned the reputation of being a 'good' child. So many classes had multiple-choice tests that I usually could guess and get by. In fact, I remember one time when I was the only one in my class to get an A on an exam. I just did what I always did with those tests I couldn't understand. I went down the pages and marked this one or that one, guessing all the way!"

12   Marvel's ability to manage her life got better and better. She received her high-school diploma and enrolled in a technical school where she was trained as a dental assistant. A tutor helped her get through her classes. After finishing the program, she found a job. She liked being a dental assistant and discovered she was good at it. In this job she was safe! She didn't have to write or read instructions to do her work.

13   Life outside of the dental office was another matter. Things she bought, such as appliances and other household items, came with instruction manuals. Expert at sewing, Marvel bought a fairly complicated sewing machine. "I thought I was going to lose my mind threading it and adjusting the tension. There were instructions in the manual, but they might as well have been in a foreign language."

14   "When I bought a computer, I practically burned out the phone lines dialing everyone I thought might be able to help me. I called the computer salesperson, friends, my sister, and 1-800-SOS-APPL day and night. I simply couldn't read the manual well enough to understand the computer's most basic uses. I would call and nervously ask, 'Why is this thing beeping at me? What did I do?' I needed to be walked though each disaster so I could keep on going."

15   The opportunities—and pitfalls—of the adult world seemed endless, requiring new and more complicated adjustments. Marvel wanted a checking account. Getting one was easy, because the bank officer simply asked her questions and filled out the forms. Marvel discovered, though, that writing out checks was stressful, especially when she had to do it in public. She developed a system of filling in store names on the checks at home or in the car before shopping—just so she wouldn't have to struggle in front of a clerk. Since spelling out "eleven" and "twelve" was always troubling, Marvel simply avoided writing checks for those amounts. As she shopped, she ran totals of her purchases in her head. Then she bought additional items or put some back on the shelves, just so the bill would be at least thirteen dollars or less than eleven.

16   Marvel's husband knew she had difficulty reading and writing, but he had no idea just how much difficulty.

He knew she had never been an "A" student, but he realized that she could manage things. For example, she addressed their wedding invitations from carefully printed lists. She wrote a form letter for her thank-you notes. Whenever a gift arrived, she copied that letter, simply filling in the blank for whatever the gift was. She had a "system," and it worked.

17   But sometimes she got caught. A few years ago Marvel won a radio contest sponsored by an insurance company. The prize was a free luncheon for all the people in her office at a restaurant of Marvel's choice. She stopped by a popular spot to check it out, thinking it would be a nice place to treat her fellow workers. A restaurant employee asked her to write down the name and address of the business so she could send a menu to Marvel's office. Marvel couldn't remember how to spell "Chicago"—the name of the street where her office is located. "I just blocked," she said. "I see 'Chicago' written out many times every day, but at that moment I froze. I turned and walked out—feeling defeated by such a simple thing as spelling 'Chicago.' I arranged to have the luncheon somewhere else."

18   Marvel Kretzmann tells about her struggle almost as though she were talking about someone else. She is upbeat, self-confident, poised°, open, and very friendly. Now in her late thirties, she realizes that difficulty reading and writing is a fairly wide-spread problem. "There are a lot of us out there," she says. "There are people who are afraid to travel because they can't read signs. Some won't apply for work because they can't fill out a job application. Others pretend they have left their glasses at home so they can take a form to someone who will read it to them. What is sad, though, is that many people assume people like us are lazy because we won't write things down in front of them. Sometimes when they see us struggle, they think we simply don't concentrate, or worse, that we are worthless. Once when I applied for a job, the person who interviewed me corrected my job application in front of me! Imagine how I felt! I told myself I couldn't work for that man, even if he offered me a job."

19   This remarkable openness and confidence did not come about by accident, nor did they come easily. After all, Marvel had spent years and years ashamed of her difficulty. How did she build her self-esteem° to such a high level? "I suddenly came face to face with the reality that life wasn't going to get any easier! In fact, it was getting harder." Marvel and her husband had bought a house, and she couldn't understand the legal papers involved. Furthermore, Marvel could see changes coming to the dental profession. One day her job would require taking notes and filling out forms. The thought also occurred to her that since she has no children, there might not be anyone around to take care of her when she was old or to cover for her when she needed help with reading or writing.

20   So Marvel decided to go back to school.

21   She found a community adult-education program that offered brush-up° classes in academic subjects. There she found just what she needed and received small-group and individual instruction. The work was intense. Teachers trained to deal with special learning needs drilled Marvel in phonics, spelling, and reading. Marvel came to school right after work and usually got there before the teachers did. The staff members who arrived first always found Marvel deep in study in the hallway. Finally they gave her a key to the classroom!

22   According to her teacher, Marvel's difficulties are typical of learning-disabled students. Such a person has a normal or an above-normal IQ°, but for some reason is unable to process math or reading and spelling. Unfortunately, the problem often isn't identified until the student is well beyond the grade levels where it could and should be more easily addressed. The problem is made worse by youthful reactions, such as bad behavior—or, in Marvel's case, extremely good behavior—and covering up.

23   Marvel is unhappy that she slipped through the system. "As an adult I can see there were great gaps in communications between my teachers and my parents—and between me and my teachers, and me and my parents on this issue! I fell through all the cracks. My teachers failed to impress on my parents very early on that I was having trouble. I didn't want my parents to think I wasn't doing well.

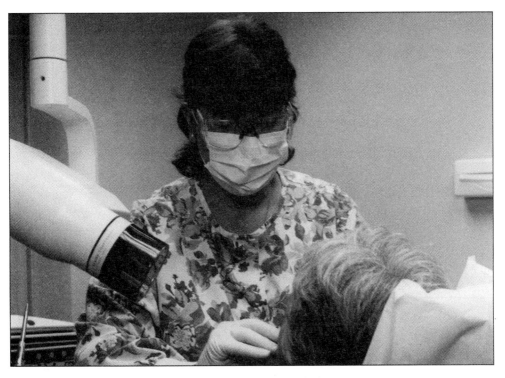

In her job as a dental assistant, Marvel works on a patient.

And I didn't have the guts to approach the teachers and say, 'Hey!' There were times I felt no teacher cared, as long as I didn't disrupt the class."

24   Marvel doesn't think much about the past, though. She is mastering her computer—by reading the instructions. She plans to attend school for another year or so to keep working on spelling and writing, "to keep it fresh." Since she went back to school five years ago, her reading has risen from the fourth-grade level to a level beyond high school.

25   Writing is still a chore, and reading is work, too. "I'm never going to write a book," Marvel says. "I can't even read a three-hundred-page novel in a week—it might take me a month or two. But that doesn't bother me. I know I have made real progress when I can set small goals and achieve them. I was so proud one time when my husband asked me to read a manual to him while he worked on my car. He looked up from under the hood and told me I was doing a great job and that school was really helping me!

26   "Thankfully, I can write letters now and make lists for shopping and for packing for vacations. I can take notes and write memos° to others and know they will be understood. I have learned to use a lot of tools, including a dictionary, a thesaurus° (which I never knew existed), and a computer. I have also learned I need lots of quiet time to do these things well.

27   "I am able to read newspapers, magazine articles, and instruction manuals, even out loud if the situation calls for it. I feel more confident read-ing stories to my nieces and nephews and my friends' children. These are tremendous rewards—all the rewards I really need to make me feel good about going back to school.

28   "It hasn't been easy, despite all the wonderful help I've had. I will never forget my first night in a writing class after going to school for reading and phonics for a couple of years. The writing teacher gave the students fifteen minutes to write a short description about their favorite place. I could think of lots of places I would love to tell people about, but I couldn't write anything more than my name at the top of the paper! After the class my teacher and I agreed I wasn't ready for this yet. I didn't feel defeated, though. I returned to the phonics and reading group. A few months later I went back. By then I was able to handle the writing class. This class was another turning point for me. My teacher helped me break the silence. At last I was able to speak freely about the secret I had been hiding all these years. Now I feel good about writing something down and then reading it out loud."

29   Marvel believes it is important for her to encourage others who share her disability. "In the School for Adults, my teachers have asked me to reach out to people who they know have the same problem. I can spot them, too. They don't talk to anyone, they keep their heads buried in books they are struggling to read, and they never mix with the other students. Sometimes when I approach people who need a lot of help, they turn away because they don't want to admit how

Marvel is teaching herself how to use a Macintosh computer.

bad their problem is. I know how they feel. I also know that it is by taking many small steps that they will make progress. There are no miracles here, just a lot of hard work!

30   "Occasionally I am asked to speak to small groups about the School for Adults and how it helped me to meet this challenge. Sometimes I feel uncomfortable and feel I'm saying, in effect, 'Hi, I'm Marvel, and I am illiterate°!' However, I believe it is important to do what I can to get the word out to others who may benefit from the program.

31   "When school was ending last spring, several people in our study work group asked me if I would organize a little class for them during the summer. I was floored°! They were actually looking up to me! But I felt that if they thought I could help them, I knew they could push me, too, so why not? We met nearly every week and practiced reading out loud, and we worked on pronunciation and word definitions."

32   How far has Marvel come? Not long ago she was invited to serve on the Advisory Council for the School for Adults. She sits as an equal with the school's director, teacher representatives, business owners, and others from the community.

33   At one meeting, the secretary was absent, and the chairman asked if someone would take notes for her. Without a moment's thought, Marvel said, "I will."

34   And she did!

WORD SKILLS QUESTIONS

Phonics and Dictionary

Questions 1–5 use words found in the following paragraph from the selection. Read the paragraph and answer the questions that follow.

"Occasionally I am asked to speak to small groups about the school for adults and how it helped me to meet this challenge. Sometimes I feel uncomfortable and feel I'm saying, in effect, 'Hi, I'm Marvel, and I am an illiterate!' However, I believe it's important to do what I can to get the word out to others who may benefit from the program." (Paragraph 30)

1. Which word has a consonant digraph and a short vowel sound?
   a. *occasionally*
   b. *challenge*
   c. *sometimes*

2. Which word is broken into syllables correctly?
   a. some-times
   b. un-co-mf-or-tab-le
   c. prog-ram

3. Which word would be found on a dictionary page with these guidewords: **somatic / sonorous**?
   a. *speak*
   b. *school*
   c. *sometimes*

Use your dictionary to answer the following question.

4. Which word is both a noun and a verb?
   a. *feel*
   b. *effect*
   c. Both of the above

Use the pronunciation key on page 119 to answer the following question.

5. In the word *important* (ĭm-pôr′tnt), the **o** is pronounced like the **o** in what common word?
   a. *pot*
   b. *toe*
   c. *for*
   d. *noise*

Vocabulary in Context

6. In the sentences below, the word *landmarks* means
   a. street signs.
   b. familiar features of the surroundings.
   c. written directions.
   d. maps.

   > "Imagine a world where you can't read the street signs. You have to find your way by using only landmarks. When you see a sign or road map, you can't understand it. . . ." (Paragraph 1)

7. In the sentences below, the word *widespread* means
   a. unimportant.
   b. unusual.
   c. common.
   d. easy to solve.

   > ". . . she realizes that difficulty reading and writing is a fairly widespread problem. 'There are a lot of us out there,' she says." (Paragraph 18)

8. In the sentences below, the word *intense* means
   a. rather easy.
   b. expensive.
   c. worthless.
   d. involving extreme effort.

   > "The work was intense. Teachers . . . drilled Marvel in phonics, spelling, and reading. Marvel came to school right after work. . . ." (Paragraph 21)

9. In the sentence below, the word *disrupt* means
   a. interfere with.
   b. attend.
   c. understand.
   d. help.

   > "There were times I felt no teacher cared, as long as I didn't disrupt the class." (Paragraph 23)

10. In the sentence below, the word *chore* means
    a. something done for fun.
    b. difficult task.
    c. mystery.
    d. reason.

    > "Writing is still a chore, and reading is work, too." (Paragraph 25)

READING COMPREHENSION QUESTIONS

Central Point and Main Ideas

1. Which sentence best expresses the central point of the selection?
   a. Learning disabilities of all types can be overcome with hard work.
   b. Kretzmann felt much shame and fear throughout her public-school education.
   c. Through hard work, Kretzmann gradually overcame her learning disability and the shame and fear it caused her.
   d. Students with learning disabilities should not have to attend the public schools in this country.

2. Which sentence best expresses the main idea of paragraph 12?
   a. The first sentence
   b. The second sentence
   c. The third sentence
   d. The last sentence

Supporting Details

3. The author states that in high school, she avoided classes that
   a. her close, helpful friends had not enrolled in.
   b. started early in the day.
   c. were too easy.
   d. involved writing assignments and heavy reading.

4. According to one of Marvel's teachers, a typical learning-disabled student
   a. is poor at sports.
   b. has few talents.
   c. has a normal or above-normal IQ.
   d. has a normal or below-normal IQ.

5. Marvel is unhappy that she
   a. slipped through the public-school system.
   b. has never made the dean's list.
   c. is not paid more for her job as a dental assistant.
   d. never married.

6. Marvel believes it is important for her to
   a. earn a degree that will enable her to work with learning-disabled students.
   b. take classes for the rest of her life.
   c. graduate from college before she is 40.
   d. encourage others who share her disability.

Relationships

7. Paragraphs 1 and 2
   a. tell a story in time order.
   b. list difficulties Kretzmann once faced.
   c. compare and contrast ways of getting around.
   d. define and illustrate the word *world*.

8. In the sentence below, the words *such as* show a relationship of
   a. addition.
   b. contrast.
   c. time.
   d. illustration.

   "Things she bought, such as appliances and other household items, came with instruction manuals." (Paragraph 13)

9. In the sentences below, the word *but* shows a relationship of
   a. addition.
   b. time.
   c. contrast.
   d. illustration.

   "She had a 'system,' and it worked. . . . But sometimes she got caught." (Paragraphs 16–17)

10. The main pattern of organization of this selection is
    a. time order.
    b. list of items.
    c. comparison-contrast.
    d. definition and example.

MAPPING ACTIVITY

Following is a map of this selection. Complete the diagram on the next page by filling in the letters of the missing major details, which are scrambled below. (Two of the items have already been filled in for you.)

a. Kretzmann learned to read at a level beyond high school.
b. Kretzmann decided to go back to school.
c. Kretzmann was in the fifth grade when she realized that she was far behind her classmates.
d. Kretzmann was trained as a dental assistant and then got a job as one.
e. Kretzmann avoided high-school classes that involved writing assignments and heavy reading.
f. Kretzmann was asked to join the Advisory Council of the School for Adults.
g. Kretzmann had two friends who took notes for her and coached her through her courses.

Central point: Marvel Kretzmann worked hard and eventually gained self-confidence and learned to read and write.

Marvel relaxes with some leisure reading.

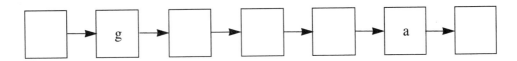

DISCUSSION QUESTIONS

1. Should Kretzmann have been "passed from grade to grade" because she was good at math? Or should she have been made to stay at a lower grade until her reading and writing skills got better?

2. Do you know someone who has a learning disability? If so, how does that person's experience compare with Kretzmann's?

3. Kretzmann says that sometimes when she is called upon to speak to small groups, she feels "uncomfortable." Why do you think this is? Would you feel uncomfortable speaking to a group? Explain.

Note: Writing assignments for this selection appear on pages 545–546.

Check Your Performance			LEARNING TO READ
Activity	*Number Right*	*Points*	*Total*
WORD SKILLS			
Phonics and Dictionary (5 items)	_____	× 10 =	_____
Vocabulary in Context (5 items)	_____	× 10 =	_____
		SCORE =	_____ %
READING COMPREHENSION			
Central Point and Main Ideas (2 items)	_____	× 8 =	_____
Supporting Details (4 items)	_____	× 8 =	_____
Relationships (4 items)	_____	× 8 =	_____
Mapping (5 items)	_____	× 4 =	_____
		SCORE =	_____ %
FINAL SCORES: Word Skills _____ %		Comprehension _____ %	

Enter your final scores into the **Reading Performance Chart: Ten Reading Selections** on the inside back cover.

2

Tickets to Nowhere
Andy Rooney

Preview

We've all heard or read about lucky people who have won millions of dollars in lotteries. One California man, for example, won over ten million dollars on his very first lottery ticket. Stories like that are enough to keep many people hopefully "investing" in the lottery week after week. But Andy Rooney, in this essay from his syndicated column, has another story to tell.

Words to Watch

his ship would come in (3): he would get lucky
come over the wires (11): be broadcast
fidgeted (12): moved nervously

1   Things never went very well for Jim Oakland. He dropped out of high school because he was impatient to get rich, but after dropping out he lived at home with his parents for two years and didn't earn a dime.

2   He finally got a summer job working for the highway department holding up a sign telling oncoming drivers to be careful of the workers ahead. Later that same year, he picked up some extra money putting fliers under the windshield wipers of parked cars.

3   Things just never went very well for Jim and he was 23 before he left home and went to Florida hoping his ship would come in° down there. He never lost his desire to get rich; but first he needed money for the rent, so he took a job near Fort Lauderdale for $4.50 an hour servicing the goldfish aquariums kept near the cashier's counter in a lot of restaurants.

4   Jim was paid in cash once a week by the owner of the goldfish business, and the first thing he did was go to the little convenience store near where he lived and buy $20 worth of lottery tickets. He was really determined to get rich.

5   A week ago, the lottery jackpot in Florida reached $54 million. Jim woke up nights thinking what he could do with $54 million. During the days, he daydreamed about it. One morning he was driving along the main street in the boss's old pickup truck with six tanks of goldfish in back. As he drove past a BMW dealer, he looked at the new models in the window.

6   He saw the car he wanted in the showroom window, but unfortunately he didn't see the light change. The car in front of him stopped short and Jim slammed on his brakes. The fish tanks slid forward. The tanks broke, the water gushed out, and the goldfish slithered and flopped all over the back of the truck. Some fell off into the road.

7   It wasn't a good day for the goldfish or for Jim, of course. He knew he'd have to pay for the tanks and 75 cents each for the fish, and if it weren't for the $54 million lottery, he wouldn't have known which way to turn. He had that lucky feeling.

8   For the tanks and the dead goldfish, the boss deducted $114 of Jim's $180 weekly pay. Even though he didn't have enough left for the rent and food, Jim doubled the amount he was going to spend on lottery tickets. He never needed $54 million more.

9   Jim had this system. He took his age and added the last four digits of the telephone number of the last girl he dated. He called it his lucky number . . . even though the last four digits changed quite often and he'd never won with his system. Everyone laughed at Jim and said he'd never win the lottery.

10   Jim put down $40 on the counter that week and the man punched out his tickets. Jim stowed them safely away in his wallet with last week's tickets. He never threw away his lottery tickets until at least a month after the drawing just in case there was some mistake. He'd heard of mistakes.

11   Jim listened to the radio all afternoon the day of the drawing. The people at the radio station he was listening to waited for news of the winning numbers to come over the wires° and, even then, the announcers didn't rush to get them on. The station manager thought the people running the lottery ought to pay to have the winning numbers broadcast, just like any other commercial announcement.

12   Jim fidgeted° while they gave the weather and the traffic and the news. Then they played more music. All he wanted to hear were those numbers.

13   "Well," the radio announcer said finally, "we have the lottery numbers some of you have been waiting for. You ready?" Jim was ready. He clutched his ticket with the number 274802.

14   "The winning number," the announcer said, "is 860539. I'll repeat that. 860539." Jim was still a loser.

15   I thought that, with all the human interest stories about lottery winners, we ought to have a story about one of the several million losers.

WORD SKILLS QUESTIONS

Phonics and Dictionary

1. Which word from paragraphs 3–5 contains *two* examples of the Two-Vowels-Together Rule (in which the first vowel is long and the second is silent)?
   a. *aquariums*
   b. *little*
   c. *reached*
   d. *daydreamed*

2. Which word from the sentence below is broken up according to the rule to divide between the words in a compound word?
   a. *wanted*
   b. *showroom*
   c. *window*
   d. *unfortunately*

   "He saw the car he wanted in the showroom window, but unfortunately he didn't see the light change." (Paragraph 6)

3. Which word from paragraph 7 has a consonant digraph and a silent letter combination?
   a. *goldfish*
   b. *known*
   c. *which*
   d. *lucky*

4. Which word from paragraph 8 is correctly broken into syllables?
   a. gold-fish
   b. ded-uc-ted
   c. en-ough
   d. mill-ion

5. Which word from paragraph 12 would be found on a dictionary page with these guidewords: **wear and tear / Weber**?
   a. *while*
   b. *weather*
   c. *wanted*
   d. *were*

Use your dictionary to answer the following question.

6. Which word from paragraph 15 is both an adjective and a noun?
   a. *thought*
   b. *human*
   c. *interest*
   d. *ought*

Use the pronunciation key on page 119 to answer the following question.

7. In the word *all* (ôl), in paragraph 15, the **a** is pronounced like the
   a. **a** in *pay.*
   b. **a** in *care.*
   c. **a** in *father.*
   d. **aw** in *paw.*

Vocabulary in Context

8. In the sentence below, the word *gushed* means
   a. dripped slowly.
   b. steamed.
   c. poured.
   d. held.

   "The tanks broke, the water gushed out, and the goldfish slithered and flopped all over the back of the truck." (Paragraph 6)

9. In the sentence below, the word *digits* means
   a. letters.
   b. single numbers.
   c. rings.
   d. area codes.

   "He took his age and added the last four digits of the telephone number of the last girl he dated." (Paragraph 9)

10. In the sentence below, the word *stowed* means
    a. discovered.
    b. bought.
    c. knew.
    d. put.

    "Jim stowed them safely away in his wallet with last week's tickets." (Paragraph 10)

READING COMPREHENSION QUESTIONS

Central Point and Main Ideas

1. Which sentence best expresses the central point of the selection?
    a. Everyone dreams of winning the lottery.
    b. The more money you invest in lottery tickets, the better your chances of winning.
    c. Jim was foolish to be so determined to get rich by winning the lottery.
    d. Jim Oakland is a very unlucky man.

2. Which sentence best expresses the main idea of paragraph 6?
    a. Jim's daydreaming caused an automobile accident.
    b. Jim was sure he would be driving a BMW soon.
    c. The old pickup had bad brakes, causing Jim to crash into the car in front of him.
    d. Many goldfish died in a car accident.

3. Which sentence best expresses the main idea of paragraph 8?
    a. Jim's boss deducted $114 from Jim's paycheck.
    b. After his boss deducted $114 from his paycheck, Jim could not afford to buy food or pay his rent.
    c. Although his reduced paycheck would not cover rent or food, Jim spent twice as much as usual on lottery tickets.
    d. Jim wanted to win the lottery more than ever.

Supporting Details

4. According to the reading, Jim dropped out of school because he
    a. was not a very good student.
    b. had to support his pregnant girlfriend.
    c. was impatient to get rich.
    d. was offered a good-paying job in Florida.

5. _____ TRUE OR FALSE? Jim's "lucky number" had once won him a little lottery money.

6. Jim slammed on his brakes because
    a. they weren't working well.
    b. he saw his boss coming.
    c. he was late in noticing that the car in front of him was stopping for a red traffic light.
    d. it was time to turn on the radio and hear the winning lottery number for that week.

7. According to the selection, Jim never threw away his lottery tickets
   a. at all.
   b. until his next paycheck.
   c. until at least a month after the drawing.
   d. so that he could write off his losses on his tax return.

Relationships

8. The word *so* in the sentence below signals a relationship of
   a. addition.
   b. time.
   c. comparison.
   d. cause and effect.

   ". . . he needed money for the rent, so he took a job near Fort Lauderdale. . . ." (Paragraph 3)

9. The words *even though* in the sentence below signal
   a. addition.
   b. comparison.
   c. contrast.
   d. cause and effect.

   "Even though he didn't have enough left for the rent and food, Jim doubled the amount he was going to spend on lottery tickets." (Paragraph 8)

10. The main pattern of organization of this selection is
    a. time order.
    b. list of items.
    c. comparison-contrast.
    d. definition and example.

MAPPING ACTIVITY

Following is a map showing events in "Tickets to Nowhere." Complete the map by filling in the missing details, which are scrambled in the list below.

- Jim quits high school.
- The winning lottery number is announced; Jim doesn't win.
- The Florida lottery jackpot becomes $54 million.
- Jim gets into an automobile accident that costs him much of his weekly salary.

Central point: Jim Oakland's determination to get rich by winning the lottery was foolish.

```
┌──────────────────────────────────────────────────────────┐
│                                                          │
│                                                          │
│                                                          │
└──────────────────────────────────────────────────────────┘
                            │
                            ▼
┌──────────────────────────────────────────────────────────┐
│  Jim moves to Florida and takes a job, hoping he'll get   │
│           lucky there and win the lottery.                │
└──────────────────────────────────────────────────────────┘
                            │
                            ▼
┌──────────────────────────────────────────────────────────┐
│                                                          │
│                                                          │
└──────────────────────────────────────────────────────────┘
                            │
                            ▼
┌──────────────────────────────────────────────────────────┐
│                                                          │
│                                                          │
└──────────────────────────────────────────────────────────┘
                            │
                            ▼
┌──────────────────────────────────────────────────────────┐
│  Jim doubles the amount of his normal investment in the   │
│                        lottery.                           │
└──────────────────────────────────────────────────────────┘
                            │
                            ▼
┌──────────────────────────────────────────────────────────┐
│                                                          │
│                                                          │
└──────────────────────────────────────────────────────────┘
```

DISCUSSION QUESTIONS

1. On balance, are lotteries good or bad? What are the positive aspects of lotteries? What are the negatives?

2. Do you know anyone like Jim, someone who depends on luck more than on hard work or ability? If so, why do you think this person relies so much on luck? How lucky has he or she been?

3. If you could have a large sum of money, would it mean more to you to have earned it or won it? Explain your answer.

Note: Writing assignments for this selection appear on pages 546–547.

Check Your Performance			TICKETS TO NOWHERE
Activity	*Number Right*	*Points*	*Total*
WORD SKILLS			
Phonics and Dictionary (7 items)	_____	× 10 =	_____
Vocabulary in Context (3 items)	_____	× 10 =	_____
		SCORE =	_____ %
COMPREHENSION			
Central Point and Main Ideas (3 items)	_____	× 8 =	_____
Supporting Details (4 items)	_____	× 8 =	_____
Relationships (3 items)	_____	× 8 =	_____
Mapping (4 items)	_____	× 5 =	_____
		SCORE =	_____ %

FINAL SCORES: Word Skills _____ %   Comprehension _____ %

Enter your final scores into the **Reading Performance Chart: Ten Reading Selections** on the inside back cover.

3

Joe Davis
Beth Johnson

Preview

From age 14 on, Joe Davis followed a path that led him closer and closer to self-destruction. He lived in a world of drugs, guns, and easy money. In this world, he had no respect for himself or sympathy for others. Today Joe Davis is, in every way, a new man. Here is the story of how Joe saved his own life.

Words to Watch

option (6): choice
shown the ropes (10): shown how things should be done
rehabilitated (10): brought back to a good and healthy life
stickup man (11): someone who robs with a gun
went downhill (13): got worse
encountered (20): met
unruly (26): disorderly
hushed (27): quiet

1   Joe Davis was the coolest fourteen-year-old he'd ever seen.

2   He went to school when he felt like it. He hung out with a wild crowd. He started drinking some wine, smoking some marijuana. "Nobody could tell me anything," he says today. "I thought the sun rose and set on me."

There were rules at home, and Joe didn't do rules. So he moved in with his grandmother.

3   Joe Davis was the coolest sixteen-year-old he'd ever seen.

4   Joe's parents gave up on his schooling and signed him out of the

tenth grade. Joe went to work in his dad's body shop, but that didn't last long. There were rules there, too, and Joe didn't do rules. By the time he was in his mid-teens, Joe was taking pills that got him high, and he was even using cocaine. He was also smoking marijuana all the time and drinking booze all the time.

5   Joe Davis was the coolest twenty-five-year-old he'd ever seen.

6   He was living with a woman almost twice his age. The situation wasn't great, but she paid the bills, and certainly Joe couldn't pay them. He had his habit to support, which by now had grown to include heroin. Sometimes he'd work at a low-level job, if someone else found it for him. He might work long enough to get a paycheck and then spend it all at once. Other times he'd be caught stealing and get fired first. A more challenging job

was not an option°, even if he had bothered to look for one. He couldn't put words together to form a sentence, unless the sentence was about drugs. Filling out an application was difficult. He wasn't a strong reader. He couldn't do much with numbers. Since his drug habit had to be paid for, he started to steal. First he stole from his parents, then from his sister. Then he stole from the families of people he knew. But eventually the people he knew wouldn't let him in their houses, since they knew he'd steal from them. So he got a gun and began holding people up. He chose elderly people and others who weren't likely to fight back. The holdups kept him in drug money, but things at home were getting worse. His woman's teenage daughter was getting out of line. Joe decided it was up to him to discipline her. The girl didn't like it. She told her boyfriend. One day, the boyfriend called Joe out of the house.

7   BANG.

8   Joe Davis was in the street, his nose in the dirt. His mind was still cloudy from his most recent high, but he knew something was terribly wrong with his legs. He couldn't move them; he couldn't even feel them. His mother came out of her nearby house and ran to him. As he heard her screams, he imagined what she was seeing. Her oldest child, her first baby, her bright boy who could have been and done anything, was lying in the gutter, a junkie with a .22 caliber bullet lodged in his spine.

9   The next time Joe's head cleared, he was in a hospital bed, blinking up at his parents as they stared helplessly at him. The doctors had done all they could; Joe would live, to everyone's surprise. But he was a paraplegic— paralyzed from his chest down. It was done. It was over. It was written in stone. He would not walk again. He would not be able to control his bladder or bowels. He would not be able to make love as he did before. He would not be able to hold people up, then hurry away.

10   Joe spent the next eight months being moved between several Philadelphia hospitals, where he was shown the ropes° of life as a paraplegic. Officially he was being "rehabilitated°"—restored to a productive life. There was just one problem: Joe. "To be rehabilitated, you must have been habilitated first," he says today. "That wasn't me." During his stay in the hospitals, he found ways to get high every day.

11   Finally Joe was released from the hospital. He returned in his wheelchair to the house he'd been living in when he was shot. He needed someone to take care of him, and his woman friend was still willing. His drug habit was as strong as ever, but his days as a stickup man° were over. So he started selling drugs. Business was good. The money came in fast, and his own drug use accelerated even faster.

12   A wheelchair-bound junkie doesn't pay much attention to his health and cleanliness. Eventually Joe developed his first bedsore: a deep, rotting wound that ate into his flesh, overwhelming him with its foul odor. He was admitted to Magee Rehabilitation Hospital, where he spent six months on his stomach while the ghastly wound slowly healed. Again, he spent his time in the hospital using drugs. This time his drug use did not go unnoticed. Soon before he was scheduled to be discharged, hospital officials kicked him out. He returned to his friend's house and his business. But then police raided the house. They took the drugs, they took the money, they took the guns.

13   "I really went downhill° then," says Joe. With no drugs and no money to get drugs, life held little meaning. He began fighting with the woman he was living with. "When you're in the state I was in, you don't know how to be nice to anybody," he says. Finally she kicked him out of the house. When his parents took him in, Joe did a little selling from their house, trying to keep it low-key, out of sight, so they wouldn't notice. He laughs at the notion today. "I thought I could control junkies and tell them 'Business only during certain hours.'"

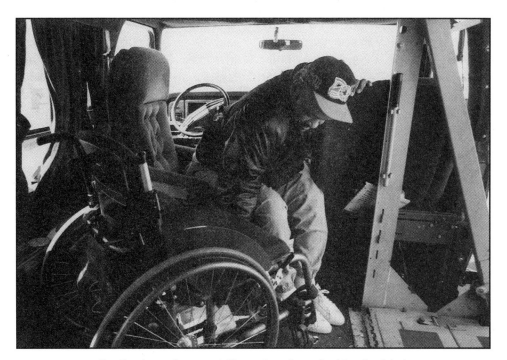

Joe Davis needs a specially equipped van for his wheelchair.

Joe got high when his monthly Social Security check came, high when he'd make a purchase for someone else and get a little something for himself, high when a visitor would share drugs with him. It wasn't much of a life. "There I was," he says, "a junkie with no education, no job, no friends, no means of supporting myself. And now I had a spinal cord injury."

14 Then came October 25, 1988. Joe had just filled a prescription for pills to control his muscle spasms. Three hundred of the powerful muscle relaxants were there for the taking. He swallowed them all.

15 "It wasn't the spinal cord injury that did it," he says. "It was the addiction."

16 Joe tried hard to die, but it didn't work. A sister heard him choking and called for help. He was rushed to the hospital, where he lay in a coma for four days.

17 Joe has trouble finding the words to describe what happened next.

18 "I had . . . a spiritual awakening, for lack of any better term," he says. "My soul had been cleansed. I knew my life could be better. And from that day to this, I have chosen not to get high."

19 Drugs, he says, "are not even a temptation. That life is a thing that happened to someone else."

20 Joe knew he wanted to turn himself around, but he needed help in knowing where to start. He enrolled in Magee Hospital's vocational rehabilitation program. For six weeks, he immersed himself in discussions, tests, and exercises to help him determine

the kind of work he might be suited for. The day he finished the rehab program, a nurse at Magee told him about a receptionist's job in the spinal cord injury unit at Thomas Jefferson Hospital. He went straight to the hospital and met Lorraine Buchanan, coordinator of the unit. "I told her where I was and where I wanted to go," Joe says. "I told her, 'If you give me a job, I will never disappoint you. I'll quit first if I see I can't live up to it.'" She gave him the job. The wheelchair-bound junkie, the man who'd never been able to hold a job, the drug-dependent stickup man who "couldn't put two words together to make a sentence" was now the first face, the first voice that patients encountered° when they entered the spinal cord unit. "I'd never talked to people like that," says Joe, shaking his head. "I had absolutely no background. But Lorraine and the others, they taught me to speak. Taught me to greet people. Taught me to handle the phone." How did he do in his role as a receptionist? A huge smile breaks across Joe's face as he answers, "Excellent."

21   Soon, his personal life also took a very positive turn. A month after Joe started his job, he was riding a city bus to work. A woman recovering from knee surgery was in another seat. The two smiled, but didn't speak.

22   A week later, Joe spotted the woman again. The bus driver sensed something was going on and encouraged Joe to approach her. Her name was Terri. She was a receptionist in a law office. On their first date, Joe laid his cards on the table. He told her his story. He also told her he was looking to get married. "That about scared her away," Joe recalls. "She said she wasn't interested in marriage. I asked, 'Well, suppose you did meet someone you cared about who cared about you and treated you well. Would you still be opposed to the idea of marriage?' She said no, she would consider it then. I said, 'Well, that's all I ask.'"

23   Four months later, as the two sat over dinner in a restaurant, Joe handed Terri a box tied with a ribbon. Inside was a smaller box. Then a smaller box, and a smaller one still. Ten boxes in all. Inside the smallest was an engagement ring. After another six months, the two were married in the law office where Terri works. Since then, she has been Joe's constant source of support, encouragement, and love.

24   After Joe had started work at Jefferson Hospital, he talked with his supervisor, Lorraine, about his dreams of moving on to something bigger, more challenging. She encouraged him to try college. He had taken and passed the high-school general equivalency diploma (GED) exam years before, almost as a joke, when he was recovering from his bedsores at Magee. Now he enrolled in a university mathematics course. He didn't do well. "I wasn't ready," Joe says. "I'd been out of school seventeen years. I dropped out." Before he could let discouragement overwhelm him, he enrolled at Community College of

Philadelphia (CCP), where he signed up for basic math and English courses. He worked hard, sharpening study skills he had never developed in his earlier school days. Next he took courses toward an associate's degree in mental health and social services, along with a certificate in addiction studies. Five years later, he graduated from CCP, the first member of his family ever to earn a college degree. He went on to receive a bachelor's degree in mental health from Hahnemann University in Philadelphia.

25   Now Joe is in his final year in the University of Pennsylvania's Master of Social Work program. Besides being a student, he is employed as a psychotherapist at John F. Kennedy Mental Health Center in Philadelphia. His dream now is to get into the "real world," the world of young men and women immersed in drugs, violence, and crime. In fact, in his field-placement work for school, Joe mentors a group of at-risk adolescent boys. Also, whenever he can, he speaks at local schools through a program called Think First. He tells young people about his drug use, his shooting, and his experience with paralysis.

26   At a presentation at a disciplinary school outside of Philadelphia, Joe gazes with quiet authority at the unruly° crowd of teenagers. He begins to speak, telling them about speedballs and guns, fast money and bedsores,

even about the leg bag that collects his urine. At first, the kids snort with laughter at his honesty. When they laugh, he waits patiently, then goes on. Gradually the room grows quieter as Joe tells them of his life and then asks them about theirs. "What's important to you? What are your goals?" he says. "I'm still in school because when I was young, I chose the dead-end route many of you are on. But now I'm doing what I have to do to get where I want to go. What are you doing?"

27   He tells them more, about broken dreams, about his parents' grief, about the former friends who turned away from him when he was no longer a source of drugs. He tells them of the continuing struggle to regain the trust of people he once abused. He tells them about the desire that consumes him now, the desire to make his community a better place to live. His wish is that no young man or woman should have to walk the path he's walked in order to value the precious gift of life. The teenagers are now silent. They look at this broad-shouldered black man in his wheelchair, his head and beard close-shaven, a gold ring in his ear. His hushed° words settle among them like gentle drops of cleansing rain. "What are you doing? Where are you going?" he asks them. "Think about it. Think about me."

28   Joe Davis is the coolest forty-four-year-old you've ever seen.

Joe goes shopping with his wife, Terri.

WORD SKILLS QUESTIONS

Phonics and Dictionary

Questions 1–5 use words found in the following passage from the selection. Read the passage and answer the questions that follow.

> Joe has trouble finding the words to describe what happened next.
> "I had . . . a spiritual awakening, for lack of any better term," he says. "My soul had been cleansed. I knew my life could be better. And from that day to this, I have chosen not to get high." (Paragraphs 17–18)

1. Which word has a silent letter combination?
   a. *had*
   b. *lack*
   c. *term*
   d. *this*

2. Which word is broken into syllables correctly?
   a. troub-le
   b. fi-nding
   c. happ-e-ned
   d. bet-ter

3. Which word would be found on a dictionary page with these guidewords: **ancillary / Angel Fall**?
   a *awakening*
   b. *any*
   c. *and*

Use your dictionary to answer the following question.

4. Which word has these parts of speech: adjective, pronoun, adverb?
   a. *next*
   b. *any*
   c. *better*
   d. *high*

Use your dictionary and the pronunciation key on page 119 to answer the following question.

5. In the word *high*, the **i** is pronounced like the **i** in what common word?
   a. *pit*
   b. *pie*
   c. *pier*

Vocabulary in Context

6. In the sentence below, the word *restored* means
   a. held back.
   b. punished.
   c. brought back.
   d. paid.

   "Officially he was being 'rehabilitated'—restored to a productive life."
   (Paragraph 10)

7. In the sentence below, the word *accelerated* means
   a. increased.
   b. grew less serious.
   c. disappeared.
   d. helped.

   "The money came in fast, and his own drug use had accelerated even
   faster." (Paragraph 11)

8. In the sentence below, the word *ghastly* means
   a. quite small.
   b. very unpleasant.
   c. caused by a gun.
   d. illegal.

   " . . . he spent six months on his stomach while the ghastly wound slowly healed." (Paragraph 12)

9. In the sentences below, the word *notion* means
   a. idea.
   b. joke.
   c. answer.
   d. cause.

   "When his parents took him in, Joe did a little selling from their house, trying to keep it low-key, out of sight, so they wouldn't notice. He laughs at that notion today. 'I thought I could control junkies . . . '" (Paragraph 13)

10. In the sentence below, the word *immersed* means
    a. totally ignored.
    b. greatly angered.
    c. deeply involved.
    d. often harmed.

    "For six weeks, he immersed himself in discussions, tests, and exercises to help him determine the kind of work he might be suited for." (Paragraph 20)

READING COMPREHENSION QUESTIONS

Central Point and Main Ideas

1. Which sentence best expresses the central point of the selection?
   a. Most people cannot improve their lives once they turn to drugs and crime.
   b. Joe Davis overcame a life of drugs and crime and a disability to lead a rich, productive life.
   c. The rules set by Joe Davis's parents caused him to leave home and continue a life of drugs and crime.
   d. Joe Davis's friends turned away from him once they learned he was no longer a source of drugs.

2. A main idea may cover more than one paragraph. Which sentence best expresses the main idea of paragraphs 21–23?
   a. The first sentence of paragraph 21
   b. The second sentence of paragraph 21
   c. The first sentence of paragraph 22
   d. The first sentence of paragraph 23

3. Which sentence best expresses the main idea of paragraph 24?
   a. It was difficult for Joe to do college work after being out of school for so many years.
   b. Lorraine Buchanan encouraged Joe to go to college.
   c. Joe overcame a lack of academic preparation and eventually received associate's and bachelor's degrees in college.
   d. If students would stay in high school and work hard, they would not have to go to the trouble of getting a high-school GED.

Supporting Details

4. Joe Davis quit high school
   a. when he was 14.
   b. when he got a good job at a hospital.
   c. when he was in the tenth grade.
   d. after he was shot.

5. Joe tried to kill himself by
   a. swallowing muscle-relaxant pills.
   b. shooting himself.
   c. overdosing on heroin.
   d. not eating or drinking.

6. According to the selection, Joe first met his wife
   a. in the hospital, where she was a nurse.
   b. on a city bus, where they were both passengers.
   c. on the job, where she was also a receptionist.
   d. at Community College of Philadelphia, where she was also a student.

7. Joe decided to stop using drugs
   a. when he met his future wife.
   b. right after he was shot.
   c. when he awoke from a suicide attempt.
   d. when he was hired as a receptionist.

Relationships

8. As suggested by the word *because,* the sentence below presents a cause and an effect. Write **C** in front of the item that is the cause. Write **E** in front of the item that is the effect.

   _____   Davis is still in school in his forties.

   _____   Davis chose a dead-end route when he was young.

   "'I'm still in school because when I was young, I chose the dead-end route many of you are on. . . .'" (Paragraph 26)

9. The word *as* in the sentence below shows a relationship of
   a. addition.
   b. time.
   c. contrast.
   d. cause and effect.

   "As he heard her screams, he imagined what she was seeing." (Paragraph 8)

10. The main pattern of organization of this selection is
    a. list of items.
    b. time order.
    c. comparison-contrast.
    d. cause and effect.

OUTLINING ACTIVITY

Following is an outline of major events in Joe Davis's life. Complete the outline by filling in the missing events, which are scrambled in the list below.

   • Joe takes a job as a receptionist.
   • Joe gets shot, which paralyzes him from the chest down.
   • Joe starts selling drugs.
   • Joe earns two college degrees.

Central point: From a life of drugs and crime, Joe Davis turned his life around in several positive ways.

   1. Joe leaves school.

   2. _____

   3. _____

4. Joe tries to commit suicide.

5. Joe gives up drugs and goes into a vocational rehabilitation program.

6. _____

7. Joe gets married.

8. _____

9. Joe works toward a master's degree in social work.

10. Joe speaks to young people, using his experiences to inspire them to improve their lives.

DISCUSSION QUESTIONS

1. What do you think was the main turning point in Joe's life, and why do you think it happened?

2. Why do you think the students Joe spoke to laughed at him as he tried to share his honest thoughts? Why did they become quieter as he continued to speak of his life? What effect do you think his presentation had on these students?

3. Joe wants young people to learn the lessons he did without having to experience his hardships. What lessons have you learned in your life that you would like to pass on to others?

Note: Writing assignments for this selection appear on page 547.

Check Your Performance   JOE DAVIS

Activity	Number Right	Points	Total
WORD SKILLS			
Phonics and Dictionary (5 items)	_____	× 10 =	_____
Vocabulary in Context (5 items)	_____	× 10 =	_____
		SCORE =	_____ %
COMPREHENSION			
Central Point and Main Ideas (3 items)	_____	× 8 =	_____
Supporting Details (4 items)	_____	× 8 =	_____
Relationships (3 items)	_____	× 8 =	_____
Outlining (4 items)	_____	× 5 =	_____
		SCORE =	_____ %

FINAL SCORES: Word Skills _____%   Comprehension _____%

Enter your final scores into the **Reading Performance Chart: Ten Reading Selections** on the inside back cover.

4

A Brother's Lesson
Christopher de Vinck

Preview

We can learn from the most unexpected sources. This story tells what one man learned from his brother, who was blind, could not speak, and was capable of doing nothing more than breathe, sleep, and eat. What could you possibly learn from such a helpless human being, you ask? Quite a lot, as you will soon find out.

Words to Watch

mute (1): unable to speak
stammered (3): spoke with pauses or repetitions without intending to
revived (6): became conscious again
plump (7): well-rounded and full in form
extent (8): the range or degree of something
confirmed (10): admitted to full membership in the church
insight (11): understanding
embrace (11): hug
hyperactive (12): overly active
sheepishly (14): in an embarrassed way
compassion (15): caring

1   I grew up in the house where my brother was on his back in his bed for almost thirty-three years, in the same corner of his room, under the same window, beside the same yellow walls. Oliver was blind, mute°. His legs were twisted. He didn't have the strength to lift his head or the intelligence to learn anything.

2   Today I am an English teacher, and each time I introduce my class to the play about Helen Keller, *The*

Miracle Worker, I tell my students about Oliver. One day, during my first year teaching, a boy in the last row raised his hand and said, "Oh, Mr. de Vinck. You mean he was a vegetable."

3   I stammered° for a few seconds. My family and I fed Oliver. We changed his diapers, hung his clothes and bed linen on the basement line in winter, and spread them out white and clean on the lawn in the summer. I always liked to watch the grasshoppers jump on the pillowcases.

4   We bathed Oliver. Tickled his chest to make him laugh. Sometimes we left the radio on in his room. We pulled the shade down over his bed in the morning to keep the sun from burning his tender skin. We listened to him laugh as we watched television downstairs. We listened to him rock his arms up and down to make the bed squeak. We listened to him cough in the middle of the night.

5   "Well, I guess you could call him a vegetable. I called him Oliver, my brother. You would have liked him."

6   One October day in 1946, when my mother was pregnant with Oliver, her second son, she was overcome by fumes from a leaking coal-burning stove. My oldest brother was sleeping in his crib, which was quite high off the ground, so the gas didn't affect him. My father pulled them outside, where my mother revived° quickly.

7   On April 20, 1947, Oliver was born—a healthy-looking, plump°, beautiful boy.

8   One afternoon, a few months later, my mother brought Oliver to a window. She held him there in the sun, the bright good sun, and there Oliver looked and looked directly into the sunlight, which was the first moment my mother realized that Oliver was blind. My parents, the true heroes of this story, learned, with the passing months, that blindness was only part of the problem. So they brought Oliver to Mount Sinai Hospital in New York for tests to determine the extent° of his condition.

9   The doctor said that he wanted to make it very clear to both my mother and my father that there was absolutely nothing that could be done for Oliver. He didn't want my parents to grasp at false hope. "You could place him in an institution," he said. "But," my parents replied, "he is our son. We will take Oliver home, of course." The good doctor answered, "Then take him home and love him."

10   Oliver grew to the size of a ten-year-old. He had a big chest, a large head. His hands and feet were those of a five-year-old, small and soft. We'd wrap a box of baby cereal for him at Christmas and place it under the tree; we'd pat his head with a damp cloth in the middle of a July heat wave. His baptismal certificate hung on the wall above his head. A bishop came to the house and confirmed° him.

11   Even now, years after his death from pneumonia, Oliver still remains the weakest, most helpless human being I ever met, and yet he was one of the most powerful human beings I ever met. He could do absolutely nothing except breathe, sleep, and eat,

and yet he was responsible for action, love, courage, insight°. When I was small my mother would say, "Isn't it wonderful that you can see?" And once she said, "When you go to heaven, Oliver will run to you, embrace° you, and the first thing he will say is 'Thank you.'" I remember, too, my mother explaining to me that we were blessed with Oliver in ways that were not clear to her at first.

12   So often parents are faced with a child who is severely retarded, but who is also hyperactive°, demanding, or wild, who needs constant care. So many people have little choice but to place their child in an institution. We were fortunate that Oliver didn't need us to be in his room all day. He never knew what his condition was. We were blessed with his presence, a true presence of peace.

13   When I was in my early twenties, I met a girl and fell in love. After a few months I brought her home to meet my family. When my mother went to the kitchen to prepare dinner, I asked the girl, "Would you like to see Oliver?" for I had told her about my brother. "No," she answered.

14   Soon after, I met Roe, a lovely girl. She asked me the names of my brothers and sisters. She loved children. I thought she was wonderful. I brought her home after a few months to meet my family. Soon it was time for me to feed Oliver. I remember sheepishly° asking Roe if she'd like to see him. "Sure," she said.

15   I sat at Oliver's bedside as Roe watched over my shoulder. I gave him his first spoonful, his second. "Can I do that?" Roe asked with ease, with freedom, with compassion°, so I gave her the bowl and she fed Oliver one spoonful at a time.

16   The power of the powerless. Which girl would you marry? Today Roe and I have three children.

WORD SKILLS QUESTIONS

Phonics and Dictionary

1. Which words from the sentence below contain consonant digraphs?
   a. *oldest, sleeping*
   b. *brother, which*
   c. *quite, ground*
   d. *sleeping, crib*

   "My oldest brother was sleeping in his crib, which was quite high off the ground, so the gas didn't affect him." (Paragraph 6)

2. The word *stove,* from the sentence below, is an example of which rule for long vowel sounds?

   a. When a word ends in vowel-consonant-**e**, the first vowel is long and the **e** is silent.

   b. When two of certain vowels are together in a word, the first one is long and the second is silent.

   c. A single vowel (other than silent **e**) at the end of a word usually has a long sound.

   " . . . she was overcome by fumes from a leaking coal-burning stove." (Paragraph 6)

3. The word *pregnant,* in the sentence below, is divided into syllables

   a. between two consonants.

   b. before a single consonant.

   c. as a compound word.

   " . . . my mother was pregnant with Oliver . . . " (Paragraph 6)

Use the entry below to answer questions 4 and 5.

pass•ing (păs´ĭng) *adj.* **1.** Moving by; going past. **2.** Of brief duration: *a passing fancy.* **3.** Cursory or superficial; casual: *a passing glance.* **4.** Satisfactory; *a passing grade.* —*n.* **1.** The act of one that passes. **2.** Death.

4. *Passing* has

   a. three parts of speech.

   b. two parts of speech and a field label.

   c. two short vowels and is accented on the first syllable.

   d. two long vowels and is accented on the first syllable.

5. Which definition of *passing* fits the sentence below?

   a. Adjective definition 1

   b. Adjective definition 4

   c. Noun definition 2

   "My parents . . . learned, with the passing months, that blindness was only part of the problem." (Paragraph 8)

Vocabulary in Context

6. In the sentence on the next page, the word *tender* means

   a. strong.

   b. easily hurt.

   c. rough.

   d. very clear.

"We pulled the shade down over his bed in the morning to keep the sun from burning his tender skin." (Paragraph 4)

7. In the sentences below, the word *overcome* means
    a. warmed.
    b. protected.
    c. impressed.
    d. overpowered.

    " . . . she was overcome by fumes. . . . My father pulled them outside, where my mother revived quickly." (Paragraph 6)

8. In the sentence below, the word *affect* means
    a. stick to.
    b. please.
    c. delay.
    d. influence.

    "My oldest brother was sleeping in his crib, which was quite high off the ground, so the gas didn't affect him." (Paragraph 6)

9. In the sentence below, the words *grasp at* mean
    a. reach for.
    b. fear.
    c. turn away from.
    d. be responsible for.

    "He didn't want my parents to grasp at false hope." (Paragraph 9)

10. In the sentence below, the word *severely* means
    a. quietly.
    b. extremely.
    c. not at all.
    d. religiously.

    "So often parents are faced with a child who is severely retarded, but who is also hyperactive, demanding, or wild, who needs constant care." (Paragraph 12)

READING COMPREHENSION QUESTIONS

Central Point and Main Ideas

1. Which sentence best expresses the central point of the selection?
   a. Parents are often forced to place very hyperactive and retarded children in institutions.
   b. Oliver's condition was caused by his mother's exposure to fumes from a coal stove.
   c. The author married Roe because she was nice to Oliver.
   d. Despite Oliver's total helplessness, de Vinck and his family benefited greatly from Oliver's presence.

2. Which sentence best expresses the main idea of paragraph 4?
   a. Despite his condition, Oliver liked to watch television.
   b. Oliver's skin was sensitive to sunlight.
   c. Oliver received lots of attention from his family.
   d. Oliver's family worried whenever he coughed.

3. Sometimes a main idea covers several paragraphs. Which sentence best expresses the main idea of paragraphs 13–16?
   a. The first girlfriend the author brought home did not want to see Oliver.
   b. The second girlfriend the author brought home did want to see Oliver and then asked to feed him.
   c. His girlfriends' reactions to Oliver helped de Vinck decide to marry his second girlfriend.
   d. The author fell in love with two girls when he was in his early twenties.

Supporting Details

4. Oliver's parents
   a. considered putting Oliver in an institution.
   b. wanted to put Oliver in an institution but could not afford it.
   c. preferred to care for Oliver themselves at home.
   d. were ordered by a doctor not to care for Oliver at home.

5. Oliver
   a. enjoyed watching television.
   b. never laughed.
   c. was hyperactive, wild, and demanding.
   d. did not require full-time care.

6. When Roe first came to visit de Vinck's house, she
    a. refused to see Oliver.
    b. started feeding Oliver immediately.
    c. asked the author if she could feed Oliver.
    d. acted embarrassed and uncomfortable.

7. _____ TRUE OR FALSE? Oliver died when he was ten years old.

Relationships

8. The word *but* in the sentences below signals a relationship of
    a. addition.
    b. comparison.
    c. contrast.
    d. cause and effect.

    "'You could place him in an institution,' he said. 'But,' my parents replied, 'he is our son.'" (Paragraph 9)

9. The relationship of the second sentence below to the first sentence is one of
    a. time.
    b. comparison.
    c. example.
    d. cause and effect.

    "When I was in my early twenties I met a girl and fell in love. After a few months I brought her home to meet my family." (Paragraph 13)

10. The overall pattern of organization of paragraphs 6–10 is

    a. time order.
    b. list of items.
    c. comparison-contrast.
    d. cause and effect.

MAPPING ACTIVITY

Major events of the selection are scrambled in the list below. Write them in the diagram in the order in which they happened.

- Oliver's mother finds out that Oliver is blind.
- Roe feeds Oliver, and de Vinck eventually marries her.
- Oliver dies.
- The author's mother is overcome by fumes.
- Oliver is born.

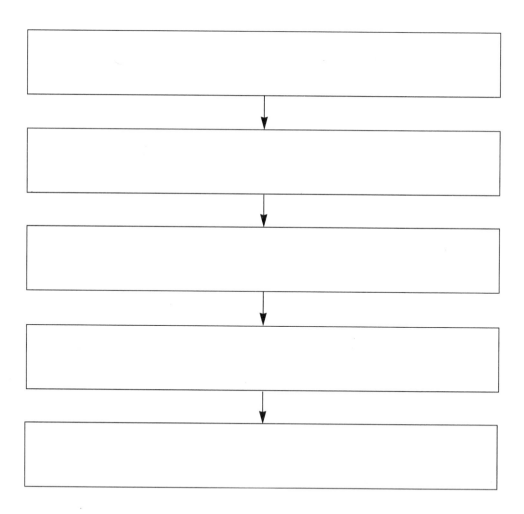

DISCUSSION QUESTIONS

1. Do you think the author's parents were correct in their decision not to put Oliver in an institution? Why or why not?

2. The author states that Oliver was "the weakest, most helpless human being I ever met, and yet he was one of the most powerful human beings I ever met." What do you think he means by this statement? Do you agree with it?

3. What was the author's first girlfriend trying to avoid by not seeing Oliver? What did it show about her as a person? What did Roe's response show about her as a person?

Note: Writing assignments for this selection appear on page 548.

Check Your Performance		A BROTHER'S LESSON	
Activity	*Number Right*	*Points*	*Total*
WORD SKILLS			
Phonics and Dictionary (5 items)	_____	× 10 =	_____
Vocabulary in Context (5 items)	_____	× 10 =	_____
		SCORE =	_____ %
COMPREHENSION			
Central Point and Main Ideas (3 items)	_____	× 8 =	_____
Supporting Details (4 items)	_____	× 8 =	_____
Relationships (3 items)	_____	× 8 =	_____
Mapping (5 items)	_____	× 4 =	_____
		SCORE =	_____ %

FINAL SCORES: Word Skills _____ % Comprehension _____ %

Enter your final scores into the **Reading Performance Chart: Ten Reading Selections** on the inside back cover.

5

How to Write Clearly
Edward T. Thompson

Preview

Do you like to write? Or is writing, in your opinion, pure torture? If you answered "torture," cheer up: you're about to receive some valuable help. Certain tricks of the trade can make writing easier and more effective for everyone. In this selection, a former editor-in-chief of *Reader's Digest* shares with you his ideas on how to write what you mean—clearly and briefly.

Words to Watch

clarity (7): clearness
objective (8): not biased
detract (8): take away from
ironically (14): in a way contrary to what is expected
i.e. (14): a Latin abbreviation meaning "that is"
delete (17): remove
mentality (19): mind
biota (21): living things
mortality: (21): death
endeavoring (22): trying
artistry (28): the work of an artist
excess: (28): extra
anecdotes (28): brief stories
belabor (28): explain in too much detail
invariably (28): always

1   If you are afraid to write, don't be.
2   If you think you've got to string together big fancy words and high-flying phrases, forget it.

3   To write well, unless you aspire to be a professional poet or novelist, you only need to get your ideas across simply and clearly.

4   It's not easy. But it is easier than you might imagine.

5   There are only three basic requirements:

6   First, you must *want* to write clearly. And I believe you really do, if you've stayed this far with me.

7   If, while you're writing for clarity°, some lovely, dramatic, or inspired phrases or sentences come to you, fine. Put them in.

8   But then with cold, objective° eyes and mind ask yourself: "Do they detract° from clarity?" If they do, grit your teeth and cut the frills.

9   Second, you must be willing to *work hard.* Thinking means work—and that's what it takes to do anything well.

10   Third, you must know and follow some *basic guidelines.*

FOLLOW SOME BASIC GUIDELINES

11   I can't give you a complete list of "do's and don'ts" for every writing problem you'll ever face.

12   But I can give you some fundamental guidelines that cover the most common problems.

1. Outline what you want to say.

13   I know that sounds grade-schoolish. But you can't write clearly until, *before you start,* you know where you will stop.

14   Ironically°, that's even a problem in writing an outline (i.e.°, knowing the ending before you begin).

15   So try this method:

- On 3" × 5" cards, write—one point to a card—all the points you need to make.

- Divide the cards into piles—one pile for each group of points *closely related* to each other. (If you were describing an automobile, you'd put all the points about mileage in one pile, all the points about safety in another, and so on.)

- Arrange your piles of points in a sequence. Which are most important and should be given first or saved for last? Which must you present before others in order to make the others understandable?

- Now, *within* each pile, do the same thing—arrange the *points* in logical, understandable order.

16   There you have your outline, needing only an introduction and conclusion.

17   This is a practical way to outline. It's also flexible. You can add, delete°, or change the location of points easily.

2. Start where your readers are.

18   How much do they know about the subject? Don't write to a level higher than your readers' knowledge of it.

19   CAUTION: Forget that old—and wrong—advice about writing to a twelve-year-old mentality°. That's insulting. But do remember that your prime purpose is to *explain* something, not prove that you're smarter than your readers.

3. Avoid jargon.

20   Don't use words, expressions, or phrases known only to people with specific knowledge or interests.

21   Example: A scientist, using scientific jargon, wrote, "The biota° exhibited a one hundred percent mortality° response." He could have written: "All the fish died."

4. Use familiar combinations of words.

22   A speechwriter for President Franklin D. Roosevelt wrote, "We are endeavoring° to construct a more inclusive society." F.D.R. changed it to, "We're going to make a country in which no one is left out."

23   CAUTION: By familiar combinations of words, I do *not* mean incorrect grammar. *That* can be unclear. Example: John's father says he can't go out Friday. (Who can't go out? John or his father?)

5. Use "first-degree" words.

24   These words immediately bring an image to your mind. Other words must be "translated" through the first-degree word before you see the image. Those are second or third-degree words.

First-degree words	Second or third-degree words
face	visage, countenance
stay	abide, remain, reside
book	volume, tome, publication

25   First-degree words are usually the most precise words, too.

6. Stick to the point.

26   Your outline—which was more work in the beginning—now saves you work, because now you can ask about any sentence you write: "Does it relate to a point in the outline? If it doesn't, should I add it to the outline? If not, I'm getting off the track." Then, full steam ahead—on the main line.

7. Be as brief as possible.

27   Whatever you write, shortening—*condensing*—almost always makes it tighter, straighter, easier to read and understand.

28   Condensing, as *Reader's Digest* does it, is in large part artistry°. But it involves techniques that anyone can learn and use.

  • *Present your points in logical ABC order.* Here again, your outline should save you work because, if you did it right, your points already stand in logical ABC order—A makes B understandable, B makes C understandable and so on. To write in a straight line is to say something clearly in the fewest possible words.

- *Don't waste words telling people what they already know.* Notice how we edited this: "Have you ever wondered how banks rate you as a credit risk? ~~You know, of course, that it's some combination of facts about your income, your job, and so on. But actually,~~ Many banks have a scoring system. . . ."

- *Cut out excess° evidence and unnecessary anecdotes°.* Usually, one fact or example (at most, two) will support a point. More just belabor° it. And while writing about something may remind you of a good story, ask yourself: "Does telling this story really help, or does it slow me down?"

  (Many people think that *Reader's Digest* articles are filled with anecdotes. Actually, we use them sparingly and usually for one or two reasons: either the subject is so dry that it needs some "humanity" to give it life; or the subject is so hard to grasp that it needs anecdotes to help readers understand. If the subject is both lively and easy to grasp, we move right along.)

- *Look for the most common word wasters:* windy phrases.

Windy phrases	Cut to . . .
at the present time	now
in the event of	if
in the majority of instances	usually

- *Look for passive verbs you can make active.* Invariably°, this produces a shorter sentence. "The cherry tree was chopped down by George Washington." (Passive verb and nine words.) "George Washington chopped down the cherry tree." (Active verb and seven words.)

- *Look for positive/negative sections from which you can cut the negative.* See how we did it here: "The answer ~~does not rest with carelessness or incompetence. It lies largely in~~ is having enough people to do the job."

- Finally, to write more clearly by using fewer words: *when you've finished, stop.*

WORD SKILLS QUESTIONS

Phonics and Dictionary

1. Which words from paragraph 28 have a consonant digraph?
   a. *people, hard,* and *grasp*
   b. *think, phrases, shorter*, and *enough*
   c. *actually, write, words*, and *stop*

2. The words *actually, sparingly, usually,* and *humanity,* in paragraph 28, are examples of which pattern for **y** as a vowel?
   a. In the middle of a word, **y** usually sounds like short **i**.
   b. At the end of a one-syllable word, **y** sounds like long **i**.
   c. At the end of a word with more than one syllable, **y** sounds like long **e**.

Use the following dictionary entry to answer questions 3–5.

jar•gon (jär′gən) *n.* **1.** Nonsensical or incoherent talk. **2.** The specialized or technical language of a profession or group.

3. *Jargon* is broken into syllables according to which rule?
   a. Divide between two consonants.
   b. Divide before a single consonant.
   c. Divide after prefixes and before suffixes.
   d. Divide between the words in a compound word.

4. *Jargon* has
   a. two syllables and is accented on the first syllable.
   b. three syllables and a usage label.
   c. two parts of speech and one schwa sound.
   d. one part of speech and one vowel sound.

5. The definition of *jargon* that applies in paragraphs 20 and 21 is
   a. definition 1.
   b. definition 2.

Vocabulary in Context

6. In the sentence below, the word *aspire* means
   a. pretend.
   b. wish.
   c. neglect.
   d. remember.

   > "To write well, unless you aspire to be a professional poet or novelist, you only need to get your ideas across simply and clearly." (Paragraph 3)

7. In the sentences below, the word *fundamental* means
   a. unusual.
   b. unknown.
   c. boring.
   d. basic.

   > "I can't give you a complete list of 'do's and don'ts'. . . . But I can give you some fundamental guidelines that cover the most common problems." (Paragraphs 11 and 12)

8. In the sentences below, the word *sequence* means
   a. circle.
   b. box.
   c. order.
   d. big pile.

   > "Arrange your piles of points in a sequence. Which are most important and should be given first or saved for last? Which must you present before others . . . ?" (Paragraph 15)

9. In the sentence below, the word *prime* means
   a. main.
   b. old.
   c. easy.
   d. not required.

   > "But do remember that your prime purpose is to *explain* something, not prove that you're smarter than your readers." (Paragraph 19)

10. In the sentences below, the word *sparingly* means
    a. at the beginning.
    b. in a limited way.
    c. pleasantly.
    d. frequently.

    > "Cut out excess evidence and unnecessary anecdotes. . . . Many people think *Reader's Digest* articles are filled with anecdotes. Actually, we use them sparingly. . . ." (Paragraph 28)

READING COMPREHENSION QUESTIONS

Central Point and Main Ideas

1. Which sentence best expresses the central point of the selection?
   a. Many people are afraid to write.
   b. Clear writing has three basic requirements.
   c. Good writers know when to stop writing.
   d. Everyone wants to write clearly.

2. Which sentence best expresses the main idea of paragraph 15?
   a. Try an outlining method that uses 3" × 5" cards to organize your points.
   b. Write one point to a card.
   c. Put the cards into piles, with each pile containing closely related points.
   d. Arrange the piles in an order.

3. Which sentence best expresses the main idea of paragraph 28?
   a. Present your points in a logical order.
   b. Don't tell people what they already know.
   c. There are a few techniques involved in writing briefly.
   d. Look for and eliminate common word wasters.

Supporting Details

4. The author states that writing well requires
   a hard work.
   b. getting your ideas across simply and clearly.
   c. learning some basic guidelines for writing.
   d. all of the above.

5. Brief writing
   a. is very boring to read.
   b. is usually easy to read and understand.
   c. avoids using any examples or anecdotes.
   d. will usually confuse readers.

6. _____ TRUE OR FALSE? According to the author, an outline should not be changed after it is written.

7. According to the author, a clear writer
   a. tells people what they already know.
   b. prefers passive verbs.
   c. makes every sentence relate to the point.
   d. uses big words and fancy phrases.

Relationships

8. Paragraphs 6, 9, and 10 all begin with
   a. addition words.
   b. comparison words.
   c. example words.
   d. cause and effect words.

9. The relationship of the second sentence below to the first sentence is one of
   a. addition.
   b. time.
   c. comparison.
   d. cause and effect.

   "This is a practical way to outline. It's also flexible." (Paragraph 17)

10. The main pattern of organization in this selection is
    a. time order.
    b. list of items.
    c. comparison-contrast.
    d. definition and example.

OUTLINING ACTIVITY

Following is a general outline for "How to Write Clearly." Complete the outline by filling in the missing major and minor details, which are scrambled in the list below.

- Know and follow some basic guidelines.
- Avoid jargon.
- Be willing to work hard.
- Use "first-degree" words.
- Be as brief as possible.

Central point: There are three basic requirements for writing well.

A. You must want to write clearly.

B. _____

C. _____

    1. Outline what you want to say.

    2. Start where your readers are.

    3. _____

    4. Use familiar combinations of words.

    5. _____

    6. Stick to the point.

    7. _____

DISCUSSION QUESTIONS

1. Of the guidelines for writing that the author gives in his article, which do you think is the most valuable—and why?

2. Do you think that the author's advice can also apply to speaking clearly? Which suggestions in particular could help make you a better speaker?

3. How do the ideas presented by the author compare with those you have used or heard about in previous classes?

Note: Writing assignments for this selection appear on page 548.

Check Your Performance		**HOW TO WRITE CLEARLY**	
Activity	*Number Right*	*Points*	*Total*
WORD SKILLS			
Phonics and Dictionary (5 items)	_____	× 10 =	_____
Vocabulary in Context (5 items)	_____	× 10 =	_____
		SCORE =	_____ %
COMPREHENSION			
Central Point and Main Ideas (3 items)	_____	× 8 =	_____
Supporting Details (4 items)	_____	× 8 =	_____
Relationships (3 items)	_____	× 8 =	_____
Outlining (5 items)	_____	× 4 =	_____
		SCORE =	_____ %

RES: Word Skills _____ %   Comprehension _____ %

the **Reading Performance Chart: Ten Reading Selections** on the inside back cover.

6

Rosa: A Success Story
Edward Patrick

Preview

This selection is about a woman who meets and conquers more obstacles than many of us have experienced. She does not spend a lot of time asking why these things are happening to her. She does what she must do to make life better for herself and her family.

Words to Watch

plantation (1): large estate where crops are grown
to no avail (3): without success
trek (3): journey
conveyed (5): communicated
sentiment (5): attitude; thought
halting (6): hesitant
preoccupied (16): deep in thought
collect myself (20): gain control of myself
immigrants (21): people who come to another country to live
oppressive (21): harsh and cruel

1   Up until six months before I met her, life for Rosa Perez had been easy. Her father was a wealthy plantation° owner in Nicaragua. Her family owned a large house with all the comforts of the rich. Then came the same type of violent civil war that has torn apart so many Latin American countries.

Rosa's father was identified as supporter of the rebel cause, and family's plantation was seized. During the government takeover, her father was shot and killed. Her mother gathered as much money as she could and fled with Rosa and her two younger brothers, Adolpho and Roberto. Their destination was the United States. Rosa's mother knew a man who knew another man who could get them through Mexico and across the U.S. border into Texas or California. There was nothing to worry about, they were told. Rosa believed it.

3   At first, things went smoothly. Twelve others joined Rosa and her family. The group had no trouble getting into and across Mexico. But just before they were to cross into California, the guide said he could go no further. Another man would take them the rest of the way. Rosa's mother protested, but to no avail°. They were led across by a man they did not know. He told them to follow his every command. They must move quickly and silently or risk detection by the Border Patrol. It was a difficult trek°. It was dark. It was cold. Coyotes howled in what all hoped was the distance. Everyone was tired and frightened.

And then came the bright lights. as they were about to cross into ⁀ited States, the U.S. Border ⁀hted the group and turned on ⁀hts on their jeeps to track ⁀eople scattered. Rosa ⁀ho and Roberto. She ⁀ould not see her ⁀ra," commanded ⁀propriately called a

"coyote." Rosa blindly followed him and watched as the lights of the jeeps sped after the others. They waited quietly for what seemed like hours. Only when he was convinced that it was safe did their guide take the five who had managed to follow him the rest of the way. Eleven were not with them, including Rosa's mother.

5   I first saw Rosa three months after this nightmare. I arrived at my office early, wanting only to unwind from the freeway drive before my first class. I was annoyed that someone was standing outside my office so early in the morning. But I spoke with her, and I soon realized that there was something special about this slender, dark-skinned young woman with large, expressive brown eyes. I didn't know then what it was I saw in her. Now I know she revealed an inner strength, conveyed° this unspoken sentiment°: "You don't know me, but you can believe in me." It was magnetic. I knew that I would help in any way I could.

6   Rosa wanted to learn English. She wanted to do more than just get by. Her halting° English told me she could manage that already. She wanted to be able to read and write the language so that she could provide for her brothers. My basic reading class had been recommended to her. She asked what materials she could get to work on even before the semester started.

7   Eager students are always easy to work with, and Rosa proved to be one of my most enthusiastic students. She kept me on my toes and constantly challenged me. She prodded me to provide more information, additional

examples, better explanations. If I used a word she didn't understand, she would stop me. She would make me explain it so that she and her classmates could grasp its meaning. If we looked for the main idea in a paragraph and her answer was different from mine, she insisted on giving the reasons why she felt she was right and I was wrong. I could not always convince her that my answer was better. But I always encouraged her to ask questions whenever she was confused or unconvinced. I looked forward to the class she had enrolled in, but I was always exhausted at its conclusion.

8 Rosa advanced from our basic reading classes to the more difficult study-skills class. Then she moved through the writing classes offered in the department. She enrolled in the Early Childhood Program at the college. This is a program which can lead to certification as a child-care worker. Her progress in her classes was reflected in a steady stream of A's and B's.

9 It took Rosa three years to complete the course work that she needed to graduate. I made plans to attend the graduation ceremonies where she would receive her associate's degree. She insisted that I attend the graduation party her friend Alberto was giving. I said I would be honored to go.

10 The ceremony was typical, with boring speeches made for proud accomplishments. The party was something special. Rosa had come a long way in the three years I had known her. She had made some wonderful friends, had found a decent job at a nearby daycare center, and had provided a good home for her two brothers.

11 Rosa greeted me when I arrived. She wanted me to meet everyone there, and she hinted at a surprise she had for me.

12 "Dr. P, may I present to you my brothers, Adolpho and Roberto."

13 *"Mucho gusto,"* I began.

14 "Right," said the smaller brother. "Call me Bobby. Nice to meet you, Doc. Say, you don't mind if me and Al 'mingle,' if you know what I mean?"

15 I knew, and I encouraged them to meet and greet the others—especially the young ladies—in attendance.

16 I commented on how quickly her brothers had adjusted to life in the States. But Rosa seemed preoccupied°. I was puzzled until I saw that we were walking toward an older woman who had the same brown expressive eyes as Rosa. It was her mother.

17 Rosa's mother had been captured by the Border Patrol and deported° to Nicaragua. There, she was jailed. Rosa had been depressed over her mother's lack of the freedom she and her brothers enjoyed. She had located her mother and worked for close to three years to get her released. I don't know all the details of how she did it. Perhaps it is best that I don't. At the moment I met her, I did not care at all about how she had attained freedom. I was just overjoyed that she was here with her children.

18 Rosa entered San Diego State University, some ninety miles away.

As often happens with students who move on, I saw very little of her. She was working hard toward a degree in early childhood education, I was on leave for a year, and our paths rarely crossed. Sometimes she would come by right before Christmas or at the end of a school year. She stopped by the office again yesterday, with a purpose. She carried two babies in her arms. The six-month-old twins were hers. Their huge, expressive brown eyes told me that before she did.

19   Rosa proudly told what had happened in the five years since her graduation. I listened enthusiastically as she told me about receiving a bachelor of arts degree, marrying Alberto, opening a child-care center with him, and giving birth to their twin sons. "And now," she said, "I want to tell you their names. This is Alberto," she said, nodding toward the larger twin. Then she looked toward the smaller one. Her eyes smiled as much as her mouth. "He is smaller, yes, but obviously more intellectual. That is why we have chosen to name him Eduardo."

20   I gasped, tried to collect myself°, but did not succeed. Rosa came to the rescue. She calmly explained that Alberto and she decided to name the baby after me because of all the help I had provided when she needed it most. I babbled something about how proud I felt. It was true.

21   Some people, I know, object to the flow of immigrants° entering our country. They forget that almost all of us came to America from somewhere else. We need every so often to be reminded of success stories like Rosa's. Like many of our ancestors, she fled an oppressive° government and poor economic conditions. She then worked hard to create a new life for herself. Hers is not an uncommon story. Many others like her have come to enrich their lives, and they have enriched our country as well.

WORD SKILLS QUESTIONS

Phonics and Dictionary

1. Which word from the sentence below has a consonant digraph and a long vowel?
   a. *first*
   b. *three*
   c. *months*

   "I first saw Rosa three months after this nightmare." (Paragraph 5)

Use your dictionary to answer the question at the top of the next page.

2. Which word from the sentence below has a long vowel and a short vowel?
   a. *she*
   b. *program*
   c. *college*

   "She enrolled in the Early Childhood Program at the college." (Paragraph 8)

Use the dictionary entry below to answer questions 3–4.

com•mand (kə-mănd´) *v.* **1.** To give orders to. **2.** To have authority over. **3.** To receive as due: *command respect.* **4.** To dominate by position; overlook. —*n.* **1.** The act of commanding. **2.** An order given with authority. **3.** *Comp. Sci.* A signal the initiates an operation defined by an instruction. **4.** Ability to control. **5.** A military unit or region under the control of one officer.

3. The word *command* has
   a. three syllables.
   b. a soft **c** and is accented on the second syllable.
   c. two parts of speech and a field label for a noun definition.
   d. three parts of speech and a usage label for a noun definition.

4. Which definition of *command* fits the sentence below?
   a. Verb definition 1
   b. Verb definition 2
   c. Noun definition 2
   d. Noun definition 5

   "He told them to follow his every command." (Paragraph 3)

5. *Command* would be found on the dictionary page with which guidewords?
   a. **Columbus Day / comet**
   b. **comeuppance / commercial bank**
   c. **commercialize / Commonwealth of Nations**
   d. **commotion / company**

Vocabulary in Context

6. In the sentence below, the word *detection* means
   a. assistance.
   b. trust.
   c. discovery.
   d. noise.

   "They must move quickly and silently or risk detection by the Border Patrol." (Paragraph 3)

7. In the sentence below, the word *prodded* means
   a. urged.
   b. left.
   c. prevented.
   d. paid.

   > "[Rosa] kept me on my toes and constantly challenged me. She prodded me to provide more information, additional examples, better explanations." (Paragraph 7)

8. In the sentence below, the word *reflected* means
   a. shown.
   b. given.
   c. sent back.
   d. hidden.

   > "Her progress in her classes was reflected in a steady stream of A's and B's." (Paragraph 8)

9. In the sentence below, the word *deported* means
   a. saved.
   b. forced out of the country.
   c. kept in the country.
   d. invited.

   > "Rosa's mother had been captured by the Border Patrol and deported to Nicaragua." (Paragraph 17)

10. In the sentence below, the word *attained* means
    a. remembered.
    b. lost.
    c. gained.
    d. defined.

    > "At the moment I met her, I did not care at all about how she had attained freedom." (Paragraph 17)

READING COMPREHENSION QUESTIONS

Central Point and Main Ideas

1. Which sentence best expresses the central point of the selection?
   a. Civil wars have destroyed many countries.
   b. Like many immigrants fleeing oppression, Rosa came to America and made a successful life for herself.
   c. Rosa finally brought her mother to the United States.
   d. Rosa married and gave birth to twins, one of whom she named after the author.

2. Which sentence best expresses the main idea of paragraph 4?
   a. The Border Patrol turned on bright searchlights.
   b. Rosa held on to her brothers but couldn't see her mother.
   c. Rosa and her brothers successfully crossed the border, but her mother was among those who did not.
   d. The guide was very cautious and waited for what seemed like hours until it was safe to continue crossing the border.

3. Which sentence best expresses the main idea of paragraphs 6–7?
   a. Rosa's English was not very good.
   b. Rosa always asked questions in class.
   c. The author encouraged Rosa to ask questions.
   d. Rosa was a very eager student.

Supporting Details

4. Of the group escaping Nicaragua with Rosa and her family,
   a. all members began a new life in the United States.
   b. the majority began a new life the United States.
   c. only five managed to begin a new life in the United States.
   d. only Rosa succeeded in reaching the United States.

5. According to the reading, Rosa's
   a. brothers had trouble adjusting to life in the United States.
   b. mother spent about three years in a Nicaraguan jail.
   c. graduation party was boring.
   d. husband has never met the author.

6. _____ TRUE OR FALSE? According to the author, Rosa's success story is unusual.

Relationships

7. *Fill in the blank:* In the sentence below, the transition word that signals a
   comparison is _____.

   ". . . Rosa seemed preoccupied. I was puzzled until I saw that we were
   walking toward an older woman who had the same brown expressive
   eyes as Rosa." (Paragraph 16)

8. The relationship of the second sentence below to the first is one of
   a. addition.
   b. time.
   c. illustration.
   d. contrast.

   "I was annoyed that someone was standing outside my office so early. . . .
   But I soon realized that there was something special about this . . . young
   woman." (Paragraph 5)

9. The relationship between the two sentences below is one of
   a. addition.
   b. time.
   c. comparison.
   d. contrast.

   "Rosa advanced from our basic reading classes to the more difficult
   study-skills class. Then she moved through the writing classes offered in
   the department." (Paragraph 8)

10. The main pattern of organization in the selection is
    a. list of items.
    b. time order.
    c. comparison-contrast.
    d. definition and example.

MAPPING ACTIVITY

Major events of the selection are scrambled in the list below. Write them in their
correct order in the diagram on the next page.

- Rosa's education toward a bachelor's degree
- Rosa's escape to the United States
- Rosa's education toward an associate's degree
- Rosa's visit with the twins
- Rosa's graduation and party

Central point: Many immigrants, like Rosa, come to America to escape oppression and then work hard to become productive citizens.

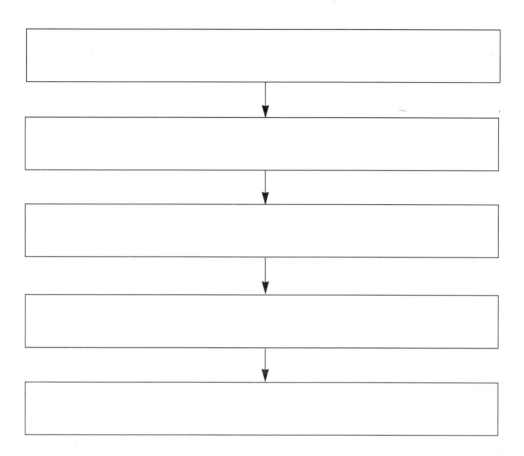

DISCUSSION QUESTIONS

1. As Rosa reached the border of the United States, she realized that her mother was not with her. Should she have looked for her mother, or was she right to cross into the United States when she did?

2. How did Rosa's education prepare her for her career? What interests and qualities would lead someone to want to work in child care?

3. The author writes that "we need . . . to be reminded of success stories like Rosa's." Do you agree? Why might being reminded of such stories be a good idea?

Note: Writing assignments for this selection appear on page 549.

Check Your Performance   ROSA: A SUCCESS STORY

Activity	*Number Right*	*Points*	*Total*
WORD SKILLS			
Phonics and Dictionary (5 items)	_____	× 10 =	_____
Vocabulary in Context (5 items)	_____	× 10 =	_____
		SCORE =	_____%
COMPREHENSION			
Central Point and Main Ideas (3 items)	_____	× 8 =	_____
Supporting Details (3 items)	_____	× 8 =	_____
Relationships (4 items)	_____	× 8 =	_____
Mapping (5 items)	_____	× 4 =	_____
		SCORE =	_____%

FINAL SCORES: Word Skills _____%   Comprehension _____%

Enter your final scores into the **Reading Performance Chart: Ten Reading Selections** on the inside back cover.

7

Knowledge Is Power
Anna-Maria Petricic

Preview

When Anna-Maria Petricic read the words "Knowledge is real power" as a student in Croatia, she was interested in the statement. She wasn't sure of its meaning, but she knew that its message was an important one. This is the story of the author's struggle to unlock the secret of that statement.

Words to Watch

proclaimed (1): announced
essence (1): central part
dismayed (4): discouraged
objective (5): unaffected by personal feelings
certified (8): guaranteed to be true
terse (9): short and direct
pretentious (10): meant to show off
imprinted (10): fixed
formidable (13): difficult
shrouded (16): covered
resolved (16): firmly decided
earnestly (17): seriously
steadily (17): firmly
quest (21): search
ascended (22): climbed

1   "Knowledge is real power," proclaimed° the bold letters on a bookmark showing Superman soaring upward from between two blocks of books. As I read this, a wave of energy swept over me. I studied the bookmark, trying to comprehend its exact meaning. It seemed as if the essence°

of life was revealed on that small piece of red and blue paper. But, as a teenager in high school, I had no idea what it meant. I only knew that this great excitement I was experi-encing had something to do with knowledge. I wanted the power that knowledge brought. For that to happen, I knew I had to attend college. I also knew that this would not be easy.

2   As a high-school student in Sisak, a town near Zagreb, Croatia, all I heard were horror stories about college. "First you sweat preparing for the entrance exams. If you survive that and are lucky enough to be accepted into college, you must deal with your teachers. They will be your enemies for the next four years. The first lesson they teach is that they will do every-thing they can to crush your confi-dence, to break your spirit, to make you quit." Such tales were commonly whispered in the high-school hallways by students aspiring to go to college.

3   I was shocked. Surely these stories could not be true. College was supposed to build my confidence in the process of attaining knowledge. Teachers were supposed to encourage me with their wisdom and their compassion. They should prepare me for all challenges, not turn me against learning. The more I heard the whispers, the more convinced I became that I must not attend college in my homeland. If I wanted knowledge, I must attend a university in America.

4   I read all I could about colleges in the United States. I was dismayed°. The costs were staggering. Then I read about a small, private university in Iowa that was offering work-study scholarships for international students. The school would cover tuition, room, and board in exchange for a twenty-hour-per-week work commitment. In return, students had to show the university that they had sufficient funds in the bank for health insurance and personal expenses. Including airfare from Croatia to America, I calculated that I would need two thousand dollars per year.

5   I could hardly contain myself. I dashed into the kitchen that cold winter evening to proudly announce the news to my mother. "I am going to school in America!" My mother looked up at me while still working at the foamy sink full of dirty dishes. "Yes? And who is going to pay for that?" My mother's voice was heavy yet coolly objective°. In my excitement, I had overlooked the fact that my mother hardly made enough money to provide for our immediate needs. I brushed that thought aside, not willing to let it spoil my enthusiasm. I wanted my mother's support. Everything else would work out somehow.

6   I eagerly wrote a letter of inquiry to the American university. Within a couple of weeks, I received a thick envelope. My mother stood beside me while I ripped it open and spread the contents on the table. I picked up the letter on top. It was from the dean of the College of Arts and Sciences. I was blinded with tears as I read the words of encouragement and warm invitation to attend the college. I felt that at this school, my desire for education would be cherished and respected. My

educational heaven was waiting in America. To get there, I knew that I had to be prepared to wage a long, hard battle. And I had to start now.

7   When she saw how understanding the university was, my mother took a strong stand of support. She vowed to do all she could to help make my dream become reality. She pointed to a row of dictionaries on the bookshelf. I reached for the Croatian-English dictionary and began the first of many long, difficult, and sometimes discouraging steps.

8   Although my English was quite good, the application forms sent by the college included many words I didn't understand. After a few hours of translating and trying to interpret meanings, my head was spinning. I needed to take the Test of English as a Foreign Language (TOEFL) and the Scholastic Aptitude Test (SAT). I also needed to send a certified° translation of my high-school transcripts. The application deadline was in April. I was not even going to get my high-school diploma until June. Suddenly, everything was moving so fast. I couldn't keep up. "Maybe I should postpone this until next year," I thought. We had little money, and I wasn't even sure I could get accepted. I could attend the University of Zagreb for a year, and then transfer the units. My mother suggested that I send a letter to the admissions officer explaining the situation.

9   After sending the letter, I went to a branch of the University of Zagreb to get information about the entrance exams. I waited for an hour in a small, crowded room thick with cigarette smoke. Two women behind the admissions desk provided meager answers to students' questions. The women were apparently upset that all these students were wasting their precious gossip time. Their sharp, terse° responses offered no help. Instead, they managed to make the students feel guilty for even asking. I gave up in my attempt to find out about the entrance exams.

10   As I walked toward the exit, I stopped to observe the college students who were in the hallway. They wore torn jeans, and they spoke in pretentious° sentences. Their eyes were dull and they had lifeless smiles imprinted° on pale faces. Burning cigarette butts between their fingers were their only well-defined feature. I did not know whether to feel pity for them or for myself. As I left the building, I was both disappointed and humiliated. I had been there for only an hour, and I wondered how I would feel after four years of classes here. My dream had spoiled me. I wanted the luxury of being treated like a human being, and I knew just the place where that would happen.

11   Shortly, I received a new letter from my admissions officer in Iowa that provided encouragement. He asked me to continue my application process and said that I should not worry about my high-school transcripts. They could be mailed as soon as I graduated. What was needed at this time were my test results.

12   A month later, I took the TOEFL and SAT at the American school in

Zagreb. I had studied hard and was satisfied with my performance. The results of both tests were sent directly to the university in America. When the admissions officer received them, he called me to offer congratulations. I had done well. My application was almost complete. Besides my transcripts, which I knew would not be a problem, I needed only one more thing: the money.

13   My mother joined forces with me in this last, but most formidable°, obstacle. She borrowed money from a friend and deposited it in my account so that I could obtain the bank's confirmation that I had the funds required by the university. However, at the last minute, my mother's friend decided that he needed his money back. I was forced to withdraw the money.

14   When I returned home from the bank, I found my mother unwrapping our old paintings, works of art by Vladimir Kirin, a famous Croatian artist who was now deceased. Mother had collected his work for as long as I can remember and had planned to open an art gallery in the artist's memory. As I walked across the room, my mother's words stopped me in my tracks. "You have to write an ad for the weekend paper," she said. These paintings meant more than anything to my mother. Yet she was prepared to sell them so that I could live my dream.

15   The ad was placed. All we had to do was wait for the phone calls. But none came. After two weeks, we ran the ad again, but nothing happened.

16   I suddenly felt afraid. Even though I could see myself walking around the campus of my new college, even though I could visualize my new classrooms and teachers, it was all still just a dream. I felt that I was looking at slowly dissolving fog. The dream world was fading away, leaving the old, gray reality. I was trapped in a truth that I could not accept. I became paralyzed as I imagined myself slowly sinking into ignorance and despair. I would become one of those lifeless, gray faces that walked daily to the bus station through the smog-shrouded° streets. I would work with people who can only afford to think about survival, people who see no values beyond the crispness of bills in their wallets. The ignorant world threatened to swallow me. Though scared to death, I resolved° not to yield. I was not just fighting for money; I was fighting for principle. I would not live a life of deliberate humiliation. I refused to expect from life only as much as others thought I should expect. I alone was responsible for making the best of my life. I had to continue my fight.

17   For the first time in my life, I earnestly° prayed for myself. I went to church in the early afternoon when I knew nobody would be there. My wooden-soled shoes echoed on the cold floor that led to the main altar. I knelt down and prayed. I prayed for *money*. That humiliated me because I have always thought it was selfish to pray for myself. My prayers had always been devoted to my friends, to my family, and to those who suffered. I

never prayed for anything for myself because I believed that if God took care of the world, I would be taken care of. Now, I prayed for the most selfish thing of all, and I hated myself for it. Full of shame, I prayed, my eyes steadily° on the ground. Finally, I gained enough strength to look up at the crucifix. I surrendered completely. I forgot all of my thoughts, and my mind began to flow toward some new space. The pressure dissolved. I felt as if I'd been let out of prison. I was free. My guilt and shame were gone, and my heart was beating with a new force. Everything was going to be fine.

18   In the meantime, my mother continued to search for funds. She called on an old friend who owned a jewelry store. He had known me since I was a little girl and bragged that he would do anything for me. He fell silent when he heard my mother's request. He was sorry, but he had just invested all of his money in a new project. He tried to comfort my mother. "I would teach her myself if she were my daughter," he boasted. "School in America. Who does she think she is? She doesn't need college. A woman shouldn't be too smart. She can marry either of my two sons. I promise she will have the freedom to go to church whenever she wants. What more could she need?" Struggling to remain civil, my mother thanked him sarcastically and walked away.

19   Time was slipping by. I had already obtained a United States visa, and I had made my air reservation. The travel agent found a cheap student rate. Despite strict regulations, she was willing to sell me a one-way ticket. My hopes were raised, but even the low-cost ticket had to be paid for. And there was precious little time.

20   That evening, my mother, brother, grandmother, and I gathered in the living room of our small apartment. I stared at the wall. My brother leaned against the doorway cursing fate. My grandmother tightly held her prayer book, her lips moving slowly. Gloomy silence threatened to break down the walls. Then, as if by magic, words I did not think about came from my lips. "Mother, what about a credit card?" In Croatia, unlike America, it was not easy to obtain a credit card. Yet my mother knew an influential officer of a local bank. Could he help us? My mother sighed and acknowledged that it was worth a try. Once again my hopes were raised.

21   I returned home from school the next day to find a sense of calm that our household had not known for weeks. Before I had a chance to ask, my mother smiled and nodded her head. My prayers had been answered. My quest° for knowledge was to become a reality.

22   Later that summer, I was on a flight to America. As the plane ascended° into the clouds, my thoughts turned from the quickly disappearing city I was leaving to the destination I knew so little about. I suddenly realized that I was all alone. I was on my own. Everything that happened from that moment on would be the result of my own actions. I was not afraid. My dream had come true,

and I was about to begin living a different reality.

23   That reality turned out to be all that I wanted: loving teachers, a real chance to pursue knowledge, and wonderful friends from all over the world. My life as a college student is better than I ever dreamed. It has not been easy. In my job with the University Food Service, I have had to work very hard. I have also had to deal with some irresponsible and uninterested students who refuse to carry out their assignments or pretend they don't understand simple instructions. I must remind myself that this is the only way to keep my scholarship. But my work has many rewards. I have become assistant director of Food Services. I have also received the first Outstanding Student-Employee Award presented by the university, and my work has been recognized by the Board of Trustees.

24   And I have begun the study of literature. This has opened up a new world for me. Every reading assignment, each class discussion has deepened my understanding of life. I am getting to know myself. I can feel the power growing inside me as I complete each assignment. I am beginning to live the magic of knowledge. In everything I learn, I find the same lesson: I can never know everything, but with what I know, I can accomplish anything. The old Superman bookmark is pasted on my door: "Knowledge is real power." Now I know what it means.

WORD SKILLS QUESTIONS

Questions 1–5 use words found in the following passage from the selection. Read the paragraph and answer the questions that follow.

Shortly, I received a new letter from my admissions officer in Iowa that provided encouragement. He asked me to continue my application process and said that I should not worry about my high-school transcripts. They could be mailed as soon as I graduated. What was needed at this time were my test results. (Paragraph 11)

Phonics and Dictionary

1. A word that contains both a consonant digraph and a consonant blend is
    a. *shortly.*
    b. *process.*
    c. *should.*
    d. *what.*

2. A word that follows the silent-**e** rule is
   a. *new.*
   b. *letter.*
   c. *he.*
   d. *time.*

3. The words *about* and *results* are divided into syllables according to which rule?
   a. When two consonants come between two vowels, divide between the consonants.
   b. When a single consonant comes between two vowel sounds, divide before the consonant.
   c. If a word ends in a consonant followed by **le**, the consonant and **le** form the last syllable.
   d. Compound words are always divided between the word they contain.

4. The word *encouragement* (**en•cour•age•ment**)
   a. has three syllables and would be found on a page with these guidewords: **EMT / encrust**.
   b. has three syllables and would be found in a page with these guidewords: **embargo / emery**.
   c. has four syllables and would be found on a page with these guidewords: **encrypt / endure**.
   d. has four syllables and would be found on a page with these guidewords: **EMT / encrust**.

5. The word *continue* (kən-tĭn′yo͞o)
   a. has four syllables and an accent on the second syllable.
   b. has four syllables and would be found on a page with these guidewords: **constitutive / contaminate**.
   c. has three syllables and an accent on the second syllable.
   d. has three syllables and two short vowel sounds.

Vocabulary in Context

6. In the sentence below, the word *comprehend* means
   a. forget.
   b. write down.
   c. understand.
   d. pass by.

   "I studied the bookmark, trying to comprehend its exact meaning." (Paragraph 1)

7. In the sentence below, the word *aspiring* means
   a. paying.
   b. hoping.
   c. remembering.
   d. forgetting.

   "Such tales were commonly whispered in the high-school hallways by students aspiring to go to college." (Paragraph 2)

8. In the sentence below, the word *attaining* means
   a. recognizing.
   b. creating.
   c. pleasing.
   d. gaining.

   "College was supposed to build my confidence in the process of attaining knowledge." (Paragraph 3)

9. In the sentences below, the word *meager* means
   a. complicated and difficult.
   b. complete.
   c. careful.
   d. brief and inadequate.

   "Two women behind the admissions desk provided meager answers to students' questions. The women were apparently upset that all these students were wasting their precious gossip time. Their sharp, terse replies offered no help." (Paragraph 9)

10. In the sentence below, the word *civil* means
    a. outraged.
    b. feminine.
    c. polite.
    d. superior.

    "Struggling to remain civil, my mother thanked him sarcastically and walked away." (Paragraph 18)

READING COMPREHENSION QUESTIONS

Central Point and Main Ideas

1. Which sentence best expresses the central point of the selection?
   a. There are big differences between Croatia and America.
   b. Education is better in the United States than in Croatia.
   c. By not giving up, the author has achieved the college experience she dreamed of.
   d. Colleges and universities should provide more low-cost opportunities for foreign students.

2. Which sentence best expresses the main idea of paragraph 2?
   a. The author spent her high-school years in Croatia.
   b. As a high-school student, the author heard horror stories about college.
   c. The author was told that college entrance exams were very difficult.
   d. The author was warned that college teachers would be her enemies.

3. Which sentence best expresses the main idea of paragraph 23?
   a. Even though she has become a successful college student, the author is disappointed with life in the United States.
   b. Despite difficulties, the author has found life as a student in the United States rewarding.
   c. The author's hard work in Food Services has paid off with an award and official recognition.
   d. The author must work hard to keep her scholarship.

Supporting Details

4. _____ TRUE OR FALSE? According to the author, in order to be accepted to the university, all she needed to show was that she had enough money.

5. According to the author,
   a. one of her mother's friends was able to help her go to college in the United States.
   b. selling precious paintings helped her raise the money she needed.
   c. the University of Zagreb was willing to offer her a scholarship.
   d. she was able to raise the money to begin college in the United States through a credit card.

6. When the author's mother called on an old friend who owned a jewelry store,
   a. he promised to help.
   b. he said he had just invested his money in another project.
   c. he said he would have helped if Anna-Maria were a boy instead of a girl.
   d. he promised to give Anna-Maria jewelry if she married one of his sons.

7. The point below is
   a. true, according to the reading.
   b. false, according to the reading.
   c. not mentioned in the reading.

   The author has to keep her job with the University Food Service in order to keep her scholarship.

Relationships

8. The sentence below expresses a relationship of
   a. cause and effect.
   b. comparison.
   c. contrast.
   d. time.

   "I never prayed for anything for myself because I believed that if God took care of the world, I would be taken care of." (Paragraph 17)

9. The relationship of the second sentence below to the first sentence is one of
   a. addition.
   b. comparison.
   c. contrast.
   d. cause and effect.

   "In my job with the University Food Service, I have had to work very hard. I have also had to deal with some irresponsible and uninterested students. . . . " (Paragraph 23)

10. The main pattern of organization of this selection is
    a. list of items.
    b. time order.
    c. comparison-contrast.
    d. definition and example.

MAPPING ACTIVITY

The following scrambled statements make up a summary of the selection. Complete the map on the next page by writing the statements in their correct order.

- Petricic decides to go to college.
- She decides that going to a special college in the United States would be better than attending the University of Zagreb.

- Finally in the United States, Petricic has found her new life to be all that she had hoped for.
- As a high-school student, Petricic is inspired by the words "Knowledge is real power."
- After much struggle, Petricic and her family find the money needed to get her to the United States.

Central point: With persistence and support, Petricic has achieved the education she wished for.

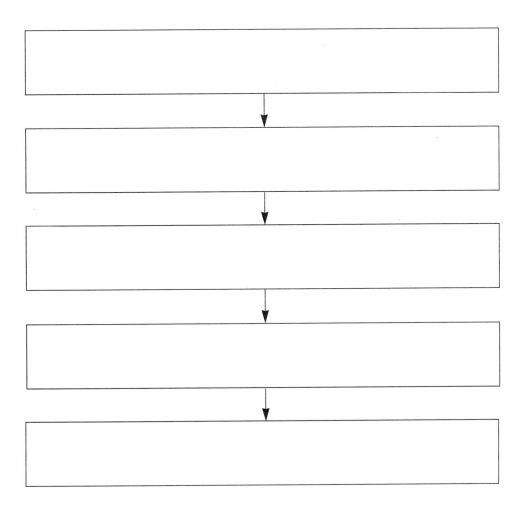

DISCUSSION QUESTIONS

1. The author writes that when she went to high school, students told horror stories about college. When you were in high school, what was your view of college? Now that you are in college, has your perception changed? If so, in what ways?

2. The author has to work while going to school. Are you working while attending school? If so, how do you make time in your life for both activities?

3. At the conclusion of the selection, the author writes that she now knows the meaning of the words "Knowledge is real power." What does that statement mean to you?

Note: Writing assignments for this selection appear on pages 549–550.

Check Your Performance		**KNOWLEDGE IS POWER**	
Activity	*Number Right*	*Points*	*Total*
WORD SKILLS			
Phonics and Dictionary (5 items)	_____	× 10 =	_____
Vocabulary in Context (5 items)	_____	× 10 =	_____
		SCORE =	_____%
COMPREHENSION			
Central Point and Main Ideas (3 items)	_____	× 8 =	_____
Supporting Details (4 items)	_____	× 8 =	_____
Relationships (3 items)	_____	× 8 =	_____
Mapping (5 items)	_____	× 4 =	_____
		SCORE =	_____%

FINAL SCORES: Word Skills _____%   Comprehension _____%

Enter your final scores into the **Reading Performance Chart: Ten Reading Selections** on the inside back cover.

8

Giving Constructive Criticism
Rudolph F. Verderber

Preview

Everyone can benefit from criticism that tells how to overcome an important fault or problem. But have you ever criticized someone in order to help and found that the other person only became annoyed and guarded? If so, this selection from the textbook *Communicate!* (Eighth Edition), by Rudolph F. Verderber, may help you to provide criticism that can be beneficial.

Words to Watch

constructive (1): helpful
receptively (3): in an interested and open-minded way
is preceded with (3): has coming before it
defensively (3): with anger
verbatim (3): word for word
detracted (3): took something away
superficial (4): unimportant
crushing (4): discouraging
patronizing (4): acting superior
hesitant (4): unwilling
on track (4): following what was planned
agenda (4): list of things to be discussed
relevant (4): meaningful
ineffective (6): not useful

1   Even though some people learn faster and better through praise, there are still times when criticism is useful—especially when a person requests it. Even when people don't ask, we are sometimes in the best position to offer critical comments to help others perform better. Unfortunately, most of us are far too free in giving criticism; we often feel the need to help others "become better persons" even if they aren't interested in hearing from us at the moment. Moreover, even when the time is right for criticism, we may not do the best job of giving it. The following guidelines should help you compose criticism that is both constructive° and beneficial.

2   **1. *Make sure that the person is interested in hearing criticism.*** The safest rule to follow is to withhold any criticism until it is asked for. Criticism will seldom help if a person is not interested in hearing it. If you believe that criticism is called for, ask whether the person is interested in hearing it. For instance, you might ask a group chairperson, "Are you interested in hearing my comments about the way you handled the meeting?" If the person answers, "Not really," then go on to a different subject. Even if the answer is yes, proceed carefully.

3   **2. *Describe the person's behavior carefully and accurately.*** Describing behavior means accurately recounting behavior without labeling the behavior good or bad, right or wrong. By describing the behavior, you lay an informative base for the criticism and increase the chances that the person will listen receptively°. Criticism that is preceded with° a description of behavior is less likely to be met defensively°. Your description shows that you are criticizing the behavior rather than attacking the person, and it points the way to a solution. For example, if DeShawn asks, "What do you think of the delivery of my report?" instead of saying "It wasn't very effective," it would be better to say something like "You tended to look down at the report as if you were reading it verbatim°— this detracted° from your really relating with your clients." This criticism does not attack DeShawn's self-concept, and it tells him what he needs to do to be more effective.

4   **3. *Preface a negative statement with a positive one whenever possible.*** When you are planning to criticize, it is a good idea to start with some praise. Of course, common sense suggests that superficial° praise followed by crushing° criticism will be seen for what it is. Thus, saying "Leah, that's a pretty blouse you have on, but you did a perfectly miserable job of running the meeting" will be rightly perceived as patronizing°. A better approach would be, "Leah, you did a good job of drawing Jarrell into the discussion. He usually sits through an entire meeting without saying a word. But you seem hesitant° to use the same power to keep the meeting on track°. By not taking charge more, you let people talk about things that were unrelated to the agenda°." Here the praise is relevant° and significant. If you cannot preface a criticism with

significant praise, don't try. Prefacing criticism with empty praise will not help the person accept your criticism.

5   **4.** *Be as specific as possible.* The more specific the criticism, the more effectively a person will be able to deal with the information. In the situation just discussed, it would not have been helpful to say, "You had some leadership problems." This comment is so general that Leah would have little idea of what she did wrong. Moreover, she may infer that she is, in your eyes, incapable of leadership. If the point was that Leah wasn't in control, say so; if Leah failed to get agreement on one item before moving on to another, say so.

6   **5.** *Restrict criticism to recent behavior.* People are not generally helped by hearing about something they did last week or last month. With the passage of time, memories fade and even change, and it may be difficult to get agreement about the behavior being criticized. If you have to spend time re-creating a situation and refreshing someone's memory, the criticism will probably be ineffective°.

7   **6.** *Direct criticism at behavior the person can do something about.* It is pointless to remind someone of a shortcoming over which the person has no control. It may be true that Jack would find it easier to prepare arguments if he had taken a course in logic, but pointing this out to him will not improve his reasoning. Telling him he needs to work on stating main points clearly and backing them up with good evidence is helpful because he can change these behaviors.

8   **7.** *If possible, include a statement that shows how the person could correct the problem.* Don't limit your comments to what a person has done wrong. Tell the person how what was done could have been better. If Gail, the chairperson of a committee, cannot get her members to agree on anything, you might suggest that she try phrasing her remarks to the committee differently, for example, "Gail, when you think the discussion is ended, say something like 'It sounds as if we agree that our donation should be made to a single agency. Is that correct?'" By including a positive suggestion, you not only help the person improve—which is the purpose of constructive criticism—you also show that your intentions are positive.

WORD SKILLS QUESTIONS

Phonics and Dictionary

Questions 1–5 use words found in the following passage from the selection. Read the paragraph and answer the questions that follow.

> *Direct criticism at behavior the person can do something about.* It is pointless to remind someone of a shortcoming over which the person has no control. It may be true that Jack would find it easier to prepare arguments if he had taken a course in logic, but pointing this out to him will not improve his reasoning. Telling him he needs to work on stating main points clearly and backing them up with good evidence is helpful because he can change these behaviors. (Paragraph 7)

1. Which word is broken into syllables correctly?
   a. some-one
   b. ab-out
   c. rem-ind
   d. bac-king

2. Which rule tells how to divide the following words into syllables: *pointless, remind, pointing, clearly, helpful*?
   a. Divide between two consonants.
   b. Divide before a consonant followed by **le**.
   c. Divide after prefixes and before suffixes.
   d. Divide between the words in a compound word.

3. Which word would be found on a dictionary page with these guidewords: **chamfer / chanson**?
   a. *can*
   b. *course*
   c. *clearly*
   d. *change*

Use your dictionary to answer the following question.

4. Which word is three parts of speech: preposition, adverb, and adjective?
   a. *about*
   b. *over*
   c. *which*
   d. *because*

Use your dictionary and the pronunciation key on page 119 to answer the following question.

5. In the word *logic*, the **i** is pronounced like the **i** in what common word?
    a. *pit*
    b. *pie*
    c. *pier*
    d. *item*

Vocabulary in Context

6. In the sentence below, the word *compose* means
    a. avoid.
    b. create.
    c. predict.
    d. receive.

    "The following guidelines should help you compose criticism that is both constructive and beneficial." (Paragraph 1)

7. In the sentences below, the word *withhold* means
    a. provide.
    b. continue with.
    c. not give.
    d. make a list of.

    "Make sure that the person is interested in hearing criticism. The safest rule to follow is to withhold any criticism until it is asked for." (Paragraph 2)

8. In the sentences below, the word *preface* means
    a. replace.
    b. ask.
    c. begin.
    d. end.

    "Preface a negative statement with a positive one whenever possible. When you are planning to criticize, it is a good idea to start with some praise." (Paragraph 4)

9. In the sentence below, the word *restrict* means
    a. ask for.
    b. learn about.
    c. limit.
    d. avoid.

    "Restrict criticism to recent behavior. People are not generally helped by hearing about something they did last week or last month." (Paragraph 6)

10. In the sentence below, the word *shortcoming* means
    a. gift.
    b. comment.
    c. fault.
    d. wise move.

> "It is pointless to remind someone of a shortcoming over which the person has no control." (Paragraph 7)

READING COMPREHENSION QUESTIONS

Central Point and Main Ideas

1. Which sentence best expresses the central point of the selection?
   a. It is a good idea to compliment someone before criticizing him or her.
   b. Seven guidelines can help you provide constructive criticism.
   c. Criticism usually does more harm than good.
   d. You can criticize anyone if you are kind.

2. Most of the main ideas of the paragraphs in this textbook reading are
   a. contained in the first paragraph of the reading.
   b. implied, not stated directly.
   c. stated at the ends of paragraphs.
   d. stated at the beginning of numbered paragraphs and written in italics.

Supporting Details

3. According to the selection, the purpose of constructive criticism is to
   a. keep a discussion going.
   b. make you look better.
   c. help someone think through his or her past behavior.
   d. help someone perform better.

4. _____ TRUE OR FALSE? The author feels that if you don't have significant praise for someone, you should not offer praise before criticizing that person.

5. According to the reading, the comment "You had some leadership problems" is too
   a. general.
   b. specific.
   c. nasty.
   d. obvious.

6. The author feels it's best to criticize behavior that
    a. you yourself have experienced.
    b. happened a month ago.
    c. hasn't happened yet.
    d. the person can do something about.

7. _____ TRUE OR FALSE? According to the author, you should limit your comments to what a person has done wrong.

Relationships

8. In the sentences below, the word *moreover* shows a relationship of
    a. addition.
    b. time.
    c. comparison.
    d. cause and effect.

    " . . . we often feel the need to help others 'become better persons' even if they aren't interested in hearing from us at the moment. Moreover, even when the time is right for criticism, we may not do the best job of giving it." (Paragraph 1)

9. In the sentence below, the words *rather than* show a relationship of
    a. addition.
    b. comparison.
    c. contrast.
    d. cause and effect.

    "Your description shows that you are criticizing the behavior rather than attacking the person. . . . " (Paragraph 3)

10. The main pattern of organization of this selection is
    a. time order.
    b. list of items.
    c. comparison-contrast.
    d. definition and example.

OUTLINING ACTIVITY

Following is a general outline of "Giving Constructive Criticism." Complete the outline by filling in the missing major supporting details, which are scrambled in the list below.

- Be as specific as possible.
- If possible, include a statement that shows how the person could correct the problem.
- Make sure that the person is interested in hearing criticism.
- Restrict criticism to recent behavior.
- Preface a negative statement with a positive one whenever possible.

Central point: Several tips tell how to provide constructive criticism.

1. _____

2. Describe the person's behavior carefully and accurately.

3. _____

   _____

4. _____

5. _____

6. Direct criticism at behavior the person can do something about.

7. _____

   _____

DISCUSSION QUESTIONS

1. Which of the seven tips provided by the author do you think is the most helpful? Explain why you chose this one.

2. Do you agree with the author's statement that "there are . . . times when criticism is useful"? Why or why not?

3. The author suggests that there are times when people request criticism. Why would they do this? Have you ever asked to be criticized—or been asked to criticize someone else? If so, what were the circumstances?

Note: Writing assignments for this selection appear on pages 550–551.

Check Your Performance — GIVING CONSTRUCTIVE CRITICISM

Activity	*Number Right*	*Points*	*Total*
WORD SKILLS			
Phonics and Dictionary (5 items)	_____	× 10 =	_____
Vocabulary in Context (5 items)	_____	× 10 =	_____
		SCORE =	_____ %
COMPREHENSION			
Central Point and Main Ideas (2 items)	_____	× 8 =	_____
Supporting Details (5 items)	_____	× 8 =	_____
Relationships (3 items)	_____	× 8 =	_____
Outlining (5 items)	_____	× 4 =	_____
		SCORE =	_____ %

FINAL SCORES: Word Skills _____ %   **Comprehension** _____ %

Enter your final scores into the **Reading Performance Chart: Ten Reading Selections** on the inside back cover.

9

A Love Affair with Books
Bernadete Piassa

Preview

How much of a difference do you think reading can make in your life? Consider this story, written by a woman who grew up in Brazil and read everything she could get her hands on. As she grew older, she didn't lose her love for books. In this reading, she tells why she reads so much and describes the impact reading has had on her life.

Words to Watch

enchanted (1): magical
devoured (5): took in with great enthusiasm
intriguing (6): interesting
illicit (9): not permitted
sadistic (9): cruel
horizon (12): view of the world
seduces (13): attracts
abyss (13): bottomless hole
precision (13): exactness
subversive (15): turning people against something

1   When I was young, I thought that reading was like a drug which I was allowed to take only a teaspoon at a time, but which, nevertheless, had the effect of carrying me away to an enchanted° world where I experienced strange and forbidden emotions. As time went by and I took that drug

again and again, I became addicted to it. I could no longer live without reading. Books became an intrinsic part of my life. They became my friends, my guides, my lovers—my most faithful lovers.

2   I didn't know I would fall in love with books when I was young and started to read. I don't even recall when I started to read and how. I just remember that my mother didn't like me to read. In spite of this, every time I had an opportunity I would sneak somewhere with a book and read one page, two pages, three, if I was lucky enough, always feeling my heart beating fast, always hoping that my mother wouldn't find me, wouldn't shout as always: "Bernadete, don't you have anything to do?" For her, books were nothing. For me, they were everything.

3   In my childhood I didn't have a big choice of books. I lived in a small town in Brazil, surrounded by swamps and farms. It was impossible to get out of town by car; there weren't any roads. By train it took eight hours to reach the next village. There were airplanes, small airplanes, only twice a week. Books couldn't get to my town very easily. There wasn't a library there, either. However, I was lucky: My uncle was a pilot.

4   My uncle, who owned a big farm and also worked flying people from place to place in his small airplane, had learned to fly, in addition, with his imagination. At home, he loved to sit in his hammock on his patio and travel away in his fantasy with all kinds of books. If he happened to read a

bestseller or a romance, when he was done he would give it to my mother, who also liked to read although she didn't like me to. But I would get to read the precious book anyway, even if I needed to do this in a hiding place, little by little.

I remember very well one series   5
of small books. Each had a green cover with a drawing of a couple kissing on it. I think the series had been given to my mother when she was a teenager because all the pages were already yellow and almost worn-out. But although the books were old, for me they seemed alive, and for a long time I devoured° them, one by one, pretending that I was the heroine and my lover would soon come to rescue me. He didn't come, of course. And I was the one who left my town to study and live in Rio de Janeiro, taking only my clothes with me. But inside myself I was taking my passion for books which would never abandon me.

I had been sent to study in a   6
boarding school, and I was soon appalled to discover that the expensive all-girls school had even fewer books than my house. In my class there was a bookshelf with maybe fifty books, and almost all of them were about the lives of saints and the miracles of Christ. I had almost given up the hope of finding something to read when I spotted, tucked away at the very end of the shelf, a small book already covered by dust. It didn't seem to be about religion because it had a more intriguing° title, *The Old Man and the Sea*. It was written by an author whom I had never heard of before: Ernest Hemingway.

Curious, I started to read the book and a few minutes later was already fascinated by Santiago, the fisherman.

7   I loved that book so much that when I went to my aunt's house to spend the weekend, I asked her if she had any books by the man who had written it. She lent me *For Whom the Bell Tolls*, and I read it every Sunday I could get out of school, only a little bit at a time, only one teaspoon at a time. I started to wait anxiously for those Sundays. At the age of 13 I was deeply in love with Ernest Hemingway.

8   When I finished with all his books I could find, I discovered Herman Hesse, Graham Greene, Aldous Huxley, Edgar Allan Poe. I could read them only on Sundays, so, during the week, I would dream or think about the world I had discovered in their books.

9   At that time I thought that my relationship with books was kind of odd, something that set me apart from the world. Only when I read the short story "Illicit° Happiness," by Clarice Lispector, a Brazilian author, did I discover that other people could enjoy books as much as I did. The story is about an ugly, fat girl who still manages to torture one of the beautiful girls in her town only because her father is the owner of a bookstore, and she can have all the books she wants. With sadistic° refinement, day after day she promises to give to the beautiful girl the book the girl dearly wants, but never fulfills her promise. When her mother finds out what is going on and gives the book to the beautiful girl, the girl runs through the streets hugging it and, at home, pretends to have lost it only to find it again, showing an ardor for books that made me exult. For the first time I wasn't alone. I knew that someone else also loved books as much as I did.

10   My passion for books continued through my life, and it had to surmount another big challenge when, at the age of thirty-one, I moved to New York. Because I had almost no money, I was forced to leave all my books in Brazil. Besides, I didn't know enough English to read in this language. For some years I was condemned again to the darkness; condemned to live without books, my friends, my guides, my lovers.

11   But my love for books was so strong that I overcame even this obstacle. I learned to read in English and was finally able to enjoy my favorite authors again.

12   Although books have always been part of my life, they still hold a mystery for me, and every time I open a new one, I ask myself which pleasures I am about to discover, which routes I am about to travel, which emotions I am about to sink in. Will this new book touch me as a woman, as a foreigner, as a romantic soul, as a curious person? Which horizon° is it about to unfold to me, which string of my soul is it bound to touch, which secret is it about to unveil for me?

13   Sometimes, the book seduces° me not only for the story it tells, but also because of the words the author uses in it. Reading Gabriel García Márquez's short story "The Handsomest

Drowned Man in the World," I feel dazzled when he writes that it took "the fraction of centuries for the body to fall into the abyss°." The fraction of centuries! I read those words again and again, infatuated by them, by their precision°, by their hidden meaning. I try to keep them in my mind, even knowing that they are already part of my soul.

14   After reading so many books that touch me deeply, each one in its special way, I understand now that my mother had a point when she tried to keep me away from books in my childhood. She wanted me to stay in my little town, to marry a rich and tiresome man, to keep up with the traditions. But the books carried me away; they gave me wings to fly, to discover new places. They made me dare to live another kind of life. They made me wish for more, and when I couldn't have all I wished for, they were still there to comfort me, to show me new options.

15   Yes, my mother was right. Books are dangerous; books are subversive°. Because of them I left a predictable future for an unforeseeable one. However, if I had to choose again, I would always choose the books instead of the lackluster life I could have had. After all, what joy would I find in my heart without my books, my most faithful lovers?

WORD SKILLS QUESTIONS

Phonics and Dictionary

Questions 1–5 are based on the following paragraph from the selection. Read the paragraph and answer the questions that follow.

But my love for books was so strong that I overcame even this obstacle. I learned to read in English and was finally able to enjoy my favorite authors again. (Paragraph 11)

1. Which word has two long vowel sounds?
   a. *overcame*
   b. *even*
   c. *obstacle*
   d. *enjoy*

2. Which word is broken into syllables correctly?
   a. overc-ame
   b. e-ven
   c. E-ng-lish
   d. ab-le

3. Which word would be found on a dictionary page with these guidewords: **afterward / aggrieved**?
   a. *and*
   b. *able*
   c. *authors*
   d. *again*

Use your dictionary to answer the following question.

4. Which word is three parts of speech: conjunction, preposition, and adverb?
   a. *but*
   b. *strong*
   c. *and*
   d. *again*

Use your dictionary and the pronunciation key on page 119 to answer the following question:

5. In the word *able,* the **a** is pronounced like the **a** in what common word?
   a. *pat*
   b. *pay*
   c. *care*
   d. *father*

Vocabulary in Context

6. In the sentence below, the word *intrinsic* means
   a. rare.
   b. efficient.
   c. unpleasant.
   d. essential.

   "Books became an intrinsic part of my life. They became my friends, my guides, my lovers. . . ." (Paragraph 1)

7. In the sentence below, the word *appalled* means
   a. shocked.
   b. unwilling.
   c. pleased.
   d. proud.

   " . . . I was soon appalled to discover that the expensive all-girls school had even fewer books than my house." (Paragraph 6)

8. In the sentence below, the word *dearly* means
   a. foolishly.
   b. with great humor.
   c. rudely.
   d. sincerely.

   " . . . she promises to give to the beautiful girl the book the girl dearly wants . . . " (Paragraph 9)

9. In the sentence below, the word *ardor* means
   a. passion.
   b. doubt.
   c. kindness.
   d. improvement.

   "When her mother . . . gives the book to the beautiful girl, the girl runs through the streets hugging it . . . showing an ardor for books. . . . I knew that someone else also loved books as much as I did." (Paragraph 9)

10. In the sentence below, the word *surmount* means
    a. remain.
    b. select.
    c. overcome.
    d. search for.

    "My passion for books continued throughout my life, and it had to surmount another big challenge when . . . I moved to New York." (Paragraph 10)

READING COMPREHENSION QUESTIONS

Central Point and Main Ideas

1. Which sentence best expresses the central point of the selection?
   a. Piassa discovered that reading books can be dangerous.
   b. Books have greatly enriched Piassa's life and helped her dare to live a nontraditional life.
   c. Piassa learned that in order to read the best works, one must learn to speak English.
   d. Piassa's experiences show that anyone can learn to read.

2. Which sentence best expresses the main idea of paragraph 4?
   a. Piassa's mother did not like Piassa to read books.
   b. Piassa read the books her mother received from her uncle, who also loved books.

     c. Piassa's uncle was a pilot who also loved reading.

     d. Piassa's uncle owned a farm and also flew people from place to place.

3. Which sentence best expresses the main idea of paragraph 13?

     a. The first sentence

     b. The second sentence

     c. The next-to-last sentence

     d. The last sentence

Supporting Details

4. The author states that in her childhood,

     a. she had a large selection of books.

     b. she did not have a large selection of books.

     c. her mother ordered her to read certain books.

     d. she had only one book to read.

5. Piassa says that at the age of 13, she was deeply in love with

     a. Ernest Hemingway.

     b. Edgar Allan Poe.

     c. her uncle.

     d. a Brazilian author named Clarice Lispector.

6. _____ TRUE OR FALSE? According to the author, when she moved to New York, she knew enough English to read many books in the English language.

7. The author says her mother was right in considering books to be dangerous because they

     a. kept Piassa from playing with other children.

     b. have words children should not see.

     c. led her to reject the life her mother had planned for her.

     d. were extremely expensive in Brazil.

Relationships

8. As suggested by the word *because,* the sentence below presents a cause and an effect. Write **C** in front of the item that is the cause. Write **E** in front of the item that is the effect.

     _____ Piassa had almost no money.

     _____ She had to leave all her books in Brazil.

     "Because I had almost no money, I was forced to leave all my books in Brazil." (Paragraph 10)

9. The relationship of the second part of the sentence on the next page (after the comma) to the first part is one of

     a. time.

     b. addition.

c. contrast.

d. cause and effect.

" . . . she promises to give to the beautiful girl the book the girl dearly wants, but never fulfills her promise." (Paragraph 9)

10. The main pattern of organization of this selection is
    a. time order.
    b. list of items.
    c. comparison-contrast.
    d. definition and example.

MAPPING ACTIVITY

Major events in Piassa's life are scrambled below. Write them in the diagram in their correct order.

- Piassa goes to boarding school in Rio de Janeiro.
- Piassa lives in a small town in Brazil, where she learns to love reading.
- Piassa learns to read in English and is able to read her favorite authors again.
- Piassa moves to New York.

Central point: Reading books has been very rewarding to Piassa and has led her to give up a traditional life for a more adventuresome one.

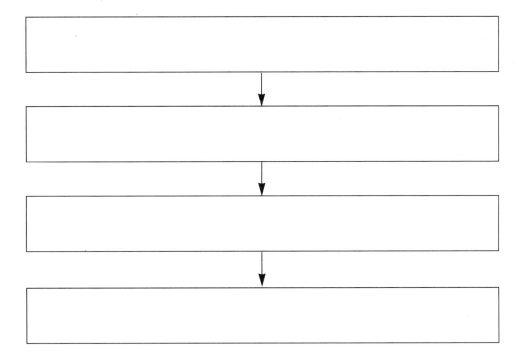

DISCUSSION QUESTIONS

1. The author's mother discouraged her from reading. As you were growing up, were you encouraged to read or discouraged from reading? Explain why you think this was so and how it affected you.

2. What was reading like for you in school? Explain why it was a positive or a negative experience.

3. Piassa writes, "I would dream or think about the world I had discovered" in the books of Herman Hesse and other authors. Do you think it is good to be so focused on books and reading? Why or why not?

Note: Writing assignments for this selection appear on page 551.

Check Your Performance		A LOVE AFFAIR WITH BOOKS	
Activity	*Number Right*	*Points*	*Total*
WORD SKILLS			
Phonics and Dictionary (5 items)	_____	× 10 =	_____
Vocabulary in Context (5 items)	_____	× 10 =	_____
		SCORE =	_____%
COMPREHENSION			
Central Point and Main Ideas (3 items)	_____	× 8 =	_____
Supporting Details (4 items)	_____	× 8 =	_____
Relationships (3 items)	_____	× 8 =	_____
Mapping (4 items)	_____	× 5 =	_____
		SCORE =	_____%

FINAL SCORES: Word Skills _____% Comprehension _____%

Enter your final scores into the **Reading Performance Chart: Ten Reading Selections** on the inside back cover.

10

Child-Rearing Styles
Virginia Nichols Quinn

Preview

Raising a child is arguably the most important responsibility a parent will ever undertake. Yet there are different ways to raise a child. Which way should a parent choose? This excerpt from the textbook *Applying Psychology* (Third Edition) defines and explains three common types of child-raising systems. As you read, think about the system you were raised under, the system you will use (or have used) with your children, and the advantages and disadvantages of each system.

Words to Watch

mittens (1): hand-coverings that enclose the thumb and four fingers separately
comply (1): obey
confront (2): challenge
cautioned (3): warned
obscure (4): not easily understood
initial (4): beginning
conformity (5): agreement

1   Psychologist Diana Baumrind describes three styles of child rearing. Think about your own childhood. How did your parents discipline you? Discipline is a way of regulating behavior. Did they use a set of rigid rules? If you were told what to do without any reasons or explanations, your parents were using an *authoritarian* approach. In an authoritarian environment, a parent might tell a child to wear mittens°. If the child asks "Why?" the parent would reply "Because I said so!" If the child does

not comply°, the mittens are forced on, and the child is spanked for not adhering to the rule. The parents would use the same method to be certain the child ate balanced meals, went to bed on time, shared toys, and completed chores. The child would not be given choices. In an authoritarian home, parents might make the decisions and use external force and punishment to be sure that rules are kept.

2   Perhaps your home atmosphere was far looser and less structured. In a *permissive approach*, little or no discipline is used. If your parents chose this rearing style, you had few rules, limits, or boundaries. A child raised by permissive parents would be asked, "Would you like to wear mittens today?" and would be allowed to wear them or not wear them regardless of the weather. Similarly, the child would choose meals and bedtime and participate with other children and family activities as he or she desired. This style of child rearing is sometimes chosen by parents who were raised in an authoritarian atmosphere. They resent the approach used on them and select a permissive style in protest against their own parents' methods. Some parents are afraid to confront° their children. Others believe that children must learn by their own mistakes. Such parents, as well as those who are too busy or uninterested, will often choose a permissive approach.

3   Both the authoritarian style and the permissive style of child rearing are extremes. Most American parents choose a middle ground. If you were raised in the United States, chances are you were reared in a more *democratic* environment. In a democratic home, children are given rules and restrictions, but the rules are usually accompanied by an explanation. A child might be cautioned° to wear mittens because the weather is cold or to go to bed because everyone feels better after a good rest. If the child can give a good reason for not keeping a rule, parents will listen and perhaps grant an exception. The aim in a democratic approach to discipline is to have children learn to control their own behavior.

4   But not all cultures share this value of independent control in children. The Zincantecos, a Mayan group in southern Mexico, value total obedience in children. American students who must learn from authoritarian teachers in Zincantan have difficulty adjusting. One college student described her problems in learning to weave from a Zincanteco teacher:

"When I began taking back-strap loom weaving from Tonik, an older Zincanteco woman, I became increasingly restless, when after two months of what I called observation and what she called learning, I had not touched the loom. Many times she would call my attention to an obscure° technical point, or when she would finish a certain step she would say, "You have seen me do it. Now you have learned." I wanted to shout back, "No, I haven't! Because I have not tried it myself." However, it was she who decided when I was ready to touch the loom, and my initial° clumsiness brought such comments as, *"Cabeza de pollo!"* (chicken head). "You have not watched me! You have not learned!"

5   Authoritarian parenting is common in Asian American and Hispanic homes. Since most American schools are based on democratic methods, students from these authoritarian settings have the same difficulties adjusting to a democratic environment that the American student (described above) faced adjusting to an authoritarian environment. The emphasis on independence and self-direction in American schools is the opposite of the family emphasis on obedience and conformity° and may put these youngsters at a disadvantage. Changing cultural surroundings can change attitudes about methods of discipline. One researcher noted that while parental strictness (authoritarian discipline) is seen as a sign of love within Korea, the same level of strictness is resented by Korean American and Korean Canadian teenagers.

WORD SKILLS QUESTIONS

Phonics and Dictionary

Questions 1–5 use words found in the following passage from the selection. Read the passage and answer the questions that follow.

In an authoritarian environment, a parent might tell a child to wear mittens. If the child asks "Why?" the parent would reply "Because I said so!" If the child does not comply, the mittens are forced on and the child is spanked for not adhering to the rule. The parents would use the same method to be certain the child ate balanced meals, went to bed on time, shared toys, and completed chores. The child would not be given choices. In an authoritarian home, parents might make the decisions and use external force and punishment to be sure that rules are kept. (Paragraph 1)

1. The words *mittens* and *certain* are divided into syllables according to which rule?
   a. Divide between two consonants.
   b. Divide before a single consonant.
   c. Divide after prefixes and before suffixes.
   d. Divide between the words in a compound word.

2. How is the word *adhering* broken into syllables?
   a. ad-he-ring
   b. adh-er-ing
   c. ad-her-ing
   d. a-dher-ing

3. The word *comply* would be found on a dictionary page with the guidewords
   a. **comparable / complement**.
   b. **complementary / compound number**.
   c. **compound sentence / concentration camp**.
   d. **concentric / concrete**.

Use your dictionary to answer the following question.

4. Which of these words has three parts of speech: noun, adjective, verb?
   a. *child*
   b. *rule*
   c. *time*
   d. *certain*

Use your dictionary and the pronunciation key on page 119 to answer the following question.

5. In the word *comply*, the **o** is pronounced like the **o** in which common word?
   a. *pot*
   b. *toe*
   c. *for*
   d. *gallop*

Vocabulary in Context

6. In the sentence below, the word *rigid* means
   a. sincere.
   b. easy to understand.
   c. strict.
   d. weak.

   "Did they use a set of rigid rules? If you were told what to do without any reasons or explanations, your parents were using an *authoritarian* approach." (Paragraph 1)

7. In the sentence below, the words *adhering to* mean
   a. understanding.
   b. liking.
   c. saying.
   d. obeying.

   "If the child does not comply, the mittens are forced on and the child is spanked for not adhering to the rule." (Paragraph 1)

8. In the sentence below, the word *resent* means
   a. welcome.
   b. forget.
   c. feel angry at.
   d. wish to use.

   "They resent the approach used on them and select a permissive style in protest against their own parents' methods." (Paragraph 2)

9. In the sentence below, the words *accompanied by* mean
   a. going along with.
   b. different from.
   c. without.
   d. hidden.

   "In a democratic home, children are given rules and restrictions, but the rules are usually accompanied by an explanation." (Paragraph 3)

10. In the sentence below, the word *grant* means
    a. agree to.
    b. refuse.
    c. take back.
    d. prove.

    "If the child can give a good reason for not keeping a rule, parents will listen and perhaps grant an exception." (Paragraph 3)

READING COMPREHENSION QUESTIONS

Central Point and Main Ideas

1. Which sentence best expresses the central point of the selection?
   a. Most people follow the same child-rearing strategies that their parents used.
   b. A psychologist has identified three types of child rearing.
   c. Most American families use the democratic child-rearing style.
   d. Children respond best to the child-rearing strategy that their own culture favors.

2. Which sentence best expresses the main idea of paragraph 3?
   a. The democratic approach to child rearing is the most common approach used in the United States.
   b. The democratic approach, used by most Americans, provides rules for children but includes the explanations and exceptions needed to let children learn to control their own behavior.

    c. In a democratic family, children are encouraged to help make the rules.

    d. Children raised under the democratic approach would never have to wear mittens if they didn't want to.

3. Which sentence best expresses the main idea of paragraphs 4 and 5?
    a. A Mayan group in southern Mexico values total obedience in children.
    b. In Asian American and Hispanic homes, authoritarian parenting is common.
    c. In a different cultural environment, people may have trouble learning, and attitudes about discipline may change.
    d. While many educators favor a hands-on approach, others believe in learning only by watching, not by doing.

Supporting Details

4. According to the author, discipline is a way of
    a. preventing problems.
    b. controlling parents.
    c. controlling behavior.
    d. punishing children.

5. _____ TRUE OR FALSE? The permissive approach is sometimes chosen by parents who are angry about having been raised in an authoritarian way.

6. *Fill in the blank:* Most American parents discipline their children using the

    _____ approach.

7. According to the selection, authoritarian parenting is common in
    a. African American and Asian American homes.
    b. Asian American and Hispanic homes.
    c. most American homes.
    d. most foreign countries.

Relationships

8. In the sentences below, the word *however* shows a relationship of
    a. time.
    b. comparison.
    c. contrast.
    d. cause and effect.

      " ' . . . Now you have learned.' I wanted to shout back, 'No, I haven't! Because I have not tried it myself.' However, it was she who decided when I was ready to touch the loom. . . .'" (Paragraph 4)

9. *Fill in the blank:* In the sentences on the next page, the word that shows a relationship of comparison is _____.

"A child raised by permissive parents would be asked, 'Would you like to wear mittens today?' and would be allowed to wear them or not wear them regardless of the weather. Similarly, the child would choose meals and bedtime and participate with other children and family activities as he or she desired." (Paragraph 2)

10. The main pattern of organization in this selection is
    a. time order.
    b. list of items.
    c. cause and effect.
    d. definition and example.

OUTLINING ACTIVITY

The three styles of child rearing described in the reading are outlined below. Complete the outline by filling in the missing major and minor details, which are scrambled in the following list.

- The aim of this system is to have children learn to control their own behavior.
- The democratic approach to child rearing provides children with rules and restrictions, and explanations of the rules.
- The permissive approach to child rearing uses few or no rules.
- Parents who believe that children must learn from their mistakes use this approach.
- In this system, a child is not given choices.

Central point: Psychologist Diana Baumrind describes three styles of child rearing.

A. In the authoritarian approach to child rearing, children are expected to follow a set of rigid rules.

    1. _____
    2. Parents make the decisions and use force to make sure the rules are followed.

B. _____
    1. This style is often chosen by parents who were raised in an authoritarian atmosphere.
    2. Some parents who are afraid to confront their children use this approach.

    3. _____
       _____
    4. Parents who are too busy or uninterested use this approach.

C. _____

_____

1. If a child has a good reason for not following a rule, parents may grant an exception.

2. _____

DISCUSSION QUESTIONS

1. Which method of discipline do you think is best, and why? If you have children, explain how you use (or have used) this method.

2. Should parents alter their child-rearing system based upon the needs of each of their children? What do you think would happen if parents used one system with one child and a different system with another child?

3. How important do you think discipline is in raising a child? How important has discipline been in your life?

Note: Writing assignments for this selection appear on pages 551–552.

Check Your Performance			**CHILD-REARING STYLES**
Activity	*Number Right*	*Points*	*Total*
WORD SKILLS			
Phonics and Dictionary (5 items)	_____	× 10 =	_____
Vocabulary in Context (5 items)	_____	× 10 =	_____
		SCORE =	_____ %
COMPREHENSION			
Central Point and Main Ideas (3 items)	_____	× 8 =	_____
Supporting Details (4 items)	_____	× 8 =	_____
Relationships (3 items)	_____	× 8 =	_____
Outlining (5 items)	_____	× 4 =	_____
		SCORE =	_____ %
FINAL SCORES: Word Skills _____ %		Comprehension _____ %	

Enter your final scores into the **Reading Performance Chart: Ten Reading Selections** on the inside back cover.

Part III

FOR FURTHER STUDY

1

Word Parts

Learning common word parts will help your pronunciation, spelling, and vocabulary. You will be able to pronounce and spell more words because you will recognize common parts used in those words. And because word parts have meanings, knowing them can help you figure out the meaning of a word you don't know.

There are three types of word parts:

1 Prefixes
2 Suffixes
3 Roots

This chapter will help you learn ten of each, thirty common word parts in all.

PREFIXES

A **prefix** is a word part that is added to the beginning of a word. When a prefix is added to a word, it changes the word's meaning. For example, the prefix *un* means "not." So when *un* is added to the word *known*, a word with the opposite meaning is formed: *unknown*.

Another prefix is *mis*, which can mean "badly." When *mis* is added to *fortune,* the resulting word is *misfortune*, which means "bad fortune." So you can see that knowing the meaning of a prefix can help you figure out the meaning of the word it is in.

On the next page are ten common prefixes and their meanings. Alternative forms of some prefixes are shown in parentheses. The practice that follows will help you learn these prefixes.

Prefixes	Examples
ex—out, from	exit
in (im)—within, into; not	inside; improbable
pre—before	prepare
post—after	postgraduate
sub—below, under	submarine
super—over, above, beyond	superior
mis—badly; wrong	mislead; misunderstand
mono—one	monotony
un—not	unwanted
re—again, back	rewrite, respond

➤ *Practice 1*

Carefully read the meanings of each pair of prefixes. Then, in each sentence, complete the partial word (in *italics*) with the prefix that fits. Write the full word in the space provided. The first one is done for you.

1 ex—out, from *Example:* exit
2 in or **im**—within, into; not *Examples:* inside; improbable

  a. The girls at first decided to (. . . *clude*) _____exclude_____ Ginger from their party because they knew she would want to watch television all night.

  b. The girls then voted to (. . . *clude*) _____ Ginger when she said she would bring the popcorn and chips.

  c. If your driver's license has (. . . *pired*) _____, you'd better not drive until you get it renewed.

  d. At the bank, many people don't want to wait for a human teller, so instead they use an (. . . *personal*) _____ bank machine.

3 pre—before *Example:* prepare
4 post—after *Example:* postgraduate

  a. Because lightning (. . . *cedes*) _____ thunder by several seconds, we see the flash before we hear the boom.

  b. At the end of her letter, my daughter wrote a sweet (. . . *script*) _____: "P. S. I love and admire you."

  c. The football field was flooded after the storm, so the school had to (. . . *pone*) _____ the season's first game.

d. Many people skip over the (. . . *face*) _____ of a book and begin reading at the first chapter.

5 sub—below, under   *Example:* submarine
6 super—over, above, beyond   *Example:* superior

a. The best thing about the (. . . *way*) _____ is that it's so fast that you don't have to stay on it long.

b. That movie had one ghost too many; I got bored by all the (. . . *natural*) _____ events.

c. The carpenter explained that he would have to install a (. . . *floor*) _____ before putting down the linoleum.

d. Alice is a born (. . . *visor*) _____: she loves to watch over other people's work.

7 mis—badly; wrong   *Examples:* mislead; misunderstand
8 mono—one   *Example:* monotony

a. Scott is so afraid of making a (. . . *take*) _____ that he never raises his hand in class.

b. My history instructor always reads his lectures in a (. . . *tone*) _____; this single tone of voice shows that he is as bored with his lectures as his students are.

c. (. . . *gamy*) _____ is not limited to humans. Some animals also have only one mate throughout their lives.

d. That dog is going to (. . . *behave*) _____ unless you take him for a walk right now.

9 un—not   *Example:* unwanted
10 re—again, back   *Examples:* rewrite, respond

a. "Never (. . . *peat*) _____ yourself," my English teacher said. "Never, never, never."

b. As (. . . *likely*) _____ as it may seem, the male seahorse gives birth, carrying the eggs inside him until after they hatch.

c. After working a double shift at the hospital, Ramon was (. . . *able*) _____ to keep his eyes open during psychology class.

d. Because our electric blender makes so much noise, I've lent it to a neighbor in the hope that she'll never (. . . *turn*) _____ it.

SUFFIXES

A **suffix** is a word part that is added to the end of a word. Like prefixes, suffixes can change the meanings of words. For instance, by adding the suffix *less* (which means "without") to the word *life*, we get a word with the opposite meaning: *lifeless*.

Also, a suffix can change a word's part of speech. The suffix *ly*, for instance, can change the adjective *sad* to the adverb *sadly*.

Below are ten common suffixes and their meanings. Alternative forms of some suffixes are shown in parentheses. The practice that follows will help you learn these suffixes.

Suffixes	*Examples*
able (ible)—able to be	enjoyable, edible
ion (tion)—state of being; act of	limitation, celebration
er (or)—a person who does something	dancer, mayor
ist—a person skilled at something	artist, therapist
ful—full of	joyful, suspenseful
less—without	homeless
ism—a practice; a belief or set of principles	terrorism, communism
ment—state of being	engagement
ish—similar to	foolish
ly—in a certain manner, at a certain time	loudly, hourly

➤ Practice 2

Carefully read the meanings of each pair of suffixes. Then, in each sentence, complete the partial word (in *italics*) with the suffix that fits. Write the full word in the space provided.

11 able (ible)—able to be   *Examples:* enjoyable, edible
12 ion (tion)—state of being; act of   *Examples:* limitation, celebration

a. If a task seems too large to handle, try to break it down into (*manage* . . .)

_____ parts.

b. The hunter did such a good (*imitat* . . .) _____ of a deer's love-call that another hunter shot him.

c. My daughter finds it (*comfort* . . .) _____ to read with her head hanging over the side of the bed and her book on the floor.

d. Rose saw her high-school boyfriend at her class (*reun . . .*) _____, and now they are dating again.

13 er (or)—a person who does something   *Examples:* dancer, mayor
14 ist—a person skilled at something   *Examples:* artist, therapist

a. As a (*visit . . .*) _____ to the rocket base, I had to pass through three security checks before seeing my first rocket.

b. A research (*scient . . .*) _____ lives for the day he or she discovers something that will benefit humanity.

c. The (*wait . . .*) _____ at Ella's Country Diner was so rude that I complained to the owners.

d. Elton John is not only an outstanding showman; he is also a talented (*pian . . .*) _____.

15 ful—full of   *Examples:* joyful, suspenseful
16 less—without   *Example:* homeless

a. On Thanksgiving everyone feels (*thank . . .*) _____ — except the turkey.

b. Francisco and Susana are both so unpleasant that the world would be (*grate . . .*) _____ if they married each other.

c. Before he smashed up his car, Amanpal was a (*care . . .*) _____ driver. Since then, he drives more cautiously than anyone else I know.

d. When I had the flu, I felt (*help . . .*) _____ —I had trouble moving, thinking, and breathing.

17 ism—a practice; a belief or set of principles   *Examples*: terrorism, communism
18 ment—state of being   *Example*: engagement

a. Mr. Bell practices (*Catholic . . .*) _____, and his wife practices Judaism.

b. After thirty years of (*imprison . . .*) _____, Eli was not sure if he could live in the real world.

c. There was a lot of (*excite . . .*) _____ at work today—two people angrily told the boss they were quitting.

d. Our neighborhood group helps the police deal with the problems of theft and (*vandal . . .*) _____.

19 ish—similar to   *Example:* foolish
20 ly—in a certain manner, at a certain time   *Examples:* loudly, hourly

a. Harry's (*child . . .*) _____ behavior at the party was more like that of a three-year-old than a thirty-year-old.

b. Sharks are attracted by soft music such as waltzes, but they leave (*immediate . . .*) _____ if they hear rock music.

c. Actor Brad Pitt's success is due in part to his (*boy . . .*) _____ smile.

d. Phone companies look forward to Mother's Day even more (*eager . . .*) _____ than mothers do; it's the day on which the most long-distance phone calls are made.

ROOTS

A **root** is a word's basic part and carries its fundamental meaning. Sometimes two roots combine to form a word. The word *telegraph*, for example, is made up of two roots: *tele* (which means "from a distance") and *graph* (which means "write").

Prefixes and suffixes also combine with roots to make words. For instance, the prefix *pre* (meaning "before") and the root *dict* (meaning "say") form the word *predict*. And the root *aud* (meaning "hear") and the suffix *ible* (meaning "able to be") form *audible*, which means "able to be heard."

Below are ten common roots and their meanings. Alternative forms of some roots are shown in parentheses. The practice that follows will help you learn these roots.

Roots	Examples
bene (bon)—good, well	benediction, bonus
port—carry	transport
bio—life	biology
ven (vent)—come	revenue, invent
man (manu)—hand	manage, manufacture
ped (pod)—foot	pedestal, tripod
auto—self	automatic
tele—far, over a distance	telescope
spect—look	inspect
aud (audi, audit)—hear	audience, auditorium

➤ *Practice 3*

Carefully read the meanings of each pair of roots. Then, in each sentence, complete the partial word (in *italics*) with the root that fits. Write the full word in the space provided.

21 bene (bon)—good, well   *Example:* benediction, bonus
22 port—carry   *Example:* transport

  a. I bought a (... *able*) _____ radio that I can carry to the beach.

  b. Jogging is supposed to be good for the body, but I don't see what's (... *ficial*) _____ about blisters and muscle cramps.

  c. The mass murderer was known to his neighbors as a very gentle, (... *volent*) _____ man who fed leftover pizza to squirrels.

  d. My suitcase was so heavy that I asked a (... *er*) _____ to carry it to the airport ticket line.

23 bio—life   *Example:* biology
24 ven (vent)—come   *Example:* revenue, invent

  a. (... *feedback*) _____ is a method that teaches people to control some body functions, including blood pressure.

  b. A successful (*con ... tion*) _____ will have people come together to share their ideas.

  c. For our Fourth of July parade, people of all ages come together on the main (*a ... ue*) _____.

  d. Reading his (... *graphy*) _____, the actor remarked, "Well, I never knew I've had such an exciting life."

25 man (manu)—hand   *Examples:* manage, manufacture
26 ped (pod)—foot   *Examples:* pedestal, tripod

  a. The giant organ had so many switches and keys that it required great skill to (... *ipulate*) _____ them all.

  b. Some (... *dlers*) _____ used to go from town to town on foot to sell their wares.

  c. Jeri enjoys having attractive nails, so she has a (... *icure*) _____ twice a month.

  d. Too many drivers forget that (... *estrians*) _____ have the right of way in a crosswalk.

27 **auto**—self   *Example:* automatic
28 **tele**—far, over a distance   *Example:* telescope

   a. Modern technology has produced a (. . . *vision*) _____ so small that it's part of a wristwatch.

   b. It was Karl Benz of Germany, not Henry Ford, who invented the (. . . *mobile*) _____; Ford invented the assembly line.

   c. In his (. . . *biography*) _____, *Why Me?* Sammy Davis, Jr., writes about how he had to fight racism in the early stages of his career.

   d When my parents blamed me for our unusually high (. . . *phone*) _____ bill, I said, "Can I help it if I have so many friends?"

29 **spect**—look   *Example:* inspect
30 **audi (audit)**—hear   *Examples:* audience, auditorium

   a. In addition to books, many libraries lend various types of (. . . *o-visual*) _____ materials, such as language tapes and videocassettes.

   b. So many singers wanted a role in the Broadway musical that over three hundred showed up for the (. . . *tion*) _____.

   c. The game lasted so long that most (. . . *ators*) _____ had gone home; only a few dozen people stayed to see the end.

   d. Benjamin Franklin invented the first (. . . *acles*) _____ with two-part lenses, for seeing both near and far.

➤ *Review Test 1*

To review what you have learned in this chapter, answer each of the following questions. Circle the letter of the answer you think is correct.

1. The prefix *un* (as in *unlucky*) means
   a. below.
   b. not.
   c. back.

2. When a prefix is added to a word, it changes the word's
   a. ending.
   b. meaning.
   c. part of speech.

3. A suffix can change
   a. a word's part of speech.
   b. a word's meaning.
   c. both of the above.

4. The suffix *-ist* (as in *violinist*) means a
   a. person skilled at something.
   b. belief or practice.
   c. state of being.

5. The basic meaning of a word is carried in its
   a. prefix.
   b. suffix.
   c. root.

➤ *Review Test 2*

Use the word parts in the box to complete the words in the following sentences. Use each word part only once.

bio — life	**ment** — state of being
ex — out, from	**pre** — before
ible — able to be	**spect** — look
in — within, into	**sub** — below, under
ism — a belief or practice	**tele** — far, over a distance

1. A fortuneteller (. . . *dicted*) _____ that I'd soon suffer a financial loss; then he charged me fifty dollars.

2. When actress Judy Garland's personal items were auctioned, they brought in $250,000, (. . . *cluding*) _____ $125 for her false eyelashes.

3. A fourteenth-century book on table manners warns that "one who blows his nose in the tablecloth" lacks (*refine* . . .) _____.

4. Before using dried mushrooms in a recipe, you should (. . . *merge*) _____ them in water for a short time.

5. Certain colors that are (*vis* . . .) _____ to bees and butterflies cannot be seen by humans.

6. Martin's continued bad behavior finally got him (. . . *pelled*) _____ from school.

7. A nature photographer may invest hundreds of dollars on a (. . . *photo*) _____ lens for a camera so that he or she can take pictures of wildlife from a safe distance.

8. For my (. . . *logy*) _____ project, I observed the way mold grows on unwashed dishes.

9 The spiritual practice of (*Hindu* . . .) _____ includes the belief that when someone dies, his or her soul begins a new life.

10. One of nature's most beautiful (. . . *acles*) _____ is thousands of monarch butterflies coming together at their winter home.

➤ *Review Test 3*

Use the word parts in the box to complete the words in the following passage. Read the passage through one time before trying to complete the words. Use each word part once.

bene — good, well	**man** — hand
ful — full of	**or** — a person who does something
ion — state of being	**re** — again, back
less — without	**un** — not
ly — in a certain manner	**ven** — come

In the days of the great sailing ships, one narrow channel was known for its rough, rocky waters. Hundreds of ships had been wrecked when their captains tried to steer through it (*cautious . . .*) (1) _____.

One day, a dolphin appeared at its entrance. Placing himself at the front of a ship, he guided it safely through. From then on, sailors learned to watch and wait for the dolphin to help them (*. . . age*) (2) _____ the trip, rather than travel through the channel (*. . . assisted*) (3) _____.

The sailors named the dolphin Jack, and he aided many ships. But when Jack approached a ship called the *Penguin*, he was shot by a drunken (*sail. . .*) (4) _____. Jack swam away, trailing blood. Now ships had to struggle through the channel without the (*. . . fit*) (5) _____ of Jack's help.

Weeks later, Jack (*. . . appeared*) (6) _____, ready to continue guiding ships. There was, however, one (*except . . .*) (7) _____. Whenever the *Penguin* approached, Jack stayed away, (*fear . . .*) (8) _____ of being shot again. Without Jack to guide it safely through the channel, the *Penguin* was (*help . . .*) (9) _____. (*E . . . tually*) (10) _____, it sank.

➤ *Review Test 4*

Phany Sarann was caught in a terrible war in Southeast Asia. Destruction and cruelty were all around her. She knew she needed a way out and believed that education and learning English were her salvation. This is her story, one of courage in the face of severe hardships.

Words to Watch

Following are some words in the reading that do not have strong context support. Each word is followed by the number of the paragraph in which it appears and its meaning there. These words are indicated in the reading by a small circle (°).

communal (3): public
trudged (3): walked in a slow, struggling manner
stalks (3): stems
porridge (3): a soft food made with meal and milk or water
guerrillas (5): rebel fighters
bribe (8): an illegal payoff
adequate (8): acceptable
forbade (12): would not allow
gritted (13): closed tightly

FROM HORROR TO HOPE

Phany Sarann

1   For the hundredth time, I closed my bedroom door, collapsed on the bed, and started to sob. Covering my face, I tried to cry silently, so my aunt and uncle wouldn't hear. Once again I asked myself why they were so cruel to me. Didn't they remember that they had invited me to work for them in America in exchange for my college education? Since my uncle had gone to college in Cambodia, why didn't he understand that education was so important to me, too? My life had already been too full of challenges. Having gone through so much and come so far, would I be defeated now?

2   When Pol Pot's Khmer Rouge soldiers* took charge of my life and my country in 1975, they forced people like my family, who lived in

---

*The murderous dictator Pol Pot and his military group, the Khmer Rouge, ruled the country of Cambodia for four years and were responsible for the deaths of over one million people.

the city of Phnom Penh, to move to the countryside. My father understood that we would be gone for a long time, so he made sure we took everything possible with us. Somehow, somewhere, he found a tractor and trailer. Since my three sisters and I were little, we rode on the wagon while my older brother and the adults walked behind. The horrible April weather cooked us and turned the dirt roads to dust. We settled first in a remote mountainous region near the Cambodian-Thai border, where we had to carry all our water from a muddy canal about half an hour's walk away. Later the Khmer Rouge moved us to a site along a river. There, at least, we could catch fish to eat. Soon my father was trading smoked fish for oranges, coffee, rice, and medicine.

3   After a year, the local authorities sent an oxcart to move our family again. They said it was because our settlement was too crowded, but my mom said the real reason was that my dad would not respect their authority. Dad hated having the uneducated local people control everything. The crops we grew, the chickens we raised, the people we talked to, the places we could and could not go, and even the family's children— all were controlled not by us, but by the authorities. After we were moved, we were all together for a few months, but then the Khmer Rouge began to separate our family. My brother and oldest sister were sent to a labor camp to dig canals by hand. My father was sent away for months to cut wood for the communal° kitchens. While I missed him, I was too hungry to feel much of anything but emptiness. My mother had to work in the rice fields all day, but thankfully she could come home at night. There were no schools and no hospitals. Many of our companions died of starvation, disease, and exhaustion. Even tiny children worked: as soon they were big enough to walk, they joined us in the rice fields. Day after day we trudged° behind the rice cutters, collecting the stalks° that they had missed. All our dreams were about finding food. The rice we harvested was hidden away or exported while we were given only one cup of watery porridge° a day. To survive, we ate whatever we could find: rats, crickets, caterpillars, snakes, frogs, and boiled banana tree bark. Our only hope was that some day our country would be rescued from the Khmer Rouge.

4   The horror grew worse when my father was accused of stealing one of our own chickens. My parents heard that my father would soon be "taken," which we knew meant executed, so he decided to escape. On the day he ran away, my sister and I met him on our way back from the fields. "Look after yourselves and tell your mother that I am leaving," he said. "I do not know when I will see you again."

5   In March of 1979, Vietnamese and Cambodian troops came to set us free. It took us two days to walk from the village back to town, and since I did not have shoes, I tried to make some from layers of leaves. When they fell apart, I cried and limped along on blistered feet. At first, we thought our nightmare was over because there were

no more killings and nobody was forcing us to work. But we were starving. My mother exchanged her diamond ring for rice to feed our hungry family. After the rice was gone, we began a series of moves, trying to find a place where life would be better. But there was no peace, because the Khmer Rouge guerrillas° and the new government troops were at war. Finally we arrived again in our old home of Phnom Penh.

6   All this time we kept hoping to see my father's face again. But in late 1981 we all wept to learn of his death. He had been shot by the Khmer Rouge as he swam across a river to escape them. There would be no more support from the man who was the most important part of our family. My mother was very sad; nevertheless, she struggled hard to bring up four daughters by herself.

7   That same year, we three younger girls began school. My sisters eventually quit in favor of going to work, but I felt that getting an education was the most important goal in my life. Struggling through high school was especially difficult because my family did not understand why I was doing it. Traditionally, Cambodians believe that education is important only for boys, so daughters are not encouraged to go to school. Many times when I came home from school, exhausted from studying, my mom would complain. "What makes you tired?" she would ask. "You just go there, sit and listen, but do nothing! But I have to carry heavy loads and move all the time!" My mother also kept reminding me that she could not support me past

high school. How could I continue my education? Then, after I graduated from high school in 1989 and my mother offered to buy me a small stall at the local market, I had an idea. I told her, "I will not sell things at the market, but if I do all the housework and all the cooking for the whole family, can I keep on studying? If I study English now, I can find a good job to support myself later." While she did not give me an answer, she did not make me go to the market either.

8   Even without my mother's support, I kept trying to get into college. However, I soon found how corrupt the educational system was. If I didn't have the money to pay a bribe°, I would not be admitted even though my test scores were adequate°. I sadly gave up the thought of college, but I started studying English in a private class. I would wake up every morning at 4:30 and ride my bicycle through the cold, dark streets to my class. I never wanted to get out of bed and go out into the cold. I was also scared people might hurt me and take my bike. But I went anyway. Soon, I found four Cambodians who wanted to speak English, so I began teaching them what I was learning. Life was full of challenges, but I was learning English and earning money too.

9   I realized how much more I had to learn when I took a job working for the United States Agency for International Development (USAID). After each staff meeting, I left the room with an aching head and an unsure feeling about what I was supposed to do. Having to make presentations in English was like a

nightmare for me. Writing reports in English was the worst of all. The simplest report took me hours and hours because I spent so much time checking words in a dictionary.

10   After a year my uncle, who had immigrated to Houston, Texas, asked me to come to work in his doughnut shop. In exchange, he promised to pay for my education in America. In great excitement, I quit my good job at USAID, said farewell to my family and friends, and came to Texas. This seemed like a dream come true—not only would I receive a good education, but I would meet many new people and have wonderful new experiences.

11   But the reality of my life in America was nothing like my dreams. Before school began, I worked hard seven days a week. When the school term started, I worked every weekend. I arranged hot doughnuts on the shelves, filled napkin boxes, made coffee, cleared tables, and sold doughnuts. Many times each day I washed all the trays we used for displaying and serving doughnuts. The hot water burned my hands, but my uncle and aunt refused to let me wear gloves, for fear they would slow me down.

12   Instead of treating me like a member of their family, my uncle and aunt regarded me with great suspicion. Because they were afraid I would steal money from the registers, they gave me working clothes with no pockets. Regularly, they searched my room, went through my belongings, and even opened and read my mail. Even my little bit of free time was not my own. I was allowed to go only to classes. When I asked to go to the Buddhist temple to honor my father on Cambodian New Year's Day and the Day of the Dead, the answer was "no." My dreams of making new friends evaporated too. My uncle and aunt forbade° me to say anything but "hi" or "good morning" to people who came in the doughnut shop. I felt I was living in a prison with no walls.

13   Once the shop was closed, the work continued. My uncle and aunt expected me to keep house for their family. I had to prepare their main meal every day and clean up after it. Three times a week, I mopped the floors and scrubbed the fixtures. I also swept and dusted all through the house once a week. How could they have forgotten to tell me that they also expected me to do all of this? But I swallowed my anger, gritted° my teeth, and kept quiet.

14   After ten months of this life, my uncle announced that he could not pay for my tuition anymore and that I had to go back to Cambodia. The excuse was a lie; I knew his business was making money. This sad experience with my aunt and uncle taught me not to trust people just because they are relatives.

15   While I felt angry, used, and scared, I also felt the freedom of the decision before me. Would I let my uncle force me to return to Cambodia? I decided the answer was no. I left my uncle's house and moved in with Nancy Dean, my former English teacher. Hearing of my plight, my former boss at USAID offered me a plane ticket to Michigan, where I could live with her parents and continue my education.

16   How excited I was to travel to Michigan, and how nervous—I had never met the people I was going to live with. However, the minute I got off the plane and met Gale and Roberta Lott, I knew a new life was about to begin. Gale and Roberta treat me as one of their children. The special attention they give me makes me feel complete for the first time in my life. Good things have continued to happen since I enrolled at Lansing Community College. I like all my classes, people are very friendly, and I have found a part-time job in the Student and Academic Support office.

17   My past has been full of challenges; some of these I could control, and some I could not. Learning to deal with challenges has made me a stronger person with the confidence to realize my dreams. I plan to transfer to a university and graduate with a bachelor of arts degree and then return to my homeland. I hope that a degree from an American university will help me move into a leadership role in Cambodia. Since education for women is still not valued there, my next challenge will be to make my culture understand that educating women will make my country a better place for everyone.

Word Part Questions

Use the word part clues you learned in this chapter to answer the following questions. Circle the letter of your choice.

1. In the sentence below, the word *uneducated* means
   a. able to be educated.
   b. well educated.
   c. not educated.

   "Dad hated having the uneducated local people control everything." (Paragraph 3)

2. In the sentence below, the word *starvation* means
   a. before being starved.
   b. without being starved.
   c. the state of being starved.

   "Many of our companions died of starvation. . . ." (Paragraph 3)

3. In the sentence below, the word *cutters* means
   a. people who are full of cutting.
   b. people who cut.
   c. people who do not cut.

   "Day after day we trudged behind the rice cutters, collecting the stalks that they had missed." (Paragraph 3)

4. In the sentence below, the word *exported* means
   a. taken above.
   b. correctly taken.
   c. taken out to another place.

   "The rice we harvested was hidden away or exported while we were given only one cup of watery porridge a day." (Paragraph 3)

5. In the sentence below, the word *eventually* means
   a. at a time that came later.
   b. at a great distance.
   c. in a skilled way.

   "That same year, we three younger girls began school. My sisters eventually quit in favor of going to work. . . . " (Paragraph 7)

6. In the sentence below, the words *reminding me* mean
   a. telling me again.
   b. telling me inside.
   c. telling me over a distance.

   "My mother also kept reminding me that she could not support me past high school." (Paragraph 7)

7. In the sentence below, the word *sadly* means
   a. without being sad.
   b. done in a sad way.
   c. before being sad.

   "I sadly gave up the thought of college. . . . " (Paragraph 8)

8. In the sentence below, the word *unsure* means
   a. very sure.
   b. not sure.
   c. sure ahead of time.

   "I left the room with an aching head and an unsure feeling about what I was supposed to do." (Paragraph 9)

9. In the sentence below, the words *immigrated to* mean
   a. moved into.
   b. moved out of.
   c. moved because of beliefs.

   "After a year my uncle, who had immigrated to Houston, Texas, asked me to come to work in his doughnut shop." (Paragraph 10)

10. In the sentence below, the word *regularly* means
   a. like regular people.
   b. according to regulations.
   c. in a regular way.

   "Regularly, they searched my room, went through my belongings, and even opened and read my mail." (Paragraph 12)

Reading Comprehension Questions

Vocabulary in Context

1. In the sentence below, the word *harvested* means
   a. gathered.
   b. stole.
   c. ate.

   "The rice we harvested was hidden away or exported while we were given only one cup of watery porridge a day." (Paragraph 3)

2. In the sentences below, the word *corrupt* means
   a. difficult.
   b. dishonest.
   c. strong.

   " . . . I soon found how corrupt the educational system was. If I didn't have the money to pay a bribe, I would not be admitted. . . ." (Paragraph 8)

3. In the sentences below, the word *evaporated* means
   a. came true.
   b. disappeared.
   c. were similar.

   "My dreams of making friends evaporated, too. My uncle and aunt forbade me to say anything but 'hi' or 'good morning' to people who came in the doughnut shop." (Paragraph 12)

Central Point and Main Ideas

4. Which sentence best expresses the central point of the selection?
   a. People would have a better life if they stayed in the country where they were born.
   b. Phany Sarann overcame extreme difficulties and succeeded in getting an education.

    c. People never know what challenges they will face in life.

    d. When the Khmer Rouge soldiers took charge of Cambodia, life became horrible for the author and her family.

5. The main idea of paragraph 9 is expressed in its

    a. first sentence.

    b. second sentence.

    c. next-to-last sentence.

    d. last sentence.

Supporting Details

6. According to the selection, the author

    a. did not believe her uncle when he said he could not pay for her tuition.

    b. was fired from her job at USAID.

    c. never went to school in Houston.

    d. was forced to move back to Cambodia from the United States.

7. _____ TRUE or FALSE? The author moved from Houston to Cambodia to Michigan.

Relationships

8. The relationship expressed in the sentence below is one of

    a. addition.

    b. contrast.

    c. cause and effect.

    d. illustration.

        "Instead of treating me like a member of their family, my uncle and aunt regarded me with great suspicion." (Paragraph 12)

9. The relationship expressed in the sentence below is one of

    a. time.

    b. comparison.

    c. cause and effect.

    d. addition.

        "After ten months of this life, my uncle announced that he could not pay for my tuition anymore. . . . " (Paragraph 14)

10. The overall pattern of organization of this selection is

    a. list of items.

    b. time order.

    c. cause and effect.

    d. definition and example.

Discussion Questions

1. Was Phany's mother right in not supporting Phany's desire to continue her education by going to college? What was her mother's point of view? What was Phany's point of view? Why do you think their views were so different?

2. What were the reasons Phany's uncle first wanted her to come to the United States? Why do you think he changed his mind and wanted to send her back to Cambodia?

3. Phany's job at her uncle's doughnut shop turned out to be a nightmare. What is the worst job you have ever had? What made it so terrible? Describe one or two incidents that show just how awful the job was.

Note: Writing assignments for this selection appear on page 552.

To the Student: If you enjoyed Phany's story and would like to read more stories like hers, turn to page 511 for a special offer from Townsend Press.

Check Your Performance			**WORD PARTS**
Activity	*Number Right*	*Points*	*Score*
Review Test 1 (5 items)	_____	× 2 =	_____
Review Test 2 (10 items)	_____	× 2.5 =	_____
Review Test 3 (10 items)	_____	× 2.5 =	_____
Review Test 4 (20 items)	_____	× 2 =	_____
		TOTAL SCORE =	_____%

WORD PARTS: Test 1

Use the word parts in the box to complete the words in the sentences below. Use each word part only once.

auto — self	**mono** — one
bene — good, well	**ped** — foot
er — a person who does something	**re** — again, back
ex — out, from	**un** — not
ion — act of	**ven** — come

1. A (research . . .) _____ found that students tend to learn better when lectures contain some humor.

2. Some lakes and rivers have become so (. . . clean) _____ that they have actually caught fire.

3. My new (. . . matic) _____ camera advances the film by itself each time I take a picture.

4. A skirt with an elastic waistband can (. . . pand) _____ to fit women of many sizes.

5. Before starting my car in cold weather, I need to pump the gas (. . . al) _____ a few times.

6. Jay Leno performs alone at the beginning of the Tonight Show, when he gives his (. . . logue) _____.

7. Whenever my mother tells me that the (. . . fits) _____ will outweigh the drawbacks, I know she's about to ask me to do something unpleasant.

8. Sometimes course (registrat . . .) _____ seems to last longer than the courses themselves.

(Continues on next page)

499

9. To *(. . . fresh)* _____ themselves, some Japanese workers take yawn breaks: They all raise their arms and yawn at the same time—for thirty seconds.

10. Many people attended the spy *(con . . . tion)* _____; however, no one was willing to wear a name-tag.

WORD PARTS: Test 2

Use the word parts in the box to complete the words in the following passage. Read the passage through one time before trying to complete the words. Use each word part once.

er — a person who does something	**ist** — a person skilled at something
ex — out, from	**ly** — in a certain manner
ful — full of	**re** — again
in — within	**spect** — look
ion — state of being	**tele** — far, over a distance

When a murder takes place, how do the police get information about the killer? First, they *(in . . .)* (1) _____ the scene of the crime. Maybe the murderer left some fingerprints on a *(. . . phone)* (2) _____, an ashtray, or a glass. Other clues that point to specific individuals *(. . . clude)* (3) _____ footprints (perhaps showing the pattern of wear in a shoe), hairs, and traces of blood. A close examination of the victim's body can also be very *(use . . .)* (4) _____. A stab wound may be matched to the blade of a particular knife. *(Similar . . .)* (5) _____, *(special . . . s)* (6) _____ can determine from a bullet wound the kind of gun that was used and the distance from which the bullet was fired. And once the bullet is *(. . . tracted)* (7) _____ from the body, it too will show marks that link it to only one gun. Increasingly, the methods for tracking down *(kill . . . s)* (8) _____ offer more than clues; they offer sure *(identificat . . .)* (9) _____. It is

(Continues on next page)

hoped that such exact police methods will persuade many would-be criminals to *(. . . consider)* (10) _____ their plans.

WORD PARTS: Test 3

Use the word parts in the box to complete the words in the sentences below. Use each word part only once.

able — able to be	**mono** — one
audi — hear	**pre** — before
ish — similar to	**sub** — below, under
ly — in a certain manner	**super** — over, above, beyond
mis — badly, wrong	**tele** — far, over a distance

1. The *(. . . ence)* _____ starting clapping as soon as the famous actress walked onstage and spoke her first line.

2. When the bus turned on its side, several passengers were *(serious . . .)* _____ injured.

3. Looking through the powerful *(. . . scope)* _____, we could see Saturn's rings.

4. According to a survey, the average person spends about a year of his or her life searching for *(. . . placed)* _____ objects.

5. Because she was *(. . . occupied)* _____ with an earlier assignment, Laurel didn't hear the teacher ask her a question.

6. Today, many reporters travel with a small *(port . . .)* _____ computer.

7. The lecturer spoke in such a *(. . . tone)* _____ that he almost put the students to sleep.

8. The scholarship is awarded on the basis of both financial need and *(. . . ior)* _____ grades.

(Continues on next page)

9. The car was so *(. . . standard)* _____ that within months the fuel pump needed replacing and the bumper fell off.

10. Whenever I catch my *(devil . . .)* _____ son snatching a piece of candy, he says, "I was taking it for you, Mommy."

WORD PARTS: Test 4

Use the word parts in the box to complete the words in the following passage. Read the passage through one time before trying to complete the words. Use each word part once.

aud — hear	**man** — hand
ex — out, from	**ment** — state of being
ful — full of	**pre** — before
in — within	**re** — again, back
ly — in a certain manner	**spect** — look

Last night in a dream, an angel came to me and asked, "Would you like to see hell?" After *(. . . paring)* (1) _____ myself to see a terrible *(. . . acle)* (2) _____, I went with the angel. Suddenly we stood *(. . . side)* (3) _____ a large room draped with blue velvet. In the middle of this *(beauti . . .)* (4) _____ room was a huge golden pot filled with sweet-smelling food. Many people sat around the pot. Each held a spoon of silver. The spoons' handles were so long that the people could reach the pot and scoop out food. They couldn't, however, *(. . . age)* (5) _____ to bring the food to their mouths. The only *(. . . ible)* (6) _____ sounds were moans of pain. I realized that everyone was starving.

"Now would you like to see heaven?" asked the angel. I *(eager . . .)* (7) _____ agreed. To my *(amaze . . .)* (8) _____, the next room I saw looked just like the first—with the same golden pot

(Continues on next page)

and the same silver spoons. However, here everyone appeared to be (. . . *tremely*) (9) _____ happy. The people were talking and laughing and looked well-fed.

Puzzled, I said, "In the other room there was only misery. Here there is only joy. How can this be?" With a wise smile, the angel (. . . *plied*) (10) _____, "Here they feed each other."

WORD PARTS: Test 5

A. Use the word parts in the box to complete the words in the sentences below. Use each word part only once.

---

bio — life   **less** — without
ism — a belief or practice   **port** — carry
ist — a person skilled at something

---

1. The stock-market crash of 1929 left many people *(penni . . .)* _____—they had no money at all.

2. Actor and *(humor . . .)* _____ Robin Williams is known for his zany routines.

3. One type of *(vegetarian . . .)* _____ excludes all dairy products and eggs.

4. To know about chemical reactions in the body, doctors must study *(. . . chemistry)* _____.

5. When the elevator broke down, the *(. . . er)* _____ had to walk up four flights of stairs to get our luggage to us.

(Continues on next page)

B. (6–10.) Use the word parts in the box to complete the words in the following passage. Read the passage through one time before trying to complete the words. Use each word part once.

er — a person who does something	**sub** — below, under
ful — full of	**un** — not
spect — look	

According to the American Kennel Club the Labrador retriever is the nation's most popular breed. What does this mean if you want a Lab puppy? Be very *(care . . .)* (6) _____ before you buy. When a breed is known to be number one, a flood of people look for puppies. *(. . . fortunately)* (7) _____, this usually attracts the dishonest type of *(breed . . .)* (8) _____ who raises *(. . . standard)* (9) _____ puppies just for the profit. These dogs have few of the qualities that made the breed popular. The best advice is to buy a puppy from a reputable source, and always *(in . . .)* (10) _____ the puppy first.

WORD PARTS: Test 6

A. Use the word parts in the box to complete the words in the sentences below. Use each word part only once.

ible — able to be	**tele** — far, over a distance
pod — foot	**un** — not
pre — before	

1. The kitten at the animal shelter looked so *(. . . loved)* _____ that I just had to adopt her.

2. The woman's feet hurt, so she went to the *(. . . iatrist)* _____ to have her corns removed.

3. The lawyer urged the jury not to *(. . . judge)* _____ the defendant, but to wait for all the facts before making up their minds.

4. The acrobat is so *(flex . . .)* _____ that he can wrap his legs around his head.

5. The Learning Center contains a *(. . . conference)* _____ room where staff members can talk on a special TV to people on other campuses.

(Continues on next page)

B. (6–10.) Use the word parts in the box to complete the words in the following passage. Read the passage through one time before trying to complete the words. Use each word part once.

ful — full of	**post** — after
less — without	**re** — again, back
ly — in a certain manner	

High-school reunions provide an opportunity to *(. . . acquaint)*
(6) _____ yourself with former classmates. However, some
people are a little nervous when attending a reunion. So here are some tips
for a *(success . . .)* (7) _____ experience. First, pamper
yourself; make yourself look your best. Second, wear something that
makes a statement. Buy a stunning *(strap . . .)* (8) _____
dress or a sharp silk suit. Next, try to be outgoing. Keep in mind that you
are a worthwhile person, and speak to other people *(confident . . .)*
(9) _____. But even if you have had a fantastic life,
don't act superior. Take the time to find out what your classmates have
done in their *(. . .-high-school)* (10) _____ years.
Finally, go with the attitude that you are going to have a good time. That is
the main reason for attending reunions.

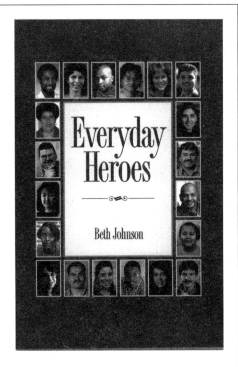

2

Combined-Skills Tests

Following are twelve tests that cover the skills taught in Part I of this book. Each test consists of a short reading passage followed by questions on any of the following: phonics, dictionary use, vocabulary in context, main ideas, supporting details, and relationships.

Note that tests 1 through 6 have questions on phonics and dictionary use as well as reading comprehension. Tests 7 through 12, the "Advanced Combined Skills" tests, have questions that involve only reading comprehension skills.

COMBINED SKILLS: Test 1

After reading the passage, circle the letter of the best answer to each question. (For your convenience, the passage is reprinted on the second page of the test.)

[1]In 1991, a total eclipse of the sun occurred over Mexico, providing scientists with a rare opportunity to watch its effects. [2]The duration of the event was more than six minutes. [3]Birds stopped singing. [4]Bees stopped flying. [5]Furthermore, flowers began to close their petals. [6]Grazing animals began to head home. [7]Scientists were able to gather data that they will be studying for years. [8]The next total eclipse in North America will not occur until 2017.

1. Which word or words have a hard *c* sound?
   a. *Mexico*
   b. *occur*
   c. *close*
   d. All of the above

2. Which word from sentences 7 and 8 is broken into syllables correctly?
   a. ab-le
   b. da-ta
   c. tot-al
   d. unt-il

3. Which word would be found on a dictionary page with these guidewords: **Sirius / skateboard**?
   a. *sun*
   b. *scientists*
   c. *six*
   d. *singing*

4. In sentence 2, the word *duration* means
   a. known reason.
   b. location.
   c. memory.
   d. length of time.

5. The topic sentence of the paragraph is sentence
   a. 1.
   b. 2.
   c. 6.
   d. 8.

(Continues on next page)

[1]In 1991, a total eclipse of the sun occurred over Mexico, providing scientists with a rare opportunity to watch its effects. [2]The duration of the event was more than six minutes. [3]Birds stopped singing. [4]Bees stopped flying. [5]Furthermore, flowers began to close their petals. [6]Grazing animals began to head home. [7]Scientists were able to gather data that they will be studying for years. [8]The next total eclipse in North America will not occur until 2017.

6. _____ TRUE OR FALSE? The paragraph suggests that there is still much for scientists to learn about eclipses.

7. According to the paragraph, the eclipse
   a. lasted six minutes.
   b. lasted over six minutes.
   c. did not influence animals.
   d. is the last one scientists will ever see.

8. The relationship of sentence 5 to sentence 4 is one of
   a. time order.
   b. addition.
   c. illustration.
   d. contrast.

COMBINED SKILLS: Test 2

After reading the passage, circle the letter of the best answer to each question. (For your convenience, the passage is reprinted on the second page of the test.)

[1]Fire-walking involves taking five steps over hot coals. [2]The traditional belief is that in order to walk over the hot coals, you must condition your mind. [3]The theory is that with proper mental fitness, you will not feel the pain. [4]Yet science has come up with another explanation. [5]The coals that are used are made of wood. [6]Though they look hot, they do not conduct heat well. [7]Thus walking five short steps over the coals does not take enough time to get burned toes or blisters on the bottom of the feet.

1. Which word has a long vowel sound?
   a. *five*
   b. *steps*
   c. *hot*
   d. *that*

2. Which syllable rule applies to the words *order, mental,* and *bottom?*
   a. Divide between two consonants.
   b. Divide before a single consonant.
   c. Divide after prefixes and before suffixes.
   d. Divide between the words in a compound word.

Use your dictionary to answer the following question.

3. _____ TRUE OR FALSE? The word *hot* is both an adjective and an adverb.

4. In sentence 2, the word *condition* means
   a. close.
   b. search.
   c. prepare.
   d. notice.

(Continues on next page)

¹Fire-walking involves taking five steps over hot coals. ²The traditional belief is that in order to walk over the hot coals, you must condition your mind. ³The theory is that with proper mental fitness, you will not feel the pain. ⁴Yet science has come up with another explanation. ⁵The coals that are used are made of wood. ⁶Though they look hot, they do not conduct heat well. ⁷Thus walking five short steps over the coals does not take enough time to get burned toes or blisters on the bottom of the feet.

5. Which of the following statements best expresses the main idea of the paragraph?
   a. Fire-walking is dangerous.
   b. Tradition and science have differing explanations for fire-walking.
   c. Difficult activities can be accomplished with proper mental fitness.
   d. Traditional beliefs are usually opposed by science.

6. According to tradition, the act of fire-walking is
   a. unhealthy.
   b. lengthy.
   c. a religious experience.
   d. a mental challenge.

7. The relationship of sentence 4 to sentence 3 is one of
   a. time.
   b. addition.
   c. comparison.
   d. contrast.

8. The paragraph is organized as a
   a. series of steps in fire-walking.
   b. comparison of two views on fire-walking.
   c. contrast of two views on fire-walking.
   d. definition of "fire-walking" with examples.

COMBINED SKILLS: Test 3

After reading the passage, circle the letter of the best answer to each question. (For your convenience, the passage is reprinted on the second page of the test.)

[1]The Worm Concern is an unusual recycling business that is benefiting the environment in a couple of ways. [2]The business takes in waste such as lawn clippings, tree trimmings, table scraps, and manure. [3]All of this is then fed to six acres of common earthworms. [4]The worms convert the garbage into an inexpensive, rich fertilizer. [5]This organic recycling has cut down on the amount of trash dumped into landfills. [6]Also, it has provided a first-class soil for lawns and gardens.

1. Which group contains words with a long vowel sound?
   a. *an, that, clippings*
   b. *ways, tree, also*
   c. *earthworms, landfills, first-class*
   d. *convert, rich, cut*

2. Which word from the paragraph is divided correctly?
   a. tab-le
   b. ear-thworms
   c. con-vert
   d. lan-dfills

3. Which word would be found on a dictionary page with these guidewords: **soda water / soldier**?
   a. *such*
   b. *scraps*
   c. *six*
   d. *soil*

4. In sentence 4, the word *convert* means
   a. change.
   b. put.
   c. carry.
   d. permit.

5. The topic sentence of the paragraph is sentence
   a. 1.
   b. 2.
   c. 5.
   d. 6.

(Continues on next page)

[1]The Worm Concern is an unusual recycling business that is benefiting the environment in a couple of ways. [2]The business takes in waste such as lawn clippings, tree trimmings, table scraps, and manure. [3]All of this is then fed to six acres of common earthworms. [4]The worms convert the garbage into an inexpensive, rich fertilizer. [5]This organic recycling has cut down on the amount of trash dumped into landfills. [6]Also, it has provided a first-class soil for lawns and gardens.

6. According to the paragraph, organic recycling
   a. is expensive.
   b. results in more room in landfills.
   c. requires chemicals.
   d. is a nonprofit activity.

7. Sentence 2 contains a transition that signals
   a. time.
   b. comparison.
   c. illustration.
   d. cause and effect.

8. The relationship of sentence 3 to sentence 2 is one of
   a. time.
   b. addition.
   c. comparison.
   d. contrast.

COMBINED SKILLS: Test 4

After reading the passage, circle the letter of the best answer to each question. (For your convenience, the passage is reprinted on the second page of the test.)

¹The odor of food draws bears. ²As a result, bears are often found around campsites. ³Fish and Game officials have suggestions about what to do and not to do if you see a bear. ⁴First of all, they suggest that if the bear has not sensed your presence, back away downwind. ⁵Do not run, as the bear is likely to give chase. ⁶If the bear sees you, stand up and raise your arms, so that you look as large as you can. ⁷Don't crouch down thinking the bear will avoid you if you appear small. ⁸If the bear charges, try yelling forcefully and throwing rocks at the bear. ⁹Don't run away even then—the bear is faster than you. ¹⁰If the animal attacks you, cover your head and neck and bring your legs up into your chest. ¹¹Don't lie flat on the ground looking as if you are dead. ¹²The bear is not likely to fall for this, and you may pay for it with a grave injury.

1. Which group is made up of words that contain a digraph?
   a. *suggest, large, charges*
   b. *fish, chase, throwing*
   c. *food, do, you*
   d. *campsites, downwind, injury*

2. Which words would be broken into syllables according to the rule to divide before a single consonant?
   a. *odor, result, around*
   b. *campsites, downwind*
   c. *forcefully, throwing, likely*
   d. *suggest, appear, attacks*

3. The word *throwing* would be found on a dictionary page with which guide-words?
   a. **therein / thing**
   b. **throaty / thunderclap**
   c. **thine / thorax**
   d. **thundercloud / tidewater**

4. In sentence 12, the word *grave* means
   a. known.
   b. small.
   c. serious.
   d. recent.

5. The topic sentence of the paragraph is sentence
   a. 1.
   b. 2.
   c. 3.
   d. 10.

(Continues on next page)

519

[1]The odor of food draws bears. [2]As a result, bears are often found around campsites. [3]Fish and Game officials have suggestions about what to do and not to do if you see a bear. [4]First of all, they suggest that if the bear has not sensed your presence, back away downwind. [5]Do not run, as the bear is likely to give chase. [6]If the bear sees you, stand up and raise your arms, so that you look as large as you can. [7]Don't crouch down thinking the bear will avoid you if you appear small. [8]If the bear charges, try yelling forcefully and throwing rocks at the bear. [9]Don't run away even then—the bear is faster than you. [10]If the animal attacks you, cover your head and neck and bring your legs up into your chest. [11]Don't lie flat on the ground looking as if you are dead. [12]The bear is not likely to fall for this, and you may pay for it with a grave injury.

6. According to the paragraph, if a bear sees you, you should
   a. run as fast as you can.
   b. make yourself look as large as possible.
   c. play dead.
   d. try to get downwind of the animal.

7. The relationship between sentences 1 and 2 is one of
   a. time.
   b. comparison.
   c. contrast.
   d. cause and effect.

8. The paragraph is organized as a
   a. story told in time order.
   b. list of suggestions on how to behave when you see a bear.
   c. contrast between bears and people.
   d. discussion of the causes and effects of bears' behavior.

COMBINED SKILLS: Test 5

After reading the passage, circle the letter of the best answer to each question. (For your convenience, the passage is reprinted on the second page of the test.)

¹A Bowling Green State University poll surveyed young men and women to find out what they considered romantic. ²The survey, which listed the top ten activities for men and women, found some similarities and some differences. ³Kissing, cuddling, hugging, and taking walks were favored by both men and women. ⁴Both also chose sending or receiving flowers, candlelit dinners, and sending or receiving cards or love letters. ⁵Saying "I love you," getting surprise gifts, and slow dancing rounded out the women's list but were not on the men's list. ⁶On the other hand, sitting by a fireplace, holding hands, and making love were found on the men's list but not on the women's.

1. In which word does **y** sound like long **i**?
   a. *young*
   b. *they*
   c. *saying*
   d. *by*

2. Which word would be broken into syllables according to the rule to divide between the words in a compound word?
   a. *women*
   b. *kissing*
   c. *fireplace*
   d. *holding*

Use your dictionary to answer the following question.

3. The word *surprise*
   a. can be both a verb and a noun.
   b. is found on a page with these guide words: **surely / surveying**.
   c. is accented on the second syllable.
   d. is all of the above.

4. In sentence 5, the words *rounded out* mean
   a. were omitted from.
   b. ruined.
   c. completed.
   d. delayed.

(Continues on next page)

[1]A Bowling Green State University poll surveyed young men and women to find out what they considered romantic. [2]The survey, which listed the top ten activities for men and women, found some similarities and some differences. [3]Kissing, cuddling, hugging, and taking walks were favored by both men and women. [4]Both also chose sending or receiving flowers, candlelit dinners, and sending or receiving cards or love letters. [5]Saying "I love you," getting surprise gifts, and slow dancing rounded out the women's list but were not on the men's list. [6]On the other hand, sitting by a fireplace, holding hands, and making love were found on the men's list but not on the women's.

5. Which statement best expresses the main idea of this paragraph?
   a. A survey found that there are similarities and differences in what men and women find romantic.
   b. One survey shows how differently men and women think about romance.
   c. Young men and women agree and disagree about a variety of things, including romance.
   d. Women have a better understanding of what is romantic than men.

6. According to the paragraph,
   a. hugging was on the women's list, but not the men's.
   b. making love was on both lists.
   c. slow dancing was on the women's list, but not the men's.
   d. taking walks was on the women's list, but not the men's.

7. The relationship of sentence 6 to sentence 5 is one of
   a. time.
   b. comparison.
   c. cause and effect.
   d. contrast.

8. The main pattern of organization of this paragraph is
   a. time order.
   b. comparison-contrast.
   c. cause and effect.
   d. definition and example.

COMBINED SKILLS: Test 6

After reading the passage, circle the letter of the best answer to each question. (For your convenience, the passage is reprinted on the second page of the test.)

¹A drought can be disastrous to farmers. ²Crops that don't get enough water fail to grow properly, leading to little or no income for the farmers. ³However, some farmers have found crops that are drought-resistant. ⁴One is canola, a plant whose oil is being touted as a healthy cooking oil. ⁵Another plant requiring much less water than most plants is buffalo gourd. ⁶It needs to be planted only once and continues to produce plants yearly. ⁷Lubricating oil and fuel can be made from buffalo gourd. ⁸Kenaf, another hearty grower, can be used in the production of newspapers. ⁹It prevents newsprint from coming off on readers' hands. ¹⁰Several drought-resistant plants, then, hold special promise for farmers.

1. Which word has a digraph that sounds like **f**?
   a. *farmers*
   b. *enough*
   c. *healthy*
   d. *kenaf*

2. The word *buffalo* is broken into syllables in this way:
   a. buff-al-o.
   b. buff-a-lo.
   c. buf-fa-lo.
   d. buf-fal-o.

Use your dictionary and the pronunciation key below to answer the following question.

ŏ **pot**   ō **toe**   ô **paw, for**

3. The **o** in the word *promise* sounds like the **o** in
   a. *pot.*
   b. *toe.*
   c. *paw.*

4. In sentence 4, the word *touted* means
   a. promoted.
   b. replaced.
   c. avoided.
   d. rejected.

5. The main idea of this paragraph is expressed in sentence
   a. 1.
   b. 2.
   c. 7.
   d. 10.

(Continues on next page)

523

[1]A drought can be disastrous to farmers. [2]Crops that don't get enough water fail to grow properly, leading to little or no income for the farmers. [3]However, some farmers have found crops that are drought-resistant. [4]One is canola, a plant whose oil is being touted as a healthy cooking oil. [5]Another plant requiring much less water than most plants is buffalo gourd. [6]It needs to be planted only once and continues to produce plants yearly. [7]Lubricating oil and fuel can be made from buffalo gourd. [8]Kenaf, another hearty grower, can be used in the production of newspapers. [9]It prevents newsprint from coming off on readers' hands. [10]Several drought-resistant plants, then, hold special promise for farmers.

6. Buffalo gourd is a source of
   a. a healthy cooking oil.
   b. lubricating oil.
   c. a special kind of newsprint.
   d. water.

7. Sentence 2 expresses a relationship of
   a. time.
   b. comparison-contrast.
   c. cause and effect.
   d. definition and example.

8. The paragraph is mainly organized as a
   a. series of events in the order in which they happened.
   b. definition of "drought" with examples.
   c. list of some drought-resistant crops.
   d. discussion of the causes and effects of droughts.

ADVANCED COMBINED SKILLS: Test 1

After reading the passage, circle the letter of the best answer to each question. (For your convenience, the passage is reprinted on the second page of the test.)

[1]Two of America's most beloved presidents were assassinated—Abraham Lincoln and John F. Kennedy. [2]There are a number of striking coincidences in President Lincoln's and President Kennedy's lives. [3]Lincoln was elected president in 1860, one hundred years before Kennedy was elected president. [4]Both had a vice president named Johnson. [5]Andrew Johnson was Lincoln's vice president. [6]Lyndon Johnson was Kennedy's. [7]Both Johnsons were Southern Democrats who had served in the U. S. Senate. [8]Andrew Johnson was born in 1808, and Lyndon Johnson was born in 1908. [9]Furthermore, both Lincoln and Kennedy were advocates of civil rights and racial equality. [10][7]Each was shot in the head on a Friday and in the presence of his wife. [11]John Wilkes Booth, Lincoln's killer, was born in 1839, a hundred years before Kennedy's killer, Lee Harvey Oswald, was born. [12]Both assassins were themselves killed before they could be brought to justice.

1. In sentence 2, the word *striking* means
   a. hitting.
   b. dull.
   c. common.
   d. remarkable.

2. In sentence 9, the word *advocates* means
   a. victims.
   b. critics.
   c. supporters.
   d. historians.

3. The topic sentence of the paragraph is sentence
   a. 1.
   b. 2.
   c. 3.
   d. 10.

4. According to the paragraph, Lincoln and Kennedy
   a. were both born in Illinois.
   b. had the same birthday.
   c. both had a vice president who had served in the Senate.
   d. were both Southerners.

5. _____ TRUE OR FALSE? Both Lincoln and Kennedy were killed by men who themselves were killed.

(Continues on next page)

[1]Two of America's most beloved presidents were assassinated—Abraham Lincoln and John F. Kennedy. [2]There are a number of striking coincidences in President Lincoln's and President Kennedy's lives. [3]Lincoln was elected president in 1860, one hundred years before Kennedy was elected president. [4]Both had a vice president named Johnson. [5]Andrew Johnson was Lincoln's vice president. [6]Lyndon Johnson was Kennedy's. [7]Both Johnsons were Southern Democrats who had served in the U. S. Senate. [8]Andrew Johnson was born in 1808, and Lyndon Johnson was born in 1908. [9]Furthermore, both Lincoln and Kennedy were advocates of civil rights and racial equality. [10,7]Each was shot in the head on a Friday and in the presence of his wife. [11]John Wilkes Booth, Lincoln's killer, was born in 1839, a hundred years before Kennedy's killer, Lee Harvey Oswald, was born. [12]Both assassins were themselves killed before they could be brought to justice.

6. President Kennedy's vice president was
   a. Andrew Johnson.
   b. John Wilkes Booth.
   c. Lyndon Johnson.
   d. Lee Harvey Oswald.

7. The relationship of sentence 9 to the several sentences before it is one of
   a. time.
   b. comparison.
   c. contrast.
   d. addition.

8. The main pattern of organization of the paragraph is
   a. comparison.
   b. contrast.
   c. cause and effect.
   d. definition and example.

ADVANCED COMBINED SKILLS: Test 2

After reading the passage, circle the letter of the best answer to each question. (For your convenience, the passage is reprinted on the second page of the test.)

¹In ice hockey, skaters using special sticks try to knock a hard rubber disk called a puck into a net that is guarded by a player called a goalie. ²Goalies wear a helmet and mask to protect themselves from being hurt if they are hit by a puck. ³They began to wear such protective gear after Bobby Hull started playing in the National Hockey League.

⁴Hull had a shot that put fear into goalies. ⁵It was clocked at a hundred miles per hour. ⁶Not only did the shot terrorize everyone around Hull; he said that once he made a shot that scared even him. ⁷That time, Hull wound up and slapped the puck, which took off toward the goalie and then rose. ⁸The goalie tried to get out of the way but could not. ⁹As he tried to move, the puck hit him on the side of the face and then ripped into his ear. ¹⁰The ear was severed and so had to be sewn back on. ¹¹From then on, that goalie began wearing a facemask whenever his team played against Hull. ¹²Other goalies followed, and eventually all goalies were wearing helmets and masks.

1. In sentence 3, the word *gear* means
   a. a machine part.
   b. equipment.
   c. underclothing.
   d. netting.

2. In sentence 10, the word *severed* means
   a. bleeding.
   b. struck hard.
   c. missed.
   d. cut off.

3. Which statement best expresses the main idea of this paragraph?
   a. A National Hockey League goalie once had his ear cut off by a puck.
   b. Unusual events often change the way a game is played.
   c. One of Bobby Hull's shots led to goalies' wearing helmets and masks.
   d. Bobby Hull's shots put terror into the heart of National Hockey League goalies.

4. According to the paragraph, goalies did not wear helmets and masks
   a. until after Bobby Hull came into the league.
   b. until the league required it.
   c. unless Bobby Hull was playing.
   d. because they were not allowed to.

5. _____ TRUE OR FALSE? According to the paragraph, all members of ice hockey teams eventually wore facemasks.

(Continues on next page)

¹In ice hockey, skaters using special sticks try to knock a hard rubber disk called a puck into a net that is guarded by a player called a goalie. ²Goalies wear a helmet and mask to protect themselves from being hurt if they are hit by a puck. ³They began to wear such protective gear after Bobby Hull started playing in the National Hockey League.

⁴Hull had a shot that put fear into goalies. ⁵It was clocked at a hundred miles per hour. ⁶Not only did the shot terrorize everyone around Hull; he said that once he made a shot that scared even him. ⁷That time, Hull wound up and slapped the puck, which took off toward the goalie and then rose. ⁸The goalie tried to get out of the way but could not. ⁹As he tried to move, the puck hit him on the side of the face and then ripped into his ear. ¹⁰The ear was severed and so had to be sewn back on. ¹¹From then on, that goalie began wearing a facemask whenever his team played against Hull. ¹²Other goalies followed, and eventually all goalies were wearing helmets and masks.

6. Sentence 8 expresses a relationship of
   a. time.
   b. addition.
   c. comparison.
   d. contrast.

7. The relationship of sentence 11 to sentence 10 is one of
   a. time.
   b. contrast.
   c. comparison.
   d. illustration.

8. The main pattern of organization of the second paragraph is
   a. time order.
   b. list of items.
   c. comparison-contrast.
   d. definition and example.

ADVANCED COMBINED SKILLS: Test 3

After reading the passage, circle the letter of the best answer to each question. (For your convenience, the passage is reprinted on the second page of the test.)

¹The Food and Drug Administration has opened a division called the Office of Criminal Investigations. ²This office was set up to discover consumer cheating. ³The first task for the office was to check claims by people who said they had found syringes in cans of Pepsi-Cola. ⁴One hundred investigators worked to verify the claims of numerous people nationwide. ⁵The examiners used techniques that would get fast results. ⁶In most cases, people admitted within two days that their claims were untrue. ⁷Despite the fact that hundreds of claims were made against Pepsi, not one of them was been proved true. ⁸Moreover, over forty of those who made claims have been arrested for trying to swindle the company.

1. In sentence 4, the word *verify* means
   a. hide.
   b. check the truth of.
   c. delay.
   d. read about.

2. In sentence 8, the word *swindle* means
   a. buy.
   b. improve.
   c. cheat.
   d. confuse.

3. Which statement best expresses the main idea of this paragraph?
   a. A federal division demonstrated great skill in its very first case.
   b. There are many divisions within the Food and Drug Administration.
   c. Many consumers claimed that they had found syringes in cans of Pepsi-Cola.
   d. It took the most experienced investigators in the government to solve a difficult case.

4. According to the paragraph, the Office of Criminal Investigations
   a. found that few claims in the Pepsi-Cola case were true.
   b. has been paid for by the Pepsi-Cola company.
   c. had as its first case a Pepsi-Cola investigation.
   d. was recently transferred to the Food and Drug Administration.

(Continues on next page)

[1]The Food and Drug Administration has opened a division called the Office of Criminal Investigations. [2]This office was set up to discover consumer cheating. [3]The first task for the office was to check claims by people who said they had found syringes in cans of Pepsi-Cola. [4]One hundred investigators worked to verify the claims of numerous people nationwide. [5]The examiners used techniques that would get fast results. [6]In most cases, people admitted within two days that their claims were untrue. [7]Despite the fact that hundreds of claims were made against Pepsi, not one of them was been proved true. [8]Moreover, over forty of those who made claims have been arrested for trying to swindle the company.

5. People claimed that in cans of Pepsi-Cola, they had found
   a. bugs.
   b. syringes.
   c. pieces of glass.
   d. hair.

6. _____ TRUE OR FALSE? The investigators often used techniques that were effective but produced slow results.

7. Sentence 7 expresses a relationship of
   a. time.
   b. comparison.
   c. contrast.
   d. addition.

8. The relationship of sentence 8 to sentence 7 is one of
   a. time.
   b. addition.
   c. contrast.
   d. cause and effect.

ADVANCED COMBINED SKILLS: Test 4

After reading the passage, circle the letter of the best answer to each question. (For your convenience, the passage is reprinted on the second page of the test.)

¹How can you tell if someone is lying? ²The polygraph test is designed to be a simple way to prove if someone is lying or telling the truth. ³The test involves a machine that is hooked up to a person by wires and straps. ⁴Questions are asked, and bodily responses are recorded. ⁵Usually, no more than ten questions are asked. ⁶Two or three of the questions are pointed—for instance, "Did you steal the picture?" ⁷The remaining questions may not seem important, but they are meant to help the questioner determine the truthfulness of the subject. ⁸Supporters of polygraph tests claim that they have a 95 percent accuracy rating. ⁹However, opponents of polygraph tests dispute this view. ¹⁰They say that a good liar and anyone accustomed to taking the test can beat a polygraph, thus making it useless.

1. In sentence 6, the word *pointed* means
   a. meant to confuse.
   b. long.
   c. short.
   d. about the matter at hand.

2. In sentence 9, the word *dispute* means
   a. agree with.
   b. notice.
   c. oppose.
   d. use.

3. Which sentence best expresses the main idea of the paragraph?
   a. The polygraph is a machine used as a lie detector.
   b. People who give polygraph tests must be very skilled in the operation of the machine and in asking questions.
   c. An important part of a polygraph test is a series of questions intended to help the questioner discover dishonesty.
   d. There is disagreement over the accuracy of the polygraph test, which is designed to tell when people are lying.

(Continues on next page)

[1]How can you tell if someone is lying? [2]The polygraph test is designed to be a simple way to prove if someone is lying or telling the truth. [3]The test involves a machine that is hooked up to a person by wires and straps. [4]Questions are asked, and bodily responses are recorded. [5]Usually, no more than ten questions are asked. [6]Two or three of the questions are pointed —for instance, "Did you steal the picture?" [7]The remaining questions may not seem important, but they are meant to help the questioner determine the truthfulness of the subject. [8]Supporters of polygraph tests claim that they have a 95 percent accuracy rating. [9]However, opponents of polygraph tests dispute this view. [10]They say that a good liar and anyone accustomed to taking the test can beat a polygraph, thus making it useless.

4. According to the paragraph, during a polygraph test
   a. no more than ten questions are ever asked.
   b. the subject's legs are hooked up to the polygraph machine.
   c. a person used to taking polygraph tests will finish more quickly than someone unaccustomed to the tests.
   d. some physical responses of the person taking the test are recorded.

5. _____ TRUE OR FALSE? Everyone agrees that polygraph tests have a 95 percent accuracy rating.

6. According to the paragraph, opponents of polygraph tests believe that
   a. the polygraph machine can physically harm people.
   b. some people can tell a lie which the polygraph machine doesn't record as a lie.
   c. ten questions are too few to ask during a polygraph test.
   d. the polygraph machine is useful in some instances.

7. The relationship of the second part of sentence 6 (after *pointed*) to the first part is one of
   a. time.
   b. contrast.
   c. cause and effect.
   d. illustration.

8. The relationship of sentence 9 to sentence 8 is one of
   a. time.
   b. contrast.
   c. comparison.
   d. illustration.

ADVANCED COMBINED SKILLS: Test 5

After reading the passage, circle the letter of the best answer to each question. (For your convenience, the passage is reprinted on the second page of the test.)

[1]San Francisco Bay isn't what it used to be. [2]Sailing ships from around the world have brought with them diverse sea animals. [3]These different organisms have changed the population of the bay. [4]For instance, New Zealand slugs with no natural enemies have eliminated the oysters that were once plentiful in the bay. [5]Similarly, Russian jellyfish are eating microscopic organisms that native fish eat. [6]Green crabs from the Atlantic Ocean were brought in by a company that had packed lobsters in seaweed. [7]The crabs hid in the seaweed and began multiplying when the seaweed was thrown into the bay. [8]Scientists report that very few original inhabitants remain in the bay.

1. In sentence 2, the word *diverse* means
   a. varied.
   b. local.
   c. private.
   d. dead.

2. In sentence 3, the word *organisms* refers to
   a. ships.
   b. animals.
   c. seas.
   d. oysters.

3. Which of the following best expresses the main idea of this paragraph?
   a. San Francisco Bay has an unusual mixture of sea animals.
   b. Sea animals from around the world have changed the population of San Francisco Bay.
   c. The original inhabitants of San Francisco Bay have chosen to leave it.
   d. Creatures with no natural enemies have taken over San Francisco Bay and will soon spread to other locations.

4. According to the paragraph, the New Zealand slugs
   a. are eaten by fish.
   b. hide in seaweed.
   c. have no natural enemies.
   d. are original inhabitants of the bay.

(Continues on next page)

[1]San Francisco Bay isn't what it used to be. [2]Sailing ships from around the world have brought with them diverse sea animals. [3]These different organisms have changed the population of the bay. [4]For instance, New Zealand slugs with no natural enemies have eliminated the oysters that were once plentiful in the bay. [5]Similarly, Russian jellyfish are eating microscopic organisms that native fish eat. [6]Green crabs from the Atlantic Ocean were brought in by a company that had packed lobsters in seaweed. [7]The crabs hid in the seaweed and began multiplying when the seaweed was thrown into the bay. [8]Scientists report that very few original inhabitants remain in the bay.

5. _____ TRUE OR FALSE? Russian jellyfish hid in the seaweed and began to multiply when the seaweed was thrown into the bay.

6. The relationship of sentence 4 to sentence 3 is one of
   a. addition.
   b. time.
   c. contrast.
   d. illustration.

7. The relationship of sentence 5 to sentence 4 is one of
   a. addition.
   b. comparison.
   c. cause and effect.
   d. illustration.

8. The paragraph's main pattern of organization is
   a. time order.
   b. list of items.
   c. comparison.
   d. definition and example.

ADVANCED COMBINED SKILLS: Test 6

After reading the passage, circle the letter of the best answer to each question. (For your convenience, the passage is reprinted on the second page of the test.)

[1]Air travel today is made possible by a powerful and efficient engine developed over sixty years ago. [2]In 1939, the jet engine was developed at the same time by two inventors who had never met or spoken to each other. [3]Hans von Ohain was a German inventor. [4]His counterpart was a British citizen named Frank Whittle. [5]Though each had thought up the same invention, the lives of these men took different paths. [6]In Germany, Hans von Ohain was able to continue his work with government support. [7]He convinced Adolf Hitler that World War II would be won if he could perfect a quiet turbine engine that would make planes fly faster. [8]Von Ohain's progress was slowed as Germany began to lose the war, and Germany never used the jet engine. [9]In contrast, Frank Whittle's government responded less positively. [10]Whittle was unable to convince the British government that the jet engine he developed would revolutionize flying. [11]Nevertheless, he continued to work on the engine throughout the war. [12]Once the war ended, Whittle found buyers for this invention.

1. In sentence 4, the words *his counterpart* mean
   a. someone with a role similar to his.
   b. a friend he once had.
   c. a coworker.
   d. a person he knew well.

2. Which statement best expresses the main idea of this paragraph?
   a. Because of its inability to develop a jet engine, Germany lost World War II.
   b. The two inventors of the jet engine had different career paths.
   c. The jet engine is an invention that has changed the world.
   d. It usually takes many years for inventions to become accepted by the world.

3. According to the paragraph, Frank Whittle
   a. knew of the work being done by Hans von Ohain.
   b. was not liked by the British government.
   c. kept working on the jet engine throughout World War II.
   d. was tempted to move from Britain to Germany.

4. _____ TRUE OR FALSE? Frank Whittle convinced Adolf Hitler that World War II would be won if a turbine engine that would make planes fly faster could be developed.

(Continues on next page)

[1]Air travel today is made possible by a powerful and efficient engine developed over sixty years ago. [2]In 1939, the jet engine was developed at the same time by two inventors who had never met or spoken to each other. [3]Hans von Ohain was a German inventor. [4]His counterpart was a British citizen named Frank Whittle. [5]Though each had thought up the same invention, the lives of these men took different paths. [6]In Germany, Hans von Ohain was able to continue his work with government support. [7]He convinced Adolf Hitler that World War II would be won if he could perfect a quiet turbine engine that would make planes fly faster. [8]Von Ohain's progress was slowed as Germany began to lose the war, and Germany never used the jet engine. [9]In contrast, Frank Whittle's government responded less positively. [10]Whittle was unable to convince the British government that the jet engine he developed would revolutionize flying. [11]Nevertheless, he continued to work on the engine throughout the war. [12]Once the war ended, Whittle found buyers for this invention.

5. Frank Whittle
   a. had a lot of government support for his work.
   b. stopped working on his invention during the war.
   c. eventually found buyers for his jet engine.
   d. all of the above.

6. Sentence 5 expresses a relationship of
   a. time.
   b. addition.
   c. comparison-contrast.
   d. cause and effect.

7. The relationship of sentence 11 to sentence 10 is one of
   a. addition.
   b. illustration.
   c. contrast.
   d. comparison.

8. The paragraph compares and contrasts two
   a. countries.
   b. engines.
   c. inventors.
   d. wars.

3
Writing Assignments

A BRIEF GUIDE TO EFFECTIVE WRITING

Here in a nutshell is what you need to do to write effectively.

Step 1: Explore Your Topic Through Informal Writing

To begin with, explore the topic that you want to write about or that you have been assigned to write about. You can examine your topic through **informal writing**, which usually means one of three things.

First, you can **freewrite** about your topic for at least ten minutes. In other words, for ten minutes write whatever comes into your head about your subject. Write without stopping and without worrying at all about spelling or grammar or the like. Simply get down on paper all the information about the topic that comes to mind.

A second thing you can do is to **make a list of ideas and details** that could go into your paper. Simply pile these items up, one after another, like a shopping list, without worrying about putting them in any special order. Try to accumulate as many details as you can think of.

A third way to explore your topic is to **write down a series of questions and answers** about it. Your questions can start with words like *what, why, how, when*, and *where*.

Getting your thoughts and ideas down on paper will help you think more about your topic. With some raw material to look at, you are now in a better position to decide on just how to proceed.

Step 2: Plan Your Paper with an Informal Outline

After exploring your topic, plan your paper using an informal outline. Do two things:

1 **Decide on and write out the point of your paper.** It is often a good idea to begin your paragraph with this point, which is known as the topic sentence. If you are writing an essay of several paragraphs, you will probably want to include your main point somewhere in your first paragraph. In a paper of several paragraphs, the main point is called the central point, or thesis.

2 **List the supporting reasons, examples, or other details that back up your point.** In many cases, you should have at least two or three items of support.

Step 3: Use Transitions

Once your outline is worked out, you will have a clear "road map" for writing your paper. As you write the early drafts of your paper, use **transitions** to introduce each of the separate supporting items (reasons, examples, or other details) you present to back up your point. For instance, you might introduce your first supporting item with the transitional words *first of all.* You might begin your second supporting item with words such as *another reason* or *another example.* And you might indicate your final supporting detail with such words as *last of all* or *a final reason.*

Step 4: Edit and Proofread Your Paper

After you have a solid draft, edit and proofread the paper. Ask yourself several questions to evaluate your paper:

1 Is the paper **unified**? Does all the material in the paper truly support the opening point?

2 Is the paper **well supported**? Is there plenty of specific evidence to back up the opening point?

3 Is the paper **clearly organized**? Does the material proceed in a way that makes sense? Do transitions help connect ideas?

4 Is the paper **well written**? When the paper is read aloud, do the sentences flow smoothly and clearly? Has the paper been checked carefully for grammar, punctuation, and spelling?

WRITING ASSIGNMENTS FOR THE TWENTY-ONE READINGS

Note: Your instructor may also permit you to write a paper based on one of the discussion questions that follow each reading.

The Struggle Continues

1. Juan says he believes in "success through education." Write a paragraph telling about a time in your life in which your education was (or is) helpful to you.

   Begin with a sentence in which you state a specific time that your education has helped you (or helps you now), for example:

   My education was helpful to me when I applied for the job I have now.

   My education is helpful when I assist my daughter with her homework.

   In your paragraph, give details about exactly how your education helped you in the situation you are describing. In addition, you might wish to describe what the situation might have been like if you had *not* had your level of education.

2. Imagine not being able to read. Write a paragraph about how you would be affected by your inability to read. Organize your paragraph in one of two ways:

   - By time order. Describe what your day as a nonreader would be like from the time you get up through the time you go to bed.

   - By categories. Describe what your day as a nonreader would be like in three or four different settings (for instance, at home, at work, at school, and driving somewhere).

   Your main point might be similar to this:

   If I couldn't read, life would be much more difficult in many ways.

   Before you write your paragraph, spend some time exploring all the little ways that reading affects your life, such as the following:

   - Reading the directions on a food package

   - Reading street signs

   - Reading store signs

   - Reading the news or sports section of a newspaper

   Alternatively, write a paragraph about how your life would be affected by an inability to write. For this paragraph, consider the ways writing is useful in your life, such as for creating to-do lists, notes to friends, and e-mail.

A Lesson in Love

1. The little girl in the reading obviously trusted her mother very much. Write a paragraph about a person you have deeply trusted. In your paragraph, tell who this person was, what his or her relationship was to you, and what it was about the person that inspired such trust in you. Provide at least one example that shows why you feel as you do (or felt) about the person.

   Begin with your main point, which might go something like this:

   My grandmother was a person I trusted with all my heart.

   A paragraph with the above point would continue by stating why the grandmother was so trustworthy ("I knew she would never lie to me, even if the truth wasn't what I wanted to hear"). It would also contain at least one detailed example of a time the grandmother told the writer the truth when it might have been easier not to.

2. "A Lesson in Love" tells of a frightening incident in which the people involved faced the possibility of death. Write a paper describing the most frightening incident you have ever experienced.

   In order to make your reader understand what you experienced, your paragraph should answer most (if not all) of the following questions:

   - Was the incident human-made (like a car accident) or an act of nature (like a tornado)?
   - How did you become involved?
   - Were you immediately very frightened, or did your fear grow?
   - How serious was the actual danger? Was your life threatened?
   - How did you get out of the situation?

   Begin your paragraph with a sentence that states your main point, including the nature of the incident. Here's an example of such a statement:

   The most terrifying experience I have ever had happened when my car stalled on railroad tracks.

Friendship and Living Longer

1. "Friendship and Living Longer" states that we especially need friends and relatives when we face major life changes. Think about a time when you experienced a difficult change—for example, when you began a new job, moved to a new town, changed schools, or lost a loved one. Now think about the person who, more than anyone else, helped you adjust to the situation. Write a paragraph about how this friend helped you through the difficult period.

   Begin with your main point, which might be worded something like this one:

The support of my best friend, Angela, really helped me deal with my parents' divorce.

Then describe why the situation was difficult for you and specific ways the friend or relative helped you. You might conclude with how you think the situation would have been different without that person's support.

2. The company of friends and family is essential to our well-being. Sometimes, however, privacy is just as important. Write a paper that begins with this point:

There are times when it is important to me to be alone.

Describe one or two such times (for example, when you have to make a decision or when you're very tired), how you like to spend such private time, and what the benefits of privacy at those times are. Include at least one or two specific examples of private times you have experienced, to help your reader get a sense of how such quiet time plays a role in your life.

Discovering Words

1. Write a paragraph about one of your significant early memories of reading. Maybe it involves being read to by a parent or teacher. Maybe it's about reading the back of a cereal box at breakfast. Maybe it's about a favorite childhood book. Or maybe it's about the frustration of trying to read in school. Begin your paragraph with a sentence that summarizes the memory you are writing about. Here are some examples:

One of my best early memories of reading is of my Grandpa reading me stories.

When I was very young and realized I could read street signs, I felt wonderful.

Fear and confusion are what I felt when I tried to read in elementary school.

Follow your first sentence with a description of what happened and how you felt about it. Be sure to include details that will help your reader understand when and where this event occurred.

2. Malcolm X writes that reading made him feel free. What activity makes you feel especially free? Is it reading, as with Malcolm? Walking alone through the city? Driving your car? Running? Dancing? Painting? Making music?

Write a paragraph that explains what makes you feel free. Use descriptive words that help the reader experience what you experience. Everyone has a different understanding of what it means to feel free, so be sure to explain what it is about this experience that is so appealing to you.

Papa

1. Papa was a strong character who seemed to command respect from everyone in his family. Whom do you know who has such a strong character—someone who seems to inspire respect in the people around him or her? Write a paragraph describing this person and his or her effect on people. (Remember as you are selecting your subject that, like Papa, a person of strong character is not necessarily boastful or successful in a material way. Rather, a person of genuinely strong character is often quietly self-confident.)

   As you write your paragraph, provide examples from your subject's life that show the effect he or she has had on others.

2. The author makes it clear that Papa was a "natural-born teacher." Write a paragraph about someone you know who seems born for a particular role in life—for example, a natural-born athlete, salesman or saleswoman, preacher, actor, nurse, or comedian.

   Begin with your main point, a statement such as this:

   From the time he was a little boy, everyone agreed that my cousin Mark was a natural-born carpenter.

   Follow up with examples that illustrate how the person was talented in the area named. Make your examples specific. Don't stop with a general comment such as "He was always good at building things." Instead, go on to provide a specific example, such as "When he was only nine years old, he built a pine bookshelf that my aunt still uses today."

Classroom Notetaking

1. Draw a line down the middle of a notebook page. On the top left-hand side, write, "Things I do." On the top right-hand side, write, "Things I don't do." In the first column, list the notetaking tips from the selection that you already use. In the second column, list those things you don't do now, but according to the article, might help you take better notes.

   Then write a paragraph that explains how the notetaking tips that you do use help you. For the things you don't do, explain which ones you'd like to try, and why.

2. The author says that the best lecturers "combine knowledge with expert showmanship" and are "informative and entertaining speakers." Write a paragraph about a teacher you have had who is both well-informed and entertaining. Provide at least two detailed illustrations of how this teacher has kept your attention. Come to some conclusion about how the teacher's attitude affected your learning.

Or instead write a paragraph describing a teacher who was outstandingly boring. Provide several detailed examples of how this teacher failed to be "informative and entertaining." In your conclusion, tell about how your learning in that class was affected.

Business Dining

1. "Business Dining" provides valuable tips that can help a diner make a favorable impression. Naturally, the opposite is also possible. Write a lighthearted paragraph on the topic of how to make an *awful* impression during a business meal. Just as the author of "Business Dining" gives suggestions on how to deal politely with such issues as ordering, alcohol, making use of silverware, and payment, you will write about how to deal with some of those issues as rudely as possible.

2. Knowing some basic rules of etiquette can help us get along without embarrassment in a situation. Have you ever been in a situation where you *did not* understand the etiquette and were embarrassed as a result? Perhaps it happened when you were dining in a fancy restaurant, visiting an unfamiliar place of worship, or spending time with people from another culture. Write a paper about the incident. In it, be sure to touch on the following points:

   - Where the incident occurred
   - How you embarrassed yourself
   - How a misunderstanding of etiquette led to your embarrassment
   - How people around you responded
   - What you learned from the incident

Learning Survival Skills

1. What career plans have you made so far? Write a paragraph about your plans and how your college classes relate to those plans. If you are not sure yet about your career choice, write about a likely possibility.

   In your paragraph, describe your interests and how they have led to your plans for a career. Then explain how your program of study will contribute to your success. Here are some sample topic sentences for such a paragraph:

   My interest in animals and science has led me to enroll in a program to become a veterinary assistant.

   Because I have always loved art and design, I am earning a degree in graphic arts.

   I intend to earn a double degree in horticulture and business because my dream is to have my own landscaping company.

2. Coleman writes, "A lot of people are their own worst enemies." Whom do you know whose own behavior is harmful to himself or herself? Here are a few examples of behavior by people who are their own worst enemies:

- They skip class and miss assignments, even though they are in danger of flunking out of school.

- They are constantly late for work, even though they need the job.

- They act ill-tempered and unfriendly, but complain that nobody likes them.

Write a paragraph about how the person you have chosen is his or her own worst enemy. In the paragraph, introduce the person, and explain how you know him or her. Next, describe the harmful behavior. Be specific. For example, don't just say someone is unfriendly—give a detailed example or two of that person's unfriendly behavior. You might wish to conclude by suggesting some positive behavior changes that person could make and how they would help him or her.

Migrant Child to College Woman

1. Throughout her life, Maria Cardenas has forced herself to do things that were very difficult for her. For example, she made herself learn to read on her own. She forced herself to begin college, despite her fears. She did these things because she believed the long-term benefits would be more important than any short-term discomfort.

    When have you made yourself do something difficult, even though it would have been easier not to? Maybe it's been one of these:

- Apologizing for something you did wrong

- Starting a new class or job

- Moving to a new town

- Speaking up for yourself to someone who was treating you badly

Write a paragraph about what you did and why. In it, answer these questions:

- What did I do that was difficult?

- Why did I find doing it so hard or frightening?

- Why did I think doing it would be worthwhile?

- How did I feel about myself after I'd done it?

2. Maria feels a strong drive to help migrant children. She wants to help them learn to speak English and to "stand on their own two feet."

    If you were offered the chance to help a particular group of people, who would it be? What kind of help would you most like to offer them? Write a paragraph in which you explain what group you would help and why and, finally, what you would like to do to help the people in this group.

Or instead, if you are now a volunteer with a particular group, write a paragraph about your experiences with that group. Tell why you decided to volunteer, what you actually do, and what your rewards are from the experience. Remember to give specific examples from your experience to support your general points.

Life Over Death

1. Think of an animal that has played a role in your life. Perhaps it was a pet in your own home or in the home of someone you visited frequently. Perhaps it was a neighborhood animal that you often observed outdoors. Write a paragraph about one characteristic of that animal, such as any of the following:

   - Cleverness
   - Playfulness
   - Stupidity
   - Stubbornness
   - Laziness
   - Loyalty

   Begin with a topic sentence that names the animal and the characteristic. For instance, that sentence might be similar to this one:

   My sister's kitten, Muffin, is the most affectionate animal I've ever known.

   Then, describe two or three specific events or behaviors that are good examples of the characteristic you have chosen.

2. The author of "Life Over Death" felt he "had no choice"—that he *had* to help the injured cat. For this assignment, write a letter to the author telling him about a time you also did something because you thought it was the only right thing to do. A topic sentence for this letter could be worded something like this:

   When my sister lost her job, I had no choice—I had to invite her and her children to live with me for a while.

   After your topic sentence, describe the situation that faced you, and then explain the decision you made. Conclude by telling what finally happened.

Learning to Read: The Marvel Kretzmann Story

1. When Marvel realized her life was getting more difficult rather than easier, she returned to school—a decision that changed her life. Like Marvel, we all have made decisions that changed our lives, such as the decision to do any of the following:

   - Marry or divorce
   - Move to another town
   - Have a child
   - End a destructive relationship
   - Get a new job
   - Go back to school

Write a paragraph about a life-changing decision you have made and its effects. In your paper, answer the following questions:

- What decision did I make?

- Why did I make it?

- What happened to me as a result of my decision?

- If I had it to do over again, would I make the same decision?

Begin by choosing a decision you might wish to write about. Next, check to see if you have enough supporting details to write about that decision. To do so, you might write down the above questions and list as many answers to each as you can think of.

2. Marvel is surprised to find herself looked up to by fellow students who also have difficulty reading. When she says, "You can do it!" they seem to believe her more readily than they would believe someone else.

Whom do you know (perhaps yourself?) who has struggled with an obstacle and was later able to help others with that same problem? Write a paragraph that includes the following:

- The person's problem

- How he or she learned to deal with it

- How that person later helped someone else deal with the same problem

Tickets to Nowhere

1. Write a paragraph about a time when you had good luck. Perhaps you found a twenty-dollar bill, or you happened to meet the person you are currently dating or are married to, or you lucked into a good-paying job. Whatever you write about, explain the circumstances fully, providing enough detail to let readers know why your experience was such a fortunate one. Your topic sentence may begin as follows:

A time I had incredibly good luck was the day that _____.

2. As Andy Rooney describes him, Jim is a man who has relied on luck to make good things happen in his life, rather than on hard work or realistic planning. Do you know someone who sort of drifts along in life, hoping for a lucky break but doing little to make it happen? Write a paragraph describing how this person goes about his or her life. Introduce that person in your topic sentence, as in this example:

My sister's former husband relies on luck, not work or planning, to get ahead in life.

Then give several specific examples of the person's behavior. Conclude by providing one or more suggestions on what the person might do in order to create his or her own "good luck."

An alternative is to write about someone who *has* made his or her own "good luck" through careful planning and hard work.

Joe Davis

1. Like Joe Davis, many of us have learned painful lessons from life. And like him, we wish we could pass those lessons on to young people to save them from making the same mistakes. Write a letter to a young person in which you use your own experience as a lesson. Begin with a topic sentence stating the lesson you'd like to teach, as in these examples:

   - My own experience is a lesson on why it's a bad idea to get involved with drugs and the people who take them.

   - I hope you can learn from my experience that dropping out of high school is a big mistake.

   - I know from firsthand experience that teenage girls should not let their boyfriends pressure them into a sexual relationship.

   As you develop your letter, describe in detail the hard lesson you learned and how you learned it.

2. One of Joe's goals is to regain the trust of the friends and family members he abused during his earlier life. Have you ever given a second chance to someone who treated you poorly? Write a paragraph about what happened. In your paragraph, answer the following questions:

   - What did the person do to lose your trust? Was it an obviously hurtful action, like physically harming you or stealing from you, or something more subtle, like embarrassing you or hurting your feelings?

   - Why did you decide to give the person another chance? Did the person apologize? Did you decide the mistreatment was not as bad as you first thought?

   - What happened as a result of your giving the person a second chance? Did he or she treat you better this time? Or did the bad treatment start over again?

   Conclude your paragraph with one or more thoughts about what you learned from the experience.

A Brother's Lesson

1. We often think of a hero as someone who has done something daring or dangerous—like rushing into a burning building to save a child. But when the author of this piece calls his parents "true heroes," it's clear he is thinking of another definition of *hero*.

   What is your definition? Write a paragraph in which you first explain how you define the word *hero*. What characteristics does a hero have? What sets a hero apart from other people? Then introduce as an example a person whom you see as a hero. Tell what this person has done in order to be a hero, according to your definition.

2. Oliver had a powerful influence on de Vinck's views of "action, love, courage, insight." Who has had a great influence on your views? Describe this person, and explain how he or she has affected your values or goals. Include at least one example of how you have been influenced by this person—just as de Vinck shows how Oliver influenced his choice of a wife.

How to Write Clearly

1. What are the biggest obstacles that stand between you and writing clearly? Write a paragraph that explains the two or three things you find hardest about writing clearly. Your topic sentence should state the obstacles you will discuss, for example:

   > For me, the hardest parts of writing clearly are organizing my material, finding the right words, and being brief.

   In your paragraph, follow up each of your points with one or more examples from your writing experiences at school or at work.

2. Before people write, says the author, they should create an outline—a plan for what they are going to put on paper. What other activities benefit from making a plan? Write about planning any of the following or another topic of your choosing.

   - Putting on a large party
   - Moving into a new house or apartment
   - Going on a family vacation
   - Going on a special date
   - Preparing a fancy meal
   - Creating a new vegetable garden

   In your paragraph, describe the steps that should be taken in order for the activity to be successful. Your topic sentence might be worded something like this one:

   > The following plan will help you put on a successful New Year's Eve party.

Rosa: A Success Story

1. Edward Patrick writes, "Almost all of us came to America from somewhere else." What do you know about your family's arrival in this country? Write a paragraph that tells what you know about your first relatives in the United States. Answer as many of the following questions as you can:

   - Who were your first relatives in the United States?

   - Where did they come from?

   - When did they arrive?

   - Why did they come to the United States?

   - What was life here like for them at first?

   If you don't know much about your first relatives in the United States, write instead about the earliest generation you do know about.

2. Rosa's college classes prepared her for a career in child care. If you want your education to lead to a specific career, write a paragraph about that career and why you've picked it. Give specific examples of the type of work you'd like to do and why. If you're not sure about the career you want, write about one or two that you're considering. Your topic sentence for this paragraph might be worded like either of these:

   I'm aiming for a career in accounting for several reasons.

   Although I haven't made a final decision, I'm considering the pros and cons of a career as a chef.

Knowledge Is Power

1. The author would not have been able to attend a college in the United States without the support of her mother. Who has helped you most in your quest for an education? That help may be very practical—such as paying bills or providing a place to stay—or it may be emotional support and encouragement. Write a paragraph explaining who this person is. Give specific examples of how he or she has helped you. Here are some sample topic sentences for this assignment:

   By reassuring me when I get discouraged, my husband is my greatest supporter as I seek an education.

   My boss has been the biggest help to me since I started college, because he (or she) has allowed me to work on a flexible schedule and has helped me with some expenses.

2. Anna-Maria was inspired by a bookmark that said, "Knowledge is power." Choose another familiar saying, such as one of the following:

> A stitch in time saves nine.
>
> Too many cooks spoil the broth.
>
> A little knowledge is a dangerous thing.
>
> A fool and his money are soon parted.
>
> Fools rush in where angels fear to tread.
>
> The acorn doesn't fall far from the tree.
>
> One bad apple can spoil the whole bunch.

Write a paragraph about an incident from your own experience that demonstrates the truth of the saying you choose. Begin with a topic sentence that mentions both the saying and the incident, like this:

> The time my brother won a large sweepstakes prize showed the truth of the saying "A fool and his money are soon parted."

Then describe the incident in detail. Be sure to emphasize the relationship between the saying and what happened. Conclude by restating the saying as it applies to the incident, for example:

> In this case, my brother certainly played the fool in being so quickly separated from his money.

Giving Constructive Criticism

1. Rudolph Verderber provides detailed suggestions for giving positive, helpful criticism. Write a paragraph on what *not* to do when giving criticism. One way to prepare for this assignment is to list a number of ways of criticizing that are not constructive. Then pick out two or three ways for which you can provide persuasive details from your own experience. Your topic sentence might look like either of these:

> From my experiences with a former boss, I learned several ways people should not give criticism.
>
> Two common ways of criticizing do more harm than good.

2. We have all been criticized at some point in life. Write a paragraph about a time when criticism motivated you to improve. Begin with a topic sentence that states briefly what happened, like this one:

> One time criticism helped me is when my little sister told me how much she hated my smoking.

Follow your topic sentence with a detailed account of what happened. Be sure your paragraph answers these questions:

- Who criticized me?

- What for?

- What did he or she say to me?

- How did I feel at first?

- What made me decide to change the behavior that was criticized?

- How did I feel later about what had happened?

A Love Affair with Books

1. Piassa lists several books that she will never forget. What have you read that sticks in your memory? A novel? A short story? A newspaper or magazine article? A textbook chapter? Write a paragraph about what you remember and why. Your topic sentence may look like this:

   I will never forget a short story called "Eve in Darkness."

   In your paragraph, describe when you read the material, what it was about, and why you found it so memorable. Include specific ideas or images that impressed you.

2. Write a paragraph that begins with one of the following topic sentences:

   - My family encouraged me to read when I was growing up.

   - My family environment discouraged me from reading as I was growing up.

   - Reading in school was a positive experience for me.

   - Reading in school was a negative experience for me.

   Develop your paper with colorful, convincing details, as Piassa has done in her story. Through such details, make your reader see, hear, and feel the things you experienced as a young reader.

Child-Rearing Styles

1. Were you raised more according to the authoritarian, the permissive, or the democratic method? Write a paragraph in which you state which approach was most commonly used in your home. Begin with a topic sentence such as this one:

   My father definitely used an authoritarian approach as he raised my brother and me.

   Then illustrate your main point with two or three incidents from your childhood.

2. What two families have you observed in which the parents use very different approaches in raising their children? Write a paragraph that contrasts those two child-rearing styles. In your paragraph, answer these questions:

- Who are the two families?
- How would I describe the difference between their parenting styles?
- What are some examples of the very different ways they treat their children?
- How do the children seem affected by their parents' child-rearing styles?
- Overall, which method do I think is better for the children?

From Horror to Hope

1. At first, Phany's uncle's invitation to work in his doughnut shop seemed kind. Later, though, Phany felt that her uncle and aunt had only wanted to use her. Have you ever found that someone who seemed friendly or helpful really wished to take advantage of you? Write a paragraph about the incident. Begin with a topic sentence, like the one below, that tells in general how you were used.

   > I was flattered when a popular girl at school started being nice to me, but soon I realized she only wanted to use me to meet my good-looking cousin.

   Your paragraph should answer the following questions:

   - Who was involved in the incident?
   - What was your first impression of that person's behavior toward you?
   - How did you realize you were being taken advantage of?
   - How did you respond at that point?

2. If you had a chance to meet Phany, what would you like to say to her? Write her a letter in response to her story. In your letter, you might do some of the following:

   - Tell her what parts of her story you think were most memorable, touching, or troubling.
   - Share an experience of your own that you think she could relate to because it is in some way similar to something she has gone through.
   - Tell her what you think of her plan to return to Cambodia to work on behalf of women's education there.
   - Tell her what kind of person you think she must be, judging from her story.

   Begin with a topic sentence that covers most or all of the details of your letter, such as either of these examples:

   > I greatly admire your persistence and goals.

   > Because of some of my own experiences, I believe I know how you feel about how your uncle and aunt treated you.

Limited Answer Key

An important note: To strengthen your reading skills, you must do more than simply find out which of your answers are right and which are wrong. You also need to figure out (with the help of this book, the teacher, or other students) *why* you missed the questions you did. By using each of your wrong answers as a learning opportunity, you will strengthen your understanding of the skills. You will also prepare yourself for the review and mastery tests in Part I and the word skills and reading comprehension questions in Part II, for which answers are not given here.

ANSWERS TO THE PRACTICES IN PART I

1   Phonics I: Consonants

Practice 1: Sounds of **c**

2. hard	6. hard
3. soft	7. soft
4. hard	8. hard
5. soft	9. hard
	10. soft

Practice 2: Sounds of **g**

2. hard	6. hard
3. soft	7. soft
4. hard	8. soft
5. soft	9. hard
	10. hard

Practice 3: Blends That Begin with **s**

A. 1. a**sleep**   4. **squ**eal
   2. cri**sp**   5. we**st**
   3. ma**sk**

B. 1. in**st**ance   4. **sk**iing
   2. **sp**orts   5. ju**st**
   3. **st**renuous

Practice 4: Blends That End in **l**

A. 1. ab**l**aze   4. imp**l**y
   2. c**l**ass   5. inf**l**ame
   3. g**l**ass

B. 1. f**l**ag   4. G**l**ory
   2. acc**l**aimed 5. p**l**enty
   3. b**l**ack

Practice 5: Blends That End in **r**

A. 1. ac**r**oss   4. jawb**r**eaker
   2. ent**r**ance   5. t**r**ade
   3. f**r**og

B. 1. d**r**iveway   4. t**r**ansmission
   2. b**r**akes   5. p**r**oblems
   3. g**r**ab

Practice 6: Other Blends

A. 1. bu**mp**er   6. pu**nt**
   2. ha**nd**cuff   7. sa**nk**
   3. mi**ld**

B. 1. diffi**cult**   4. co**ld**er
   2. **camp**   5. Disney**land**
   3. ra**ft**

553

Practice 7: Consonant Digraphs

1. mouth	6. crashed
2. **Chinese**	7. **cholesterol**
3. starfish	8. phony
4. shop	9. **Chicago**
5. phrase	10. rough

Practice 8: Silent Letters

1. know	6. crumbs
2. Wheaties	7. muggy
3. lamb	8. wholesale
4. knead	9. message
5. check	10. write

2 Phonics II: Vowels

Practice 1A: Short **a** Sound

3. ă	6. X
4. ă	7. ă
5. X	8. X
	9. ă
	10. X

Practice 1B: Short **e** Sound

3. X	6. ĕ
4. ĕ	7. X
5. X	8. X
	9. ĕ
	10. ĕ

Practice 1C: Short **i** Sound

3. ĭ	6. X
4. X	7. ĭ
5. ĭ	8. X
	9. ĭ
	10. X

Practice 1D: Short **o** Sound

3. X	6. ŏ
4. X	7. X
5. ŏ	8. ŏ
	9. X
	10. ŏ

Practice 1E: Short **u** Sound

3. ŭ	6. ŭ
4. X	7. X
5. ŭ	8. X
	9. ŭ
	10. X

Practice 2: Rule for Short Vowel Sounds

1. stop	6. Nevada
2. back	7. butter
3. hungry	8. bad
4. fat	9. think
5. rubber	10. body

Practice 3A: Long **a** Sound

3. X	6. ā
4. ā	7. X
5. ā	8. X
	9. X
	10. ā

Practice 3B: Long **e** Sound

3. ē	6. ē
4. X	7. X
5. X	8. ē
	9. X
	10. ē

Practice 3C: Long **i** Sound

3. ī	6. X
4. X	7. X
5. ī	8. ī
	9. X
	10. ī

Practice 3D: Long **o** Sound

3. ō	6. X
4. ō	7. ō
5. X	8. X
	9. ō
	10. X

Practice 3E: Long **u** Sound

3. X	6. X
4. ū	7. ū
5. ū	8. X
	9. ū
	10. X

Practice 4: Silent-e Rule

1. pine	4. unsafe
2. like	5. brave
3. notebook	

Practice 5: Two-Vowels-Together Rule

1. train	4. soap
2. Greece	5. team
3. day	

Practice 6: Final Single Vowel

1. als**o**
2. sp**i**der
3. **o**ver
4. **e**rase
5. f**a**mous

Practice 7: Sounds of **y**

4. ē
5. ī
6. ĭ
7. y
8. ē
9. y
10. ĭ

Practice 8: Long and Short Vowels and Vowels Followed by r

4. ā
5. r
6. r
7. ē
8. ŭ
9. r
10. ĭ

Practice 9: Long and Short **oo**

3. o͞o
4. o͝o
5. o͞o
6. o͝o
7. o͝o
8. o͞o
9. o͞o
10. o͝o

3   Phonics III: Syllables

Practice 1: Numbers of Vowels, Vowel Sounds, and Syllables

1. 2   1   1
2. 2   1   1
3. 2   1   1
4. 2   1   1
5. 2   2   2
6. 2   1   1
7. 3   3   3
8. 2   1   1
9. 3   2   2
10. 3   2   2

Practice 2: Dividing Between Two Consonants

1. can-dy
2. nap-kin
3. har-bor
4. trum-pet
5. muf-fin

Practice 3: Dividing Between Three Consonants

1. cen-tral
2. ad-dress
3. com-plete
4. at-tract
5. ob-scure

Practice 4: Dividing Before a Single Consonant

1. bo-nus
2. i-tem
3. fi-nal
4. ma-jor
5. u-nit

Practice 5: Dividing Before a Consonant and **le**

1. i-dle
2. rip-ple
3. pur-ple
4. ti-tle
5. gar-gle

Practice 6: Dividing After Prefixes and Before Suffixes

1. mis-sion
2. ad-vice
3. un-bend
4. play-ful
5. ex-port
6. na-tion
7. mind-less
8. con-sist
9. re-act
10. dis-ease

Practice 7: The Suffix **-ed**

1. separate
2. not separate
3. not separate
4. separate
5. separate

Practice 8: Dividing Between the Words in a Compound Word

1. note-book
2. rain-coat
3. pop-corn
4. work-shop
5. sea-shell

4   Dictionary Use

Practice 1

A. 1. blush, boat
2. dodo, dogcart
3. lilac, limousine
4. rainwater, ragtime
5. weightlifting, wedding

B. 6. b
7. a
8. c
9. b
10. c

Practice 2

1. revise
2. kidnap
3. carry
4. giant
5. really
6. schoolteacher
7. please
8. coming
9. believe
10. tunnel

Practice 3

1. hic•cup, 2
2. min•i•mal, 3
3. dis•pos•al, 3
4. in•sen•si•tive, 4
5. com•mu•ni•ca•tion, 5

Practice 4

1. pot
2. pit
3. cut
4. pat
5. pet

Practice 5

1. mag·net   măg′nĭt
2. jan·i·tor   jăn′ĭ-tər
3. en·cour·age ĕn-kûr′ĭj
4. spec·u·late spĕk′yə-lāt′
5. trou·ble·mak·er trŭb′əl-mā′kər

Practice 6

1. noun, verb
2. noun, adjective, verb
3. adjective, adverb
4. conjunction, adjective, noun
5. adjective, noun, verb

Practice 7

1. hid, hidden *or* hid, hiding
2. one-upped, one-upping
3. skinnier, skinniest
4. worse, worst
5. parties; [informal] partied, partying

Practice 8

A. 1. Definition 2   3. Definition 1
   2. Definition 1

B. 4. a; *Informal:* a short rest period
   5. c; *Music:* A thin, upright piece of
      wood in some stringed instruments
      that supports the strings above the
      sounding board

Practice 9

1. Old English, "trousers"
2. Old Spanish, "northeast wind"
3. Latin, "short"

Practice 10

1. breeze
2. cinch, pushover, snap, walkaway,
   walkover
3. *Informal:* Something, such as a task, that
   is easy to do

5   Vocabulary in Context

Practice 1

1. *Examples:* a length of 100', a width of 15',
   a depth of 10'; c
2. *Examples:* actor Tom Cruise, tennis star
   Patrick Rafter, singer Janet Jackson; b
3. *Examples:* giant pandas, snow leopards,
   koala bears; a

4. *Examples:* quotations which were never
   said, events which never occurred; c
5. *Examples:* the thumbs-up sign, hands on
   the hips, a shrug of the shoulders; c
6. *Examples:* mountain climbing, deep-sea
   diving; c
7. *Examples:* belching in public, talking
   loudly in a movie theater; a
8. *Examples:* exercising daily, eating
   nutritious foods; c
9. *Examples:* the student on your left has a
   bad cough, the student on your right sighs
   out loud, the student behind you kicks
   your chair; b
10. *Examples:* purring, licking their owners'
    hands, rubbing against their owners' legs;
    c

Practice 2

1. steady customer   6. came between
2. job   7. admit
3. strengthens   8. fearful
4. ridiculous   9. unwilling
5. fair   10. false belief

Practice 3

1. simple; c   7. lack of
2. famous; a   preparation; c
3. unrelated; b   8. criticized; c
4. out of order; b   9. strict; a
5. serious; c   10. active; b
6. mild; b

Practice 4

1. a   6. a
2. b   7. a
3. b   8. b
4. a   9. c
5. c   10. b

6   Main Ideas

Practice 1

1. pet   6. bedding
2. shape   7. greeting
3. direction   8. noise
4. beverage   9. command
5. high-risk job 10. punishment

Practice 2 (Answers will vary; below are some possibilities.)

1. Michelle Pfeiffer, Denzel Washington
2. tiger, elephant
3. fax machine, postage meter
4. chocolate cake, fruit salad
5. Detroit, Tallahassee
6. New Year's Day, Memorial Day
7. Mars, Jupiter
8. cousin, grandmother
9. microwave, refrigerator
10. tomatoes, corn

Practice 3 (Answers to the second part of each item will vary; below are some possibilities.)

1. *General term:* bird; sparrow
2. *General term:* furniture; chair
3. *General term:* vehicle; car
4. *General term:* weather; rain
5. *General term:* snack; potato chip
6. *General term:* writing tool; pencil
7. *General term:* dance; polka
8. *General term:* insect; grasshopper
9. *General term:* cosmetics; eye shadow
10. *General term:* job; waiter

Practice 4

1. b	4. a
2. a	5. b
3. c	

Practice 5

1. b	6. c
2. a	7. b
3. c	8. a
4. a	9. c
5. c	10. c

7 Supporting Details

Practice 1

Group 1
  a. SD
  b. MI
  c. SD

Group 2
  a. MI
  b. SD
  c. SD

Group 3
  a. SD
  b. SD
  c. MI

Group 4
  a. SD
  b. MI
  c. SD

Practice 2 (Wording of details may vary.)

Passage 1

1. The desire to achieve
3. The desire to associate with other people

Words that introduce a list: several powerful motives

Words that introduce
  First major detail: One
  Second major detail: Another
  Last major detail: A third

Passage 2

1. the delinquent group
  a. Dislike authority figures
2. a. Known for their high regard for education
3. The most popular: the fun subculture
  b. Interested in material goods, like clothes and cars

Words that introduce a list: one of three subcultures

Words that introduce
  First major detail: One
  Second major detail: The next
  Third major detail: Last of all

Practice 3 (Wording of details may vary.)

A. 1. Spanish—in 20 countries
  3. English—in 44 countries

B. *Head:* . . . on tests

Arrive early	Follow test-taking strategies
Focus on new material	Outline essay answers

  Words that introduce
  First major detail: First
  Second major detail: Another
  Third major detail: Third

Practice 4 (Wording of details may vary.)

A. 1. c
  2. b
  3. a
  4. floating on air
  5. air-conditioned domes

B. 6. b   9. Finally
  7. One   10. B
  8. Second

8 Finding Main Ideas

Practice 1

1. 2   4. 2
2. 1   5. 1
3. 5

Practice 2

1. a   4. d
2. c   5. b
3. c

Practice: Level 1

1. 1   4. 2
2. 6   5. 3
3. 1

Practice: Level 2

1. 1   4. 6
2. 3   5. 2
3. 3

Practice: Level 3

1. 1   4. 2
2. 4   5. 3
3. 4

Practice: Level 4 (Unstated Main Ideas)

1. b   4. b
2. d   5. b
3. d

9 Relationships I

Practice 1

1. also   4. Another
2. Other   5. Moreover
3. In addition

Practice 2 (Wording of answers may vary.)

A. **Main idea heading:** . . . of stress in young people
   1. Unusual tiredness
   2. Temper tantrums
   3. Forgetting known facts

B. **Main idea heading:** . . . contained in pizza
   • Crust is rich in B vitamins
   • Cheese contains proteins and calcium

Practice 3

1. before   4. until
2. After   5. next
3. Then

Practice 4 (Wording of answers may vary.)

A. 2. Then cut a patch the same size and shape from a leftover or unnoticeable piece of carpet.
   3. . . . burlap the same size as the patch.
   4. Place the burlap where you cut out the damaged piece of carpet.
   5. Finally, glue the carpet patch to the burlap.

B. *(Wording of answers may vary.)*
   • . . . there were over 80,000 in California hoping to "strike it rich."
   • By 1860, California's population had grown to 380,000.

10 Relationships II

Practice 1

1. just like   4. however
2. Even though   5. as
3. Despite

Practice 2

A. 1. Comparing
   2. Men's and women's bad driving
   3. equally, similarly

B. **Main idea heading:** . . . stepfamilies and "natural" families

	Ways they are different
Backgrounds that tend to be alike	Stepfamily includes more people

Practice 3

1. cause   4. because
2. so that   5. Therefore
3. As a result

Practice 4

A. C Greater emphasis on being efficient and clean
   E More time spent on dusting, cleaning and scrubbing
   C Greater variety of foods available
   E More time spent on food preparation

B. **Main idea heading:** . . . being
   unemployed
   3. Increased alcohol and tranquilizer
      abuse
   4. . . . heart disease

Practice 5

1. such as   4. Once
2. For instance   5. For example
3. including

Practice 6

A. 1. charisma
   2. 1
   3. 4
   4. 2

B. **Heading:** . . . the ability to renew lost
   body parts
   • An octopus can regrow lost tentacles.
   • One leg of a sea star that includes part
     of its center can regenerate a whole
     new body.

ANSWERS TO THE PRACTICES IN PART III

1   Word Parts

Practice 1

1–2. b. include
      c. expired
      d. impersonal

3–4. a. precedes
      b. postscript
      c. postpone
      d. preface

5–6. a. subway
      b. supernatural
      c. subfloor
      d. supervisor

7–8. a. mistake
      b. monotone
      c. Monogamy
      d. misbehave

9–10. a. repeat
      b. unlikely
      c. unable
      d. return

Practice 2

11–12. a. manageable
       b. imitation
       c. comfortable
       d. reunion

13–14. a. visitor
       b. scientist
       c. waiter
       d. pianist

15–16. a. thankful
       b. grateful
       c. careless
       d. helpless

17–18. a. Catholicism
       b. imprisonment
       c. excitement
       d. vandalism

19–20. a. childish
       b. immediately
       c. boyish
       d. eagerly

Practice 3

21–22. a. portable
       b. beneficial
       c. benevolent
       d. porter

23–24. a. Biofeedback
       b. convention
       c. avenue
       d. biography

25–26. a. manipulate
       b. peddlers
       c. manicure
       d. pedestrians

27–28. a. television
       b. automobile
       c. autobiography
       d. telephone

29–30. a. audio-visual
       b. audition
       c. spectators
       d. spectacles

Acknowledgments

The American Heritage Dictionary, Third Paperback Edition. Sample page, pronunciation key, and entries on pages 117, 120, 123, 125, 126, 132, 133, 135, 138, 139, and 143. Copyright © 1994 by Houghton Mifflin Company. Reprinted by permission from *The American Heritage Dictionary*, Third Paperback Edition.

Angel, Juan. "The Struggle Continues." Reprinted by permission.

Buscaglia, Leo. "Papa," from *Papa, My Father*, by Leo F. Buscaglia. Copyright © 1989 by Slack, Inc. Reprinted by permission.

Cardenas, Maria. "Migrant Child to College Woman." Reprinted by permission.

Chan, Vicky. "Friendship and Living Longer." Reprinted by permission.

Coleman, Jean. "Learning Survival Skills." Reprinted by permission.

de Vinck, Christopher. "A Brother's Lesson." Reprinted by permission of the author and *The Wall Street Journal,* copyright © 1985, Dow Jones & Company, Inc.

Drafke, Michael W. and Stan Kossen. "Business Dining," from *The Human Side of Organizations*, 7th edition. Copyright © 1998 by Addison Wesley Longman, Inc. Reprinted by permission of Addison Wesley Longman.

Hawley, Casey. "A Lesson in Love." Reprinted by permission.

Johnson, Beth. "Joe Davis." Reprinted by permission.

Malcolm X with Alex Haley. "Discovering Words," from *The Autobiography of Malcolm X* by Malcolm X, with the assistance of Alex Haley. Copyright © 1964 by Malcolm X and Alex Haley. Copyright © 1965 by Alex Haley and Betty Shabazz. Reprinted by permission of Random House, Inc.

Patrick, Edward. "Rosa: A Success Story." Reprinted by permission.

Petricic, Anna-Maria. "Knowledge Is Power." Reprinted by permission.

Piassa, Bernadete. "A Love Affair with Books." Reprinted by permission.

Quinn, Virginia Nichols. "Child-Rearing Styles," from *Applying Psychology.* Copyright © 1984 by The McGraw-Hill Companies. Reprinted by permission.

Rooney, Andy. "Tickets to Nowhere." © Tribune Media Services, Inc. Reprinted by permission.

Sarann, Phany. "From Horror to Hope." Reprinted by permission.

Sherry, Mary. "Learning to Read: The Marvel Kretzmann Story." Reprinted by permission.

Thompson, Edward T. "How to Write Clearly." Reprinted by permission of the International Paper Company.

Verderber, Rudolph F. "Giving Constructive Criticism," from *Communicate!,* 8th edition, by R. F. Verderber. Copyright © 1996 by Wadsworth Publishing. Reprinted by permission.

White, Clarissa. "Classroom Notetaking." Reprinted by permission.

Index